Oracle Cloud Infrastructure: A Guide to Building Cloud Native Applications

Oracle Cloud Infrastructure: A Guide to Building Cloud Native Applications

Jeevan Gheevarghese Joseph
Adao Oliveira Junior
Mickey Boxell

Pearson

Oracle Cloud Infrastructure: A Guide to Building Cloud Native Applications

Jeevan Gheevarghese Joseph, Adao Oliveira Junior, Mickey Boxell

Copyright© 2024 Pearson Education, Inc.

Published by Oracle Press
Hoboken, New Jersey

For information about buying this title in bulk quantities, or for special sales opportunities (which may include electronic versions; custom cover designs; and content particular to your business, training goals, marketing focus, or branding interests), please contact our corporate sales department at corpsales@pearsoned.com or (800) 382-3419.

For government sales inquiries, please contact governmentsales@pearsoned.com.

For questions about sales outside the U.S., please contact intlcs@pearson.com.

Library of Congress Control Number: 2023944840

ISBN-13: 978-0-13-790253-8
ISBN-10: 0-13-790253-0

1 2023

General Manager
Mark Taub

Director, ITP Product Management
Brett Bartow

Executive Editor
Nancy Davis

Managing Editor
Sandra Schroeder

Development Editor
Christopher Cleveland

Senior Project Editor
Tonya Simpson

Copy Editor
Krista Hansing

Technical Editor
Peter Jausovec

Editorial Assistant
Cindy Teeters

Cover Designer
Chuti Prasertsith

Composition
codeMantra

Indexer
Timothy Wright

Proofreader
Jennifer Hinchliffe

Warning and Disclaimer

This book is designed to provide information about Oracle Cloud Infrastructure. Every effort has been made to make this book as complete and as accurate as possible, but no warranty or fitness is implied.

The information is provided on an "as is" basis. The authors, Oracle Press, and Pearson shall have neither liability nor responsibility to any person or entity with respect to any loss or damages arising from the information contained in this book or from the use of the discs or programs that may accompany it.

The views expressed in this book are those of the author or authors and do not necessarily reflect the views of Oracle.

Oracle does not make any representations or warranties as to the accuracy, adequacy or completeness of any information contained in this work, and is not responsible for any errors or omissions.

Feedback Information

At Oracle Press, our goal is to create in-depth technical books of the highest quality and value. Each book is crafted with care and precision, undergoing rigorous development that involves the unique expertise of members from the professional technical community.

Readers' feedback is a natural continuation of this process. If you have any comments regarding how we could improve the quality of this book, or otherwise alter it to better suit your needs, you can contact us through email at feedback@oraclepress.com. Please make sure to include the book title and ISBN in your message.

We greatly appreciate your assistance.

Trademark Acknowledgments

Oracle, Java, MySQL and NetSuite are registered trademarks of Oracle Corporation and/or its affiliates. All other trademarks are the property of their respective owners.

Screen displays of copyrighted Oracle software and services have been reproduced herein with the permission of Oracle Corporation and/or its affiliates.

All terms mentioned in this book that are known to be trademarks or service marks have been appropriately capitalized. Oracle Press or Oracle Corporation cannot attest to the accuracy of this information. Use of a term in this book should not be regarded as affecting the validity of any trademark or service mark.

Pearson's Commitment to Diversity, Equity, and Inclusion

Pearson is dedicated to creating bias-free content that reflects the diversity of all learners. We embrace the many dimensions of diversity, including but not limited to race, ethnicity, gender, socioeconomic status, ability, age, sexual orientation, and religious or political beliefs.

Education is a powerful force for equity and change in our world. It has the potential to deliver opportunities that improve lives and enable economic mobility. As we work with authors to create content for every product and service, we acknowledge our responsibility to demonstrate inclusivity and incorporate diverse scholarship so that everyone can achieve their potential through learning. As the world's leading learning company, we have a duty to help drive change and live up to our purpose to help more people create a better life for themselves and to create a better world.

Our ambition is to purposefully contribute to a world where

- Everyone has an equitable and lifelong opportunity to succeed through learning
- Our educational products and services are inclusive and represent the rich diversity of learners
- Our educational content accurately reflects the histories and experiences of the learners we serve
- Our educational content prompts deeper discussions with learners and motivates them to expand their own learning (and worldview)

While we work hard to present unbiased content, we want to hear from you about any concerns or needs with this Pearson product so that we can investigate and address them.

Please contact us with concerns about any potential bias at https://www.pearson.com/report-bias.html.

Figure Credits

Contents at a Glance

Contents

About the Authors

Jeevan Gheevarghese Joseph is a senior principal product manager in the Containers and Kubernetes Services group within Oracle Cloud Infrastructure. He focuses on product strategy for containers and Kubernetes platforms at OCI. Jeevan also works with strategic customers as an advisor to help them make the most of Oracle's tooling and technology platforms. Jeevan's interests include application architecture, developer tooling, automation, and cross-product integration. Before his current role, he held positions in the Oracle A-Team and Oracle Data Cloud. He routinely speaks at developer events and industry conferences.

Adao Oliveira Junior has been working in the technology industry for more than two decades, with five years of experience in cloud native solutions. He is a senior principal solutions architect who excels at gathering high-level requirements and turning them into technical solutions, aiding customers and partners worldwide. Adao has held various positions, including sales engineering and product manager, in organizations like Oracle A-Team and OCI Developer Adoption. He is a well-known figure in the cloud native field and has made significant contributions to open-source projects and the Kubernetes community. Adao holds multiple Kubernetes certifications, including CKS, CKA, CKAD, and KCNA, as well as other computer and cloud industry certifications.

Mickey Boxell is a senior principal product manager in the Containers and Kubernetes Services group within Oracle Cloud Infrastructure. He has been a member of the Kubernetes release team for many releases, including as the communications coordinator for Kubernetes 1.24 and the docs lead for Kubernetes 1.27. Mickey has worked in the cloud platform and infrastructure space for the past decade. He has spoken at numerous developer meetups and conferences, contributed to many open-source projects, and worked directly with many customers to help implement Oracle technology.

About the Technical Reviewer

Drawing from more than 15 years of experience in software development and technology, **Peter Jausovec** specializes in the cloud-native space, Kubernetes, and service meshes. He is an international speaker, book author, and creator of popular Kubernetes, Istio, and Envoy courses. Peter regularly shares his technical knowledge and insights on cloud-native technologies through his blog on learncloudnative.com.

Dedications

Jeevan: I dedicate this book to my loving family. To my amazing wife, Annie, for being the rock in my life and my shoulder to lean on. Thank you for your constant support through the endless late nights and missed weekends. To my wonderful daughter, Eva, for the sheer joy you bring us. I hope I can make up for every bedtime story and good night hug I missed. To my parents, who gave me wings, pointed at the sky, and were unafraid to let me fly: Appa, I wish you were here to see this.

Adao: To my beloved family, you have been my rock throughout this entire journey. Your unwavering support and love have kept me going. This book is dedicated to you as a small token of my appreciation for all you have done for me. Thank you for inspiring me to pursue my passions and believing in me when I didn't believe in myself. I love you all more than words can express.

Mickey: I would like to give a huge thank you to my family for their support. To my fiancée, Rainy, thank you for always brightening my day. To my parents, Kris and Tim, thank you for shaping me into the person I am today.

Acknowledgments

Jeevan: Thanks to Brad Posner, who told me that I could write a book. Without your encouragement, this idea would not have taken shape.

I sincerely thank my coauthors, Adao and Mickey. This book would still be just an idea without you guys. Special thanks to our technical reviewers, Peter Jausovec, and Matt Vander Vliet, who both had an immense impact on keeping this book on point.

Thanks to Loïc Tregan, Matt Vander Vliet, Adao Junior, and Peter Jausovec. I still remember the day MuShop started in a meeting room. MuShop and its success inspired this book, and none of it would have been possible without this team.

To all my colleagues from the Oracle A-Team. It's a privilege to have worked with all of you and learned from the legends that you are. #ATeamForever

A special thanks to the mentors that I've had over the years. Ric Smith, Stefan Krantz, Yogesh Bhootada, Loïc Tregan, and Brad Posner—thank you for all the support, direction, and help you have given me over the years to grow and expand my horizons.

Special thanks to Nancy Davis, executive editor at Pearson, and Christopher Cleveland, our development editor. You believed in us when we didn't ourselves.

Last but not least, a special thanks to the Containers and Kubernetes team at OCI for their tireless dedication toward building a rock-solid product. I'll also use this opportunity to thank my current and past colleagues in Oracle Cloud Infrastructure for building a world-class platform and executing a vision for a hyperscale cloud that can scale fast and democratize the cloud provider ecosystem.

Adao: I want to express my heartfelt gratitude to Jeevan and Mickey, who worked tirelessly to make this book a reality. Your dedication, hard work, and unwavering support have been invaluable throughout this journey. I am truly blessed to have such a fantastic team of individuals who share my passion for this project.

Special thanks to Nancy Davis, executive editor at Pearson, and Christopher Cleveland, our development editor. Your creativity, insights, and attention to detail have brought this book to life. I am grateful for your unwavering commitment to excellence and your willingness to go above and beyond to ensure its success.

I would also like to thank our technical reviewers, Peter Jausovec and Matthew Vander Vliet. Your support and wisdom have been instrumental in helping us achieve our goals. The MuShop project that we started together was a great inspiration for this book.

Finally, I want to thank my family and friends for their unwavering support and encouragement. Your love and belief in me have constantly inspired and motivated me.

Thank you, everyone, for your hard work, dedication, and support throughout this journey. This book would not have been possible without you.

Mickey: I would like to begin by thanking Jeevan and Adao for bringing me into this project. This book would not have been possible without your knowledge and dedication. I would also like to say thank you to Diane Anderson, for helping me develop good working habits and guiding me at the start of my career; to the Cloud Native Labs team, for giving me space to grow and develop my understanding of cloud native technology; to Jesse Butler, for mentoring me and always being there to help even long after we parted teams; to Jonathan Schreiber and Jon Reeve, for taking a chance on me as a new product manager; and to Devika Nair, for helping me refine my craft.

Introduction

Cloud native development has become the de-facto architecture of choice for newly built applications. Cloud native development gives enterprises the capability to fully realize the advantages of leveraging a cloud platform and enables quick iteration and portability. Cloud native development takes a different and modern approach to designing, building, deploying, and managing applications. This approach places automation, elasticity, and resiliency front and center by leveraging cloud platforms such as Oracle Cloud Infrastructure (OCI).

OCI is a next-generation cloud designed to run any application faster and more securely, for less. It is one of the fastest-growing cloud platforms, in terms of customer growth and global geographical footprint. OCI includes tools and utilities for building new cloud native applications and also running existing enterprise applications without rearchitecting them. OCI is built around the pillars of AI and autonomous systems, enterprise security, and open standards.

Goals and Approach

Whether you are new to the cloud paradigm or new to just OCI, this book aims to give you a complete rundown of the services in OCI that help you build cloud native applications. Because lines between infrastructure engineers and developers are blurring, the book covers both infrastructure services and developer services, as well as how to manage them in the context of a cloud native application development environment.

For application developers, this book covers modern cloud native application design paradigms for those who are new to developing on the cloud, within the context of the services offered by OCI. Readers who are familiar with cloud native toolchains and paradigms will find the book useful for exploring the OCI-specific services and features that help them make the most of moving their workloads on to OCI.

Readers new to OCI will be introduced to OCI's central concepts, including tenancies and compartments. This introduction orients you with OCI terminology and offers insights into common patterns for access control and resource organization. Some OCI services, such as identity and access management, are covered in detail: They are pervasive concepts, and understanding these systems is key to being productive on OCI. Other supporting services are mentioned only briefly in comparison in the context of supporting cloud native application development. The book covers the automation platforms and practices that are key to being productive when operating cloud native applications and infrastructure at scale. The book then dives deeply into cloud native platforms such as the managed Kubernetes service and serverless platforms. Each chapter includes complete coverage of the relevant services and best practices for using them. Throughout the book, we use example code or snippets to demonstrate concepts and operational procedures. We include several real-world examples of running or configuring popular open-source tools on OCI. Finally, we use all the concepts and services discussed in the book to implement a coherent application that we have open-sourced. This example application puts into practice the learnings around infrastructure automation and the application development explored earlier in the book. The application serves as a blueprint for new application developers who might be just getting started or as a reference point for those who are comparing OCI's services against other market offerings.

Who Should Read This Book?

This book is written for developers, DevOps professionals, architects, or anyone who wants to understand the various developer-focused features of OCI. Familiarity with OCI is not assumed, and familiarity with the general cloud services model is helpful but not required. The book focuses on the cloud native services and platforms offered by OCI but does not cover every OCI feature or platform.

How This Book Is Organized

The book is organized to give readers who are new to OCI and cloud native development a structured journey that starts with the basics of OCI, proceeds through infrastructure automation tools, and then dives deep into cloud native application development platforms. Readers who are familiar with other cloud platforms can benefit from the introduction to OCI and then move freely to other topics and areas of interest. The final chapter walks through an open-source example application, complete with infrastructure automation code, that readers can use as a learning tool or a reference point for implementing specific features.

Book Structure

The book is organized into 10 chapters:

Chapter 1, Introduction to Oracle Cloud Infrastructure: This chapter introduces the reader to Oracle Cloud Infrastructure. Basic concepts and terminology in OCI are introduced, along with identity and access management. This chapter does not attempt to exhaustively cover OCI at a high level; instead, it covers the critical basics so that the reader is familiar with foundational OCI constructs in the chapters that follow. The goal of this chapter is to orient readers with OCI, and it is relevant to both readers who have prior experience with other cloud platforms and readers who are new to cloud-based development.

Chapter 2, Infrastructure Automation and Management: This chapter covers infrastructure automation in OCI. Infrastructure management plays an important role in cloud-based development, including when it comes to designing applications for ephemeral and API-driven infrastructure. This chapter covers the OCI APIs and popular tools such as Terraform that you use to interact with OCI in a programmatic manner.

Chapter 3, Cloud Native Services on Oracle Cloud Infrastructure: This chapter provides a bird's-eye view of the various services typically used for building cloud native applications and supporting services in that ecosystem. Several of the key services discussed in this chapter are covered in more depth in subsequent chapters; this chapter provides the big picture of the various cloud native tools and services available at your disposal in OCI.

Chapter 4, Understanding Container Engine for Kubernetes: Cloud native application development has coalesced around Kubernetes so much that it has become the most common runtime service for running a cloud native application on any cloud. This chapter introduces Container Engine for Kubernetes, which is OCI's managed Kubernetes service. The fundamental concepts and features of the service are covered in this chapter.

Chapter 5, Container Engine for Kubernetes in Practice: This chapter dives deeper into Container Engine for Kubernetes and looks at how to operate and run clusters at scale. Advanced usage scenarios and configurations are also covered in this chapter.

Chapter 6, Securing Your Workloads and Infrastructure: As cloud native applications become more distributed, include multiple technology stacks, and evolve in parallel with the infrastructure, new approaches to securing the applications and the underlying infrastructure are required. This chapter introduces open-source and OCI native security tools and processes to secure your workloads and data.

Chapter 7, Serverless Platforms and Applications: This chapter introduces OCI's serverless platforms. These platforms transparently handle infrastructure management. They offer developers varying degrees of agility and control and have been designed from the start to offer quick-and-easy cloud native development workflows. This chapter covers OCI services such as Functions and Container Instances, as well as their use cases and best practices.

Chapter 8, Observability: Cloud native systems are always in flux, as they scale and flex to meet workload demands and optimize cost. This chapter tackles the challenge of observing constantly changing applications and infrastructure using common observability tools and platforms. The chapter covers OCI infrastructure and application observability services, such as metrics and log analytics. Apart from the native tooling that OCI provides, this chapter looks at popular open-source tools for observability and shows how to integrate OCI metrics and logging with these open-source tools.

Chapter 9, DevOps and Deployment Automation: One of the biggest drivers for adopting cloud native architecture is the increased development velocity and faster evolution of your applications. This is facilitated by agile tools that can constantly update your distributed code bases, validate the security of your software supply chain, and continuously deploy updates to your workloads without interrupting business.

This chapter covers the operation and lifecycle management of owning a cloud native workload. OCI features and services such as the DevOps platform are discussed in this chapter. This chapter also looks at the GitOps approach to lifecycle management and shows how to implement such an approach on OCI with open-source tools.

Chapter 10, Bringing It Together: MuShop: The final chapter in this book gives you a tour of MuShop, a set of sample applications built to showcase the approaches and tools described in this book. It models an online shop that consists of a set of polyglot microservices. The application architecture demonstrates how a group of services can interact and communicate to form a cohesive application. It shows how failures in a distributed system such as this can be safely handled, how individual parts of the applications can be upgraded and scaled, and how the system as a whole (including the infrastructure) can be secured and monitored. The source code for the application is open and published on GitHub, and this chapter walks you through both the code and the various application design elements of MuShop.

Code Examples and Cloud Resources

Throughout the book, we showcase code snippets to demonstrate concepts and configuration options. However, code can be verbose when presented in its complete form, and it is often unproductive to wade through large chunks of code to locate a few lines that demonstrate a concept. For this reason, the code examples in the book have been kept as brief as possible. This also helps draw your attention to the essential code elements in each context. While this makes for a better reading experience, we also understand that, in many cases, you might want to see the code in its complete form to experiment with it in a live environment easily. We have placed several of these lengthy code examples, scripts, and utilities in a public GitHub repository. You will find the GitHub repository at

https://github.com/building-cloud-native-apps

We also present a complete cloud-native application example that demonstrates the development practices and infrastructure automation practices cohesively. This application and its associated resources are available at

https://github.com/oracle-quickstart/oci-cloudnative

These examples are a powerful learning tool when combined with the Always Free Tier of service offered by Oracle Cloud Infrastructure. This gives you access to the services provided by Oracle Cloud Infrastructure and can help you build hands-on experience and practice the concepts described in this book. You can sign up for the free trial with the included Always Free Tier at

https://www.oracle.com/cloud/free/

1

Introduction to Oracle Cloud Infrastructure

Oracle Cloud Infrastructure (OCI) offers a comprehensive platform of public cloud services that enable enterprises, Independent Software Vendors (ISVs), and startups to create cloud-scale solutions that are secure, highly available, and geographically distributed on one of the fastest-growing cloud provider footprints.

Cloud adoption can empower your organization to improve business agility and promote innovative solutions. However, every cloud infrastructure platform uses its own architecture and terminology. This makes the process of getting started on a cloud platform equally challenging for both new users and users who have worked on other cloud platforms. Understanding these terms also helps you understand how OCI is distributed across the globe, how it organizes resources, and how it secures access to them. If you are new to working on a cloud platform, this section introduces the basic OCI terminology. On the other hand, if you are familiar with other cloud platforms, many of these terms and concepts might sound familiar; however, they might also differ in small but important ways when compared to similar terms or concepts in other cloud platforms.

The OCI service portfolio is broad, encompassing infrastructure services, security and identity services, developer platforms, analytics platforms, machine learning and artificial intelligence (AI) platforms, media services, and more. Figure 1-1 shows a high-level overview of the various classes of services that are available in OCI. This book focuses on building cloud-native applications and discusses the services and platforms in OCI that help you build modern, distributed, and resilient applications. These include services such as Oracle Container Engine for Kubernetes (OKE), Oracle Container registry, OCI messaging and observability platforms, OCI service mesh, API gateways, and more. These services build on the foundational concepts of how resources are distributed, organized, secured. This chapter covers these foundational concepts in OCI and introduces its vocabulary. To get the most from OCI's services, this chapter also presents a set of best practices for effectively planning and executing your OCI adoption.

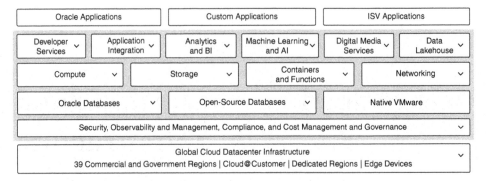

Figure 1-1   A High-Level Overview of the Services OCI Offers

Realms, Regions, and Availability Domains

OCI as a cloud platform is organized into multiple *realms*. An example of a realm, and the most common realm for most users of OCI, is the OCI commercial realm. Most users do not even realize that realms exist, because they most often interact with just the commercial realm. A realm is a logical construct that is spread across geographies and physical data centers. Realms are completely isolated from each other, even when they might share a physical location. Examples of other realms include the government realms for the United States, the United Kingdom, and more. These realms have a different geographical spread than the commercial realm.

A realm is made up of one or more *regions*. Regions are geographical areas around the globe where OCI has a presence. At the time of writing, the OCI commercial realm is spread across more than 45 regions across the globe and is used by OCI commercial customers (see Figure 1-2). The OCI approach to regions is to have regions close to customers. The OCI fundamental design and architecture prioritizes the speed and efficiency of launching new regions, allowing OCI to rapidly scale its footprint across the globe. The OCI focus on enterprise workloads prioritizes data sovereignty and business continuity requirements for customers, which drives its strategy of building multiple cloud regions in every country.

Regions themselves are a logical grouping of one or more *availability domains*, which are physical data centers located within the same relative geographical area. Some regions have multiple availability domains, which means that the region has multiple physical data centers that are connected by a fully encrypted low-latency/high-bandwidth network. Cloud resources can be regional in nature, as with a Kubernetes cluster, or they can be specific to an availability domain, as with a node (compute instance) within that cluster. Figure 1-3 shows the OCI region presence at the time of writing.

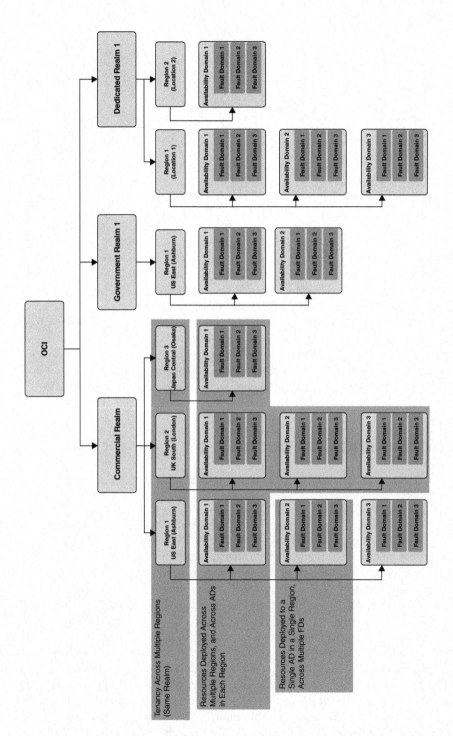

Figure 1-2 OCI Realms, Regions, and Availability Domains

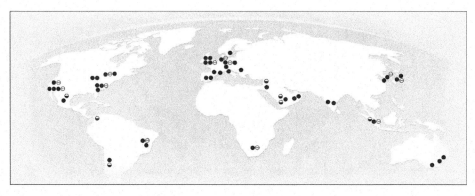

Figure 1-3   Oracle Cloud Infrastructure Global Footprint

An availability domain offers a construct known as a *fault domain* for applications to implement fault tolerance and high availability. Every availability domain has three fault domains that offer completely isolated physical hardware grouping. Each fault domain has its own hardware resources, including power distribution units, cooling, and more, within a single availability domain. This enables you to ensure that redundant resources you use are isolated at a hardware level, protecting your workloads from hardware failure and maintenance outages. Depending on the type of workloads and their characteristics, fault tolerance and high availability can be implemented within a single availability domain, spanning multiple availability domains within a region or even spanning the workload across multiple regions.

Tenancies and Compartments

A *tenancy* is a partition within an OCI realm that identifies a single customer subscription. A tenancy is created when you subscribe to OCI and is secure and isolated from other tenancies. A tenancy can subscribe to any region that is part of its realm and use the resources from any of the subscribed regions. It also acts as the top aggregate unit for cost management and budgeting tools that OCI provides out of the box. These included tools, such as the tenancy explorer, can aggregate resource use across regions to give users insights into their tenancy's resource use across all geographies.

Most organizations use a single tenancy and usually want to have a management model that is similar to their existing processes. This generally means that they carve up the tenancy and give individual departments or business units more autonomous control over their own collections of resources; the global infrastructure team then sets standards on usage quotas, security posture, and more. In other words, administrators usually compartmentalize their workloads or business units. OCI offers a construct for this exact purpose. Within a tenancy, you can organize your resources into *compartments*. Compartments are not just for organizing resources; they also let you manage who has access to perform various operations on resources within a compartment. This lets administrators create *policies* that govern how an organization's members access and interact with the resources. Compartments can be hierarchical: They can have nested compartments up to six levels deep. The root of all compartments is tenancy itself. As a simple example, an administrator could designate one group of users to have only read-only access to resources within a compartment, grant another group access to modify certain resources, and allow yet another group complete control, including the capability to create and terminate resources. Although this model is common, other models are also possible, depending on an organization's structure and what is conducive for the users. For instance, a large organization might operate as a set of independent business units that own their individual tenancies. Likewise, another organization could be horizontally integrated, with multiple shared databases colocated in a compartment that is managed by a team of database administrators (DBAs).

A cloud resource, or simply a *resource*, is any service or object that users create in OCI and that represents some capability. For instance, a Kubernetes cluster, a compute instance, a network security group, and a user account are all examples of resources. The various services that make up OCI offer APIs and tooling built on the APIs to enable users to interact with and manipulate these resources. Oracle assigns a unique identifier called an Oracle Cloud Identifier (OCID) to all resources. Users can use OCIDs to identify and operate on specific resources when using the OCI API, the command-line interface (CLI), or tools such as Terraform. OCIDs are structured as follows:

```
ocid1.<RESOURCE TYPE>.<REALM>.[REGION][.FUTURE USE].<UNIQUE ID>
```

An example OCID for a block volume could look like `ocid1.volume.oc1.iad.xxxx[truncated]xxxx` and an example OCID for a User could look like `ocid1.user.oc1..xxxx[truncated]xxxx`. Note that the *region* identifier in an OCID is optional and is present only for region-specific resources such as block volumes or compute instances (they are always located in a specific region). Global resources, such as a user, do not have this identifier because the user is not localized to any region but instead is valid across all regions to which the tenancy has subscribed.

Controlling Access to Resources

A common challenge for infrastructure teams is figuring out how to give their users a certain amount of autonomy without compromising their security posture. This is more challenging than it sounds. It starts with the task of identifying users, who can be human or nonhuman. The users can be transient because team members are generally added and removed or because a particular person's access changes over time. General industry principles such as the principle of least access promote an access pattern in which users are given the least privileges to accomplish their tasks and are restricted to the most specific resources for the shortest duration of time. This presents several challenges, such as needing to be very specific about the resources that a user can effect and further narrowing access to specific types of operations on those resources that are allowed and specific time frames.

To address these needs, OCI provides a built-in identity and access management (IAM) capability. OCI IAM enables you to manage access to your cloud resources in a declarative manner that spans regions. IAM provides resources such as *users*, *groups*, and *policies*. A *user* resource in OCI represents a subject that authenticates with OCI and works with OCI resources. A *group* resource in OCI is simply made up of zero or more users, making it simple to manage access for a collection of users by treating them as a logical collection. A user can be a part of multiple groups. IAM uses *policies* to describe access control, and it confers privileges to groups, never individual users. A user starts out as not a member of any group and, hence, has no privileges (other than perhaps changing passwords). When a user is added to a group, the user is conferred the privileges that the policy has granted to the group; if a user is a member of multiple groups, the user gets the widest permissions that are allowed by the totality of the group memberships.

Policies are designed to be intuitive and human readable, which makes it easy to create and maintain policies over time. Policies follow this structure:

```
Allow group <group_name> to <verb> <resource-type> in compartment
  <compartment_name>
```

Figure 1-4 shows a policy made up of several policy statements.

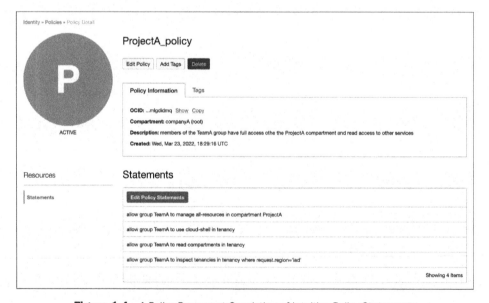

Figure 1-4   A Policy Document Consisting of Intuitive Policy Statements

Notice that the policy statements always start with the word `allow`. By default, there are no permissions; all policies *add* permissions and never take away permissions. In a policy statement, you can refer to *group names* using their OCIDs or names, and you can include multiple groups (comma separated) within the same statement.

The *verbs* indicate what types of operations are granted by the policy. Verbs can be `inspect`, `read`, `use`, and `manage`. Both `inspect` and `read` verbs allow nonmutating operations and essentially grant read-only access. The difference between them is that `inspect` restricts the amount of data you can read about the resource, whereas `read` allows the user to get complete metadata about a resource. The `use` verb grants use of the resource and limited modifications to resources, but it limits this to existing resources; it does not include the ability to create or delete resources. Furthermore, the `use` verb does not cover modifications that are equivalent to creation and deletion.

The various verbs attempt to aggregate API operations for each service in a generic manner. Ultimately, OCI is a cloud platform, and every resource provided by the platform is manipulated through the APIs that it exposes. The types of operations that are available for each resource differ, so the various verbs for each resource can also have different meanings. For instance, consider the verb `use` in the context of networking and in the context of storage: They could mean different things. Therefore, OCI documentation[1] provides a complete reference for each service and how the various verbs affect each resource. The various verbs and their effects in general terms can be summarized as follows:

- **inspect:** Fetch a limited amount of data about a resource
- **read:** Fetch the complete metadata for a resource
- **use:** Interact with the resource, without being able to create or delete it
- **manage:** Operate with complete control over the resource

To illustrate these verbs in action, consider the act of updating the Kubernetes version used by a Kubernetes cluster running on Container Engine for Kubernetes. This is not covered by the `use` verb and requires the permissions conferred by the `manage` verb. On the contrary, consider the act of generating a `kubeconfig` file. The cluster exists, and generating a `kubeconfig` file does not modify the cluster in any way. Therefore, a user who has permissions to `use` clusters can request the configuration required to connect to it. The `manage` verb, on the other hand, confers permissions to perform any action on the resource, including upgrading it to a newer version, creating new clusters, and terminating existing ones.

The verb in a policy statement is followed by the *resource type*. This can be a very specific resource or a more generalized family of related resources. Although it is good practice to individually identify the resources the policy affects, many times resources are closely related and often managed together. In these cases, a single policy statement can refer to a family of resources that the policy statement will affect equally. The primary advantage of using family resource types is the capability to write fewer policies and ease policy management. The downside is that if OCI adds a new resource to a family, the existing policies will automatically apply to the new resource, which is sometimes undesirable. As an example, consider the following resource types:

- `clusters`: Represent Kubernetes clusters running on Oracle Container Engine for Kubernetes.

- `cluster-node-pools`: Represent a pool of nodes that act as worker nodes for deploying and running workloads in this cluster. A cluster may have many node pools.
- `cluster-work-requests`: Consist of resources that track long-running tasks, such as upgrading your cluster or scaling your node pool, and other cluster management operations that are executed asynchronously.

These three resource types are related to each other and can be collectively addressed as the `cluster-family` aggregate resource type. In the future, if another resource type that is closely related to these is added, the `cluster-family` aggregate resource type could encompass that resource type as well. In other words, the aggregate resource type's scope can change as the services expand and evolve.

Using these resource types individually, we can craft policies that give various groups access to very specific operations. This approach might be well suited for organizations that have clear responsibility boundaries or are required to isolate access for regulatory reasons. Such an organization might choose to use policy statements as follows:

```
Allow group k8s_admin to manage clusters in compartment project_A
Allow group k8s_admin to manage cluster-node-pools in compartment project_A
Allow group k8s_admin to manage cluster-work-requests in compartment project_A
Allow group k8s_ops to read clusters in compartment project_A
Allow group k8s_ops to read cluster-node-pools in compartment project_A
Allow group k8s_ops to read cluster-work-requests in compartment project_A
```

These policy statements identify two groups, `k8s_admin` and `k8s_ops`. The `k8s_admin` group has full control over these resources, whereas the `k8s_ops` group has the ability to read the resources and their metadata. Note that both groups have access to the same resource types, but their level of access or the operations that members of each group are allowed to perform are different. Using the aggregate resource type, the same policy statements can be rewritten as follows:

```
Allow group k8s_admin to manage cluster-family in compartment project_A
Allow group k8s_ops to read cluster-family in compartment project_A
```

An agile team in which developers take on multiple roles might find it easier to create relatively coarse-grained policies that permit the same level of access to all the resource types within the family. It is important to note that, when using an aggregate resource type such as `cluster-family`, if the aggregate resource type adds a new individual resource type to it, these policies will now grant access to that new resource type, which did not exist at the time the policy was written. Therefore, you should take care when using aggregate resource types: Over time, the policy could potentially give users access to more resources (but always closely related ones) than at the time of its writing. Being more specific might be verbose, but it is usually more precise and consistent with the intent. The contrary view to this approach could be that an aggregate would only ever add resources that are closely related and, therefore, if a closely related new resource type is added in the future, it might invariably trigger an updating of the policy to include the new resource type. The choice here depends on your preference, established organizational processes, and security posture.

The final part of the preceding policy syntax is the scope of the policy statement—in other words, where and at what level this policy should be applied. This is typically a compartment. In the preceding example, the permissions are granted to the groups k8s_admin and k8s_ops for all resource types in the cluster-family in the compartment named ProjectA. This keeps the policies you write simple to read, understand, and maintain, yet keeps them flexible enough that you can implement an access pattern to give users the least amount of privileges to accomplish their tasks to the most specific resources. The privileges granted by a policy statement are limited to classes of operations (verbs) and scoped to groups of users. The resources to which the access is granted are limited to the resource types and scoped to the compartment specified. When an authenticated user attempts to perform an operation on OCI—regardless of whether the API is used directly or a higher-level abstraction is used (such as the Software Development Kits [SDKs], CLI, Terraform, Ansible, or the web console)—the IAM system checks whether the user (or, more specifically, any group that the user belongs to) is allowed to perform the requested operation.

Policies also offer advanced syntax elements that are a lot more granular and nuanced than the simple syntax you have seen so far. As part of a policy statement, you can specify one or more conditions that must be met for access to be granted. These conditions are based on variables that represent either the access request itself or the resource on which the action is taken. The variable that encapsulates the request parameters and characteristics is named request. The variable that represents the resource being acted upon is named target. Using these variables enables you to make policies a lot more fine-grained. As an example, consider the following policy:

```
Allow group vendor-admins to manage clusters in tenancy
    where all { request.utc-timestamp.time-of-day between '17:00:00Z' and
  '01:00:00Z',
                      target.compartment.id != 'OCID_for_production_compartment',
                      request.permission != 'CLUSTER_DELETE'}
```

This policy enables members of the group vendor-admins to manage clusters in the tenancy if they meet some conditions. The conditions are combined with the all keyword, indicating that all the conditions need to be met if access is to be granted. First, the group is granted the permission only when the requests are made during a specific time interval of the day. Second, the users are allowed to manage clusters in any compartment except the production compartment. Last, the CLUSTER_DELETE permission is not granted. This uses the notion of permission, which allows you to be very specific in your policy statements. *Permissions* represent the operations that a user is allowed to perform on a resource. These operations depend on the resource itself. Verbs such as use and manage, in the context of a specific service, are simply bundles of these permissions. The Oracle documentation comprehensively covers these advanced constructs.[2]

Similar to groups, OCI supports a construct called a dynamic group. *Dynamic groups* are defined in terms of a set of matching rules. All resources that match the rules are considered members of the group. For instance, consider a dynamic group named build-nodes that is defined by a matching rule that matches all instances in a specific compartment named build-nodes. The matching rule might look as follows:

```
instance.compartment.id = '<compartment_ocid for the build-nodes compartment>'
```

Now consider the following policy:

```
allow dynamic-group build-nodes to use devops-repository in compartment
    Project-A
```

Any instance created in the compartment `build-nodes` is automatically a member of the dynamic group. When the instance in this compartment tries to access a `devops-repository` in the Project-A compartment, its permissions are checked and IAM will resolve it as having access. This access is granted because the instance that is requesting access is part of the dynamic group `build-nodes` and the dynamic group is given access through the policy.

Cloud Guard and Security Zones

Cloud Guard is an OCI service that constantly examines your OCI resources, looking for potential security issues, configurations that increase the attack surface, or user activity that deviates from normal. When Cloud Guard detects a problem, it can alert you or take corrective actions itself. The general workflow in Cloud Guard is to define a scope for the resources to target, usually a compartment. When that is set, Cloud Guard continues to monitor the resources it is targeting, using a set of detectors. The detectors' behavior is encapsulated in a set of rules bundled as a recipe. When rule violations are detected, it raises a problem. Responders then can take an appropriate action, based on rules defined in a responder recipe. This flow and behavior are fully customizable. You can use Oracle-provided detector recipes to watch for issues or build your own ruleset as a recipe. Similarly, the actions that are taken can be customized by either using the Oracle-provided recipes or building your own. Figure 1-5 shows the Cloud Guard dashboard that organizes the high-level report from Cloud Guard, enabling you to drill down into the problems that are detected.

Even though Cloud Guard constantly watches over its list of targets using the detectors you specify, it can be useful to set some ground rules to prevent policy violations instead of simply detecting and remediating them. Security zones provide exactly this capability. Security zones work by validating operations, such as creating or updating resources in real time to deny operations that would result in a violation of the zone's rules. Security zones are created by attaching a security zone recipe to a compartment. Security zone recipes are a collection of security zone policies that are applied to the security zone.

Figure 1-5 Cloud Guard Dashboard

For example, a security zone policy such as deny block_volume_without_vault_ key forces block volumes created in a security zone to require a customer-managed encryption key instead of the default Oracle-managed encryption key. These policies are not always intrusion oriented; for instance, the policy deny database_without_backup enforces all databases within that security zone to have automatic database backup configurations. Security policies are categorized into several groups, based on the security principles they help implement. You can create your own recipes using these policies to meet your specific security requirements. Apart from the custom recipes you can create, all tenancies come with a default recipe named Maximum Security Recipe that includes all available security zone policies.

When creating a new tenancy or starting with OCI, it is often good practice to enable Cloud Guard. Enabling Cloud Guard is an easy process that involves the tenancy owner granting the Cloud Guard service permissions to introspect resources within the tenancy. Although these services are part of OCI, they still require customers to acknowledge and provide privileges so that they can introspect customer-owned resources. Cloud Guard requires minimal permissions to monitor the resources in your tenancy. With Cloud Guard enabled, you can also use security zones, which requires an added set of permissions. Both Cloud Guard and security zones provide default configurations that you can customize to your needs or use as is when you get started.

Service Limits and Cost Management

A basic understanding of service limits, quotas, budgets, and other guardrails and cost-management features in OCI can come in handy as you scale your workloads on OCI. Every tenancy is preconfigured at its creation with a set of limits for each resource type, called *service limits*. When you reach the service limit for a resource, OCI does not allow you to create more of that resource. These limits exist to protect users from accidentally creating too many resources. Service limits are updated automatically, based on consumption patterns, but they also can be updated by raising a request from the OCI web console.

Whereas service limits are set by Oracle, *compartment quotas* are limits that you can set on compartments. Compartment quotas are set through policies. Consider the following policy:

```
set compute-core quotas gpu-a10-v2-count to 20 in compartment Project-A
```

This policy caps the number of GPUs for shapes in the VM.GPU.A10 and BM.GPU.A10 series to 20 in the compartment named Project-A. Compartment quotas are typically used when a project or a team is given its own compartment and the admin wants to cap the resource usage for the project or team by setting a compartment quota. When the quota has been reached, no more resources of that kind will be provisioned in that compartment. In the preceding example, `gpu-a10-v2-count` is the quota for the number of GPUs that are available through compute shapes such as VM.GPU.A10 and BM.GPU.A10. These are GPU-enabled compute shapes; a tenancy admin might want to use quotas to ensure that all projects and teams have access to these resources so that no single team can monopolize its use or overconsume them.

These quota policies can be used to set a quota (`set`), unset a quota (`unset`, typically to override a tenancy-wide quota), or remove access to a resource within the specified compartment (`zero`). It is important to note that, when the compartment quota has been reached, the tenancy still has resources that can be consumed in other compartments. The tenancy administrator, or any user who has access to manage compartment quotas, is in full control of these limits. Each service exposes certain resource quotas; the OCI documentation provides a complete reference.[3]

Limiting resource usage often can be a harsh step, especially when your goal is to minimize friction and increase team velocity while staying informed about resource usage and projections. To address this, OCI comes with features that help you track your cost across multiple dimensions. A *budget* is a construct that can be used to create your own soft limits on resources so that you can keep track of your infrastructure spending and create alerts to give you a heads-up. Alerts can be triggered when your spending crosses thresholds that you set. Administrators and users who have been given access to the feature can manage budgets using a consolidated view in OCI and also receive email alerts. Unlike compartment quotas, which are always set at a compartment level, budgets offer the flexibility of using cost-tracking tags or compartments to track spending. Budgets are not evaluated in real time and they update periodically (usually hourly). Each budget shows the current spend as well as a forecast for the spend, along with the last time the budget was evaluated. Figure 1-6 shows the alert options for a budget.

Because budgets are based on costs and spending instead of limits placed on resources themselves, they can be used alongside compartment quotas in a complementary manner.

When bringing new workloads to OCI, it is typically easier to set a budget and work within that constraint. This is because, when bootstrapping a new workload, developers might not have a good handle on the resources required and the work typically involves a lot of initial flux in determining resource consumption, sizing, and setting up and tearing down ad-hoc environments. This is also the phase where you need the most velocity to build momentum for your team. You can keep tabs on the spending patterns using a budget. Then when you get a good sense of what your typical resource consumption is, you can set quotas to tighten the rules. This avoids accidental resource consumption, say, by a misbehaving automation.

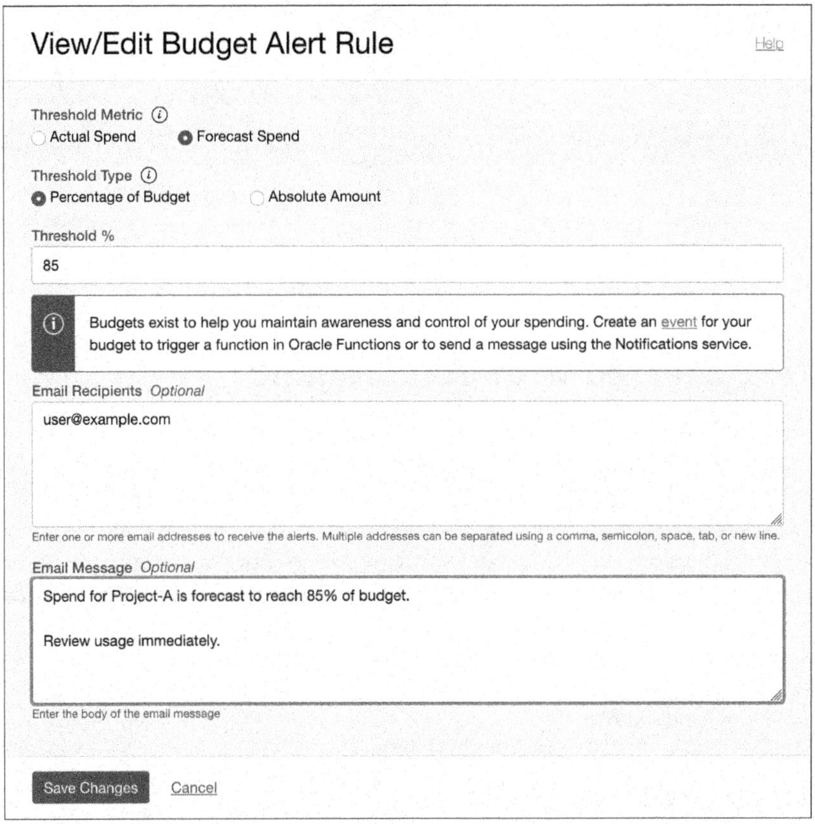

Figure 1-6   Creating a Budget Alert Rule

Apart from these services, OCI also includes many governance and compliance features. Tenancy explorer is a service that enables you to examine your tenancy to get a cross-region view of your resource usage. Cloud Advisor, shown in Figure 1-7, automatically and continuously analyzes your tenancy to find cost optimizations, performance improvements, and security posture improvements. Transparent billing offers analysis tools within the console that enable you to explore your spending in multiple dimensions.

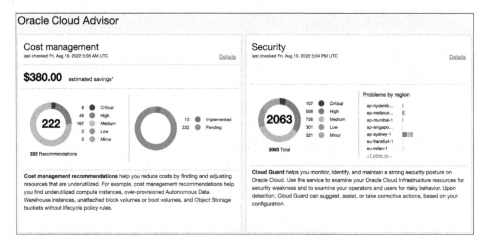

Figure 1-7   Oracle Cloud Advisor Dashboard

Getting Started with Your Tenancy

Having covered the basic OCI terminology and concepts, this chapter moves on to look at how you can start setting up your tenancy to support development teams, create application environments, track costs, and set budgets. The first step is to sign up for an account. OCI offers a paid tier, a trial, and an always-free tier. The paid tier offers the full breadth of metered services, and you have multiple options to pay as you go and leverage existing licenses you might have. The trial (at press time) offers a 30-day window with a $300 credit to your account. The always-free tier limits the resources you can use, but these are available to you without charges for an unlimited time. After you have activated your account, you can log in through https://cloud.oracle.com and see your cloud service dashboard.

Setting Up Users and Groups

When a tenancy is created, the email address you provided is added as the first user in the tenancy, and this user is added to the Administrators group. The Administrators group is a superuser group that, by default, has complete privileges over the entire tenancy. If you provided your email address when you signed up for your tenancy, then you are automatically an administrator once the tenancy has been created. Administrators can add other users and groups. The identity system can also be federated to an external identity provider.

Users can always change or reset their own console password, as well as manage their own API keys. An administrator does not need to create a policy to give a user those abilities.

To manage credentials for users other than yourself, you must be in the Administrators group or some other group that has permission to work with the tenancy. Having permission to work with a compartment within the tenancy is not sufficient. For more information, see the Administrators Group and Policy.[4]

IAM administrators (or anyone with administration privileges to the tenancy) can use either the console or the API to manage all aspects of both types of credentials, for themselves and all other users. This includes creating an initial one-time password for a new user, resetting a password, uploading API keys, and deleting API keys.

Setting Up API Keys and Auth Tokens

As a Developer or a DevOps engineer, one of the first actions to take after you have logged into your account, is to set up your API keys. The API key is a standard 2048-bit RSA key pair in PEM format. You upload the public key to your user profile and keep the private key securely. Every API call you make to OCI is signed by the private key, and OCI verifies the signature using the public key associated with your profile. The API keys securely authenticate you with the OCI APIs and are essential when you work with OCI tooling such as the command-line interface, Terraform, or the various SDKs. You can use the console to generate the private/public key pair for you (see Figure 1-8). If you already have a key pair, you can choose to upload the public key as well. OCI tooling such as the OCI CLI or external tools such as Terraform use these API keys to sign the requests to OCI APIs and identify the user making the API calls. Because developers and DevOps engineers commonly work with multiple tenancies, regions or identities, these API keys and associated information are typically stored in a configuration file as *profiles* to easily switch between the configurations and identities. When you use the console to add the key pair, the console also generates a configuration file snippet that you can save. The configuration file typically has the following elements:

- `user:` The OCID that represents the user who owns this key
- `fingerprint:` The public key's digest in two-digit groups
- `tenancy:` The tenancy's OCID
- `region:` The default region to use
- `key_file:` The path on your file system where the private key file is located

Auth Tokens are Oracle-generated token strings that can be used when a third party or API does not support key-based authentication and when OCI signature-based authentication cannot be used. Consider the example of using Docker to pull a container image from an image repository with the `docker pull <image>` command. OCI provides a private image repository that is Docker compatible. Docker, however, uses usernames and passwords to authenticate with repositories, not the more secure key-based authentication that OCI prefers. In this scenario, you can use an auth token. Auth tokens do not expire, and each user can have up to two auth tokens at any given time. Similar to API keys, users have the capability to create, update, and delete their own auth tokens. Administrators, on the other hand, have the capability to manage auth tokens for other users as well. Figure 1-9 shows a user profile with two auth tokens. The purpose of these tokens is clear from their descriptions; however, the actual token itself can no longer be viewed. If the token is lost, the user can delete and re-create another token.

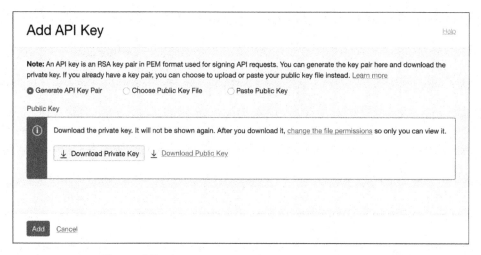

Figure 1-8   Generating an API Key Pair from the Console

Auth Tokens

Description	Created	
OCIR - Cloud Shell	Thu, Sep 28, 2023, 17:04:29 UTC	⋮
OCIR - Dev Machine	Sun, Oct 8, 2023, 21:24:27 UTC	⋮

Displaying 2 Tokens

Figure 1-9   Generating Auth Tokens

Planning How Your Teams Will Use OCI

As you prepare to onboard your team to OCI, it is prudent to consider a plan for how you will manage your tenancy and set it up so that multiple teams can work within it efficiently. You should consider how your IT and development organizations are structured and create a synergistic strategy for managing your tenancy. This includes planning how your users are grouped and designing an efficient compartment structure that makes it conducive for developers and DevOps teams to collaborate effectively. Development teams typically want quick and friction-free access to resources, whereas

DevOps and SecOps teams have resource management and security posture as their top priorities. Designing an efficient compartment structure and a set of policies that manage access to these compartments is critical to ensuring success for the various stakeholder teams.

On one end of the spectrum, you can put all your resources into the root compartment. This would make the setup process simple, but at the same time it makes fine-grained access control more difficult. Although this might be useful during evaluation and basic prototyping with OCI, its untenable for real-world use in an enterprise setting. The other extreme would be having too many compartments with resources that are used and managed by the same groups located across several compartments, resulting in very complex policies needed to manage the right level of access to the resources and compartments. Both these extremes are uncommon for real-world use.

One common strategy would be to set up compartments and policies that align with the workloads. For instance, imagine that your team is bootstrapping a new project codenamed Hydra. You could create a new compartment named Hydra and then create groups such as Hydra-Devs, Hydra-Ops, Hydra-Admins, and Hydra-ReadOnly. All resources pertaining to the Hydra project, from core services such as networks, to developer lifecycle services such as DevOps, to application runtimes such as Kubernetes clusters, are all located within the compartment. The users on the project are grouped into the various groups. Some users could be taking on multiple roles by being a part of multiple groups. This compartment and group structure makes it easy to create policies that apply to each group and give them varying levels of access to the resources in the compartment. As an example, consider the following policy statements:

```
Allow group Hydra-Admins to manage all-resources in compartment Hydra
Allow group Hydra-Ops to manage cluster-family in compartment Hydra
Allow group Hydra-Ops to manage devops-family in compartment Hydra
Allow group Hydra-Devs to use cluster-family in compartment Hydra
Allow group Hydra-Devs to use devops-family in compartment Hydra
Allow group Hydra-Devs to manage devops-repository in compartment Hydra
Allow group Hydra-ReadOnly to inspect all-resources in compartment Hydra
```

The example shows that Hydra-Admins can act as superusers within the compartment. This is often desirable to scale the team of tenancy admins while maintaining the principle of least access. A few users who belong to this group can assume the administrator role, but only within the confines of the Hydra project. The Hydra-Ops team has access to manage both the `cluster-family` as well as the `devops-family`. This means that members of this group can create and manage OKE clusters as well as code repositories (git), build pipelines, and more. The group Hydra-Devs can access these same resources but cannot make administrative changes such as creating or modifying the clusters; however, it can create code repositories. The Hydra-ReadOnly group can view all resources in the compartment but cannot otherwise affect them. This model makes it easy to create a sandboxed environment for each workload and enables administrators to create clear and concise policies, making them easy to understand and manage. This approach can be thought of as a *vertical model* because all layers of the stack for a particular workload are managed together.

Similar to organizing compartments and user groups around workloads, another common approach is to organize around the existing organizational structures. These cases might use compartments such as Networking, Databases, and Middleware, and user groups such as Network-Admins, DBAs, and DevOps that own and operate their own collection of resources for which they are responsible. In this model, the resources that are managed by a group are colocated in a compartment even when these are used by separate workloads. That is, regardless of which application they are associated with, all databases are in the same compartment and are administered by the same set of DBAs, which might feel familiar to organizations that follow a similar model in their enterprises. This model also makes it easier to manage policies for shared resources, such as databases that multiple applications use. Such an approach can be thought of as a *horizontal model* because it typically groups the management of a class of resources horizontally across workloads. This model can support organizational structures that already operate with these horizontal dependencies.

These are broad approaches that generalize common usage patterns. Each organization and each team's dynamics are different, so it is a worthwhile exercise to plan how you want to organize your resources, group your users, and manage access. In addition to the approaches described here, the Oracle documentation covers other approaches and includes an OCI Cloud Adoption Framework that addresses best practices and provides concrete guidance across several pillars of success, such as business and people strategies, process design, technology implementation, and operations.

Summary

This chapter just scratched the surface of OCI, but it gives you a sense of the scale at which you can operate; how the platform itself is structured; and what controls are available to manage your workloads, organize your teams, and provide access in a secure and efficient manner. This offers a starting point for you to explore more features in OCI and form preliminary ideas on how you can shape OCI to fit your deployment process and workflows. Elasticity and resiliency are keystones for a cloud native application. The next chapter discusses the infrastructure automation tools and platforms in OCI that enable you to scale infrastructure as your application's needs change at runtime.

References

1 OCI Policy Reference: https://docs.oracle.com/en-us/iaas/Content/Identity/Reference/policyreference.htm

2 Advanced Policy Features : https://docs.oracle.com/en-us/iaas/Content/Identity/policiesadvfeatures/policyadvancedfeatures.htm

3 Available Quotas by Service: https://docs.oracle.com/en-us/iaas/Content/Quotas/Concepts/resourcequotas_topic-Available_Quotas_by_Service.htm

4 Administrators Group and Policy: https://docs.oracle.com/en-us/iaas/Content/Identity/Concepts/overview.htm#The

2

Infrastructure Automation and Management

One of the primary ways in which cloud-based infrastructure differs from traditional infrastructure is in its use of APIs to provision and manage infrastructure. This means that the traditional hardware procurement and refresh cycle can now be replaced with a simple API call. This simple but powerful construct opens the door to significant advantages and optimization in infrastructure management. Users no longer have to preplan for infrastructure needs; instead, they can provision infrastructure just in time. This also unlocks cost savings in elastically scaling infrastructure based on metrics or other criteria. The advantages of these optimizations also cascade into modern application design practices that can programmatically scale infrastructure along with applications based on real-time need.

One Set of APIs, Different Ways to Call Them

As with any other cloud provider, Oracle Cloud Infrastructure (OCI) provides application programming interfaces (APIs) for all its infrastructure resources. This means that every single infrastructure resource that OCI provides can be created and managed using its APIs. On top of these APIs, OCI provides software development kits (SDKs) for various programming languages, which make the process of calling these APIs from your favorite programming language easy and enables you to create a new breed of software that can provision and manage hardware by itself. For example, if you have a Java or Python application that needs to create compute resources or set up other infrastructure, you can use the SDK to make the call to the OCI APIs from your language of choice.

Taking it one step further, domain-specific languages (DSLs) have been developed to make the process of interacting with these APIs easier. These DSLs and tools that build on top of these DSLs bring the power of cloud APIs to infrastructure professionals who have no application development background or experience.

Two such popular tools are Terraform and Ansible. Terraform uses a DSL named HashiCorp Configuration Language (HCL) to describe infrastructure and manage it. Ansible describes infrastructure and configuration in YAML format. Regardless of the format and the tools/clients used, the APIs are the primary endpoints to the cloud platform. Users interacting with OCI using a browser-based UI, a terminal-based CLI, or even infrastructure-management tools such as Terraform are simply using various channels to call the underlying APIs. As tools and technologies evolve, OCI keeps adding new ways to make it easier to call the APIs and use OCI.

The examples and later chapters in the book make extensive use of Terraform for infrastructure management. This chapter covers Terraform basics and the managed services in OCI that use Terraform.

A Quick Terraform Primer

Terraform is an infrastructure-management tool from HashiCorp that helps you implement practices for managing infrastructure as code to create and manage reproducible infrastructure in the cloud and even across cloud providers. It works on the principle of defining infrastructure as it should exist (in a desired state) using a configuration language. This definition is then passed on to the Terraform tool, which makes appropriate cloud API calls to converge on the desired infrastructure state expressed in the configuration.

A user starts by defining the infrastructure topology and specifying how these resources are connected and configured using the Terraform language. This concise and human-readable configuration language forms the blueprint of the infrastructure that you want to create.

The Terraform language is expressed using the HashiCorp Configuration Language (HCL) syntax, which is also used in other HashiCorp products. This configuration file, often simply called the Terraform configuration, is typically source controlled to maintain a history of the changes to the desired infrastructure state. When Terraform configurations are paired with a source control system to store and track changes to the codified infrastructure, and a CI/CD tooling to manage the deployment of this infrastructure, you can quickly create a workflow that manages immutable, consistent, and repeatable environments. Figure 2-1 illustrates the Terraform workflow.

Terraform interacts with external services such as cloud providers, Software as a Service (SaaS) services, and other APIs using plug-in modules called providers. A *provider* abstracts the cloud- or service-specific detail and models the resource mapping for the Terraform configuration language. Every Terraform provider adds a set of resource types and data sources that Terraform can use. You can use these resource types and data sources in the configuration to manage or query the respective cloud resources using Terraform. The Terraform Registry is the main repository of publicly available Terraform providers and hosts the OCI provider for Terraform.

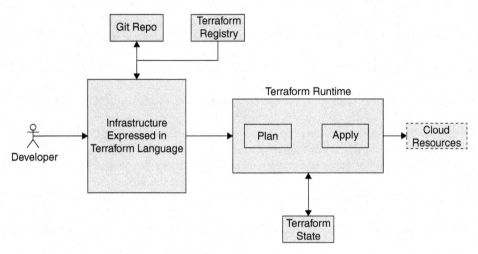

Figure 2-1   Terraform Workflow

The Terraform Registry also acts as a repository for common cloud resource configurations that are designed to be reusable. These reusable configurations are called Terraform modules. Modules make it easy to ensure consistency and replicate organizational standards in your configurations. Modules can also cut down on duplicated resource definitions, making it easier to maintain these configurations over time. Consider an organization in which multiple teams are creating and using cloud resources such as networks. The organization might want to enforce specific configurations for all the networks that are created. When using a Terraform provider directly, users have full control over the resource parameters and may choose to configure that resource in any manner they choose. When using a Terraform module, however, many of the configuration options for the resource are already chosen by the module developer, and a minimal set of configuration options is presented to the user. In most cases, a module is functional in nature. This means that a module might have multiple resources, such as compute instances, load balancers, storage volumes, and more to quickly and consistently create a complete subsystem. Terraform modules make it easy for the user to create the resource with minimal input while adhering to the organizational standards.

When the desired configuration has been expressed in the Terraform language, the Terraform runtime can process that configuration to construct cloud API calls and execute those API calls against a cloud platform such as OCI. Because the configuration is expressed in terms of the resources and data sources supported by a provider, Terraform calls on the respective providers to make the actual API calls. Terraform configurations are required to declare the specific providers they use within the configuration, and Terraform initializes the providers when it runs. The same Terraform configuration can also use multiple providers, which makes it possible to interact with several services and cloud vendors within the same configuration to create and manage multicloud deployments. Terraform can validate the configuration, as well as do a dry run, by executing a `terraform plan` to see what impact running the configuration, executing a `terraform apply`, would have on the existing infrastructure.

Figure 2-2 illustrates the typical cycle for managing infrastructure with Terraform. It starts with defining your infrastructure as code using the Terraform language. Next, you pass this configuration to Terraform and run a `plan`, which causes Terraform to inspect the existing resources and figure out the changes that need to be applied to converge the configuration to the one that has been provided. The result of the plan is the set of actions to be performed on cloud resources, such as what resources are to be created, modified, or deleted. If the plan looks valid and the actions that will be performed are acceptable, the developer can run an `apply`, which causes the plan to be applied. During the `plan` and `apply` operations, Terraform calls on the providers to make the API calls to query the existing resources or manage them on the remote cloud platforms. Resources can also be destroyed after their purpose has been fulfilled, which is common for ephemeral resources in the cloud. Using Terraform to destroy resources also ensures that no resource is overlooked or left behind because Terraform keeps tracks of every resource it creates. For instance, suppose that you write a Terraform configuration that creates a couple of compute instances and a load balancer that points to them. The first time this configuration is applied, all resources in the configuration are created. The configuration described in the Terraform files as code using the Terraform language now matches the resources created in the cloud. Now, if the developer updates the definition to include a third compute instance and updates the load-balancer definition to point at all three instances, Terraform will create a plan to add a new instance and to update the existing load balancer to include the newly created instance. Terraform will also figure out that it needs to create the instance first so that the instance's IP address can be used as a back end for the load balancer to direct traffic. When you no longer need these resources, you can destroy them or scale down the resources. The code you created for the infrastructure can be run at any time to re-create the exact same resource configuration whenever you need it.

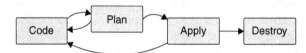

Figure 2-2 The Typical Lifecycle for Managing Infrastructure with Terraform

This lifecycle can also address drift in your configurations. Drift is the change in configuration that is usually manually applied to your infrastructure, outside of what Terraform has been configured to do. For instance, consider a load balancer that is configured to listen on port 443. Now consider an operator that manually updates the configuration to open port 80 as well. This change is not described in the Terraform configuration; therefore, the next time Terraform runs, Terraform will detect this change and recommend reverting it to the original state by closing that port. This makes it easy to ensure that your infrastructure configurations are always well known, reproducible, and expressed as code that can be audited.

The power of implementing infrastructure as code is fully realized when you introduce a source control management system to store and track changes to the codified infrastructure and optional CI/CD tooling to manage the deployment of this infrastructure. You then have a complete workflow to create and manage immutable, consistent, and repeatable environments. No one needs to guess what configuration changes have happened to the infrastructure over time. Adopting this model means that the only way to manage the infrastructure is through Terraform, and Terraform is expressed as code with full version history and provenance tracked by the source control system.

This level of automation opens a new realm of possibilities for application development teams to become more agile than ever while optimizing cost. In a testing environment, for example, tests generally are not running continuously, which results in resource waste. With the help of automation tools such as Terraform and a CI/CD platform, application teams can create a test environment when required, run these tests, and destroy the environment after the tests have been completed. Because the infrastructure is described as code, it can consistently be re-created any number of times in any location. This portability also enables application teams to quickly create consistent environments across regions. These new opportunities help application teams expand quickly and consistently across the globe, create disaster recovery processes that are cost-optimized by running a scaled-down version of the infrastructure in the primary site, and more.

A Basic Introduction to the Terraform Language

Terraform configurations can be expressed using the Terraform language (using the HCL syntax) or using JavaScript Object Notation (JSON). Although expressing configurations in JSON makes it easier to parse using a variety of tools, the native Terraform language using the HCL syntax is more common and more expressive. Throughout this book, we use the more commonly used native syntax instead of JSON.

Terraform configurations written using the native language (HCL) are organized into blocks. *Blocks* are of different kinds and can represent an object such as a cloud resource, an output definition, a variable, or a provider configuration. Listing 2-1 provides an example.

Listing 2-1   Elements of the Terraform Language

```
# Block 1
variable "tenancy_ocid" {
    default = "xxxx.xxxx.xxxx.xxxx"
}
# Block 2. Note that arguments for the provider definition have been truncated
  for brevity.
provider "oci" {
  tenancy_ocid = var.tenancy_ocid

  ...
```

```
    . . .
}
# Block 3
resource "oci_core_vcn" "my_vcn" {
  cidr_block = "10.0.0.0/16"
    . . .
    . . .
}


# Block 4
resource "oci_core_subnet" "public" {
  vcn_id = oci_core_vcn.my_vcn.id
  cidr_block = cidrsubnet(var.vcn_cidr, 8, 0)
    . . .
    . . .
}
data "oci_identity_availability_domains" "test_availability_domains" {
    compartment_id = var.tenancy_ocid
}
```

Block 1 defines a *variable* named `tenancy_ocid` and provides a default value for it using the argument `default`. This variable can be referenced from other parts of the code as `var.tenancy_ocid`.

Block 2 declares and configures a *provider*. This block references the variable defined in the listing as `var.tenancy_ocid`. The intention of the developer here is to build a configuration that can be run against multiple tenancies by turning the `tenancy_id` into a variable that can be changed at runtime.

Block 3 is a *resource* block that represents a cloud resource. In this case, the `oci_core_vcn` resource models a virtual cloud network in OCI and is named `my_vcn`. The CIDR block argument is provided with an explicit value.

Block 4 is also a *resource* block, and this one represents a subnet. Subnets are created inside (virtual) networks. In Block 4, the network to which this subnet should belong is identified by the `vcn_id` argument. Note the value of this argument: `oci_core_vcn.my_vcn.id`. It is clearly pointing to the VCN created in Listing 2-1, identified by its resource type and name: `oci_core_vcn.my_vcn`. However, the `id` attribute is not present; the `id` attribute is provided by the `oci_core_vcn` resource. The provider documentation lists the attributes that can be used to configure each resource type.[1]

It is also worth pointing out that arguments can be updatable or non-updatable, depending on the behavior of the cloud resource. In the previous example, the `vcn_id` argument for the resource is non-updatable. After the subnet is created, if the value is changed and Terraform is executed again, Terraform will notice the change. This effectively means that the subnet will be created under a different VCN. Terraform will delete the existing subnet and create a new subnet with the new arguments. Here, it makes sense because the updated configuration effectively means that a subnet is to be moved from one VCN to another and that the cloud provider does not support an "in-place" update to happen for this property of the resource. Another example could be updating the tags on a resource. Tags can be updated in place and thus will not trigger the re-creation of a resource. After the Terraform configuration to model the cloud resources has been created, you perform a dry run with Terraform. Performing a `terraform plan` shows the exact changes that will be effected. To make the changes that the dry run has outlined, a `terraform apply` can be executed.

Terraform State Tracking

Terraform tracks the state of your infrastructure using a `.tfstate` file. This state file is used to create associations between the cloud resources you create when you run the Terraform configuration and the entries defined in the configuration. In the previous example, when you create the actual subnet in OCI, the subnet's identity (OCID) is associated with the definition `"oci_core_subnet" "public"`. In the future, if the definition or configuration properties of the subnet change, Terraform will use this association to know which subnet in the VCN (identified by its OCID) to update or re-create the resource.

Before taking any action, Terraform runs a refresh to reconcile the state of the external real infrastructure resources with what is defined in the configuration. The state file is used for this reconciliation as well. If the external real infrastructure has been changed manually outside Terraform, there will be a delta between the state that Terraform has been tracking and the state that is on the real infrastructure. This *drift* detection capability in Terraform can greatly enhance the security posture by detecting unapproved infrastructure configuration changes, keeping the infrastructure in a well-known reproducible state. The state file also tracks dependencies between resources. In the previous example, if the VCN were to be re-created, the subnets would need to be re-created as well; Terraform automatically knows this because it tracks the dependencies between the resources in the state file.

By default, the Terraform state file is stored in a file named `terraform.tfstate`. For most real use, however, the default location is inadequate—especially when working in teams. Consider two developers running a Terraform configuration in parallel. They could be creating duplicate resources because they are using their own state files and are unaware of each other's changes. Terraform supports remote state to solve this problem and offers several options to configure and store state remotely. Aside from making the state changes transparent to everyone in the team, remote state storage can also use locking. Locking the state protects teams from performing multiple simultaneous Terraform executions at the same time, thus ensuring that each Terraform run begins with the most recent updated state. Terraform can use one of several back ends to manage remote state; each back end provides support for a different storage system.

OCI object storage can be used as a remote state back end in Terraform. This allows Terraform to use the OCI object storage as the storage back end for Terraform state, making it consistent across all users of the Terraform configuration. Terraform can leverage OCI Object Storage using the HTTP back end or the S3 back end. Table 2-1 compares the two storage options.

Table 2-1   .tfstate Storage Option Comparison

HTTP Back End	S3 Remote State Back End
Uses standard HTTP methods	Uses Object Storage S3-compatible APIs
Requires a preauthenticated request and no additional authentication	Requires additional per-user authentication

> **Note**
>
> Terraform state files can potentially contain sensitive data, especially if you use Terraform to manage access keys, passwords, or cryptographic keys. Even without such data, the state file contains a complete blueprint for your cloud infrastructure and its topology. For this reason, it's always preferable to consider the state file as a sensitive document.

The OCI Terraform Provider

The OCI Terraform provider[2] is the component that connects Terraform to OCI services. It models the OCI services and APIs as Terraform objects such as resources and data sources that can be used in Terraform configurations. The OCI provider is open source and is available through the Terraform Registry, which hosts the providers for all major platforms and services. Developers and DevOps engineers can use the OCI Terraform provider to manage OCI resources wherever you use a Terraform distribution, including with Terraform Cloud and the OCI Resource Manager. The Terraform runtime and the OCI provider are also available for installation through Oracle's public YUM repositories.

Setting Up the OCI Terraform Provider

When installing on OCI compute instances, the quickest way to install Terraform CLI and the OCI provider is to use the YUM repositories. The tools are included in the developer repository, which is usually disabled by default. Depending on the version of Oracle Linux, you can enable the repository and install the packages with the following commands:

For Oracle Linux 8:

```
sudo yum-config-manager --enable ol8_developer &&\
sudo yum install terraform
```

For Oracle Linux 7:

```
sudo yum-config-manager --enable ol7_developer &&\
sudo yum install terraform
```

Optionally, you can install the OCI Terraform provider using YUM, although it might be preferable to manage versions of the provider for each Terraform configuration basis by letting Terraform download and manage the Terraform provider as part of initialization for each configuration. The Terraform provider for OCI is available in the Oracle YUM repositories with the package name `terraform-provider-oci` and can be installed with the following command:

```
sudo yum install terraform-provider-oci
```

Note

If you work in a highly sensitive environment, you might want to consider the FIPS-compatible version of the OCI provider. The FIPS-compatible version of the provider ensures that traffic from Terraform to OCI service API endpoints transits over a TLS connection established with an HTTP client using FIPS-certified encryption. The FIPS version of the OCI Terraform provider uses the FIPS 140-2 certified Oracle Cloud Infrastructure Cryptographic Library for Kubernetes instead of the Go native cryptography implementation. Install the FIPS-compatible provider as follows

```
sudo yum-config-manager --enable ol8_developer &&\

sudo yum install terraform &&\

sudo yum install terraform-provider-oci-fips
```

To install Terraform CLI manually on your workstation, you can download it directly from HashiCorp (https://www.terraform.io/downloads) for your specific operating system.

After Terraform is installed, when it encounters a configuration that uses the OCI provider in a provider block, Terraform downloads the provider as part of the `terraform init` process. You can also pin your configuration to a specific version of the provider. This is useful when you want to ensure that you always use a provider version that you have tested your configuration with or when you need to maintain software versioning for compliance reasons. When you always use the latest version of a provider, you can potentially get unexpected behavior if a provider makes a non-backward-compatible change. You can pin the provider version by specifying the version in the `required_providers.oci.version` argument, as shown in Listing 2-2.

Listing 2-2　Configuring the OCI Provider

```
terraform {
  required_providers {
    oci = {
```

```
      source  = "hashicorp/oci"
      version = ">= 4.50.0"
    }
  }
}


provider "oci" {

  # variables are not shown

  region = var.region
  tenancy_ocid = var.tenancy_ocid
  user_ocid = var.user_ocid
  fingerprint = var.fingerprint
  private_key_path = var.private_key_path
}
```

The configuration in Listing 2-2 shows that the version of the provider required is set as version 4.50.0 or later. You can also see that the provider has been initialized with a set of provider configuration arguments that include the following:

- region: The OCI region where this configuration will be applied
- tenancy_ocid: The tenancy OCID against which this configuration will be applied
- user_ocid, fingerprint, private_key_path: API signing key credentials for authenticating with OCI

Using API keys is the default and most common method for authenticating Terraform with OCI. If you have the OCI CLI installed,[3] the Terraform provider can optionally use the OCI CLI configuration file for authentication. This can be handy because the OCI CLI configuration file supports profiles to work with multiple OCI tenancies or to use different identities to authenticate with OCI, enabling you to switch between identities and tenancies while externalizing the authentication information from your Terraform code. You can configure the provider to use the OCI CLI configuration, as demonstrated in Listing 2-3. The default configuration filename and location is ~/.oci/config. You change this by setting the environment variable OCI_CLI_CONFIG_FILE to point to a CLI configuration file at an arbitrary location.

Listing 2-3   Using the CLI Configuration to Provide Authentication Information

```
provider "oci" {
  tenancy_ocid = var.tenancy_ocid
  config_file_profile= 'profile_name_in_CLI_configuration_file'
}
```

Authenticating Without API Keys

When using automation systems and CI/CD tools, using an API key might not be desirable. In these cases, you can consider *Instance Principal*–based authentication. This authentication method is applicable only if Terraform is being executed from an OCI compute instance. This relies on Instance Principals in OCI and the policies that govern them. When using Instance Principals, you do not need to provide the arguments used for API key-based authentication. Your OCI Provider configuration could look like Listing 2-4.

Listing 2-4   Using Instance Principals to Provide Authentication Information

```
provider "oci" {
    auth = "InstancePrincipal"
    region = "${var.region}"
}
```

You can also use the token-based authentication driven by the OCI CLI. This method avoids the use of an API signing key and provides an interactive way to authenticate users. This authentication method uses the OCI CLI *session authenticate* flow that uses an OAuth implicit grant flow to authorize Terraform.

Managing OCI Resources with Terraform

When you have Terraform installed and configured, you can start creating Terraform configurations for OCI. The OCI Terraform provider defines several resources and data sources that enable you to interact with the cloud resources offered by OCI. *Resource* blocks in Terraform represent a cloud resource such as a compute instance or a load balancer. *Data sources* provide data about cloud resources. They are typically used to *query* a cloud provider to get data about one or more resources so that the Terraform code can make choices based on that data.

To understand this, consider a real scenario. You need to create two compute instances, one that uses an ARM-based CPU and another that uses an Intel/AMD-based CPU. These are different CPU architectures and require different versions of the operating systems to be installed on them. Listing 2-5 is a Terraform code snippet that makes the instance shape a variable. If the user chooses an instance based on the ARM architecture, the OS image is different than if the user had chosen a shape that uses the x86 architecture.

Listing 2-5   Using Data Source to Create More Dynamic Configurations

```
# Only relevant attributes are shown below.


resource "oci_core_instance" "RStudio" {
```

```
  display_name      = "MyInstance"
  shape             = var.instance_shape
  source_details {
    source_type = "image"
    source_id   = data.oci_core_images.InstanceImageOCID.images[0].id
  }
}

data "oci_core_images" "InstanceImageOCID" {
  compartment_id          = var.compartment_ocid
  operating_system        = var.instance_os
  operating_system_version = var.linux_os_version
  shape                   = var.instance_shape
}

variable "instance_shape" {
  description = "Instance shape"
}

variable "instance_os" {
  description = "Operating system."
  default     = "Oracle Linux"
}

variable "linux_os_version" {
  description = "Operating system version."
  default     = "7.9"
}
```

To use the latest version of the operating system image available for each architecture, you can use a data source. The set of parameters and filters in a data source lets you identify a resource (in this case, the operating system image that satisfied your conditions) without having to hard-code anything. The data source for the images accepts the shape as an argument and lists only images that are compatible with the provided shape. This data obtained by the data source can be used by the compute instance resource so that the instance uses a compatible operating system image.

The OCI Terraform provider defines resources and data sources for almost all services that are available through the OCI API.

Simplifying Infrastructure Management with the Resource Manager Service

You already saw how OCI resources can be managed through infrastructure-management tools such as Terraform. The OCI provider for Terraform allows Terraform to hook into the OCI APIs and manage OCI resources using a Terraform language. You also learned how Terraform itself manages state and how to use OCI object storage for shared state when using teams. These approaches still assume that the developers have the tooling installed and configured. Large teams can still run into issues when trying to standardize Terraform versions and their execution environments and trying to coordinate between developers, despite having state file locking.

To address these shortcomings, OCI offers a fully managed Terraform platform called Resource Manager Service. The Resource Manager Service is a managed Terraform platform that can manage Terraform configurations as *stacks* that encapsulate multiple resource definitions. Stacks are first-class OCI resources that enable teams to coordinate their infrastructure management activity. Stacks can be based on Git repositories, ZIP files, or Terraform configuration files uploaded to the Resource Manager Service.

Resource Manager keeps track of the Terraform configuration and provides lifecycle management, as in managing the execution of the plan and apply stages. As a managed service, it provides the execution environment for developers to run Terraform configurations, removing the need to maintain local tooling. Developers can also run multiple Terraform configurations in parallel using Resource Manager. Additionally, Resource Manager keeps track of the Terraform state file, enabling team-based development. The Resource Manager Service manages the Terraform execution environment and the execution process, enabling coordinated infrastructure management for teams. Figure 2-3 shows the various aspects of the Resource Manager Service.

Stacks also enable the developer to optionally omit certain Terraform provider configuration parameters, such as the user_ocid, from the Terraform definition. This is because stacks themselves are OCI resources that an authenticated and authorized user is accessing, and the service can fill in some of the provider initialization parameters from the execution context. This makes stacks more portable because they can use their execution environment to infer these values. Take a look at the example in Listing 2-6.

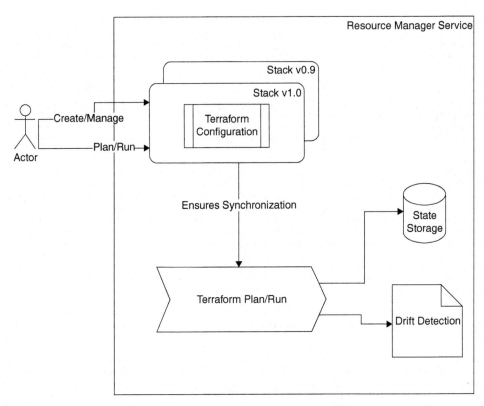

Figure 2-3   Resource Manager Service Components

Listing 2-6   OCI Provider Configuration with Terraform

```
provider "oci" {

    # variables are not shown

    region = var.region
    tenancy_ocid = var.tenancy_ocid

    # Authentication parameters

    user_ocid = var.user_ocid
    fingerprint = var.fingerprint
    private_key_path = var.private_key_path
}
```

The same configuration can be expressed in Resource Manager, as shown in Listing 2-7.

Listing 2-7   OCI Provider Configuration When Using Resource Manager Service

```
provider "oci" {

    # variables are not shown

    tenancy_ocid = var.tenancy_ocid
    region = var.region

    # The authentication parameters are not required since the Resource Manager
    authenticates the user.
}
```

As you can see, the authentication parameters have been omitted from the configuration. This is possible because the omitted values can be inferred by the service and passed on to the Terraform runtime.

Resource Manager not only manages Terraform executions and lifecycle, but it also provides valuable additional integration with other OCI services and features. These include generating Resource Manager stacks from resource creation wizards, resource discovery, and drift detection. The following sections cover these concepts in more detail.

Helm and Kubernetes Providers

As a managed platform, Resource Manager Service manages the Terraform providers that can be used through Resource Manager. Apart from the OCI provider, several popular third-party providers are supported, including Ansible, Vault, TLS, Kubernetes, and Helm. In later chapters, you interact with both the Helm and Kubernetes providers for Terraform.

The Kubernetes provider for Terraform adds support for creating and managing Kubernetes objects as Terraform resources. Creation, modification, and deletion of resources produces the same effect on the Kubernetes objects. The provider makes it possible to manage Kubernetes objects in a Kubernetes cluster, much the same as it enables you to manage infrastructure resources on a cloud provider. The example in Listing 2-8 shows a PodSpec as a Terraform resource. The `kubernetes_pod` resource is provided by the Kubernetes provider for Terraform and models a standard Kubernetes PodSpec.

Listing 2-8   Managing Kubernetes Resources Through Terraform

```
resource "kubernetes_pod" "test" {
  metadata {
    name = "nginx"
  }

  spec {
    container {
      image = "nginx:1.7.9"
      name  = "example"

      port {
        container_port = 8080
      }

      liveness_probe {
        http_get {
          path = "/nginx_status"
          port = 8080
        }

        initial_delay_seconds = 3
        period_seconds        = 3
      }
    }
  }
}
```

Listing 2-9 shows the equivalent PodSpec.

Listing 2-9   Managing Kubernetes Resources Through PodSpec

```
apiVersion: v1
kind: Pod
metadata:
  name: nginx
spec:
  containers:
  - name: nginx
```

```
image: nginx:1.7.9
ports:
- containerPort: 8080
livenessProbe:
  httpGet:
    path: /nginx_status
    port: 8080
  initialDelaySeconds: 3
  periodSeconds: 3
```

Similar to the Kubernetes provider, but perhaps more useful in the context of automation, is the Helm provider. Helm itself is a way to package, deploy, and manage complex application deployments on Kubernetes. A set of Kubernetes objects such as pods, services, and config-maps that together make up an application are parametrized and managed as a Helm release. The example in Listing 2-10 shows how a packaged Helm chart, the template for generating Kubernetes manifests that make up the application, is defined as a Terraform resource. Creation of the resource implies creation of the release—or, in other words, deployment of the application Helm chart.

Listing 2-10 Managing Helm Releases Using Terraform

```
resource "helm_release" "nginx_ingress" {
  name       = "nginx-ingress-controller"

  repository = "oci://ghcr.io/nginxinc/charts"
  chart      = "nginx-ingress"
  version    = "0.18.0"

  set {
    name  = "service.type"
    value = "ClusterIP"
  }
}
```

The equivalent Helm command follows:

```
helm install nginx-ingress-controller oci://ghcr.io/nginxinc/charts/nginx-
  ingress --version 0.18.0 —set service.type=ClusterIP
```

The support for the Helm and Kubernetes providers makes it possible for developers to create solutions that automate not just infrastructure provisioning, but also the deployment and management of cloud native workloads as resources managed through Terraform. The Kubernetes best practice at the time of this writing is to keep the infrastructure components and Kubernetes/Helm provider-managed resources (Kubernetes objects and Helm charts) as separate Terraform modules.

The complete list of supported providers are documented[4] and are frequently updated as new providers are added.

Generating Resource Manager Stacks

Resource Manager is integrated with other OCI resource creation wizards in the OCI console to make the process of generating resource definitions easy. A good example is the Oracle Container Engine for Kubernetes (OKE). OKE is a service that requires multiple supporting resources, such as networks, and offers many configuration options when you create a cluster. Instead of creating the cluster manually, which makes the cluster difficult to reproduce because of the sheer number of available options, you can use Terraform to encapsulate all the options and configuration, which can be then managed as a Resource Manager stack. However, if you're not familiar with the Terraform language, the cluster re-creation workflow in the console conveniently provides a way to export the configuration of a cluster as a Resource Manager stack after the input is gathered. Thus, you can provide all the configuration options for the cluster to the cluster re-creation wizard, which then exports that configuration to a Resource Manager stack. The stack can then be executed, creating an OKE cluster along with all the required components, such as VCNs, security lists, node pools, nodes, placement configurations, and so on.

Resource Discovery

If you already have a hand-crafted solution created in OCI using a set of resources, the resource discovery feature in Resource Manager can generate a Terraform configuration out of these existing resources to make the solution more portable and easier to replicate across environments and regions. Resource discovery works at the compartment level; the compartment provided to the service is considered the source compartment. Resource discovery generates a Resource Manager stack along with a Terraform state file that represents all the supported resources that belong to the given source compartment. The discovery process does not descend into nested compartments or support multiple source compartments for the same stack.

It is also important to note that, in most cases, the stacks generated by resource discovery provide a starting point for the code representing the resources and require slight modifications to be run. For instance, sensitive information such as passwords used when creating a database are not included in the generated code, for obvious security reasons. Resource attributes whose values are omitted from the generated stack are placed in an `ignore_changes` meta-argument in a nested lifecycle block for the resource definition. Similarly, resources that have been terminated or are otherwise inactive are generally excluded from the generated stack. Figure 2-4 shows the option for creating a stack that captures resources from a specified compartment.

Note

`lifecycle` is a nested block for meta-arguments in Terraform that can appear in any resource block. The `ignore_changes` meta-argument identifies a list of attributes that may change outside Terraform after the resource is created. This signals to Terraform that changes to these values are acceptable and do not warrant an update to reset the values. In the case of resource discovery, attributes without values are placed in the `ignore_changes` list to ensure that a Terraform plan will still run without failure. When creating the resources, the developer should provide appropriate values because many of these, such as passwords, could be mandatory parameters for resource creation. Where appropriate, the developer can also move them out of the `ignore_changes` list.

Choose the origin of the Terraform configuration. The Terraform configuration outlines the cloud resources to provision for this stack. Learn more

○ My Configuration
  Upload Terraform configuration files.

○ Template
  Select an Oracle-provided template or private template.

○ Source Code Control System
  Select a Terraform configuration from GitHub or GitLab.

● Existing Compartment
  Create a stack that captures resources from the selected compartment (resource discovery).

Stack Configuration ⓘ

Compartment for Resource Discovery

[Select a Compartment   ⌄]

Region for Resource Discovery

[us-ashburn-1   ⌄]

Terraform Provider Services ⓘ
● All
○ Selected

Services   Select All Clear All

[Select...   ⌄]

Note: Subcompartments are not used in stack creation.

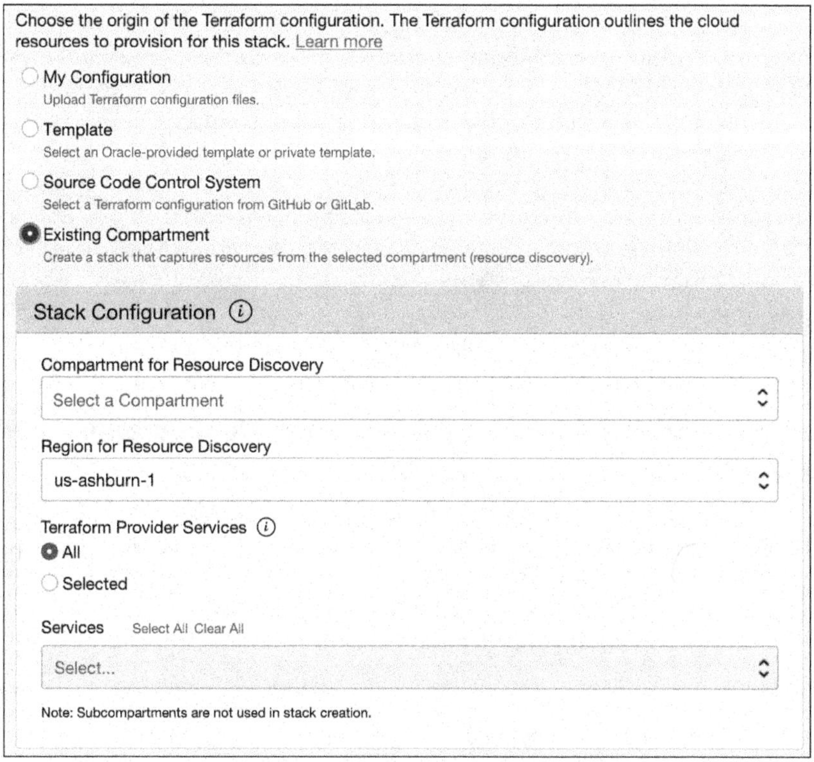

Figure 2-4   Resource Discovery in the Resource Manager Service

Drift Detection

A critical feature that the OCI Resource Manager provides to streamline infrastructure management at scale is *drift detection*. As the name suggests, this feature can compare actual infrastructure and its parameters with the expected infrastructure configuration to identify drift or deviations.

As your cloud-based infrastructure scales, a compelling motivator will be moving toward an elastic model to optimize cost and infrastructure usage with infrastructure-as-code practices. Imagine that you're managing your infrastructure through code. You expect your infrastructure to be in sync with that code, which is fundamental to realizing immutable infrastructure. Infrastructure automation makes it easy to implement immutable infrastructure, but it does not prevent users with access to the infrastructure from making ad-hoc changes to it, such as opening a port on your network security list. A fully mature practitioner will have multiple checks and balances and will have well-defined supporting processes such as security policies to keep infrastructure secure and immutable. Even in these cases, a malicious user or attacker could try to make changes to the infrastructure and compromise it.

Periodically verifying the infrastructure against the configuration defined in the code therefore provides a checkpoint that the infrastructure is still compliant with the definitions. A deviation could point to ad-hoc changes, configuration that is not yet captured in the code, or, in the worst case, a potential intrusion or attack on your infrastructure. The drift detection feature in Resource Manager performs this validation by comparing the current state of the resources with the last executed state for the stack. Drift detection produces a report of the drift that shows the actual resources and their parameters compared to the configuration in the stack. Changes are highlighted to make it easier to identify the changes, and the stack is marked as *Drifted* if drift is detected. Drift detection reports are run as asynchronous work requests, and their progress can be tracked through these work requests. The latest drift detection report is available on the stack details page or through the More Actions menu; historical reports are available from their work requests. Figure 2-5 shows a drift detection report highlighting how the actual configuration has drifted from the expected configuration.

Generating a User Interface from Terraform Configurations with a Custom Schema[5]

The Resource Manager Service goes beyond just managing the lifecycle for Terraform configurations. It can also extend the OCI console UI to make Terraform execution more approachable to end users. This enables developers to create Terraform configuration-based solutions that can be configured and deployed by end users who have no Terraform experience with an intuitive UI.

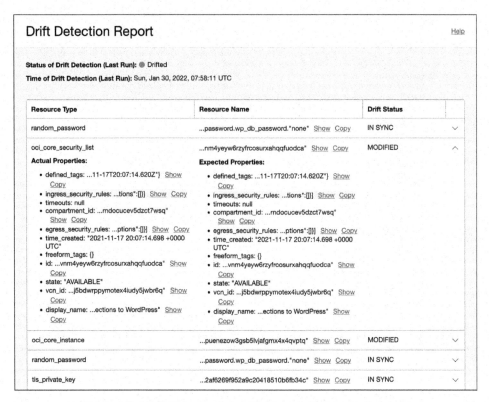

Figure 2-5 Drift Detection Report Highlighting Changes to Resources

When a stack is loaded, the Resource Manager Service inspects the Terraform configuration in it to identify the variable declarations and other user input required for the stack to execute. On the standard command line, Terraform prompts the user to provide input through the terminal. Resource Manager, on the other hand, renders a text input box on the console UI for the user to provide variable values. Although this is perfectly acceptable in some cases, developers can include an optional schema file along with a stack. The schema file describes how the variables and outputs of the terraform configuration look and behave. Figure 2-6 shows how Resource Manager can render Terraform variables as intuitive onscreen controls.

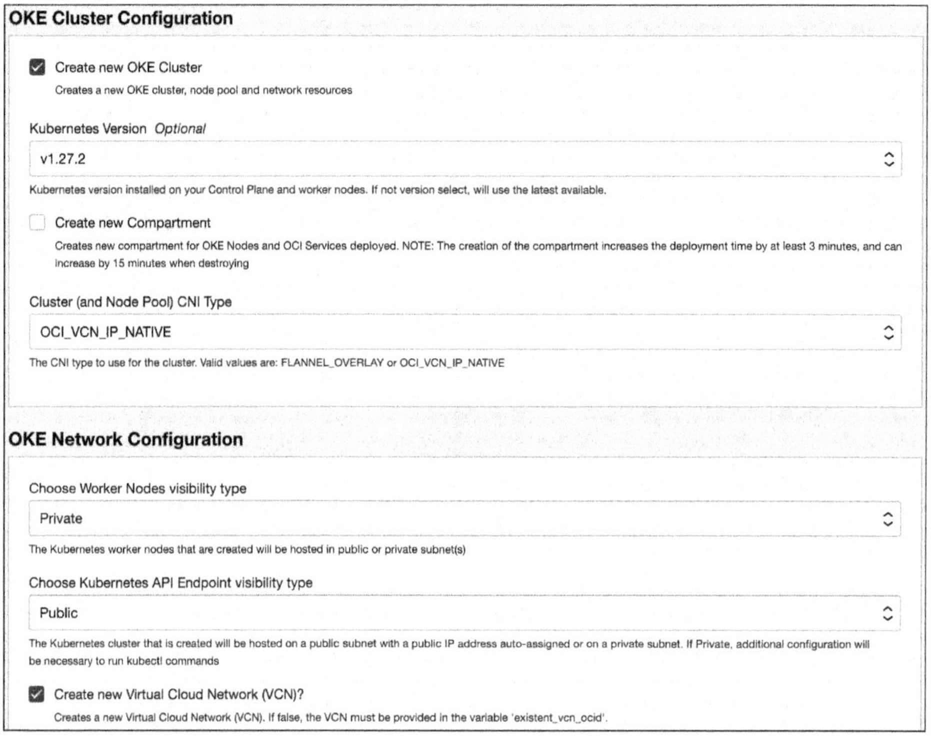

Figure 2-6   Resource Manager Rendering Terraform Variables with the Help of UI Hints Provided in the Schema File

The schema file should be written in YAML and included at the root of the stack. The YAML document contains UI hints and structure that help the Resource Manager service to extend the OCI console UI to support much more complex input fields, queries, and validation. Each schema document defines keys for various purposes. The values can be of various types, such as *string*, *numeric*, *enum*, types that query OCI APIs for existing resources, or an expression that can be evaluated into values.

Listing 2-11 provides an example of a schema file.

Listing 2-11   Example Schema File for Terraform Stacks

```
# Stack Metadata


title: "MuShop Cloud Native App"
description: "Microservices demo App for Oracle's Container Engine for Kubernetes
  (OKE)"
schemaVersion: 1.1.0
version: "20190304"
```

```
# Variable Groups

variableGroups:
  - title: "General Configuration"
    variables:
      - app_name
      - password
      - show_advanced
    visible: true

outputs:
  service_ip:
    type: link
    title: Application Login
    description: Open the login page for the application

primaryOutputButton: service_ip

# Variables
variables:
  app_name:
    type: string
    title: "Cluster Name Prefix"
    required: true
    visible:
      and:
        - create_new_oke_cluster

  app_password:
    type: password
    required: true
    title: Admin Password
    description: The password for the admin user
    pattern: "^(?=.*[!@#%^*_+\\-:?.,\\[\\]\\{\\}])(?=.*[0-9])(?=.*[a-z])(?=.*
[A-Z])(?!.*[$\\(\\)]).{8,32}$"
    visible: true
```

```
node_pool_shape:
  type: oci:core:instanceshape:name
  title: "Select a shape for the Worker Nodes instances"
  required: true
  dependsOn:
    compartmentId: compartment_ocid
  visible:
    and:
      - create_new_oke_cluster
```

A typical schema file like the one in the example is structured into at least four sections:

- Stack metadata.
- Variable groups: These are denoted by `variableGroups`.
- Output section: Output groups can group outputs into various sections for display after the stack has been applied.
- Variable metadata: The `variables` key specifies the display properties and behavior of variables in the Terraform configuration.

The next pages look at each section in detail.

Stack Metadata

The stacked metadata includes information about the stack itself. It uses keys such as `title`, `description`, `version`, and `logoUrl` that can provide metadata about a stack, including its purpose and publisher information, along with how to display the stack in the OCI console. The metadata for the stack is shown on the console UI at the time the stack is loaded and provides a description of the functionality that the stack provides. Listing 2-12 shows an example.

Listing 2-12 Stack Metadata in a Schema File

```
title: "MuShop Cloud Native App"
description: "Microservices demo App for Oracle's Container Engine for Kubernetes
  (OKE)"
schemaVersion: 1.1.0
version: "20190304"
locale: "en"
logoUrl: <URL/URL encoded data>
```

Variable Groups

This element groups variables into various sections for display on the UI, such as grouping all networking parameters together. The variable groups are listed under the key `variableGroups`, which is at the root of the document. The example in Listing 2-13 has three separate variable groups, called General Configuration, OKE Cluster Configuration, and OKE Worker Nodes. Each variable group has a `title`, which forms the title for the section of input fields in the UI, and a list of variables. The list of variables is a reference to the variable definitions that are listed further down in the document. Each of the variable groups can also have a `visible` attribute that can be evaluated to a Boolean that toggles the display of the entire section.

Listing 2-13 Variable Groups Can Help Structure Related Terraform Variables on the User Interface

```
variableGroups:
  - title: "General Configuration"
    variables:
      - app_name
      - password
      - show_advanced
    visible: true


  - title: "OKE Cluster Configuration"
    variables:
    - create_new_oke_cluster
    - existent_oke_cluster_compartment_ocid
    - existent_oke_cluster_id
    - k8s_version


  - title: "OKE Worker Nodes"
    variables:
    - num_pool_workers
    - node_pool_shape
    - node_pool_name
```

In the example, the first variable group is the General Configuration. Here you can see that this group has two keys defined, the `title` and `variables`. The section is presented to the user under a section with the title specified here, and the section will render the variables listed in the `variables` list. The display of the individual variables listed—app_name, password, and show_advanced—depends on these variables' metadata defined in the `variables` section at the root of the document. Figure 2-7 shows the OKE Worker Nodes variable group and demonstrates how a variable group is rendered.

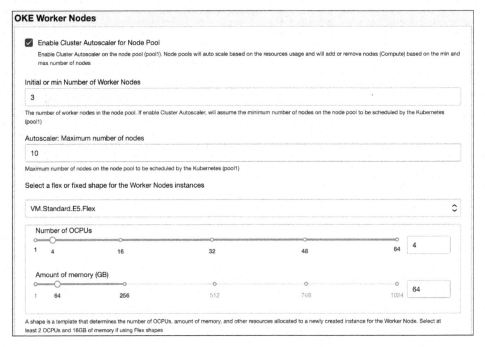

Figure 2-7   OKE Worker Nodes Variable Group

Output Section

The variable group section is followed by the output section. Here, we see two separate outputs defined. Outputs from the stack are displayed on the Application Information tab on the stack page after the stack has been run at least once. Listing 2-14 shows an example.

Listing 2-14   The Output Section Provides Structure to Terraform Outputs

```
outputs:
  service_ip:
    type: link
    title: Application Login
    description: Open the login page for the application

  generated_ssh_private_key:
    title: Generated Private Key
```

```
description: The auto-generated private key. Save this to a file to SSH into
the instance.
type: copyableString
visible: true
```

The first output in the example is called the `service_ip` and has attributes that include `type`, `title`, and `description`. The `title` and `description` provide the metadata for displaying the value of the output on the UI. The type determines how the value itself is rendered; here, it is rendered as a hyperlink. The other output is named `generated_ssh_private_key` and is of type `copyableString`. When rendering the value, it will be shortened for better display, along with Show and Copy buttons for users to easily see or copy the value.

You also see a primary output button. The Application Information tab can optionally render a button on the Information area, which is determined by the `primaryOutputButton`. In this example, it references the `service_ip`, which means that the `service_ip` will be rendered as the primary output button on the Application Information tab. The button text uses the `title` for the `service_ip`; clicking the button opens the hyperlink that is the value for the `service_ip`.

Variable Definitions

The variables used in the Variable Groups are defined here, and these correspond to the variables declared in the Terraform configuration. Variable definitions provide metadata for the variables, such as their type. Types such as numeric, string, and password affect both how the variable is rendered on the UI and its behavior. The attributes of a variable definition can include expressions that depend on other attributes as well. For instance, it is possible to specify that the app name should be visible if the `create_new_oke_cluster` variable is `true`, as shown in Listing 2-15.

Listing 2-15 Variable Definitions Provide Metadata to Influence the Look and Behavior for Terraform Variables

```
app_name:
  type: string
  title: "Cluster Name Prefix"
  required: true
  visible:
    and:
      - create_new_oke_cluster
```

The definition of the `app_password` variable in Listing 2-16 specifies that it is of type `password`, which provides a hint to the Resource Manager to render it as a password field on the UI. It is also marked as a `required` variable, which means that a value is expected from the user; the UI will display an error if the user does not provide one. For this variable, the title and description give the UI hints to display this variable onscreen. The title provides the prompt in the description that supplies a small textual description under the input field. The pattern is a regular expression to validate the text input on this field. If the value provided by the user does not match this regular expression, the service rejects the value and an error is displayed onscreen identifying the field that failed the validation.

Listing 2-16   Variable Definitions Can Validate Input Data

```
app_password:
    type: password
    required: true
    title: Admin Password
    description: The password for the admin user
    pattern: "^(?=.*[!@#%^*_+\\-:?.,\\[\\]\\{\\}])(?=.*[0-9])(?=.*[a-z])(?=.*[A-Z])
(?!.*[$\\(\\)]).{8,32}$"
    visible: true
```

Resource Manager supports several other types of variables, including Booleans, OCI resources, and enumerations. Listing 2-17 shows the usage of some of these types and how they can interact with each other.

Listing 2-17   Variable Definitions Can Reference Other Variables to Create Complex UI Behavior

```
show_advanced:
    type: boolean
    title: "Show advanced options?"
    description: "Shows advanced options, such as customer-managed encryption keys"
    visible: true


create_new_oke_cluster:
    type: boolean
    title: "Create new OKE Cluster"


existent_oke_cluster_compartment_ocid:
    type: oci:identity:compartment:id
    title: "Existent OKE Cluster Compartment"
    description: "The compartment where you find the existent OKE Cluster"
```

```
    default: compartment_ocid
    required: true
    visible:
      not:
        - create_new_oke_cluster

existent_oke_cluster_id:
    type: oci:container:cluster:id
    title: "Existent OKE Cluster"
    required: true
    dependsOn:
      compartmentId: existent_oke_cluster_compartment_ocid
    visible:
      not:
        - create_new_oke_cluster

k8s_version:
    type: oci:kubernetes:versions:id
    dependsOn:
        compartmentId: compartment_ocid
        clusterOptionId: "all"
    title: "Kubernetes Version"
    required: true
    visible:
      and:
        - create_new_oke_cluster
        - show_advanced

num_pool_workers:
    type: integer
    title: "Number of Worker Nodes"
    minimum: 1
    maximum: 1000
    required: true
    visible:
```

```
and:
  - and:
    - create_new_oke_cluster
  - not:
    - cluster_autoscaler_enabled
```

The `show_advanced` variable is of type `boolean`. Booleans are presented and rendered as check boxes that represent their value. Other variables can use the value of Boolean variables to determine their visibility and other properties. OCI resource variable types are special variables that provide querying capabilities into OCI resources.

The variable `existent_oke_cluster_compartment_ocid` is of type `oci:identity:compartment:id`. This is a hint for the Resource Manager to query the OCI compartment IDs and show them in a drop-down list when this variable is rendered on the UI. The user can select a compartment from the list of compartments shown, and the OCID for that compartment is then passed to the cluster.

Similarly, the `existent_oke_cluster_id` is of type `oci:container:cluster:id`. This allows the user to choose a cluster by name from a list of existing Kubernetes clusters rendered as a drop-down list.

The variable `k8s_version` is of a different type, called `enum`. Enums are enumerations of specific values, and this enum has four values. Resource Manager renders the enum as a drop-down list; the user can choose a value from this list that Resource Manager then provides to the Terraform variable. A selection from only these four values is possible, which avoids human errors and values that are beyond the expected set of possible valid values.

The `num_pool_workers` variable is of type `integer`, which means that it accepts only integer numbers. The UI that Resource Manager renders for these variables validates the input based on the type and its attributes. The integer type variable shown here has additional attributes, such as `minimum` and `maximum`.

This support for the notion of types in Resource Manager prevents the user from entering accidental typographical errors or incompatible values as if it were a free-form text field, as with the Terraform CLI. It also makes the process of entering values much easier for the end user. Values outside this range trigger a validation error on this component and inform users that they have made a choice outside the valid range.

Beyond the example in Listing 2-17, several types exist, each one with various supported attributes. For a full description of these, you can look at the meta schema published by Oracle.[6]

Figure 2-8 shows a portion of the UI rendered by the example in Listing 2-17.

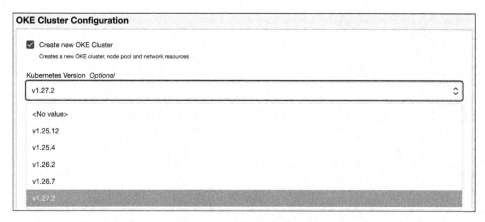

OKE Cluster Configuration

☑ Create new OKE Cluster
   Creates a new OKE cluster, node pool and network resources

Kubernetes Version *Optional*

v1.27.2

<No value>

v1.25.12

v1.25.4

v1.26.2

v1.26.7

v1.27.2

Figure 2-8   UI Portion Rendered by the Configuration in Listing 2-17

The addition of metadata and types for variables enables Terraform developers to build stacks that are presented to end users with input fields that are less prone to human errors and typographical errors. Developers segregate input fields into groups, perform validation, and create more intuitive user interfaces that turn the Terraform configurations into deployment wizards that end users can use even if they have no prior experience with Terraform. Therefore, stacks with schema files allow solution developers to create polished and complete solutions that can be delivered directly from any web page using the Deploy button or through the OCI Marketplace.

Publishing Your Stacks with Deploy Buttons

The Resource Manager Service offers developers the capability to package Terraform-based solutions into stacks and publish these stacks over multiple channels for broad consumption. For commercial applications and licensed software, Oracle offers a partner program in which Oracle partners can list their stacks as solutions in the OCI Marketplace. Customers can consume these solutions by deploying them in their own tenancies directly from within OCI.

For open-source projects or other projects for which becoming an Oracle partner is not a consideration, the Resource Manager Service offers the capability to create web-based deployment buttons that can be placed on any web page. These deployment buttons are simple hyperlinks that can be placed on any web page; when clicked, they can load the stack into the Resource Manager Service and walk the user through the deployment process.

The Deploy button flow supports three providers:

- GitHub
- GitLab
- Oracle Object Storage's preauthenticated requests

The developer builds a stack and creates a `.zip` file. The file is uploaded to any of the supported providers. The public URL for the ZIP file is used to construct the Deploy button. Listing 2-18 shows the format for creating a Deploy button. The `<package-url>` is to be replaced with the public URL for the ZIP file from any of the supported providers. For GitLab and GitHub, Resource Manager supports both a direct link to the file or a link to a file published as part of a release. In most cases, it is preferable to use the link to a file published as part of a release in the Deploy button because that uniquely identifies a versioned artifact.

Listing 2-18   A Stack Deploy Button in HTML

```
<a
href="https://cloud.oracle.com/resourcemanager/stacks/create?zipUrl=<package-
    url>"
target="_blank">
  <img
src="https://oci-resourcemanager-plugin.plugins.oci.oraclecloud.com/latest/
    deploy-to-oracle-cloud.svg"
alt="Deploy to Oracle Cloud"/>
</a>
```

Alternatively, you can use the markdown in Listing 2-19 if you need to place a Deploy button for your stack in a markdown file, such as in your project README in GitHub.

Listing 2-19   Stack Deploy Button in Markdown Format

```
[![Deploy to Oracle Cloud]
(https://oci-resourcemanager-plugin.plugins.oci.oraclecloud.com/latest/deploy-to-
    oracle-cloud.svg)
]
(https://cloud.oracle.com/resourcemanager/stacks/create
?zipUrl=<package-url>)
```

When a Deploy button is clicked, the user is taken to the OCI console. If the user is not already logged in, the user logs into the tenancy and is immediately taken to the Create Stack workflow, where the stack is loaded from the provider and ready to be deployed. The user can then proceed with configuring the stack with the required variables and kickstart a Terraform apply job to create the resources and deploy the solution. An example of this is showcased in the example application for this book.

Managing Multiregion and Multicloud Configurations

All cloud vendors provide multiple regions, for better availability and fault tolerance. Managing these cloud infrastructure resources as code simplifies and automates their lifecycle management. With infrastructure defined as code and a full-featured CI/CD system managing the lifecycle, the next logical step is to manage your infrastructure across regions and across cloud providers using the same processes. With its provider-based architecture, Terraform enables you to easily create Terraform configurations that span multiple regions within the same cloud provider or even transcend cloud providers. This capability to define infrastructure in a parameterized way and create it in any region or cloud provider opens up new possibilities in implementing a globally distributed disaster recovery strategy. For instance, you can easily implement a pilot-light strategy with primary sites created from Terraform configurations operating at scale, while the same Terraform configuration with a lower number of resources acts as a pilot-light standby in another region, ready to be scaled up when required.

The providers used in a Terraform configuration are called out and declared within the configuration. The same Terraform configuration can have provider plug-ins for multiple cloud platforms. To create a Terraform configuration that spans multiple cloud providers, you can simply declare both provider plug-ins within the Terraform configuration. At runtime, Terraform will initialize all the declared providers. Resources from all the initialized providers can be used in the Terraform configuration.

Similarly, you also want to manage resources in two separate regions for the same cloud provider. Part of any provider configuration is the region for which the provider is configured. To work with multiple regions simultaneously, you can declare the cloud provider twice with *aliases*. Using aliases, you can determine which region you are interacting with for given resources. Listing 2-20 presents an example.

Listing 2-20 Multiple Provider Instances Can Be Instantiated with Aliases to Work with Multiple Regions or Tenancies

```
provider "oci" {
    alias        = "phoenix"
    tenancy_ocid = var.tenancy_ocid
    region       = "us-phoenix-1"

    user_ocid        = var.user_ocid
    fingerprint      = var.fingerprint
    private_key_path = var.private_key_path
}
```

```
provider "oci" {
  alias       = "ashburn"
  tenancy_ocid = var.tenancy_ocid
  region      = "us-ashburn-1"

  user_ocid       = var.user_ocid
  fingerprint     = var.fingerprint
  private_key_path = var.private_key_path
}
```

A resource block can include a `provider` argument, which uniquely identifies the provider to use for that specific resource. At runtime, when Terraform encounters a resource block with a provider argument, it maps to the provider definition with a matching alias and uses that provider instance to manage the resource lifecycle. In the example in Listing 2-21, the resource block uses the argument provider set to `oci.phoenix`, which maps to the provider definition with the alias `phoenix`, which then uses the provider instance configured to use the Phoenix region.

Listing 2-21   Resource Definitions Can Refer to Specific Provider Instances by Their Alias

```
resource "oci_core_virtual_network" "my_vcn" {
  cidr_block = var.vcn_cidr
  compartment_id = var.compartment_ocid
  display_name = var.vcn
  dns_label = "myvcn"

  provider = oci.phoenix
}
```

As discussed earlier in the chapter, environment variables or the OCI CLI configuration file and its support for profiles can also be used in these cases to decouple the configuration values from the code itself. The OCI CLI configuration file shown in Listing 2-22 describes two profiles names, IAD and PHX.

Listing 2-22   OCI CLI Configuration File with Multiple Profiles

```
[IAD]
region=us-ashburn-1
tenancy=<tenancy_ocid>
user=<user_ocid>
fingerprint=<key_fingerprint>
```

```
key_file=<path to key file>

[PHX]
region=us-phoenix-1
tenancy=<tenancy_ocid>
user=<user_ocid>
fingerprint=<key_fingerprint>
key_file=<path to key file>
```

The Terraform provider configuration block shown in Listing 2-23 refers to these profiles to load the provider configuration for Terraform. Using this approach, the actual values for authenticating with OCI can be maintained outside the Terraform code itself. The Terraform code can use the provider alias to distinguish between the two profiles. This makes the Terraform code more portable, by avoiding sensitive data from the codebase and making it possible to inject these values later. In the example in Listing 2-23, the two profiles represent two regions, and with this the Terraform code can work with OCI resources in both regions by referring to the appropriate provider alias.

Listing 2-23 Provider Configuration with Multiple Regions

```
provider "oci" {
   alias        = "phoenix"
   config_file_profile= "PHX"
}

provider "oci" {
   alias        = "ashburn"
   config_file_profile= "IAD"
}
```

Summary

This chapter examined how APIs are central to the cloud platform. Regardless of how the APIs are consumed, whether through the browser-based UI, command-line tools, or infrastructure-management tools such as Terraform, APIs form the primary control surface for interacting with the cloud platform. The chapter also served as a quick primer on Terraform, the infrastructure-management tool used throughout this book. You also briefly learned about the essentials of HCL, the language used for describing resource configurations in Terraform, and saw how Terraform integrates with multiple cloud providers using its provider-based model.

Additionally, the chapter covered the OCI provider for Terraform in detail, including ways to install, configure, and authenticate with OCI. You saw how the OCI resources are represented using the OCI provider and examined some strategies to decouple authentication information from the code for the infrastructure. You also investigated how Terraform tracks infrastructure state using state files and saw how to manage state files in OCI object storage when operating in teams.

Next, the chapter introduced the Resource Manager Service, a managed service for infrastructure management using Terraform. Resource Manager automatically tracks the Terraform state and makes team-based development of infrastructure easy and seamless. You also looked at additional features of Resource Manager, including drift detection, resource discovery, and generation of Terraform code as Resource Manager stacks from existing OCI workflows.

Furthermore, this chapter covered some of the supported providers inside Resource Manager, such as Kubernetes, and Helm, which later chapters discuss. You looked at the stack metadata, in which stacks with a schema file are presented as workflows with an intuitive UI to the end users. The stack metadata provides easy UI-based validations and lookup methods for several OCI resources, as well as common expressions. You also saw how developers can publish their Resource Manager stacks as Deploy buttons that can be placed on any web page. Finally, you looked at how you can work with multiple regions or multiple cloud providers.

References

1   OCI Terraform provider: https://registry.terraform.io/providers/oracle/oci/latest/docs

2   OCI Terraform provider GitHub: https://github.com/oracle/terraform-provider-oci

3   OCI CLI installation and configuration: https://docs.oracle.com/en-us/iaas/Content/API/SDKDocs/cliinstall.htm

4   Supported Terraform Providers in OCI Resource Manager: https://docs.oracle.com/en-us/iaas/Content/ResourceManager/Concepts/providers.htm

5   Extend Console Pages Using Schema Documents: https://docs.oracle.com/en-us/iaas/Content/ResourceManager/Concepts/terraformconfigresourcemanager_topic-schema.htm

6   https://docs.oracle.com/en-us/iaas/Content/ResourceManager/Concepts/terraformconfigresourcemanager_topic-schema.htm

3

Cloud Native Services on Oracle Cloud Infrastructure

The Cloud Native Computing Foundation, a part of the nonprofit Linux Foundation, is the premier body whose charter is to foster the development of open-source and vendor-neutral cloud native projects. According to the Cloud Native Computing Foundation (CNCF):

> Cloud native technologies empower organizations to build and run scalable applications in modern, dynamic environments such as public, private, and hybrid clouds. Containers, service meshes, microservices, immutable infrastructure, and declarative APIs exemplify this approach.

Cloud native applications are defined by their resilient design, capability to elastically scale using cloud platforms, and capacity to implement efficient lifecycle management that leverages observability and automation. The technology platforms and tools that enable developers to build cloud native applications are generally termed *cloud native technologies*. The fundamental outcome and goal of the cloud native paradigm is to dramatically improve software development velocity, thereby creating innovation that disrupts traditional business models.

Several turnkey technologies and patterns characterize modern cloud native applications, including container orchestration with Kubernetes, the use of service meshes and observability, and stream- and event-based service architecture. This chapter introduces the various services in Oracle Cloud Infrastructure (OCI) that developers can use as their fundamental building blocks when building cloud native applications. The chapter covers the role each of these services plays within the cloud native paradigm so that you get a panoramic view of the cloud native ecosystem that OCI offers. OCI's fundamental focus on openness also means that these services are compliant with open standards or are built on top of industry-standard open-source platforms and are interoperable with them.

Oracle Container Image Registry

Containers are a fundamental turnkey technology that enables the creation of cloud native applications. Containers provide the capability to bundle applications and their dependencies into packages called *container images*. Container images contain the application code and its required dependencies, runtime, system settings, tools, and libraries. This packaging format makes it easy to quickly transmit application containers and run them in dynamic environments while providing a consistent execution environment for the application. Docker originally developed the container image specification and runtime. For this reason, containers and Docker are synonymous for most users. Docker donated the container image specification and the runtime to the Open Container Initiative[1] to help establish open standards as the container ecosystem evolves.

Note

This book uses the abbreviation OCI to mean Oracle Cloud Infrastructure and calls out uses of the abbreviation for Open Container Initiative when discussing container images.

At its core, a container image is a directory of files with associated metadata. The container image format[2] defines the *layers* in a specific order that make up this directory. These layers are combined with *union mounting*, a way to combine the contents of various directories, to create a directory that seems like it contains the combined contents. The order of the layers is important because the layers are overlaid on top of each other. When the same files are present on multiple layers, the file on the upper layer overwrites (or deletes) the same files on the lower layer. When creating the image, each layer that makes up the image is archived into a tar ball and compressed with GZIP. A container image *manifest* describes the various layers of the image (in their respective order) and additional metadata such as the OS and architecture. A container runtime can take this package, the container image, and create an isolated execution environment for the application contained in the container image. The container image provides all the information for a container runtime, such as the manifests to identify the file system layers, an index that provides a list of manifests for various platforms, configuration documents that describe image ordering, and more. Using this information in the container image, a container runtime can obtain all layers and configure a running container. Figure 3-1 shows this model, with an image made up of several layers of files and described by manifests and configuration documents, while a container runtime uses the information in an image to create a running container.

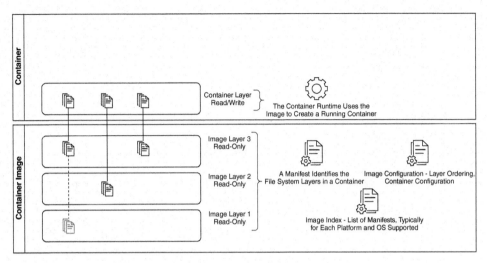

Figure 3-1 Container/Container Image Model

Container images need to be stored in a repository, where they can be requested, or "pulled." Registries provide an address for a container image—a URL that uniquely identifies a container image, called a *container reference*. Oracle Cloud Infrastructure Registry (OCIR, or Container Registry) is a managed service that provides a container image registry to store, serve, and manage container images. OCIR supports multiple image formats or specifications, including Docker V2 and the Open Container Initiative image spec. This allows OCIR to work with several container image specs and container runtimes that support these image specifications. This means that, when using OCIR, you can work with all standard container tools, such as Docker, Podman, cri-o, and containerd. Additionally, the service supports manifest lists, also known as image indexes in the Open Container Initiative specification. Manifest lists allow a single container reference to represent multiple forms of an image (multiple manifests). Each of these manifests is typically associated with a specific OS or architecture so that a container runtime can pick the manifest based on the platform that it's running on. This is crucial when working with images that are built for different CPU architectures, such as amd64 (x86) and arm64 (ARM).

A typical image reference on OCIR looks like this:

```
iad.ocir.io/idi2cuxxbkto/demo-site:1.0.1
```

Breaking this image reference into its parts, you can see the following:

- **The registry URL:** `iad.ocir.io`.
- **The namespace:** `idi2cuxxbkto`. OCI provides every tenancy with a namespace, and this is shown when you create a repository.
- **The repository:** `demo-site`.
- **The tag:** `1.0.1`. Tags point to the digest of the image manifest. A tag is a more human-readable pointer to an actual digest.

The Container Registry provides a manifest (or a manifest list) at this location for container runtimes to pull the image (its layers and its metadata). You can also use the docker manifest command to inspect the manifest (or manifest list) available at a container reference:

```
$ docker manifest inspect iad.ocir.io/idi2cuxxbkto/demo-site:1.0.1
```

```
{
    "schemaVersion": 2,
    "mediaType": "application/vnd.docker.distribution.manifest.v2+json",
    "config": {
            "mediaType": "application/vnd.docker.container.image.v1+json",
            "size": 9439,
            "digest": "sha256:8bdcd2821a78c7bf91dffe1d3f0380cd6c977efe0214c0bc6962
7611e7205881"
    },
    "layers": [
            {
                "mediaType": "application/vnd.docker.image.rootfs.diff.tar.gzip",
                "size": 208,
                "digest": "sha256:b1c13aac26c6d0816d720f6afed6292bde309137d4894819d3
c6e49265490c8c"
            },
            {
                "mediaType": "application/vnd.docker.image.rootfs.diff.tar.gzip",
                "size": 2009946,
                "digest": "sha256:c3c2acf3bfb91ca8a0220d3d411f8f91f92bc3725fd617b5f7
d962c5d06beb91"
            }
        ]
}
```

Working with OCIR

As a fully managed service, OCIR ensures that you can reliably store and serve your container images without managing or scaling the storage and other infrastructure resources typically required for running and operating a container image registry. OCIR supports both public and private access to container images managed by the service. To expose an image publicly, you do not need any resources (such as an Internet gateway or a load balancer) in your tenancy because the service is fully managed. When working with private images, you can efficiently access the registry through a service gateway in your virtual cloud network (VCN), which ensures that the resources that access the images can do so in a highly efficient and secure manner, completely within the OCI network fabric. If an image is exposed publicly, the image can still be accessed over a service gateway by resources inside OCI for better throughput, and the image will also be publicly available over the Internet. Private registries are ideal in environments where Internet access is disallowed for security reasons.

Image Signing

The ease of creating and distributing container images comes with an increased exposure to security vulnerabilities. Container images provide a way to build software packages in layers, with developers building on top of popular open-source images that provide basic functionality and runtimes (such as Java) and then laying down their application binaries and artifacts on top of these base layers to create the final image. From a security perspective, developers need to ensure not only that their own software is secure, but also that every layer in their final container image, including the layers that they built on top of, are secure and free from vulnerabilities. They also must consider the possibility of image tampering, in which a malicious actor injects security vulnerabilities into an image. Therefore, to ensure a secure container supply chain, you must ensure that the container images (and each layer that makes up an image) are free from vulnerabilities and that you can verify that the image came from a trusted source and has not been tampered with.

To ensure the provenance of container images that you use in your environments, the OCIR service supports image signing. Image signing is a way to confirm that the container images you are deploying come from a trusted source and to verify that these images have not been tampered with. With OCIR, you can use asymmetric cryptographic keys to ensure the authenticity of an image's origin and guarantee its integrity. The developer (or the CI process) building the image pushes the image to OCIR. This creates the image in OCIR and assigns an OCID for the image. Now the developer can sign the image with a master encryption key stored in the OCI Vault service and associate the signature with the image's OCID. For better security, OCIR supports only asymmetric key algorithms, such as RSA or ECDSA; symmetric key algorithms such as AES are not supported.

When a client such as a Kubernetes cluster validates the signature, the Vault service is checked to ensure that the signature is valid. The service also ensures that the user who pushed the image into the registry had access to the master encryption key at the time the image was signed. The signature is based on the content of the image; any tampering or changes to the image invalidate the signature. This gives users or systems pulling a signed image from OCIR confidence that the source of the image is trusted and that the image has not been tampered with. To further ensure security within the container image supply chain, other OCI services, such as Oracle Cloud Infrastructure Container Engine for Kubernetes (OKE), can be configured to accept only signed images. Figure 3-2 illustrates the signatures for an image in OCIR and shows the results of a signature verification. After an image in OCIR has been signed, the signature can be verified at any time.

Figure 3-2   OCIR Showing a Repository with Signed Images and Image Signature Verification

Image Scanning

OCIR also supports image scanning to identify vulnerabilities in your container images. These vulnerabilities could be within the application you are developing or within the tools or runtimes that exist on the base layers of the image you are building upon. Image scanning can be enabled on a per-repository basis by adding a scanner to the repository. The scanner looks for vulnerabilities published in the publicly available Common Vulnerabilities and Exposures (CVE) database.

The scanner is powered by the Oracle Cloud Infrastructure Vulnerability Scanning Service, and it also provides a Vulnerability Scanning REST API that you can integrate into your CI pipeline so that a build pipeline can build an image, push it to an OCIR repository, and programmatically get scanning results. This enables you to integrate image scanning into your development pipeline so that you can identify images with vulnerabilities as early as possible and then create CI/CD workflows that can prevent the images from being promoted to critical environments. Figure 3-3 shows the result of an image scan, summarizes the issues found for the image, and gives details on each CVE that has been identified.

When enabling the scanner on a repository that already has images in it, the most recent four images are scanned immediately. The scanner produces a report showing an overall risk assessment for the image based on the scan, as well as the individual vulnerabilities found and their risk levels, with pointers to the CVE database for more information on the vulnerability. OCIR automatically scans the images as new vulnerabilities are added to the CVE database and retains the scan results for a period of 13 months so that the risk level of the image can be assessed over time.

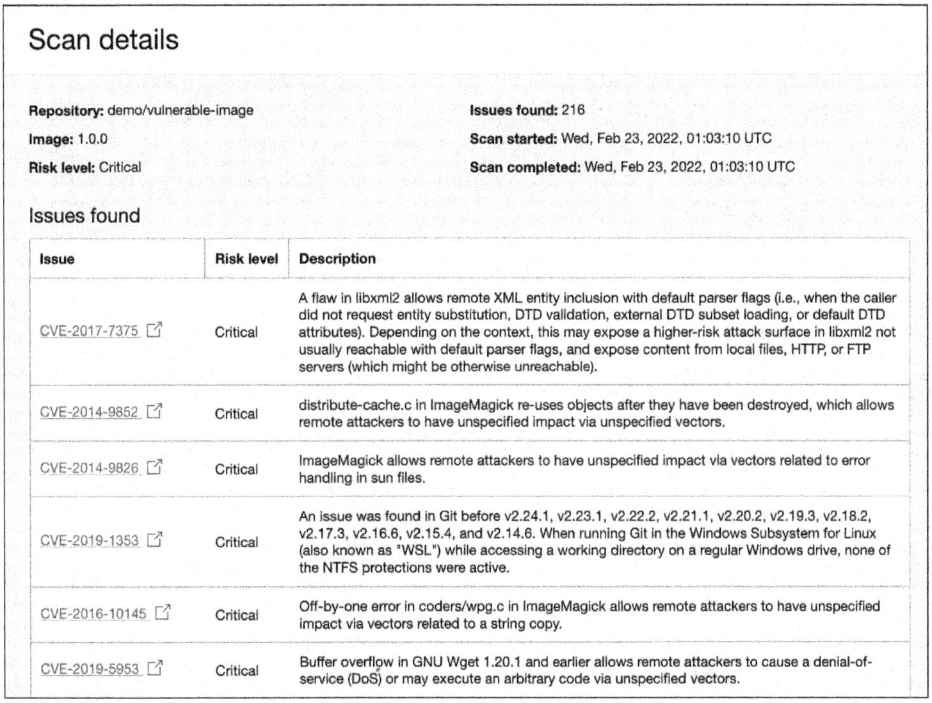

Scan details

Repository: demo/vulnerable-image

Image: 1.0.0

Risk level: Critical

Issues found: 216

Scan started: Wed, Feb 23, 2022, 01:03:10 UTC

Scan completed: Wed, Feb 23, 2022, 01:03:10 UTC

Issues found

Issue	Risk level	Description
CVE-2017-7375	Critical	A flaw in libxml2 allows remote XML entity inclusion with default parser flags (i.e., when the caller did not request entity substitution, DTD validation, external DTD subset loading, or default DTD attributes). Depending on the context, this may expose a higher-risk attack surface in libxml2 not usually reachable with default parser flags, and expose content from local files, HTTP, or FTP servers (which might be otherwise unreachable).
CVE-2014-9852	Critical	distribute-cache.c in ImageMagick re-uses objects after they have been destroyed, which allows remote attackers to have unspecified impact via unspecified vectors.
CVE-2014-9826	Critical	ImageMagick allows remote attackers to have unspecified impact via vectors related to error handling in sun files.
CVE-2019-1353	Critical	An issue was found in Git before v2.24.1, v2.23.1, v2.22.2, v2.21.1, v2.20.2, v2.19.3, v2.18.2, v2.17.3, v2.16.6, v2.15.4, and v2.14.6. When running Git in the Windows Subsystem for Linux (also known as "WSL") while accessing a working directory on a regular Windows drive, none of the NTFS protections were active.
CVE-2016-10145	Critical	Off-by-one error in coders/wpg.c in ImageMagick allows remote attackers to have unspecified impact via vectors related to a string copy.
CVE-2019-5953	Critical	Buffer overflow in GNU Wget 1.20.1 and earlier allows remote attackers to cause a denial-of-service (DoS) or may execute an arbitrary code via unspecified vectors.

Figure 3-3   Scan Results for an Image Showing the CVEs That Are Identified on That Image, with Risk Levels, Descriptions, and Links to the CVE Database

Creating Containers from Images

After a container image has been created and pushed to a container image repository, the next logical step is to create a running container from this image. A container runtime, or a container engine, is the software that can run containers on a host operating system.

Container Runtime vs Container Engine

Although the two terms are used interchangeably in many situations, they have subtle but important differences. A *container runtime* simply manages the creation and management of a container. On Linux, this includes making the system calls to create and configure the kernel features that enable resource limiting, process isolation, and more. However, this does not include capabilities such as pushing/pulling images from remote repositories. These container runtimes are sometimes known as low-level runtimes; examples include runc and crun. A *container engine*, on the other hand, comprises more tools and utilities, including CLIs for managing containers, pulling and pushing images, and so on. These are also called high-level container runtimes; examples include containerd and cri-o.

The container runtime uses the host operating system kernel's capabilities to create isolated sandboxes for processes with resource limits. The container runtime uses the metadata in the image to configure the isolated execution environment that has been created using the underlying kernel features, union mount the image layers, and configure the mount as the root file system for the isolated environment. Typically, this is done through operating system–level isolation and virtualization, such as with cgroups, namespaces, and chroot in Linux, or Hyper-V in Windows.

Oracle Cloud infrastructure offers several choices to run and manage container workloads, from the basic approach of running and managing containers on compute instances to fully autonomous and serverless offerings.

Compute Instances

The most obvious and trivial way to run a container on OCI is to create a compute instance, install a container runtime on that instance, and then use the tooling provided by the container runtime to create and manage containers. Although this is a perfectly valid model, it often involves more (and often unacceptable) management overhead for the developers because of the need to keep the container runtimes, tools, and other infrastructure components updated and patched on a rigorous schedule. However, this approach affords you the highest amount of control in managing your workloads.

The trivial method for booting a compute instance with a container runtime is to install it at first boot using `cloud-init`[3]. Listing 3-1 shows an example `cloud-init` configuration for Oracle Linux 7, to install Docker, enable the service, and start it. The example also adds the default `opc` user to the docker group so that this user can use the `docker` command without using `sudo`.

Listing 3-1   `cloud-init` Example for Bootstrapping an Oracle Linux 7 Instance with a Container Runtime

```
#cloud-config
bootcmd:
  - [ cloud-init-per, once, enable-epel,  yum-config-manager, --enable, ol7_
developer_epel]
groups:
  - docker
users:
  - default
  - name: opc
    groups: docker
    shell: /bin/bash
    sudo: ALL=(ALL) NOPASSWD:ALL
```

```
packages:
  - docker-engine
  - docker-cli

runcmd:
  - [ systemctl, daemon-reload ]
  - [ systemctl, enable, docker.service ]
  - [ systemctl, start, --no-block, docker.service ]
```

> **Note**
>
> On Oracle Linux 7, the package *docker-engine* refers to the Oracle Container Runtime for Docker. This package is based on the upstream docker releases.

Oracle Linux 8 does not feature the Oracle Container Runtime for Docker and instead uses Podman, Buildah, and Skopeo, which is a set of container tools based on the Open Container Initiative. All the tools are available conveniently in a single module that can be installed with the following command:

```
sudo dnf module install container-tools:ol8
```

This command can be used from within the cloud-init configuration as well.

Aside from using cloud-init to set up required packages, you can also create custom OS images with the tools preinstalled. This approach avoids the installation process at instance creation time. It saves several seconds when launching an instance, which can be quite significant if you have highly performance-sensitive workloads that frequently need ephemeral compute instances. Several task-based workloads belong to this category. When using this approach, an instance is created and then the required packages and settings are configured. A custom OS image is created from this instance, which now includes the packages and customizations that were applied to the instance. New instances can thus be created using the custom image as the OS image.

Container Instances

Container instances address the primary drawback of running a container runtime directly on top of infrastructure, which is the high setup and maintenance overhead associated with it. Using the methods described in the previous section, the setup process and methods can be streamlined to a certain extent. However, the maintenance of infrastructure poses an entirely different challenge. Using infrastructure directly, developers need to take on the responsibility for routinely updating, patching, and rebooting their compute instances. It is also important to keep the container runtime up to date with the latest patches and CVEs while ensuring consistent configurations of these runtimes. Sizing the infrastructure becomes another challenge in this model because you need to always ensure compute capacity for container workloads to scale dynamically while still optimizing for cost. Instance provisioning times can be orders of magnitude higher than container creation and startup times, so always having "just enough headroom" is essential to seamlessly scale the container workload. Developers also need to ensure that logs and metrics from containers can be collected and pushed to analytics tools. Workload isolation is an equally challenging problem, particularly for multitenant applications and SaaS platforms. When building multitenant applications and platforms, the shared infrastructure needs to be managed carefully to prevent data leakage and container escape attacks. These often result in solutions that require a significant amount of custom code to ensure that containers are placed in optimally sized instances, containers have room to scale when needed, shared resources are well isolated, and the fleet can be managed and patched efficiently from an operational perspective.

Container instances address these concerns by offering a service that enables you to create one or more containers without managing infrastructure. The experience is like compute instance creation, in that it enables you to specify the CPU, the memory, network, and other resource characteristics required for one or more containers and then for providing container images to run. OCI provides the compute, the container runtime, and other resources, such as networking and storage; then it uses the metadata provided to pull the images and create a running container or set of containers. Here the OCI service takes care of creating and maintaining the underlying infrastructure. The service manages activities such as OS patching and restarts, container runtime setup, network setup, storage attachment, and so on. This greatly simplifies the workflow for developers while addressing the drawbacks of the traditional approaches. From the developer's perspective, the workflow is very similar to launching a compute instance. Instead of providing an operating system image, the developer provides the CPU memory and other resource constraints, as well as the container images that need to be part of the container instance.

A container instance is a lightweight container-optimized VM that can have more than one container in it. This enables developers to start containers much faster than provisioning VMs while providing the same level of hypervisor-level isolation and avoiding the management overhead of traditional VMs. The hypervisor level allows for a better security posture, even in the face of container escape attacks. The containers within a container instance all share the CPU, network, and storage resources. This is somewhat like a *pod* in Kubernetes, although a container instance should really be thought of as a lightweight VM that can run one or more containers; it differs greatly in the level of container orchestration features when compared to platforms such as Kubernetes. Figure 3-4 shows how the container instance provides hypervisor level isolation and an environment that can run multiple containers that share the container instance's resources.

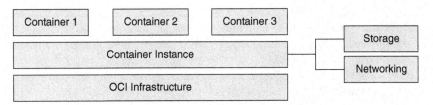

Figure 3-4 Container Instance and Hypervisor-Level Isolation

Container instances integrate with OCI features such as instance pools and autoscaling for fleet management. This means that you can create a container-based workload fleet that is consistently configured and can scale elastically. The container instance also makes it easy to access container logs and metrics for each container within the container instance and execute commands within the containers. As with containers, container instances are also immutable. When a container instance is created, changing resources such as CPU or storage is done by creating a new container instance and discarding the old one. This includes updating the image tags and changing the configurations for the containers, in keeping with standard container lifecycle management practices. This dramatically improves the workflow for developers working with container applications by providing a fully managed platform for infrastructure and container runtimes.

Ideal applications for container instances include data processing jobs such as video encoding or data analytics, build jobs, CRUD applications, event-based actions, and task automation.

Container Engine for Kubernetes

As containerized applications grow in scale, they tend to become smaller and more distributed. Modern distributed applications are designed as a network of microservices that each implement a specific feature and communicate with each other using well-defined interfaces. When combined with container-based packaging, this design paradigm enables each of these smaller services to scale, update, and expand in their features, independent of each other. This also helps increase the overall development velocity and supports a more frequent release of smaller changes. As the number of these containers rises, however, so does their management overhead; the overall application also increases in its complexity. Manually or statically wiring together the containers and keeping track of their status and health soon becomes an untenable approach. This calls for more automation to orchestrate the container workloads. For large container-based workloads that require significant higher-level abstractions and orchestration, Kubernetes is the platform of choice. Kubernetes offers much beyond container management, and it provides features such as autoscaling, resource management, service discovery, load balancing, and deployment management. Kubernetes is a CNCF graduated open-source project and can be installed and run on public cloud, hybrid, or on-premises infrastructures.

Kubernetes exemplifies the "pets versus cattle" approach. The premise is that you do not treat your infrastructure as individual hosts or resources, each with a designated purpose and name, like a pet. Instead, you see your infrastructure as a fleet of servers, with none serving any special role and all being completely replaceable. For instance, with Kubernetes, you can configure an application container so that it is allowed to use two cores and 8GB of memory to run, and you can request that three instances of the application be running at any one time. Using this configuration, called a *manifest* and typically represented in YAML, Kubernetes can create the required number of containers to meet your specification and keep track of their health. Kubernetes can move your containers as the fleet's status changes and failures occur, all without intervention. In this manner, Kubernetes enables you to describe the configuration you desire in the deployment manifests; you can then apply these manifests to a Kubernetes cluster that keeps track of the containers, nodes, and other resources and ensures that your configuration defined in the manifest is always met. Because these manifests can be versioned, releasing new changes and rolling back to previous configurations becomes trivial for most applications.

Oracle Cloud Infrastructure Container Engine for Kubernetes (OKE) is the managed Kubernetes platform for developing modern applications from Oracle. Although you can install Kubernetes on any infrastructure yourself, the installation and upkeep of the administrative and platform components in Kubernetes can be challenging. Figure 3-5 illustrates the various components of an OKE cluster.

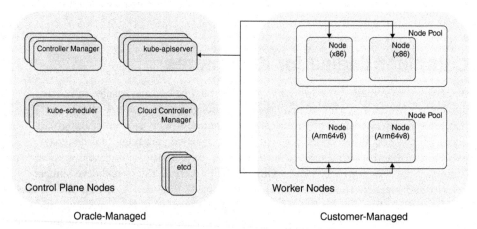

Figure 3-5 Components in an OKE Cluster, Showing the Oracle-Managed Control Plane and the Data Plane Where the User Has Full Control

As a software suite that manages container-based workloads, Kubernetes has a set of administrative components that manage and control the cluster for tasks such as keeping track of the nodes, workloads, configurations, health status, and so on. The nodes on which these control components run are called the *control plane nodes*. In a managed Kubernetes platform such as OKE, these are installed and managed by the cloud provider. The control plane nodes do not run any workloads other than the management processes for the cluster itself. Users do not have access to these nodes.

The workloads themselves run on compute instances called worker *nodes*. The cluster control plane processes monitor and record the state of the worker nodes and schedule workloads onto them. A *node pool* is a subset of worker nodes within a cluster that all have the same configuration. A cluster must have a minimum of one node pool, but a node pool need not contain any worker nodes.

OKE supports two types of node pools that differ in how the nodes in the pool are managed. *Managed* node pools have nodes that are controlled by the user. *Virtual* node pools, on the other hand, are fully managed by OCI. Managed node pools and virtual node pools address different use cases and usage models. A managed node is a compute instance of the user's choice of shape. Users have full access to these nodes, including SSH access and the capability to customize the nodes with user-created OS images and cloud-init scripts. Nodes run the kubelet process, which is responsible for ensuring that the pods scheduled on the node are running and reporting on the node health conditions acting as a node agent for Kubernetes. Virtual nodes, on the other hand, leverage Kubernetes pod configurations to create an isolated compute environment for the pod. Each Kubernetes pod is therefore isolated from other pods at a hypervisor level. The configuration of the execution environment, such as the number of CPU cores and memory, is inferred from the resource requests and limits set on the containers in the pod configuration. The execution environment for the pod is fully managed by Oracle and runs abstracted, away from the user. Virtual node pools therefore completely remove the need to manage infrastructure when deploying Kubernetes workloads and can be considered to be a serverless Kubernetes platform. Although managed nodes give users a high degree of control in accessing and managing their nodes (as with using custom cloud-init scripts to customize nodes), they come with the additional overhead of managing the node's OS and Kubernetes upgrades. Virtual nodes, on the other hand, offer an experience that is focused on your workload, with little or no infrastructure management overhead. However, that comes at the expense of having control over the configuration of nodes. A single cluster can have both provisioned and virtual node pools.

Table 3-1 offers a comparison of managed and virtual nodes.

Table 3-1 Managed versus Virtual Nodes

	Managed Nodes	**Virtual Nodes**
Infrastructure control	Users maintain control over nodes.	Users can control the workload but not the infrastructure.
Upgrades	Users upgrade the nodes.	Upgrades are fully managed by OKE.
Isolation	A node's resources are shared by the pods that run on it.	A virtual node has no physical resources. Each pod runs in its own hypervisor-level isolated compute environment.

	Managed Nodes	Virtual Nodes
Resource management	Users decide the shapes of the nodes and set resource requirements and limits for pods. The Kubernetes scheduler matches pods to nodes based on availability.	Nodes need not be created or managed. Users should set resource requirements and limits on pods, to create dedicated compute environments for each pod.

Node pools can also have placement configurations that control the placement of the nodes in the node pool. These placement configurations can be used to spread the nodes in a node pool across multiple availability domains or fault domains to ensure better resiliency. Creating multiple node pools enables you to create groups of machines within a cluster that have different configurations. Figure 3-6 shows two node pools, one with E3.Flex shapes and another with A1 bare-metal machines. Here, the first node pool is based on AMD (x86)–based Flex shape virtual machine instances; the second node pool is an ARM-based bare-metal shape. This example also demonstrates that different node pools can be of different shapes, CPU architectures, and bare metal or virtual machines. Having this flexibility in your cluster resources lets you right-size the workloads and progressively introduce infrastructure changes to your environments—for example, introducing ARM-based compute for a subset of workloads or using bare-metal or GPU–enabled nodes for compute-heavy workloads and VMs for supporting workloads. Node pools also let you control the placement of nodes across availability domains and fault domains in OCI. Figure 3-6 shows the first node pool placing nodes across all three availability domains and the second node pool restricting nodes to just two of the three availability domains.

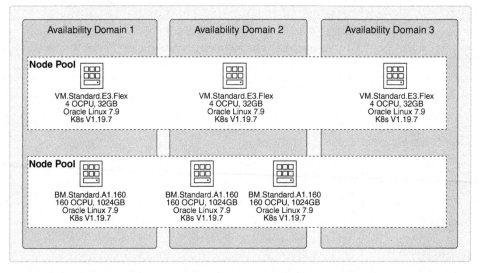

Figure 3-6   Node Pools in a Cluster Can Be Used to Control the Node Types and Their Placement, as Well as Create Clusters with Multiple Types of Nodes in Separate Node Pools

The node pools act as the control unit for scaling and can be used to scale the number of compute instances up or down, to add or remove compute capacity in the cluster. The scaling also can be automated based on metrics. Autoscaling is covered in more detail in Chapter 4, "Understanding Container Engine for Kubernetes."

Note that the number of pods that can be scheduled or placed on a node is still dependent on the network address space available on a node, up to a maximum of 110. Larger nodes with more CPU cores and memory are therefore ideal to accommodate pods with much higher resource consumption needs. The memory and network throughput are also important considerations when choosing a shape for your nodes. The maximum available memory and network bandwidth changes, based on the shape of the node and the number of OCPUs (an OCPU is a complete core, not just a hardware thread). Thus, the choice of shape for the nodes also depends on the memory and network throughput expectations for the workloads.

As one of the highest-velocity open-source projects, Kubernetes provides support for three minor versions. This support policy is sometimes also called an N-2 support policy, in which the latest version and the two preceding minor versions of Kubernetes get patches for security and bug fixes. OKE as a managed service does not force users to upgrade as new versions of Kubernetes are released, although keeping your Kubernetes version up to date with the latest security fixes and bug fixes is an important consideration. For creating new clusters, OKE always supports at least three versions of Kubernetes. Version choice for new clusters moves like a rolling window as well. When OKE adds a new version of Kubernetes as a choice for creating new clusters, the oldest version choice remains a choice for at least 30 days, beyond which it may be removed. Exiting clusters that use that version are unaffected; the removal simply means that new clusters will have newer version choices. As support for new Kubernetes versions is added to OKE, you can update the control plane to the new version with a click of a button or an API call. The control plane upgrades are completely managed by Oracle and are transparent to the user. The Oracle-managed control plane is always in a highly available configuration, and the upgrade is performed in a rolling fashion so that it does not impact the cluster's normal operations. After the control plane has been upgraded, the node pools can be upgraded as well. Chapter 4 does a deep dive into OKE, providing best practices, strategies, and tips for building and deploying applications to OKE.

Service Mesh

As we become more accustomed to microservice-based architectures and distributed applications, we start seeing applications as consisting of services that communicate with each other and forming a network of services that implement the application. This design paradigm of creating a network of services affords us a lot of advantages in flexibility, development velocity, and resiliency. However, as applications evolve, the network of microservices grows and the complexity of managing the entire application also increases. The task of ensuring reliable and secure service-to-service communication and implementing observability can have a significant impact on the development of the services. Building these features directly into the services makes them more brittle, impedes their capability to change, and slows the development of features because the application code now needs to take on additional responsibilities. In a cloud native environment, a service mesh is a tool that can be used to add cross-cutting functionality, such as security or observability, to a set of microservices.

A service mesh operates by inserting proxies between services into the network of microservices. These network proxies are typically deployed as a set of sidecar containers, or containers that are deployed alongside microservice containers. They handle the service-to-service communication between the microservices and can transparently implement security, observability, and patterns for resiliency.

Oracle Cloud Infrastructure Service Mesh is a fully managed service mesh implementation that provides security, observability, and traffic management to cloud native applications without any application changes or dependencies. OCI Service Mesh creates proxies that are containers deployed alongside your applications, in the same Kubernetes cluster. The proxies handle traffic to the application and provide telemetry, security, and load balancing across pods. The proxies communicate with each other and are aware of policies that govern communications so that they allow only permissible communications between services. Figure 3-7 shows how the proxies deployed as sidecars to microservice containers communicate with the managed components of the service mesh to provide features such as telemetry and security.

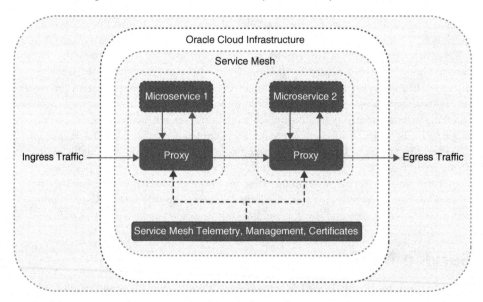

Figure 3-7   OCI Service Mesh Is Based on Proxies That Are Injected as Sidecar Containers to Your Pods

The service mesh has managed components that include an IngressGateway, VirtualServices, and VirtualDeployments, along with policy management to support customized and secure traffic routing. These are mapped to an application's services and provide abstractions for those services. When using the OCI service mesh, the applications services are mapped to virtual services and virtual deployments and associated policies. These virtual services are then bound to the existing services using binding objects. The applications are exposed using the IngressGateway, which routes traffic to the various VirtualServices. VirtualServices are in turn bound to Kubernetes services that the application exposes. A virtual service represents a customer-managed microservice in the mesh. Each virtual service has its own configuration for the service hostname, Transport Layer Security (TLS) certificates (for both client and server), and Certificate Authority (CA) bundles. A virtual deployment represents a version of a virtual service; each virtual service has up to five virtual deployments. Route tables are a virtual service feature that routes ingress traffic to specific versions of the virtual service. A virtual deployment binding associates the pods in an application cluster with a virtual deployment in your mesh. The virtual deployment binding resource allows service mesh to discover pods, backing the virtual deployment for service discovery.

The service mesh components and custom resources are installed on a Kubernetes cluster using the OCI Service Operator for Kubernetes (OSOK). OSOK is a collection of operators for OCI services that includes the operator for the service mesh. This operator provides the CRDs, roles, and other resources required to allow users to perform actions on the OCI service mesh using the Kubernetes API. With the operator installed, users can interact with the service mesh using standard tools such as kubectl.

When using the service mesh with the operator, users can apply annotations at the namespace level to enable sidecar injection for all pods in the namespace. The effect of these namespace-level annotations can be overridden at a pod level by specifying the sidecar injection on a per-pod basis.

Serverless Functions

Serverless functions are at the pinnacle of building scalable and distributed business logic implementations. They are called *serverless* simply because the server and its runtime environment are fully managed by the cloud vendor and are not exposed to the application developer. The essential idea is to create functional units of business logic that can be packaged and executed in isolation. These are generally focused, well-defined tasks such as file processing, in which a file is read from a source, minimally processed or transformed, and then either sent to a destination or takes an action in response to an event. Functions also find use in Internet of Things (IOT) applications, image processing, machine learning (ML) inferencing, and other applications. Functions usually do not exist in isolation; many times, they are chained together to create a network of functions (similar to microservices in that respect) that interact with external systems. Functions are usually time bound: They are expected to finish their execution within a slice of time, beyond which they can be terminated. In many cases, functions are also event driven. Their fundamental design of running small, time-bound processes that perform well-defined actions makes them naturally scalable and distributed when assembled into larger systems. Functions can be written in Python, Go, Java, NodeJS, and other commonly used programming languages and runtime environments. Functions should be fully self-contained and cannot depend on any outside software or code to operate other than calling other APIs. Being packaged into these self-contained units allows them to start up, execute their functionality, and then shut down quickly. Functions abstract all infrastructure management from their users, and a cloud platform (such as OCI) guarantees a secure execution environment that can scale quickly as the calls to the function increase. This also means that functions follow a very different cost model based on actual usage rather than the typical infrastructure that might be billed based on resources allocated.

Oracle Functions is a fully managed Functions-as-a-Service platform that is built on enterprise-grade Oracle Cloud Infrastructure and powered by the Fn Project open-source engine. The serverless and elastic architecture of Oracle Functions means there is no infrastructure administration or software administration for you to perform. You do not provision or maintain compute instances, nor are you responsible for operating system software patches and upgrades. Oracle Functions simply ensures that your app is highly available, scalable, secure, and monitored. With Oracle Functions, you can write code in Java, Python, Node.js, Go, and Ruby (and, for advanced use cases, bring your own Dockerfile and Graal VM). You can then deploy your code, call it directly, or trigger it in response to events, and you get billed only for the resources consumed during the execution.

Oracle Functions is based on Fn Project.[4] Fn Project is an open-source, container-native, serverless platform that can be run anywhere—in any cloud or on-premises. Fn Project is easy to use, extensible, and performant. You can download and install the open-source distribution of Fn Project, develop and test a function locally, and then use the same tooling to deploy that function to Oracle Functions. You can access Oracle Functions using the console, a Command Line Interface (CLI), and a REST API. You can invoke the functions you deploy to Oracle Functions by using the CLI or by making signed HTTP requests. Oracle Functions is integrated with Oracle Cloud Infrastructure Identity and Access Management (IAM), which provides easy authentication with native Oracle Cloud Infrastructure identity functionality.

When you have written the code for a function and it is ready to deploy, you can use a single Fn Project CLI command to perform all the deploy operations in sequence:

1. Build a Docker image from the function.
2. Provide a definition of the function in a func.yaml file that includes:
   a. The maximum length of time the function is allowed to execute
   b. The maximum amount of memory the function is allowed to consume
3. Push the image to the specified Docker registry.
4. Upload function metadata (including the memory and time restrictions and a link to the image in the Docker registry) to the Fn Server and add the function to the list of functions shown in the console.

Figure 3-8 shows how the Functions CLI interacts with the various components to deploy a new function.

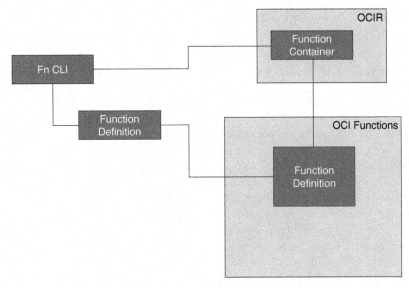

Figure 3-8   The Components of Oracle Functions

API Gateways

An API gateway provides a layer of abstraction for the Application Programming Interfaces (APIs) that your applications expose. For microservice-based applications that operate at scale, this becomes almost indispensable, although, in many ways, an API gateway predates the popularity of microservice architectures. API gateways can be software-defined, self-managed platforms that you deploy on top of infrastructure, or they can be a fully managed service delivered by a cloud provider. Regardless of the model, at its core, an API gateway is a service that provides a facade around one or more of your applications' APIs, with added features. Common features offered by API gateways include the capability to implement a common and consistent authentication and authorization model across the back-end APIs, rate limiting for APIs, caching, monitoring, API versioning, and the capability to transform both requests and responses.

The API Gateway service in OCI is a fully managed service that is implemented as a virtual network appliance that you can deploy to a regional subnet. Regional subnets are required because API gateways are always highly available, with fault tolerance built in. When deployed in regions with multiple availability domains, API gateways are automatically configured across multiple ADs for fault tolerance. In single-AD regions, an API gateway is configured across fault domains. API gateways can be public (accessible from anywhere on the Internet) or private (accessible from within the VCN). API gateways always have a private endpoint, and this is optionally exposed publicly to create a public API endpoint. You can use a single API gateway to link multiple back-end services and route inbound traffic to them. These back-end services can include HTTP APIs exposed through compute instances, load balancers, external API providers, and OCI Functions.

Components of an API Gateway

When working with the API Gateway service, you generally start with the gateway resource. This is the infrastructure component, the virtual network appliance that is managed by OCI. You can then deploy API deployment specifications on this gateway resource. An API deployment specification is a way to describe the back-end APIs as a set of *routes*. A route is the mapping from a path to one or more methods and then a back-end service. Routes capture the type of resources that provide the underlying API and how to reach that resource. For instance, an HTTP URL exposed by an application that you are running on a compute instance captures the private IP address or domain name, the port on which the service is available, and the path under which to expose or present the API and the HTTP operations that the gateway supports for the route. The API deployment spec also describes the policies that can validate and transform the requests or responses. The policies are applied to every request or response. You can also use policies to add authentication, authorization, and monitoring. When the deployment specification is deployed to a gateway resource, it becomes an API deployment. The API deployment causes the gateway to expose the API as defined in the spec and is ready to direct traffic to the back ends described in the spec. As API traffic flows in, the gateway applies the policies that are specified by the API deployment spec. You can add policies to an API deployment specification that applies globally to all routes in the API deployment specification, as well as policies that apply only to particular routes. Figure 3-9 shows how an API gateway can contain multiple API deployments with policies and routes that connect it to various back ends.

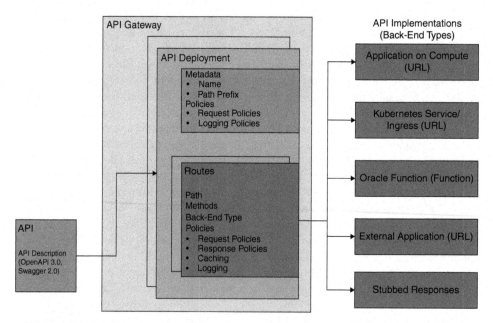

Figure 3-9   An API Gateway Can Host Multiple API Deployments, with Routes and Policies That Connect It to Various Back Ends

Apart from resources such as the gateway and an API deployment, the service exposes another resource called the *API*. As shown in Figure 3-9, an API resource can be used to create an API deployment as well. The API resource is a representation of an API description in an open format such as OpenAPI 3.0 or 2.0 (also known as Swagger 2.0). An API description like this establishes the public contract for your API, which automatically documents the endpoints, paths, HTTP operations, and type of responses to expect from the API. Representing the API contract in an open format such as OpenAPI 3.0 helps to ensure the portability and tooling for working with these APIs; these industry-standard formats have attracted an established ecosystem of tools around them. The API description format is machine readable and can be processed by tools with which you can generate documentation for the API, generate stubs for clients to call the API without an actual implementation, generate test cases and Software Development Kits (SDKs), and so on. An API resource is created by uploading an API description. The API resource can be deployed to an API gateway, creating an API deployment. When an API resource is deployed to an API gateway, the routes are created from the API description because it provides the paths, the HTTP methods supported, and expected responses. Policies and references to the actual API implementations are added to the API description when creating an API deployment. Creating API resources in the API Gateway service is optional, but it is highly recommended. You can also create an API deployment that does not initially have an API description and then add an API description later.

Working with the API Gateway Service

The workflow for using an API gateway is best demonstrated by starting with a simple API. This example shows a minimal API for product data. The API will have methods by which users can request a list of products or get the details of a single product. To build this API, a developer can start with the infrastructure resources and build an ad-hoc deployment. This is done by creating an API deployment from scratch, defining its routes, back ends, and so on. Alternatively, a developer can first define the API contract and then create the infrastructure resources and deploy the API definition to it. The best practice is to use an API-first approach, to define the API and its behavior without focusing on the implementation. This API definition defines an interface that potential consumers can start consuming even before an implementation is created. After all, the implementation for the API simply materializes the behavior described by the API definition with concrete back-end systems. The actual implementation is hidden from consumers and can potentially be swapped out, if needed. This is because the consumers always consume the API through the API Gateway, which maintains the API behavior expressed in the API definition and routes the requests to a back end that implements that behavior. After the API is defined, a developer can create the infrastructure and deploy the API definition to that infrastructure. The example presented here uses OpenAPI Spec 3.0[5] to define the API, and the code snippet in Listing 3-2 shows how an API of this nature would appear.

Listing 3-2   An Example API Definition Expressed Using the OpenAPI Spec v3 Standard

```
{
  "openapi": "3.0.0",
  "info": {
    "version": "1.0.0",
    "title": "Minimal Product API"
  },
  "paths": {
    "/products": {
      "get": {
        "summary": "get all products",
        "operationId": "getProducts",
        "responses": {
          "200": {
            "description": "An array of products",
            "content": {
              "application/json": {
                "schema": {
                  "$ref": "#/components/schemas/Products"
                }}}}}}
    },
    "/products/{productId}": {
      "get": {
        "summary": "Info for a specific product",
        "operationId": "getProductById",
        "parameters": [{
            "name": "productId",
            "in": "path",
            "required": true,
            "description": "The id of the product to retrieve",
            "schema": {
              "type": "string"
            }}
            ],
        "responses": {
          "200": {
            "description": "Expected response to a valid request",
            "content": {
```

```
            "application/json": {
              "schema": {
                "$ref": "#/components/schemas/Product"
            }}}}}}}
  },
  "components": {
    "schemas": {
      "Product": {
        "type": "object",
        "required": [
          "id",
          "name"
        ],
        "properties": {
          "id": {
            "type": "integer",
            "format": "int64"
          },
          "name": {
            "type": "string"
        }}
      },
      "Products": {
        "type": "array",
        "items": {
          "$ref": "#/components/schemas/Product"
        }}}}
}
```

OpenAPI definitions always start with the version of the OpenAPI Spec used. Explicitly setting the version is mandatory. Here, the spec version used is 3.0.0. This is followed by some API metadata in the info object. The paths section is one of the most important in the API definition; it defines the various URL paths or routes that the API exposes. The example here shows two paths: /products and /products/{productId}. Each path then defines the HTTP methods that the path will support. For each method, the definition identifies the request parameters and request body, where applicable, as in the case of PUT and POST methods. Paths can contain path parameters such as /products/{productId} or other parameter types, such as query parameters, cookie parameters, or header parameters. Each HTTP method also identifies the various possible response codes and response structures.

> **Note**
>
> Several optional elements have been removed; for brevity, the example shows only necessary attributes. The OpenAPI spec website has more details on the various attributes within the specification: https://spec.openapi.org/oas/v3.0.0.

With the API defined, the developer can now create an API resource and upload the API definition to it. After the API definition is uploaded, the API resource validates the definition to ensure that it conforms to the specification. Once validated, the API definition is ready to be deployed to an API gateway. The developer can create infrastructure resources such as the gateway at this point or use pre-existing resources. Deploying the API to an *API gateway* creates the *API deployment* resource. During deployment, the service parses the API definition and creates the routes and methods based on the definition. At this stage, the developer can specify additional information about these APIs, such as the back ends that implement the APIs or the policies that need to be applied. Figure 3-10 shows how an API deployment infers the routes and HTTP methods from the paths specified in an API spec. To get started, developers can use a stubbed-out back end; as real back-end services are built out, they can simply be switched in.

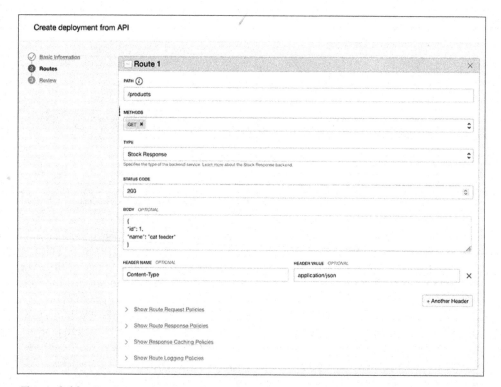

Figure 3-10   The Service Can Parse the API Spec and Populate the Routes in an API Deployment

Messaging Systems

Modern cloud native architecture that emphasizes resiliency through scalable, loosely coupled components relies on asynchronous messaging between components. Messaging-based architectures allow microservices to scale and become location transparent because systems are not connecting to each other directly; instead, they are communicating through messages brokered by a messaging system. This enables load management, elasticity, and flow control by shaping and monitoring the message queues in the system. It also enables developers to manage failures as messages. The asynchronous and nonblocking communication in message-driven architectures consumes resources only while active, delivering optimized resource usage and cost optimizations. Today several leading CNCF projects exist in the messaging space, including NATS.io and Cloud Events, providing a wide array of features, programming models, and performance characteristics.

In message-driven architectures, a message usually represents an object and its state or a change in its state. For instance, in an ecommerce application, a message that is sent from a cart service to an order service can identify an item by its ID, the quantity to be purchased, payment information, and the user who is purchasing it. The orders system can process the messages as they arrive, checking inventory, processing the payment, and sending more messages to other systems, such as a fulfillment system for the orders placed. Here, the systems are not directly communicating, nor do they know the other systems that are receiving the messages. This allows for flexible architectures—if one service were to be replaced, the other services would not even be aware of this change. This allows systems to scale independently and maintain well-defined failure boundaries, avoiding cascading failures. If a service fails, the messages intended for that failed receiver simply wait for the system to return to an operational state and pick up from the next message that is to be processed. Developers thus can work with well-defined contracts expressed as message formats, and rollout changes to parts of the system can be done with greater velocity and agility, yet without the need for highly coordinated release workflows.

Several messaging approaches offer different semantics, including message queuing and publish subscribe. These models have three key components: message producers, the messaging system, and message consumers. Message producers are applications that generate messages. Message consumers are applications that consume and process messages. They are connected by the messaging system, which provides features such as message storage, message order, at-least-once delivery, and at-most-once delivery. Note that the messaging system decouples the producer and consumer. Each component knows only about the messaging system, not about each other. This isolation of each component allows them to be independently deployed, scaled, and patched.

In message queuing, messages sent by the message producer are stored in a buffer until they are dequeued or consumed by another component. The message is processed only by the message consumer that dequeues it from the queuing system.

In the publish subscribe (Pub/Sub) model, shown in Figure 3-11, the producers (also known as publishers) publish messages onto a topic, and the message can be processed by all consumers (also called subscribers) who have subscribed to the topic. Note that in the Pub/Sub model, the same message is processed by many subscribers, unlike in a queue.

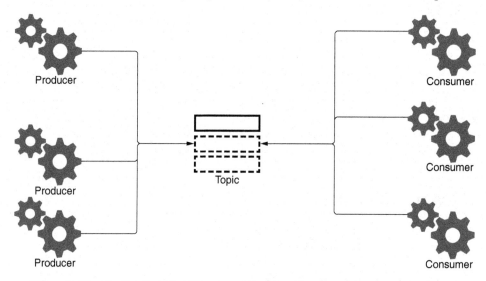

Figure 3-11   The Pub/Sub Model Connects Distributed Systems Using Messages That Are Published and Consumed on a Topic

Among these three components, the messaging system is usually the most complex. It handles message persistence, ordering, delivery guarantees, and more. The producer and the consumer interact with the messaging system using an API that the messaging system provides. The APIs provided by the messaging system aim to make the producer and consumer code as simple as possible. For most platforms, the producer API simply lets an application publish a message, and the consumer API lets an application read these messages. In practice, when there is a multitude of producers and consumers, the messaging system provides the heavy lifting of ensuring the throughput, infrastructure resources, and delivery semantics. This makes the task of running and maintaining open-source messaging systems such as Kafka and NATS appreciably complex and nontrivial. As a solution to this problem, most cloud vendors provide a fully managed messaging system that either is built on top of the open-source tools or has API compatibility with open-source tools.

Streaming

The OCI Streaming service provides a scalable messaging system with durable storage. It is a fully managed service that can be used for ingesting continuous streams of data. Streaming service is suited for building web-scale applications and microservices that use a message-driven architecture. These applications are typically designed around data that is produced and processed continually and sequentially in a Pub/Sub messaging model.

The OCI Streaming service is also suited for applications that ingest logs, metrics, and operational telemetry, as well as other fast data streams, such as website clickstreams. As a fully managed service, OCI Streaming manages all infrastructure needed to operate and scale the service, from provisioning, deployment, maintenance, and replication to configuration of the hardware and software that enables you to stream data. As a user of the service, you create a *stream* and configure the *partitions*. Streams and partitions are resources provided by the service; they are discussed in the next section. You can securely put and get your data from Streaming through SSL endpoints using the HTTPS protocol. The service ensures that user data is encrypted both at rest and in transit, and you can bring your own encryption keys that you manage in the OCI Vault service. Streams also support private endpoints, which limits the visibility of your streaming endpoint so that it is restricted within your virtual cloud network (VCN), preventing access through the Internet.

Understanding the Streaming Service

The OCI Streaming service is a fully managed service. As such, it exposes a resource called a *stream* that encapsulates the infrastructure required to operate a messaging system and manage its lifecycle. Developers first create a stream in the streaming service using the console, CLI, Terraform, or the APIs. A stream is the primary resource you interact with, and it can be thought of as an append-only log. Streams are organized into *stream pools* that provide a way to manage the settings for all the streams in a pool. If you do not explicitly associate a stream with a stream pool, the stream is created in the default stream pool.

After a stream has been created, applications can publish messages to it. In most cases, applications use the OCI SDK or the APIs directly to publish messages. You can also use the OCI console and the CLI to send messages to your stream for testing. Another popular way for applications to interact with the streaming service is to use the Kafka APIs, which the streaming service supports. Every message consists of a key and a value, both of which can be set by the developer. Listing 3-3 shows a snippet of code using the Python SDK to publish a message. Multiple publisher applications can publish messages to the stream at the same time.

Subscribers or subscriber applications can consume messages from the stream either individually or as part of a *consumer group*. The streaming APIs and SDK offer many options for consumers to control how messages are delivered to them.

As applications publish messages to a stream, these messages are distributed to *partitions* that are managed by the streaming service. Each partition stores a subset of the messages that were published. Having multiple partitions allows message consumers to consume messages from multiple partitions at the same time. Because publishers and subscribers can use partitions in parallel, the number of partitions has an impact on the message throughput of the stream. There are limits to this as well. Each partition is limited to 1MBps of data write and 5 get requests per second from each consumer group. When a new stream is created, the number of partitions it should use needs to be specified. Once created, the number of partitions in the stream cannot be changed. Messages that are published onto a stream by producers are routed and stored on one of the partitions in the stream. Figure 3-12 shows an overview of how applications can publish and receive messages using the streaming service, as well as the various components of the streaming service itself.

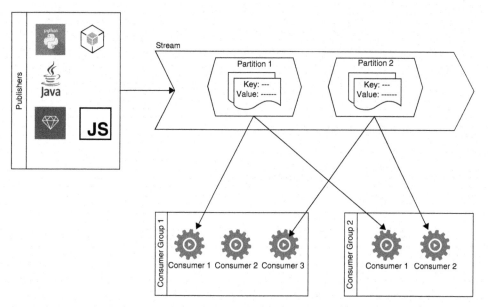

Figure 3-12   An OCI Stream Showing Various Partitions and How Publishers and Subscribers Can Communicate Using Messages

Working with the OCI Streaming Service

A producer publishes a message onto the stream. The various SDKs for languages such as Java, Python, Go, JavaScript, and TypeScript provide wrapper methods to access the streaming APIs. A single call to publish messages can include multiple messages, but the total size of payload must be 1 mebibyte (MiB) or less. Each message that is published to the stream should contain a *key* and a *value*. If there is more than one partition, the steaming service determines the partition where the message is published using the message key. Based on the key, two messages with different keys could potentially be published on the same partition; however, messages with the same key always go to the same partition. If you do not specify a key, the service considers the message to have a *null* key and generates a random key for the message. Messages with null keys trigger the generation of random keys, so these messages do not pile up within the same partition. This avoids accidental hot spots, with messages with null keys all ending up on the same partition and impacting the throughput of the system. Listing 3-3 shows a snippet of Python code that connects to a stream on the OCI Streaming service and publishes two messages with the single call. It shows the Python SDK reading the config to connect and authenticate, with OCI being loaded from a file and a streaming client being created.

Listing 3-3   Example Code to Publish a Message Using the Python SDK

```
config = oci.config.from_file()
streaming_client = oci.streaming.StreamClient(
    config, "https://service_endpoint.url")

streaming_client.put_messages(
    stream_id="<stream_OCID>",
    put_messages_details=oci.streaming.models.PutMessagesDetails(
        messages=[
            oci.streaming.models.PutMessagesDetailsEntry(
                value="FirstMessage",
                key="key_one");
            oci.streaming.models.PutMessagesDetailsEntry(
                value="SecondMessage",
                key="key_two")])
```

The `StreamClient` provides the function `put_messages`, which wraps the streaming service's API for publishing messages. It requires the stream ID, which is the OCID for the stream, as well as a list of messages to publish. As mentioned previously, there is no limit to the number of messages that can be included in this function call, as long as the total size of the payload is 1MB or less. The message keys can be up to 256 bytes. The SDKS for other languages provide similar constructs.

Note

In general, applications should strive to design message keys that help spread the messages evenly. If a vast majority of the messages produced in a system have a common attribute, then using that attribute as a message key will lead to an overwhelming number of messages in a single partition, while other partitions remain relatively idle. Better throughput could be achieved by picking keys so that a large number of unique keys can be generated and as few messages as possible share the same key. This ensures better distribution of messages across the various partitions. Messages with the same key are guaranteed to be stored in the order in which they are published and are delivered to consumers in the same order that they were produced. Because messages with the same key go to the same partition, this guarantee applies only at the partition level.

Consumer applications consume messages from a stream using the API or the SDKs in a manner similar to how a producer publishes messages onto the stream. A consumer needs to start consuming messages from some point in the stream. Consumers use a *cursor*, which is a pointer to a specific location within a stream, to do this. Messages then are consumed starting with the one that the cursor points to. The streaming service guarantees that the messages from a partition are always delivered in the same order they were produced. After a cursor has been created, the consumer uses the `GetMessages` API to fetch messages. Similar to publishing messages, a single call to the `GetMessages` API returns multiple messages. By default, the number of messages that are batched inside a single response is based on the average message size, so as to not exceed the stream's throughput. You can also specify the number of messages to be returned, as long as you do not exceed the throughput of the stream. As the number of messages returned from a call to the `GetMessages` API can vary based on the message size, the call also returns a cursor for use with the next `GetMessages` call. The cursor is returned as a response header value in the custom header `opc-next-cursor`. The next call to `GetMessages` can use the value returned in the header as the cursor parameter, to get the next batch of messages.

Individual consumers can start consuming messages from different relative points in the stream using different types of cursors. The types of cursors include ones that point to the following:

- A specific time (cursor type `AT_TIME`)
- The earliest message available on the stream (cursor type `TRIM_HORIZON`)
- A relative position within the messages on the partition, called an offset (cursor type `AT_OFFSET` or `AFTER_OFFSET`)
- Only messages published after the cursor has been created (cursor type `LATEST`)

This enables consumers to keep track of the various partitions, the position of the last message the consuming application has consumed from the partition, and from what position in the partition the consuming application needs to start in case it is interrupted or terminated and needs to restart consuming from where it left off.

Consumers can also be grouped into *ConsumerGroups* that coordinate the consumption of messages from a stream. In streams that have numerous partitions, keeping track of offsets and partitions while dynamically scaling the number of consumers can be cumbersome. ConsumerGroups can push to the streaming service most of the heavy lifting required to manage offsets and partitions when consumers are scaled up or down. This helps developers focus on what to do with messages instead of having to orchestrate message consumption. ConsumerGroups consist of multiple consumers, called *instances*. The ConsumerGroups automatically manage offset tracking, assign the various instances in the group to specific partitions, and balance the group as instances are created and removed in the ConsumerGroups. ConsumerGroups are more efficient and practical for most purposes than individual consumers simply because of the benefits they provide at no extra cost. ConsumerGroups use a cursor called a *GroupCursor*, which creates a *group name* and *instance name* association, in addition to performing the duties of a normal cursor. The first time a GroupCursor is created with a new group name, the ConsumerGroup by that name is created. When a group cursor is created with an existing group name and a new instance name, the consumer that requested the group cursor is added to the group as a new instance in the group. Each instance in a group is assigned a partition, and an instance may be assigned more than one partition. However, two instances will never be assigned to a single partition; if a ConsumerGroup has more instances than partitions, the extra instances remain idle. ConsumerGroups automatically remove instances that have not consumed messages for more than 30 seconds. In these cases, the idle instances in the ConsumerGroup are assigned to a partition whose assigned instance has been removed.

The 30-second window to request additional messages essentially means that consumers should ideally limit the number of messages requested to something that it can process within 30 seconds. If it takes longer than 30 seconds to process the message and call `getMessages` again, the service assumes that the consumer went offline and allocates the partition to an idle consumer. Data is not lost in these scenarios, though, because the default behavior of the GroupCursor is to commit messages on the next call to `getMessages`. So in a scenario in which a consumer has been terminated, fails, or cannot process all messages within 30 seconds, the messages are not considered committed (or processed). The partition is allocated to another consumer (when one comes online in the group, if there are no idle consumers), and these messages are delivered to the consumer for processing again. Some of these messages might have been processed by the failed consumer before it failed, so these messages appear as redundant to the second consumer. This also illustrates the "at least once" delivery model of the streaming service. How the consumer applications handle redundant messages is up to the consuming application, and they should be designed to account for multiple message deliveries in situations like the aforementioned one.

Listing 3-4 shows a typical ConsumerGroup using a group cursor to consume messages.

Listing 3-4   Consumer Group Using a Group Cursor

```
config = oci.config.from_file()
streaming_client = oci.streaming.StreamClient(
    config, "https://service_endpoint.url")


cursor_details = oci.streaming.models
                                    .CreateGroupCursorDetails(group_
    name="group01", instance_name="instance01",

    type=oci.streaming.models.CreateGroupCursorDetails.TYPE_TRIM_HORIZON,

    commit_on_get=True)
response = sc.create_group_cursor(sid, cursor_details)
cursor = response.data.value
while True:
        get_response = client.get_messages(
                                    stream_id="ocid1.test.oc1..xxxxx.
    streamId-Value",
```

```
                                             cursor,
                                             limit=10)


    if not get_response.data:
            return


    # Process the messages
    print(" Read {} messages".format(len(get_response.data)))
    for message in get_response.data:
            print("{}: {}".format(b64decode(message.key.encode()).decode(),
                                        b64decode(message.value.
encode()).decode()))
        time.sleep(1)
        # use the next-cursor for iteration
        cursor = get_response.headers["opc-next-cursor"]
```

Listing 3-4 shows a stream client being created. A group cursor is also created that creates a ConsumerGroup called group01. This consumer within the group (instance) is named instance01. The initial group cursor is used to call the get_messages API with a message limit set to 10. This is done to illustrate the fact that all instances in a ConsumerGroup should try to limit messages to what they can process within 30 seconds; a gap of more than 30 seconds between calls to the get_messages API causes the service to consider the instance as offline, as previously discussed. After the messages are processed, the opc-next-cursor response header is extracted to get the cursor for the next call to get_messages. Note that, in this example, with commit_on_get set to True when creating the GroupCursor, the first 10 messages that were returned are committed when the instance calls the get_messages the second time. If this instance takes too long to process the first 10 messages or it went offline unexpectedly, then these messages are not committed and they are delivered to another instance if and when one becomes available.

Service Connector Hub Integration

The Streaming service is integrated with the OCI Service Connector Hub. The OCI Service Connector Hub is a messaging bus that enables you to orchestrate data movement between services in OCI. Using the Service Connector Hub, you can define the source for the data, a set of tasks that you can optionally apply to the data to process it (such as transforming the data), and a target service to deliver the processed data. Using the service bus connector, you can enable use cases in which you can use a stream as a data source, use Serverless Functions to transform the stream's messages, and deliver the transformed messages to a target while maintaining Streaming's order guarantees.

Kafka Compatibility

Streaming is compatible with most Kafka[6] APIs, enabling you to use applications
written for Kafka to send messages to and receive messages from the Streaming service
without having to rewrite your code. Streaming makes it possible to offload the setup,
maintenance, and management of the infrastructure that hosting your own Apache Kafka
cluster requires. Streaming also takes advantage of the Kafka Connect ecosystem to
interface directly with first-party and third-party products by using out-of-the-box Kafka
source and sink connectors. At the time of writing, the service offers compatibility with
the Kafka APIs outlined in Table 3-2.

Table 3-2   OCI Streaming Compatibility with Various Kafka APIs

Compatible	Incompatible
Producer	Compaction
Consumer	Transactions
Kafka Connect	Dynamic Partition Addition
Group Management	Idempotent Production
Admin	Kafka Streams

If you use Kafka APIs to publish messages to Streaming, you can choose to do custom
partitioning and explicitly map messages to partitions. Although this gives you more
control and predictability over what messages are sent to which partitions, the Streaming
service avoids this, to keep from accumulating too many messages in the same partitions
and creating "hotspots." When developers take control over partitions with custom
partitioning, they also take on the responsibility to avoid hotspots from having too many
messages within the same partitions.

The Kafka Connect support in OCI Streaming allows developers to leverage
the Kafka Connect ecosystem of connectors to move data between systems. Several
connectors make it easy to create integrations with Oracle platforms:

- Kafka Connect JDBC, for working with the Oracle database
- Oracle Integration Cloud
- Oracle Golden Gate
- Kafka Connect Amazon S3 connectors, which can use the Oracle Object Storage
  S3-compatible APIs

When using Kafka Connect, you need to create Kafka Connect Configurations
called *harnesses* on the OCI Streaming service. A single harness can be used to configure
multiple connectors and the harness needs to be created within the same compartment as
the stream. Kafka Connect uses internal topics to track and manage connector and task
configurations, offsets, and status. These internal topics are automatically created by the
Streaming service and follow the convention `<stream ocid>-{config|offset|status}`.
These topics can be configured in the distributed worker configuration file of the
connector, typically `connect-distributed.properties`.

OCI Events Service

All OCI services emit *events*. Events can be thought of as status updates about lifecycle state or activities that these services are performing. The occurrence of a change, such as a compute instance being created ("Instance creation started") or the completion of a block volume backup ("Block Volume backup complete"), can be represented as events. Events typically capture some context about the occurrence so that the event is actionable. An example is the OCID of the compute instance that was created. A downstream system can potentially take action based on this contextual information that is captured in the event. In large distributed systems like cloud platforms such as OCI, numerous services and components can emit events that signal their normal operations; in most cases, only a few events would be interesting and acted upon. With voluminous events being produced, the Events service provides a way to listen to or filter only interesting events and then use the context captured in the event to take an action. Although any system can emit events, in the context of the OCI Events service it is the OCI services that emit events.

In a general sense, events are a way for systems to communicate facts about their operations or statuses to other systems. Although events might sound similar to a message in a messaging system, an event described using the CloudEvents format represents a fact. As a signal about the occurrence of a change in a system and bundled with contextual information about the change, an event is not particularly intended for any one consumer. An event also notably lacks intent. This contrasts with messages, which usually convey some intent from one system to another. As cloud platforms gain popularity and application design evolves to become distributed, resilient, and more aware of its surrounding systems, events play a crucial role in enabling that transition. This has also led to a proliferation of event formats, which limits the interoperability of events across platforms. The CNCF project CloudEvents is an emerging standard that aims to unify how event publishers can standardize on the format used to describe an event. This enables events to be described in a standardized manner so that developers can build systems that can interoperate and handle events across cloud platforms. The OCI event service uses the CloudEvents format to describe events. Listing 3-5 shows an OCI event that uses the CloudEvents specification.

Listing 3-5 OCI Event Using the CloudEvents Specification

```
{
    "eventType": "com.oraclecloud.computeapi.launchinstance.end",
    "cloudEventsVersion": "0.1",
    "eventTypeVersion": "2.0",
    "source": "ComputeApi",
    "eventTime": "2019-08-16T12:07:42.794Z",
    "contentType": "application/json",
    "eventID": "unique_ID",
```

```
  "extensions": {
    "compartmentId": "ocid1.compartment.oc1..unique_ID"
  }
  "data": {
    "compartmentId": "ocid1.compartment.oc1..unique_ID",
    "compartmentName": "example_compartment",
    "resourceName": "my_instance",
    "resourceId": "ocid1.instance.oc1.phx.unique_ID",
    "availabilityDomain": "availability_domain",
    "additionalDetails": {
      "imageId": "ocid1.image.oc1.phx.unique_ID",
      "shape": "VM.Standard2.1",
      "type": "CustomerVmi"
    }
  },
}
```

The structure of the event message can be broken down into two broad parts:

- **The event envelope:** The event envelope encompasses all the attributes at the top level, including the eventID, version, eventType, and other attributes. The event envelope is based on the cloud event specification, and the eventType usually provides the most basic mechanism to identify specific events to filter for processing. In the example presented in Listing 3-5, the value for eventType is com.oraclecloud.computeapi.launchinstance.end, and predictably it represents the completion of a compute instance launch.
- **The payload:** The data or *payload* that is pertinent to the event itself is contained in the data attribute. The content and structure of the JSON payload differ for each event type, to be pertinent to the event. The schema for the payload can also be versioned to support schema evolution. This is when the content of the payload and its structure change over time to support newer attributes and features. The eventTypeVersion can be used to indicate what version of the payload structure or data schema the payload is using for the event type.

Services emit events continuously. You work with events by creating rules that match only certain event types, tags, or attributes contained in the event payload itself. The filtered events are then delivered to a target service that can act on the event. The OCI event service supports Notifications, Streaming, and Functions as target services where filtered events can be delivered.

Any attribute of the event can be used to filter events into a flow of events that a developer would be interested in. The filtering is done by creating conditions. Conditions match the event message structure and produce a flow of events that match the conditions, which can now be delivered to a target service. Conditions can use various operands such as any, all, or even wildcard-based matching. Figure 3-13 shows the console with a matching rule.

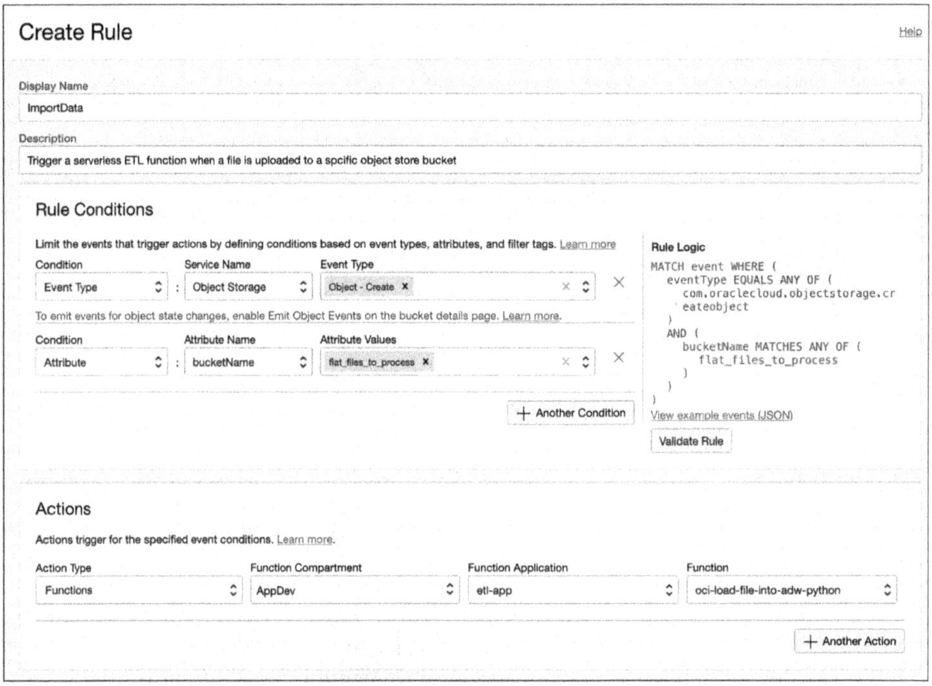

Figure 3-13   Working with the Events Service to Create a Matching Rule and an Action to Trigger When the Rule Condition Is Met

The console provides an intuitive interface to create and validate rules with sample payloads and tests for matching conditions. Here you see that a matching rule has been created for the event type com.oraclecloud.objectstorage.createobject. This event type represents an event for which a new object has been created in object storage—in other words, a new file has been uploaded to an object store bucket. The conditions further check whether the bucket where the new object has been created is named flat_files_to_process.

After events have been filtered, the filtered events are directed to one of the supported target systems, such as streaming, functions, or notifications. The broad goal here is for the downstream systems to process the event data to perform an action. For instance, when an object storage bucket has been created, the event that notifies the completion of the bucket creation could be used to run a serverless function on a regular schedule to check for data inside this bucket.

In the example, there is a single action to invoke a specific function. The event will cause the function to be triggered, and the function can take any action based on the event data. In the example, you can presume that the function will use the event payload to access the file uploaded into the object storage bucket and perform some ETL job to import the data contained in it to a database. In this example, the event-driven model with a serverless function allows developers to build completely event-driven applications that process data when data becomes available so that they do not have to worry about infrastructure management.

The same event-driven principles can be applied to a variety of situations. The event service therefore enables application developers to build applications that can react to changes in the infrastructure and events or occurrences happening in the infrastructure layer directly, and then react to them from within their applications. This means that developers can build applications that are more resilient, autonomous, and elastic, thereby making the event service an important tool in building cloud native applications.

Summary

This chapter introduced several OCI services that are key to building cloud native applications. Although not all aspects of these services are explored in detail, these brief introductions should help you to see the big picture of the various OCI services and tools at your disposal and how they may interact. A few of the key services introduced in this chapter, such as Container Engine for Kubernetes, Container Instances, and OCI Functions, are examined in much greater detail in Chapters 4, 5, and 7. It is not mandatory to use all or any of these services in all your cloud native applications; these are services that aim to help developers build loosely coupled, scalable applications at a high development velocity. Some of the managed services aim to remove as much operational overhead as possible so that developers can be less focused on handling the operational aspects and more focused on developing their applications. You should also keep in mind that OCI and the various open-source platforms and standards themselves are constantly evolving. New platforms and services may be added, and some services and standards might be eclipsed in the future by newer and more evolved versions of themselves.

References

1 Open Container Initiative: https://opencontainers.org/
2 Open Container Initiative image format specification: https://github.com/opencontainers/image-spec/blob/main/spec.md
3 Cloud Init: https://cloud-init.io/
4 Fn Project: https://fnproject.io/
5 OpenAPI Specification 3.0.0: https://spec.openapis.org/oas/v3.0.0
6 Apache Kafka: https://kafka.apache.org/

4

Understanding Container Engine for Kubernetes

In today's world, one of the qualities that sets apart successful businesses is agility, the ability to keep pace with constantly shifting trends and changing customer expectations. It's not enough for decision makers in the company to adapt; the technology supporting the company must be able to keep up as well. This is one of the areas where cloud native development shines. Cloud native is an approach or methodology that takes advantage of the scalability, resilience, and efficiency of cloud infrastructure. It enables businesses to quickly iterate without sacrificing the quality of their service to gain an advantage over their competition.

This chapter contextualizes the importance of cloud native development and container orchestration using Kubernetes and then dives into how to operate your own Kubernetes cluster using Oracle Container Engine for Kubernetes (OKE). By the end, you should have the tools you need to create clusters and nodes, deploy containers, and securely expose those containers to your users.

Monoliths and Microservices

Classic software development relies on monoliths, an approach in which applications consist of a single code base, including the business logic, data, and resources needed to run the application, and are deployed to static physical infrastructure. Monoliths contain a large amount of code, and they commonly include complex dependencies and require interactions between different components. Updating one part of the application means that operators need to build, test, and deploy the application as a whole instead of having to do so for only the specific part being iterated. Similar challenges apply to scaling: Even if only one aspect of the monolith is responsible for throttling performance and needs to be scaled, there is no capability for it to be independently scaled. The entire monolith needs to be deployed to larger or more performant hardware.

In contrast to the inflexibility of software monoliths, cloud native development relies on microservices, a software architecture approach in which applications are built as sets of small, independent services, each responsible for a specific business function and working in concert to deliver a unified experience. By decoupling monoliths into microservices, applications can be iterated faster. Each service can be developed, tested, and deployed independently. You can make changes to a single service without affecting the rest of the application. This also makes it easier to update and maintain the application. If you see a bottleneck in one aspect of architecture, that microservice can take advantage of the elasticity of the cloud to be independently scaled without the need to scale the application as a whole. Microservices are also designed to be flexible and resilient because they can be deployed on different servers and can continue to function even if one of the services fails. This makes them well suited for distributed systems and cloud environments. All of these qualities enable microservices to address the fundamental requirement of IT infrastructure that supports business agility, making them the de facto standard for cloud native software.

However, microservices can be more complex to design and manage than monolithic applications because they require more effort to coordinate the communication among the different services. They also require a more robust infrastructure to support the deployment and management of the individual services.

Containers

After choosing to adopt a microservice approach, you might ask, "How do I package my software into microservices?" Separating the software from the host can be accomplished in multiple ways. One option is to use virtual machines. A virtual machine (VM) allows a computer to run multiple operating systems simultaneously by creating one or more virtual environments on physical hardware, each of which behaves like a separate physical device.

Another option is to use containers, which enables you to package an application, along with its dependencies, runtime, and libraries, into a single unit that can be easily moved and deployed on any system that supports the container technology. A container appears to be a standalone system, with its own root file system. Containers are a combination of namespaces, control groups, and supporting OS features. Figure 4-1 shows a visual of the differences between containers and virtual machines (VMs).

Software containers are used for microservices instead of VMs for a number of reasons. Containers are much more lightweight than VMs because they do not require a separate operating system to be installed. This means that they can be started and stopped more quickly, and they take up less space on the host machine. Containers are more efficient than VMs because they share the host machine's operating system kernel and use resource isolation features to ensure that each container has access to the resources it needs to run. This means that they can run more applications on the same hardware, which can lead to cost savings. Containers enable you to define the exact dependencies and configuration required for an application to run, which means that you can deploy the application consistently across different environments, often referred to as portability.

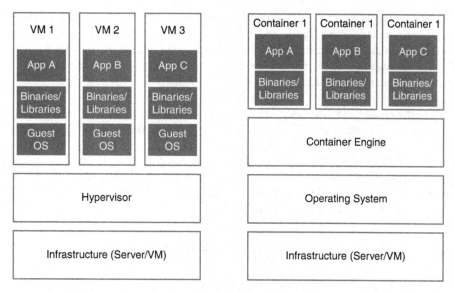

Figure 4-1   Architectural Difference Between Virtual Machines and Containers

Microservices can make it easier to develop and maintain an application because each service can be developed, tested, and deployed independently of the others. Containers are easier to scale than VMs and can be deployed to multiple servers or cloud environments without the need to reconfigure the underlying infrastructure. Additionally, you can quickly and easily adjust the number of instances of a particular microservice in response to changes in demand. Overall, the use of containers in microservice architectures helps to increase the agility, scalability, and reliability of the overall system.

However, these benefits do not come free of challenges. This leads to questions such as the following:

How do we scale to keep pace with dynamic workload demands?
When I grow from tens or hundreds of containers to thousands of containers, how can I ensure that all of my containers are healthy and running?

Container Orchestration and Kubernetes

Kubernetes is the answer to many of these questions. At a high level, Kubernetes is an open-source infrastructure abstraction used to orchestrate the deployment, scaling, and management of containerized applications. Kubernetes leverages automation and declarative configuration. It provides a consistent and easy-to-use interface for managing containerized applications, regardless of the underlying infrastructure. Kubernetes enables you to easily scale your application up or down by adding or removing containers as needed. This makes it easier to handle changes in demand or load. Kubernetes can automatically detect when a container or node has failed, and it can automatically restart the container or replace the node to keep the application running. With regard to portability, as with the containers it orchestrates, Kubernetes can run on multiple cloud platforms and also on-premises, making it easy to move applications between environments. Overall, Kubernetes makes it easier to deploy and manage containerized applications in a cloud native environment, which can help organizations increase the agility, scalability, and reliability of their applications. More tangibly, Kubernetes is cluster software with one or more control plane nodes controlling a group of worker nodes. The scheduler deploys work in the form of pods, a unit of one or more containers, to the worker nodes using various patterns.

Oracle Container Engine for Kubernetes

Every new software tool comes with a learning curve, and Kubernetes is no exception. Kubernetes comes with a new set of concepts to learn and a large number of control plane and node components that must be deployed and operated, including these:

- **Control plane components:**
  - kube-apiserver
  - etcd
  - kube-scheduler
  - kube-controller-manager
  - cloud-controller-manager
- **Node components:**
  - kubelet
  - kube-proxy
  - The container runtime

Figure 4-2 illustrates these components.

In some cases, learning about how to do this, let alone actually implementing it, can be overwhelming and prevents businesses from taking the leap to modernize their IT infrastructure. In other cases, it's simply too complex, costly, and time-consuming for businesses to build and maintain an environment like this. Managed Kubernetes offerings provide users with a simple way to automatically deploy, scale, and manage Kubernetes. Offloading responsibility to a provider enables developers to create a cluster and deploy containers quickly.

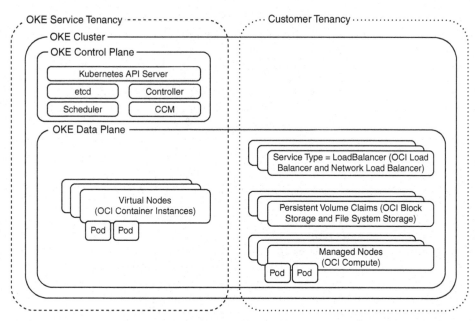

Figure 4-2   OKE Architecture, Including Components of a Kubernetes Cluster That Are Managed
by the OKE Service and Managed by Customers

Oracle Container Engine for Kubernetes (OKE) combines production-grade
container orchestration of open Kubernetes with the control, security, IAM, and high
predictable performance of Oracle Cloud Infrastructure. OKE fully manages the cluster
control plane for you and makes it easy to create and manage other components of your
cluster, including worker nodes, load balancer services, and more. You can get started
quickly by using a Quick Create cluster, which streamlines cluster creation by providing
an opinionated provisioning experience and automatically creates networking resources
on your behalf. Alternatively, you can create a cluster using existing network resources
and with a large number of configuration options using the Custom Create workflow.

OCI-Managed Components and Customer-Managed Components

A Kubernetes cluster consists of a group of nodes, physical or virtual machines, that run
cluster software. These nodes fall into two categories: a control plane and a data plane.

Control Plane

The Kubernetes control plane is a set of several components that work together to
manage the overall state of a Kubernetes cluster. The cluster control plane monitors
and records the state of the worker nodes in the cluster's data plane and distributes

requested operations to them. It runs on multiple control plane nodes configured for high availability in the OKE service tenancy. When using OKE, the cluster control plane is fully managed by Oracle.

The cluster control plane consists of these components:

- **kube-apiserver** serves as the front end for the Kubernetes control plane by exposing the Kubernetes API. This includes supporting direct API calls and requests from the Kubernetes command-line tool, `kubectl`.
- **etcd** is a distributed key-value store used to contain the configuration data for the Kubernetes cluster. It provides a reliable and highly available storage solution for the control plane.
- **kube-scheduler** watches for newly created pods and assigns pods to nodes based on resource availability and other constraints.
- **kube-controller-manager** is a collection of controller processes that manage different Kubernetes components.
- **cloud-controller-manager** connects your cluster to your cloud provider's API and runs a collection of controller processes that are specific to your cloud provider. For example, in the case of Oracle Container Engine for Kubernetes, the `oci-cloud-controller-manager` uses the nodeController to update and terminate worker nodes and the serviceController to create load balancers when Kubernetes services of `type: LoadBalancer` are created. The `oci-cloud-controller-manager` also implements a container-storage-interface, a FlexVolume driver, and a FlexVolume provisioner to manage additional OCI resources.

Data Plane

The Kubernetes data plane consists of one or more worker nodes, where you run the containerized applications deployed to your cluster. Each node is managed by the control plane and contains the node components necessary to run pods, including the following:

- **kubelet** is the agent that communicates with the cluster control plane to verify that containers are running.
- **kube-proxy** is a networking proxy used to maintain networking rules. These rules enable network communication to your pods from within and outside the cluster.
- The **container runtime** is the software responsible for running containers. In the case of OKE, this runtime is CRI-O.
- A **node pool** is a set of worker nodes within a cluster that all possess the same properties. Node pools enable you to create groups of nodes within your cluster to accommodate workloads with different requirements. For example, within the same cluster, you might create one pool of virtual machine nodes and another pool of GPU nodes for your HPC workloads. A cluster must have a minimum of one node pool, but a node pool does not need to contain any worker nodes.

When creating a node pool in an OKE cluster, you must specify the type of worker node to create:

- **Virtual nodes:** Virtual node resources are provisioned dynamically, as needed, and exist in the OKE service tenancy. Virtual nodes remove the operational overhead of upgrading your data plane infrastructure and managing the capacity of clusters, providing a "serverless" Kubernetes experience.
  - **Managed nodes:** Managed nodes are compute instances in your tenancy that are managed by a combination of you and the OKE service. Managed nodes come with the flexibility to configure them to meet your specific requirements, but you are responsible for upgrading Kubernetes and host OS versions and ensuring that capacity is properly scaled.

Billable Components

Those same categories of the control plane and data plane can be useful to understand the billable components of your cluster. Simply put, your control plane node usage is not metered, but your data plane nodes are metered and billed for their usage.

At the cluster level, you have a choice between enhanced and basic clusters. Enhanced clusters support all available OKE features, including features that are not supported by basic clusters. These features include but are not limited to virtual nodes, add-on lifecycle management, workload access to OCI resources, on-demand node cycling, and additional worker nodes per cluster. Enhanced clusters also come with a financially backed service-level agreement (SLA) tied to the availability of the Kubernetes API server. Basic clusters support all the core functionality provided by Kubernetes and Container Engine for Kubernetes but support none of the enhanced features that Container Engine for Kubernetes provides. Basic clusters come with a service-level objective (SLO) but not a financially backed SLA. A management fee is associated with using enhanced clusters, whereas basic clusters do not have a fee.

Creating a new cluster of the enhanced type enables you to use enhanced features immediately or at any point in the future. If you choose to create a new cluster of the basic type, you can still upgrade the cluster from a basic to an enhanced type at any point in time. Keep in mind that you cannot downgrade from an enhanced type cluster to a basic type cluster.

The data plane consists of worker nodes, which are charged based on the compute shape chosen for the node. In the case of virtual nodes, worker nodes are charged based on the container instance shape chosen for the node and are assessed an additional management fee per virtual node. The data plane is the primary source of costs for running an OKE cluster.

Additionally, there are charges for cluster resources you provision that are backed by OCI resources. For example, creating a Kubernetes service of type LoadBalancer results in the creation of an OCI Load Balancer resource, for which you will be charged. The same is true for other Kubernetes resources, such as persistent volumes and OCI block storage or file system storage.

Those same categories of the control plane and data plane can be useful in understanding the billable components of your cluster. Simply put, you are not charged for your control plane nodes, but you are charged for your data plane nodes.

Kubernetes Concepts

The more you know about the intricacies of the Kubernetes API, the more powerful you will become as a cluster operator. Even if ultimate knowledge of the Kubernetes API is not your goal, certain key concepts are worth knowing. The comprehensive reference for Kubernetes concepts is the excellent Kubernetes documentation itself. This book does not attempt to re-create the Kubernetes documentation. Instead, this section serves as a quick refresher for some of the most commonly used Kubernetes resources and concepts:

- **Pods:** Pods are one or more containers with shared resources, including CPU, memory, storage, and networking. The contents of a pod are always scheduled together. Pods are often created and destroyed as a result of being rescheduled onto new nodes or when new versions of an application are rolled out. Each pod has an ephemeral IP address that is assigned when the pod is first created and is released when the pod is terminated. Each pod has a universally unique identifier (UUID).
- **Deployments:** Deployments are used to specify the desired state of an application, including the number of replicas of a pod or pods that should be running at a given time. Deployments can be used to upgrade your application by rolling out new pod versions with zero downtime and to roll back to a previous state.
- **Namespaces:** A Kubernetes cluster can be organized into namespaces, to divide the cluster's resources among multiple users. Initially, a cluster has the following namespaces: default, for resources with no other namespace, and kube-system, for resources created by the Kubernetes system.
- **Services:** Services are an abstraction that defines a method for accessing a pod or pods. This is the Kubernetes way of decoupling the discovery of an application from the application instances. This allows one application to have a reliable address, regardless of whether the pods that make up the application change. Some parts of an application, such as the front ends, are typically exposed through the ingress controller or directly with an external IP address accessible from outside a cluster. Other applications might choose to use the service abstraction for service discovery because it decouples the consumer of an application service from the pods that make up the application service. Kubernetes ServiceTypes enable you to specify the way you want your pods exposed:
  - A **LoadBalancer** ServiceType creates an Oracle Cloud Infrastructure load balancer on load balancer subnets in your VCN. These load balancers are automatically configured to route to the pods. The load balancer configuration is updated when the pod configuration changes, such as when new pods are added and existing pods are deleted. Kubernetes clusters created by OKE also include

capabilities that can automatically update OCI resources such as security lists when load balancers are created and applications are exposed using them.

- A **NodePort** service is a type of service that exposes a specific port on each node in the cluster. This allows external traffic to access the service by sending requests to a node's IP address and the node port specified for the service. Node port services do not provide the same level of traffic management and load balancing as other service types, such as LoadBalancer and ClusterIP.

- A **ClusterIP** service is the default service type that is used when no other service type is specified. It assigns an IP address from an IP pool that the cluster's networking plug-in (CNI) manages. On Kubernetes clusters created by OKE, you have the choice of two CNIs: Flannel or the OCI Native CNI. This topic is covered in greater depth in the "Kubernetes Networking" section.

- **Labels and selectors:** Labels and selectors are key/value pairs attached to objects in a Kubernetes cluster. Labels are used to identify and organize Kubernetes objects, such as to explain which application a pod is associated with.

Cloud Controller Manager

The Kubernetes Cloud Controller Manager (CCM) is a controller used to implement cloud provider–specific control loops required for Kubernetes to function. For example, CCM can implement a node controller that is responsible for updating Kubernetes nodes using a cloud provider's API and deleting Kubernetes nodes that were deleted on your cloud. Kubernetes introduced the CCM project to decouple the development of cloud features from the core Kubernetes project. Early in the existence of Kubernetes, cloud providers were added in-tree in the `kube-controller-manger` binary. To increase extensibility and remove the need to directly interact with the Kubernetes code base, external cloud providers were introduced. External cloud providers are Kubernetes controllers that implement cloud provider–specific control loops required for Kubernetes to function, but for out-of-tree providers.

The OCI Cloud Controller Manager, which implements OCI-specific control loops, is an example of an external cloud provider. For example, the `oci-cloud-controller-manager` implements a NodeController, which is used to update OCI Compute nodes with cloud provider–specific labels and addresses; it also deletes Kubernetes nodes when they are deleted from OCI by scaling down a node pool or using the delete node API. It also implements a ServiceController, which is responsible for creating OCI load balancers when a service of `type: LoadBalancer` is created in Kubernetes. Another key aspect of this project is related to storage: The OCI CCM implements a Container Storage Interface, a volume provisioner, and a FlexVolume driver for Kubernetes clusters running on OCI.

The CSI plug-in for OCI enables provisioning, attaching, detaching, mounting, and unmounting of OCI block storage volumes to Kubernetes pods via the Container Storage Interface (CSI) plug-in interface. The volume provisioner enables the dynamic provisioning of OCI storage resources, such as block volumes, while the FlexVolume driver enables the mounting of OCI block storage volumes to Kubernetes pods using the FlexVolume plug-in interface.

Similar to the manner in which CCM was introduced to enable extensibility for cloud providers, CSI was developed as a standard for exposing arbitrary block and file storage systems to containerized workloads running on Kubernetes. Using CSI made it simpler for third-party storage providers, such as OCI, to write and deploy plug-ins exposing new storage systems in Kubernetes without ever having to touch the core Kubernetes code. Most OKE users have moved from using FlexVolume to using CSI.

Nodes and Node Pools

Worker nodes constitute the cluster data plane. Worker nodes are where you run the applications that you deploy in a cluster. These are compute instances with additional software that communicates with the Kubernetes control plane to make it a worker node that is known to the cluster control plane. Worker node runs a number of processes, including these:

- kubelet to communicate with the cluster control plane
- kube-proxy to maintain networking rules

The cluster control plane processes monitor and record the state of the worker nodes and distribute requested operations among them.

A node pool is a subset of worker nodes within a cluster that all have the same configuration. Node pools enable you to create pools of machines within a cluster that have different configurations. For example, you might create one pool of nodes in a cluster as virtual machines and another pool of nodes as bare metal machines. A cluster must have a minimum of one node pool, but a node pool need not contain any worker nodes. Worker nodes in a node pool are connected to a worker node subnet in your VCN.

When creating a node pool with OKE, you specify that the worker nodes in the node pool are to be created as one of the following:

- **Virtual nodes**, fully managed by Oracle. Virtual nodes provide a "serverless" Kubernetes experience, enabling you to run containerized applications at scale without the operational overhead of upgrading the data plane infrastructure and managing the capacity of clusters. You can create virtual nodes only in enhanced clusters.
- **Managed nodes**, running on compute instances (either bare metal or virtual machine) in your tenancy and at least partly managed by you. Because you are responsible for managing managed nodes, you have the flexibility to configure them to meet your specific requirements. You are responsible for upgrading Kubernetes on managed nodes and for managing cluster capacity. You can create managed nodes in both basic clusters and enhanced clusters.

Node Pool Properties

Node pools possess a set of standard properties that are inherited by worker nodes running in the pool. These properties include but are not limited to the following:

- The name of a node pool
- The version of Kubernetes to run on new worker nodes
- The number of worker nodes in a node pool and the availability domains, fault domains, and subnets in which to place them
- The image to use for new worker nodes
- The shape to use for new worker nodes
- The boot volume size and encryption settings to use for new worker nodes
- The cordon and drain options to use when terminating worker nodes
- The cloud-init script to use for instances hosting worker nodes
- The public SSH key to use to access new worker nodes

Worker Node Images and Shapes

You can customize the worker nodes in your OKE cluster by specifying the following:

- **The operating system image:** The host image includes the operating system and other software required for the instance to act as a Kubernetes worker node. Note that this option is available exclusively to managed nodes because infrastructure management is abstracted away by the service when using virtual nodes.
- **The shape:** The shape is the number of OCPUs and the amount of memory to allocate to each newly created instance to be used as a worker node. The choice of shape can also dictate other infrastructure properties, such as available network bandwidth and specialized hardware such as GPUs.

Images

Three types of images are available for use as worker node images, built for all shape architectures supported by OKE:

- **OKE images** are built on top of Oracle Linux platform images and include all the necessary configurations and required software for use as managed nodes. They are optimized to minimize the time it takes to provision managed nodes at runtime when compared to platform images and custom images. The use of OKE images reduces managed node provisioning time by more than half when compared to platform images.

  Because the Kubernetes software is prebaked onto the host image, OKE images bundle together the host OS and Kubernetes version. The Kubernetes version that you specify when creating and updating node pools must match the Kubernetes version of your chosen OKE image. In the console, this is automatically done for you.

- **Platform images** also contain the Oracle Linux operating system, but unlike with OKE images, additional Kubernetes software is not prebaked into the image. When the managed node boots up for the first time, OKE downloads, installs, and configures the required software based on the Kubernetes version you select. This is the legacy option available for worker node images.
- **Custom images** are built from OKE or Platform images but are provided by you. They give you the option to bring your own host image configurations. Unlike OKE and Platform images, custom images are not explicitly supported by OKE.

You can find the latest available images in the console in a few ways: When creating a cluster in the Custom Create workflow or when creating or editing a node pool, you can view the list of supported platform images and OKE images in the Browse All Images window (see Figure 4-3).

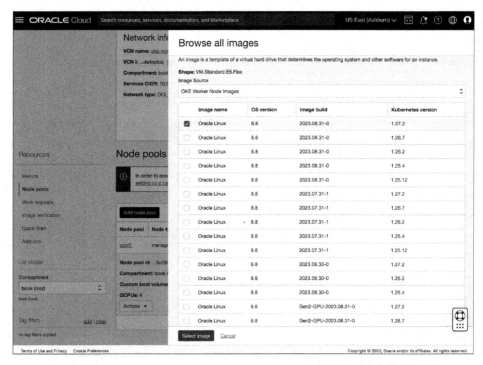

Figure 4-3   Selection of a Worker Node Host Image—Here, Oracle Linux 8 Running Kubernetes 1.27.2

Shapes

OKE supports a growing variety of shapes for use as worker nodes. These include most but not all of the shapes available through Oracle Cloud Infrastructure. The choice of shape can be important when it comes to supporting specific workloads. For example, high-performance computing or machine learning use cases can benefit from the use of GPU shapes. These shapes are divided into two categories: those supported for managed nodes and those supported for virtual nodes.

Managed Nodes

The following shapes are supported for use as managed nodes:

- Flexible shapes
- Bare metal shapes (including standard shapes and GPU shapes)
- HPC shapes (except in RDMA networks)
- VM shapes (including standard shapes and GPU shapes)
- Dense I/O shapes

The following shapes are not supported for use as managed nodes:

- Dedicated VM host shapes
- Micro VM shapes
- HPC shapes on bare metal instances in RDMA networks
- Burstable capacity for flexible shapes

Virtual Nodes

At the time of writing, the Standard.E3.Flex and Standard.E4.Flex shapes are supported for use as virtual nodes. All other shapes are not supported for use as virtual nodes.

The available shapes increase regularly. The best way to stay on top of shape availability is directly through the console or CLI. You find the latest available shapes in the console in a few ways: When creating a cluster in the Custom Create workflow or when creating or editing a node pool, you can view the list of supported shapes in the Browse All Shapes window (see Figure 4-4).

When using the CLI, you can view the supported OKE, platform, and custom images in the `data.shapes:` section of the response of the following command:

```
oci ce node-pool-options get --node-pool-option-id all
```

Note

Even if a shape is supported by OKE, you might not be able to select it in your tenancy or in a particular region because of service limits, compartment quotas, or available capacity.

Custom cloud-init

To customize your managed worker nodes, OKE gives you the option to add your own logic at node startup time. OKE uses cloud-init, the industry-standard method for cloud instance initialization, to set up compute instances as managed nodes. The first time the instance boots up, cloud-init runs the default startup script:

```
#!/bin/bash
curl --fail -H "Authorization: Bearer Oracle" -LO http://169.254.169.254/opc/v2/
  instance/metadata/oke_init_script | base64 --decode >/var/run/oke-init.sh
bash /var/run/oke-init.sh
```

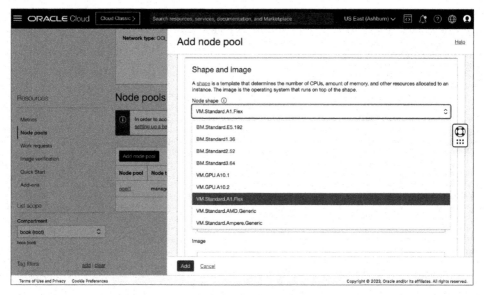

Figure 4-4   Selection of a Worker Node Shape—Here, the VM.Standard.A1.Flex Shape

You can customize the default startup script by adding your own logic either before or after the default logic. A custom cloud-init script can be used to do the following:

- Configure the kubelet running on the worker node
- Expand the boot volume with growfs
- Configure a corporate proxy or custom YUM proxies
- Install mandated security tools

The customized startup script runs when a worker node boots up for the first time. If you choose to add your own custom logic, it can be useful to test whether that logic negatively impacts the host's use as a worker node. To do so, you can run the Node Doctor script to confirm that worker nodes on newly started instances are working as expected.

> **Note**
> If you customize the default startup script, do not modify the logic provided by OKE. It can be easy to accidentally overwrite the OKE startup script, so double-check that the script is still present before you pass in your changes.

Using Custom cloud-init Script to Set kubelet-extra-args on Managed Nodes

A straightforward use of a custom cloud-init script is to use it to configure extra options on the kubelet (the primary node agent) on managed nodes. These extra options, sometimes referred to as kubelet-extra-args, include the option to configure debug log verbosity. Figure 4-5 shows how to configure a custom cloud-init script in the OCI Console.

1. In the console, navigate to create a new node pool or edit an existing node pool.
2. In the **Show Advanced Options** section, navigate to **Initialization Script**, as illustrated in Figure 4-5.
3. Begin by clicking **Download Custom Cloud-Init Script Template** to download a boilerplate script. The file contains the default logic required by OKE. You can add your own custom logic either before or after the default logic. Remember not to modify the default logic.
4. You can choose to upload this cloud-init script or paste your script directly into the console.
5. Use the following cloud-init script to configure the debug level log verbosity:

```
#!/bin/bash
curl --fail -H "Authorization: Bearer Oracle" -LO http://169.254.169.254/opc/
v2/instance/metadata/oke_init_script | base64 --decode >/var/run/oke-init.sh
bash /var/run/oke-init.sh --kubelet-extra-args "--v=4"
```

6. After clicking **Add** or **Save Changes**, depending on whether you created a new node pool or are editing an existing node pool, the cloud-init logic will be passed to a newly created node.
7. To confirm the setting of debug level log verbosity, connect to a worker node and use the `sudo systemctl status -l kubelet` command. This command returns the verbosity level as 4 for all nodes on which the preceding cloud-init script was run.

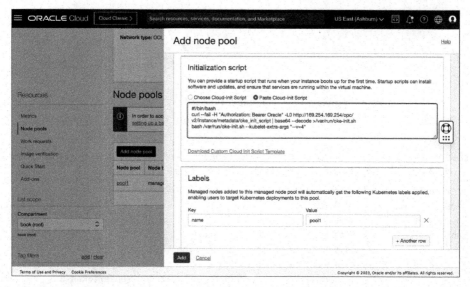

Figure 4-5 Adding a Custom cloud-init Script to a Node Pool to Modify the Verbosity of Logs Generated by the Kubelet Running on the Node

Kubernetes Labels

Kubernetes labels are key/value pairs used to specify identifying attributes of objects in a human-readable way. Labels can be used to associate objects with a particular application or a line of business to implement chargeback. Another great use for labels is to organize and select nodes when deploying applications. Each node comes with a set of default labels, including those related to the shape and architecture of the node. Labels enable you to target workloads at specific node pools. You also can use an optional node pool property to add more labels to worker nodes directly through the OKE API and using the OCI Console (see Figure 4-6). As with other node pool properties, labels are attached nodes at creation time. You can subsequently add or modify labels using the Kubernetes API.

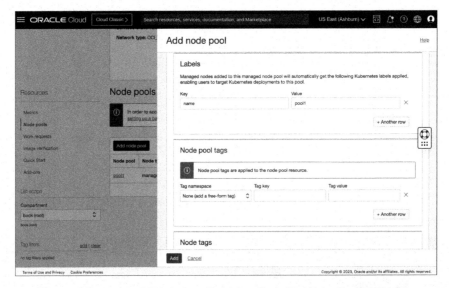

Figure 4-6   How to Add Labels to Nodes in a Node Pool Using the OCI Console

To see the labels of a given node, run kubectl describe node [node name]. Listing 4-1 shows the default labels applied to a managed node created by OKE.

Listing 4-1   Labels Automatically Added to a Managed Node Created by OKE—These Labels Will Change, Depending on the Shape Chosen for the Node Pool

```
$ kubectl describe node 10.0.10.151
Name:        10.0.10.151
Roles:       node
Labels:      beta.kubernetes.io/arch=amd64
             beta.kubernetes.io/instance-type=VM.Standard.E3.Flex
             beta.kubernetes.io/os=linux
             displayName=oke-c2usfphkqza-nctxoizruoq-seoda7iqkwa-3
             failure-domain.beta.kubernetes.io/region=uk-london-1
             failure-domain.beta.kubernetes.io/zone=UK-LONDON-1-AD-2
```

```
hostname=oke-c2usfphkqza-nctxoizruoq-seoda7iqkwa-3
internal_addr=10.0.10.151
kubernetes.io/arch=amd64
kubernetes.io/hostname=10.0.10.151
kubernetes.io/os=linux
last-migration-failure=get_kubesvc_failure
name=NC
node-role.kubernetes.io/node=
node.info.ds_proxymux_client=true
node.info/compartment.name=oracle-cloudnative
node.info/kubeletVersion=v1.25
node.kubernetes.io/instance-type=VM.Standard.E3.Flex
oci.oraclecloud.com/fault-domain=FAULT-DOMAIN-2
oke.oraclecloud.com/node.info.private_subnet=false
oke.oraclecloud.com/node.info.private_worker=true
topology.kubernetes.io/region=uk-london-1
topology.kubernetes.io/zone=UK-LONDON-1-AD-2
```

SSH Keys

SSH keys are another optional node pool property. Adding your public portion of an SSH key pair to the node pool enables you to access the nodes directly through SSH. The public key is added to all worker nodes in the cluster. If you don't specify a public SSH key, you will not have SSH access to the worker nodes. Figure 4-7 shows a user adding an SSH key to the node pool using the OCI Console. Note that you cannot use SSH to directly access worker nodes in private subnets because they have private IP addresses only; they are accessible only by other resources inside the VCN. You can use the Oracle Cloud Infrastructure Bastion service to enable external SSH access to worker nodes in private subnets.

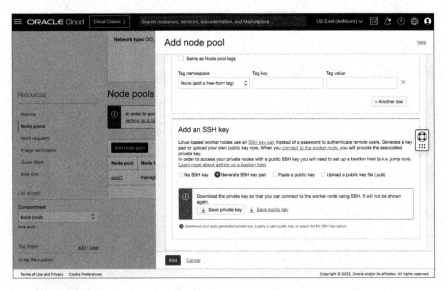

Figure 4-7 Adding an SSH Key to a Node Pool Using the OCI Console

Tagging Your Resources

Oracle Cloud Infrastructure Tagging allows you to add metadata to resources, which enables you to define keys and values and then associate them with resources. At their most basic, tags can be used to organize resources based on your business needs; however, tags opens up a lot of possibilities, from cost tracking to access control.

OCI offers tagging in two flavors: *free-form tags* and *defined tags*. Most of the advanced capabilities of tagging are applicable to defined tags, in which you create a tag namespace and then create a series of well-defined tag keys for which you can use a multitude of tag values. Although all defined tags can be used for cost analysis and usage reporting, defined tags that are designated as cost-tracking tags allow you to use them in OCI budgets. Budgets can track and forecast the cost for resources and alert you proactively when the forecast or actual consumption crosses a threshold of the budget you have set.

Consider a scenario in which you have a single cluster used by several applications or teams. You might want to implement both cost tracking and access control on a per-application (or per-team) basis on this shared infrastructure. Assume that each application is deployed on its own dedicated node pool. The applications can also create and use other resources, such as load balancers and storage, dynamically. To get an accurate estimate of the cost for each application, you can use tagging to tag the resources this application uses. Similarly, you can write access policies that restrict access for each team to only the resources that are used by their application, using tags.

Tags can be set on clusters, node pools, load balancers, and storage attachments. When creating a cluster, you can set tag defaults for the various types of resources, which you can also override with resource annotations when needed. With the resources tagged, you can implement features such as cost tracking, setting access controls, or setting budgets for the various applications. Similarly, you can use tags to keep track of the resources used by the dev, test, and prod environments for an individual application.

Tags present a flexible way of attaching additional metadata to resources: How you use these tags is up to you. This affords a tremendous amount of flexibility in the types of tags you can create and how you can leverage them.

Creating a Cluster

You can use OKE to create new Kubernetes clusters in many ways, including using the console (web UI), the CLI, automation tools such as Terraform, or the APIs directly. The console, in particular, offers two workflows to get you started: the Quick Create and Custom Create workflows (see Figure 4-8). The Quick Create workflow is the fastest way to create a new cluster. This approach automatically creates new network resources, including regional subnets for the Kubernetes API endpoint, for worker nodes, and for load balancers. This workflow is ideally suited if you are new to Kubernetes and want to get started quickly.

Note

To create a cluster, you must belong to either the tenancy's Administrators group or a group to which a policy grants the CLUSTER_MANAGE permission.

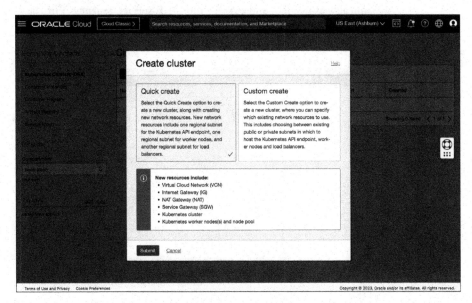

Figure 4-8   Choosing Between the Quick Create and Customer Create Workflows

Quick Create Cluster Workflow

In the Console, open the navigation menu and click Developer Services. Under Containers & Artifacts, click Kubernetes Clusters (OKE).

Step 1. Choose a compartment, and click **Create Cluster**.

Step 2. Select **Quick Create** and then click **Submit**.

Step 3. Either accept the default configurations (see Figure 4-9) or choose alternatives:

    a. Give a name to your cluster.

    b. Choose the compartment where you want your cluster control plane and related networking resources created.

    c. Choose a Kubernetes version for your cluster control plane.

    d. Specify whether you want a private or public Kubernetes API endpoint. In the case of a private subnet, the Kubernetes API endpoint will be hosted on a private subnet and assigned a private IP address. In the case of a public subnet, the Kubernetes API endpoint will be hosted on a public subnet with a public IP address automatically assigned.

e. Choose between managed and virtual nodes. Managed Kubernetes worker nodes are compute instances in your tenancy. Managed nodes come with the flexibility to configure them to meet your specific requirements, but you are responsible for upgrading Kubernetes and host OS versions and for ensuring that capacity is properly scaled. In the case of virtual nodes, the resources to execute your Kubernetes pods are provisioned dynamically, as needed, and exist in the OKE service tenancy. Virtual nodes remove the operational overhead of upgrading your data plane infrastructure and managing the capacity of clusters.

Figure 4-9   The First Step in the Quick Cluster Creation Workflow

Step 4. Depending on your chosen node type, the following steps will differ:

a. Choosing managed nodes gives you a choice between creating a private subnet or public subnet to host your Kubernetes worker nodes. It also give you a choice of image to use for your worker node hosts. These images determine the operating system and other software used for managed nodes. Selecting managed nodes also gives you expanded options for the shape of your nodes, compared to virtual nodes. Additionally, the choice of managed nodes enables you to customize the size and encryption options for the boot volumes of nodes in the node pool. Select the **Specify a Custom Boot Volume Size** check box, and enter a custom size from 50GB to 32TB to specify a custom size for the boot volume. The specified size must be larger than the default boot volume size for the selected image. If you increase the boot volume size, you must also extend the partition for the boot volume, to take advantage of the larger size using the `oci-growfs` utility. Nodes with the VM instance chosen as the shape allow you to optionally select the **Use In-Transit encryption** check box. This is not configurable for bare metal instances. Bare metal instances that support in-transit encryption have it enabled by default. Boot volumes are encrypted by default, but you can optionally use your own Vault service encryption key to encrypt the data in this volume. To use the Vault service for your encryption needs, select the **Encrypt This Volume with a Key That You Manage** check box. Then select the Vault compartment and Vault that contain the master encryption key you want to use. Also select the master encryption key compartment and master encryption key. If you enable this option, this key is used for both data-at-rest encryption and in-transit encryption.

b. Choosing virtual nodes gives you a choice of pod shape, which determines the processor type on which to run the pod. Note that you explicitly specify the CPU and memory resource requirements for virtual nodes in the pod spec. Choosing virtual nodes also gives you the option to apply taints to nodes in the virtual node pool. Taints allow virtual nodes to repel pods, thereby ensuring that pods do not run on virtual nodes in a particular virtual node pool.

c. Both options enable you to choose the number of nodes created in the default node pool. Both options also allow you to optionally specify Kubernetes labels. These labels are added to the set of default labels already on the node and are used to target workloads at specific node pools.

Click **Next** to review the details you entered for the new cluster. If you have not selected any features restricted to enhanced clusters, you can choose to create a basic cluster. To do so, check the **Create a Basic Cluster** check box on the Review page. Otherwise, leave the box unchecked to create an enhanced cluster. Click **Create Cluster** to create the new network resources and the new cluster. Click **Close** to return to the Console.

Custom Create Cluster Workflow

The Custom Create workflow gives you the most control over creating a new cluster. It allows you to explicitly define the new cluster's properties and specify which existing network resources to use, including the existing public or private subnets in which to create the Kubernetes API endpoint, worker nodes, and load balancers. Because the Custom Create workflow opens up more features and configuration options, it is better suited for more advanced scenarios, such as when you want to bring your own networking resources or when you need to configure advanced capabilities.

Step 1.   In the Console, open the navigation menu and click **Developer Services**. Under Containers & Artifacts, click **Kubernetes Clusters (OKE)**.

Step 2.   Choose a compartment and click **Create Cluster**.

Step 3. Select **Custom Create** and then click **Submit**.

Step 4. You can accept the default configurations or choose alternatives (see Figure 4-10):

a. Give a name to your cluster.

b. Choose the compartment where you want your cluster control plane and related networking resources created.

c. Choose a Kubernetes version for your cluster control plane.

Figure 4-10   The First Step in the Custom Cluster Creation Workflow

Step 5. Click **Show Advanced Options** to view other options available for cluster configuration.

a. Specify whether to allow the deployment of images from Oracle Cloud Infrastructure Registry only if they have been signed by particular master encryption keys. To enforce the use of signed images, select **Enable Image Verification Policies on This Cluster**, and then specify the encryption key and the vault that contains it.

b. **Encrypt using an Oracle-managed key:** Encrypt Kubernetes secrets in the etcd key-value store using a master encryption key that is managed by Oracle.

c. **Encrypt using a key that you manage:** Encrypt Kubernetes secrets in the etcd key-value store using a master encryption key (stored in the Vault service) that you manage.

d. Specify how to manage cluster add-ons. Select **Configure Cluster Add-ons** to enable or disable specific add-ons, select add-on versions, opt into and out of automatic updates by Oracle, and manage specific customizations. Select the appropriate cluster add-on and set options as appropriate. See "Configuring Cluster Add-ons."

    e. Specify whether to add cluster tags to the cluster, initial load balancer tags to load balancers created by Kubernetes services of type LoadBalancer, and initial block volume tags to block volumes created by Kubernetes persistent volume claims. Tagging enables you to group disparate resources across compartments and also allows you to annotate resources with your own metadata.

Step 6. After clicking **Next**, choose between VCN-native pod networking and Flannel overlay for your network type. VCN-native pod networking allows Kubernetes pods to connect directly to a VCN subnet and communicate natively through a VCN with other pods, other services, and the Internet. Flannel overlay configures an overlay network for pod communication. Note that if you choose the Flannel overlay option, you will not be able to create virtual nodes or specify a subnet for pod communication.

Step 7. Choose the networking setup for your cluster:

    a. Select an existing VCN in which to provision your cluster.

    b. Optionally, choose a Kubernetes load balancer service subnet to host load balancers. The load balancer subnet must be different from worker node subnets, can be public or private, and can be regional or AD specific.

    c. Select a public or private Kubernetes API endpoint subnet to act as a regional subnet to host the cluster's Kubernetes API endpoint. The Kubernetes API endpoint is assigned a private IP address. If you selected a public subnet for the Kubernetes API endpoint, you can also assign a public IP address to the API endpoint. Note that assigning a public IP address makes this cluster accessible from the Internet.

    d. Optionally, you can use security rules defined for one or more network security groups (NSGs) to control access to the cluster's Kubernetes API endpoint.

Step 8. After clicking **Next**, you can define the properties for node pools for your cluster.

    a. Begin by choosing a name, compartment, and Kubernetes version for your node pool. By default, the version of Kubernetes specified for the control plane nodes is selected. The Kubernetes version on worker nodes must be either the same version as that on the control plane nodes or an earlier version that is still compatible.

    b. Choose between managed and virtual nodes. Managed Kubernetes worker nodes are compute instances in your tenancy. Managed nodes come with the flexibility to configure them to meet your specific requirements, but you are responsible for upgrading Kubernetes and host OS versions and for ensuring that capacity is properly scaled. In the case of virtual nodes, the resources to execute your Kubernetes pods are provisioned dynamically, as needed, and exist in the OKE service tenancy. Virtual nodes remove the operational overhead of upgrading your data plane infrastructure and managing the capacity of clusters.

Step 9. Depending on your chosen node type, the following steps will differ:

a. Choosing managed nodes gives you a choice of creating a private or public subnet to host your Kubernetes worker nodes. It also give you a choice of image to use for your worker node hosts. These images determine the operating system and other software used for managed nodes. This also gives you expanded options for the shape of your nodes, compared to virtual nodes. Additionally, the choice of managed nodes enables you to customize the size and encryption options for the boot volumes of nodes in the node pool. Select the **Specify a Custom Boot Volume Size** check box, and enter a custom size from 50GB to 32TB to specify a custom size for the boot volume. The specified size must be larger than the default boot volume size for the selected image. If you increase the boot volume size, you must also extend the partition for the boot volume to take advantage of the larger size using the `oci-growfs` utility. Nodes with the VM instance chosen as the shape allow you to optionally select the **Use In-transit Encryption** check box. This is not configurable for bare metal instances; bare metal instances that support in-transit encryption have it enabled by default. Boot volumes are encrypted by default, but you can optionally use your own Vault service encryption key to encrypt the data in this volume. To use the Vault service for your encryption needs, select the **Encrypt This Volume with a Key That You Manage** check box. Then select the Vault compartment and Vault that contain the master encryption key you want to use. Also select the master encryption key compartment and master encryption key. If you enable this option, this key is used for both data at rest encryption and in-transit encryption.

b. Choosing virtual nodes give you a choice of pod shape, which determines the processor type on which to run the pod. Note that you explicitly specify the CPU and memory resource requirements for virtual nodes in the pod spec. Choosing virtual nodes also provides you with the option to apply taints to nodes in the virtual node pool. Taints enable virtual nodes to repel pods, thereby ensuring that pods do not run on virtual nodes in a particular virtual node pool. You must also choose the subnet that will host your virtual nodes.

c. Both options allow you to choose the number of nodes created in the default node pool. Optionally, you can specify Kubernetes labels. These labels are added to the set of default labels already on the node and are used to enable targeting workloads at specific node pools. Additionally, you must specify a placement configuration for your node pool. This configuration determines the subnets, availability domain, and (optionally) fault domain in which to place worker nodes. Finally, you must also select the subnet to be used for pod communication. Here, you can define the number of pods per node, as well as the security rules defined in the network security group (NSG) to control access to the pod subnet.

Step 10. Click **Next** to review the details you entered for the new cluster. If you have not selected any features restricted to enhanced clusters, you can choose to create a basic cluster. To do so, check the **Create a Basic Cluster** check box on the Review page. Otherwise, leave the box unchecked to create an enhanced cluster.

Step 11. Click **Create Cluster** to create the new network resources and the new cluster.

Step 12. Click **Close** to return to the console.

Using the OCI Command-Line Interface

You can also create clusters with ease using the OCI CLI. This approach enables you to create clusters using automation tools and shell scripts. It is an option for when Terraform might present a steep learning curve or when you simply want to automate the creation of these resources and you do not necessarily care about maintaining these resource configurations or tracking drift from its initial configuration.

Because the OCI CLI works on individual OCI resources, it should be noted that the Kubernetes cluster is a separate resource from the node pools that belong to the cluster. When creating clusters, you use both of these resources to create a functional Kubernetes cluster using OKE. Node pools always belong to a cluster, so you first create a cluster resource. This cluster resource represents the control plane elements that are managed by Oracle. When you have a cluster and a cluster OCID, you add a node pool to this cluster. This can be done with the cluster and node pool resources, as follows:

```
oci ce cluster create [OPTIONS] # use -- help for full list of options
oci ce node-pool create [OPTIONS]
```

The first command, `cluster create`, creates a cluster with the properties that are set by the options for this command. The second command, `node-pool create`, creates a node pool and includes a reference to the cluster OCID for the cluster created by the first command. This creates the node pool that belongs to that cluster. The CLI can also include options to manage control flow in scrips, such as to wait for an action to complete. A more complete example in Listing 4-2 showcases a variety of options that you can pass when you are creating a cluster.

Listing 4-2   Options Available When Creating an OKE Cluster Using the OCI CLI

```
oci ce cluster create \
  --name demo-cluster \
  --kubernetes-version v1.26.2 \
  --compartment-id … \
  --vcn-id … \
  --type ENHANCED_CLUSTER \
  --endpoint-public-ip-enabled true \
  --endpoint-subnet-id … \
  --service-lb-subnet-ids '["…"]' \
  --wait-for-state SUCCEEDED \
  --wait-interval-seconds 10 \
  --max-wait-seconds 600
```

The command in Listing 4-2 creates a cluster named demo-cluster in the specified compartment and attached to a specific VCN. The cluster type is specified as an ENHANCED_CLUSTER, and the Kubernetes API endpoint is configured to have a public IP address. The command also includes options to block until the creation of that cluster has entered a state named SUCCEEDED. The command waits a maximum of 600 seconds for this to occur and checks the progress every 10 seconds.

Similarly, Listing 4-3 demonstrates a more complete example for creating a node pool.

Listing 4-3   Options Available When Creating a Managed Node Pool for an OKE Cluster Using the OCI CLI

```
oci ce node-pool create \
--cluster-id … \
--name my-node-pool \
--node-image-id … \
--compartment-id … \
--kubernetes-version v1.26.2 \
--node-shape VM.Standard.E4.Flex \
--node-shape-config "{\"memoryInGBs\": 8, \"ocpus\": 1}" \
--pod-subnet-ids "[\"…\"]" \
--placement-configs "[{\"availability-domain\":\"xxxx:US-ASHBURN-AD-2\",
  \"subnet-id\":\"…\", \"faultDomains\":[\"FAULT-DOMAIN-3\", \"FAULT-DOMAIN-1\"]},
  {\"availability-domain\":\"xxxx:US-ASHBURN-AD-1\", \"subnet-id\":\"…\",
  \"faultDomains\": [\"FAULT-DOMAIN-1\", \"FAULT-DOMAIN-2\"]}]" \
--size 1 \
--region=us-ashburn-1
```

The command creates a new node pool for the cluster that is identified with the provided cluster-id. The new node pool is named my-node-pool and uses Kubernetes version 1.26.2. The shape of the nodes within the node pool is set to E4 flex; because this is a flexible shape, the shape configuration option specifies the number of CPUs and the amount of memory each of the nodes should have. The placement configuration is another JSON-formatted attribute that describes how the nodes within this node pool are to be placed across availability domains and fault domains.

When using the CLI, you might want to know the supported values for the various configuration options. You can view the supported values using the following command:

```
oci ce node-pool-options get --node-pool-option-id all
```

The command lists the various supported values for every option you can set for a node pool. The `data.sources` element in the response from the command describes the options and their possible values. These values can often change as well. For instance, the OS images are published every month, and getting the latest image is recommended when you create new clusters. Similarly, permissible values for the other options can change, as with the list of supported shapes, which is constantly being expanded to include new shapes that OCI rolls out for general use. Similarly, the supported Kubernetes versions change periodically as new versions of Kubernetes are released.

JSON-Formatted Configuration

As you can see from the previous examples, OKE exposes several configuration options to control various aspects of your cluster and its node pools. This can make CLI commands lengthy and verbose. It is often desirable to encapsulate these verbose configuration options into a single document, which can potentially be source controlled for change tracking.

To make this possible, the OCI CLI includes an option to provide the entire cluster configuration as a JSON document. This includes all the parameters that are configurable and presented to the CLI in a predefined JSON format that the CLI then parses before creating or updating the resource. To understand the expected structure of this JSON document, you can use the following commands:

```
# For the cluster resource
oci ce cluster create --generate-full-command-json-input
# For the node-pool resource
oci ce node-pool create --generate-full-command-json-input
```

This generates a JSON document template that shows the various options that can be provided. Not all options are mandatory; the official documentation describes the mandatory and optional parameters. You can customize this document with your own values and configurations. This JSON document now serves as a template for your cluster or your node pool; when you create new clusters or node pools, you can provide this JSON document as input instead of using a verbose CLI command that is hard to read and often difficult to reproduce. The example that follows demonstrates creating a cluster and a node pool from a preexisting JSON template:

```
# For the cluster resource
oci ce cluster create --from-json my-oke.json
# For the node-pool resource
oci ce node-pool create --from-json my-oke-nodes.json
```

The advantage of this approach is that the document that describes the configuration can be source controlled to track changes to it over time. It also enables automation workflows, in case you need to repeatedly stamp out clusters of predefined configurations.

When using the JSON-based configuration, option values can still be provided on the command line. If an option is configured in both the JSON document and the command line, the value specified on the command line takes precedence. Think of this as overriding the JSON template-based value with the one on the command line for that individual command invocation.

Using Custom Images for Your Nodes

Unlike using the console, using the CLI, Terraform, or the API directly enables you to also specify a custom operating system image for your nodes. Using a custom OS image for your node pool is common when you have additional software that you need to include in the base image for your Kubernetes nodes. This could be endpoint protection software such as threat monitoring and antivirus, agents for observability, or basic tools, programs, and operating system configurations that are mandated by your organization.

Under most circumstances, you want to use an official Oracle OKE image as the base for your customizations. OKE publishes operating system images for various operating system versions, with a monthly cadence. These are published as OCI images in every region, and the OCIDs of these images are published in the Oracle documentation.[1] To use one of these images as the basis for your custom image, you can import that image and customize it with tools such as Ansible. Alternatively, you can simply create a compute instance with the desired image, perform your customizations, and then create an image from the customized compute instance. Note that you should not create an image from an existing Kubernetes node on which you have performed customizations. This is because when a compute instance has joined a Kubernetes cluster as a worker node, that node has data about the specific cluster it is part of. Creating an image from this node would also capture the cluster's identity information, which would create a conflict when this image is used to create another node that needs to join a new Kubernetes cluster.

Listing 4-4 shows the CLI command to create a new compute instance using one of the publicly available OKE node images.

Listing 4-4 Process to Create a Compute Instance Using an OKE Worker Node Image

```
oci compute instance launch \
--display-name OKE_NODE_CUSTOM \
--compartment-id … \
--availability-domain xxxx:US-ASHBURN-AD-1 \
--shape VM.Standard.E4.Flex \
--shape-config "{\"memoryInGBs\": 8, \"ocpus\": 1}" \
--subnet-id … \
--image-id … # Image OCID for public OKE Image
```

This creates a compute instance using an OKE node image. This compute instance does not join any cluster because the instance was not launched by a node pool (and did not have an OKE cloud-init script) and, therefore, does not have any Kubernetes cluster information configured within it. After the compute instance has been launched, you can customize the instance with additional software or configuration. When the required customization has been done, you can generate an image from this instance that includes the customization you have performed. The image still retains the Kubernetes components, such as the kubelet, which remains uninitialized.

Now you can use your customized image to launch your OKE nodes by providing the image ID of your custom image when you create a node pool. Listing 4-5 shows a complete example of what this might look like.

Listing 4-5 The Process of Creating a Node Pool with a Customized Image Using the OCI CLI

```
oci ce node-pool create \
--cluster-id … \
--name my-node-pool \
--node-image-id … \ # OCID of your customized image
--compartment-id … \
--kubernetes-version v1.26.2 \
--node-shape VM.Standard.E4.Flex \
--node-shape-config "{\"memoryInGBs\": 8, \"ocpus\": 1}" \
--pod-subnet-ids "[\"…\"]" \
--placement-configs "[{\"availability-domain\":\"xxxx:US-ASHBURN-AD-2\",
  \"subnet-id\":\"…\", \"faultDomains\":[\"FAULT-DOMAIN-3\", \"FAULT-
  DOMAIN-1\"]}]" \
--size 1 \
--region=us-ashburn-1
```

Note

After the image has been created, it can still be edited. For instance, you can change the image's launch mode or network attachment mode. This can be useful when you work with highly network sensitive applications that need to leverage hardware-assisted networking or SRIOV networking for the network attachments made to instances launched from this image. Changing the network attachment mode from VIRTIO mode to SRIOV mode exposes the underlying virtual function from the hardware network card to the operating system directly without involving any virtualization layers.

Using the Terraform Provider and Modules

Kubernetes clusters can be created with OKE using APIs and automation as well. In fact, for most production use, you should prefer the Terraform-based automation or the OCI CLI approach. The advantage of using automation is consistency and repeatability, along with all the advantages of infrastructure as code described in Chapter 2, "Infrastructure Automation and Management." OCI provides a full-featured Terraform provider that includes the Kubernetes cluster[2] and node pool[3] resources. Data sources[4] also are available that can query the existing resources and their properties. In addition to the Terraform provider, OCI has made available a Terraform module[5] that can quickly create a cluster and its associated resources as a single unit. The module also provides several preconfigured examples to get you started quickly.

Listing 4-6 shows a snippet of the Terraform code from the example application showcased in Chapter 10, "Bringing It Together: MuShop," that is used to create an OKE cluster using Terraform. The Terraform configuration allows for extensive templating and customizations that enable you to create okay clusters and related resources in a consistent and configurable manner. The Terraform configuration expresses the desired state for the cluster and its associated resources. When the Terraform configuration is executed, Terraform introspects the existing resources and creates a plan that identifies the delta between the currently existing resources and how they need to be changed to match the intended configuration that is expressed in the Terraform configuration. Moreover, because Terraform tracks the state of these resources, you can use it to detect changes to these configurations over time. These changes that occur to the configuration overtime are called drift. Terraform can be rerun to return the configuration to its intended state. Note that although most properties of the resource can be updated in place, some properties of a resource might cause Terraform to delete the resource and then re-create it. When working with Kubernetes clusters, it is important to understand what these properties are so that inadvertently updating a property does not result in the deletion and recreation of a resource such as a node pool.

Listing 4-6   Snippet of Terraform Code from an Example Application

```
resource "oci_containerengine_cluster" "oke_cluster" {
  compartment_id    = local.oke_compartment_ocid
  kubernetes_version = (var.k8s_version == "Latest") ? local.k8s_latest : var.
  k8s_version
  name              = "${var.app_name} (${random_string.deploy_id.result})"
  vcn_id            = oci_core_virtual_network.oke_vcn[0].id
  endpoint_config {
    is_public_ip_enabled = (var.cluster_endpoint_visibility == "Private") ? false
  : true
    subnet_id            = oci_core_subnet.oke_k8s_endpoint_subnet[0].id
    nsg_ids              = []
  }
  options {
    service_lb_subnet_ids = [oci_core_subnet.oke_lb_subnet[0].id]
    add_ons {
```

```
    is_kubernetes_dashboard_enabled = var.is_kubernetes_dashboard_enabled
    is_tiller_enabled               = false # Default is false, left here for
  reference
  }
  admission_controller_options {
    is_pod_security_policy_enabled = var.is_pod_security_policy_enabled
  }
  kubernetes_network_config {
    services_cidr = lookup(var.network_cidrs, "KUBERNETES-SERVICE-CIDR")
    pods_cidr     = lookup(var.network_cidrs, "PODS-CIDR")
  }
}
image_policy_config {
  is_policy_enabled = false
}
}
```

Automation and Terraform Code Generation

If you are new to Terraform and the learning curve looks steep, the OCI console offers a way for you to still get the benefits of infrastructure as code. Both the Quick Create and Custom Create workflows offer a Save as Stack option at the end of the workflow (see Figure 4-11). Choose this option to generate Terraform code that captures the configuration you specified for the cluster and its components in the console. The generated Terraform code with the configuration values is packaged as a resource manager stack. This stack can be executed from within the Oracle Resource Manager service, which runs Terraform to build a Kubernetes cluster based on the configuration that was captured. Now you can also use the features of Resource Manager, such as drift detection, to ensure that your clusters' configuration is not drifting from its expected values due to manual or ad-hoc changes.

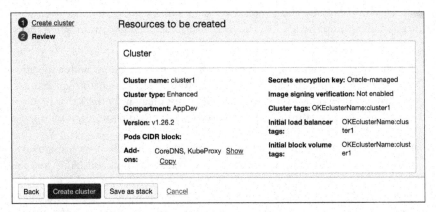

Figure 4-11 Summary of the Resources That Will Be Created Using the Oracle Resource Manager Service; the Save as Stack Generates a Terraform Configuration from the Options Provided to the Wizard

Asynchronous Cluster Creation

Regardless of the method you use to create a cluster, the act of setting up a new Kubernetes cluster control plane, and subsequently the data plane, is asynchronous. This means that the cluster creation API returns immediately (regardless of whether it is invoked through the console, CLI, or Terraform) and the cluster moves into a provisioning state. The progress of cluster creation can be tracked through a work request that is available under the cluster details page. The data plane or the node pools are created when the control plane creation is complete. In most cases, however, you do not need to wait for the data plane to be fully provisioned before deploying workloads. When the Kubernetes API endpoint is available, you can deploy pods or other Kubernetes resources to the cluster even if no data plane nodes are available. The resources simply remain in pending status until those data plane nodes are available.

Cluster Topology Considerations

OKE offers a set of flexible options in structuring your cluster topology. Various choices can help you decide how and where you create your data plane nodes, to meet your objectives. For example, you might choose to have a topology with a node pool that places its nodes across availability domains, a topology that restricts the node to a single availability domain, or a topology for which you need multiple node pools, each connected to a separate subnet for network-level isolation. The Node Pool resource in OKE provides these options for creating a wide range of topologies.

Using Multiple Node Pools

Because each node pool can be configured with a unique set of parameters, using multiple node pools enables you to deploy workloads running in the same cluster to the pool that best matches the needs of the workloads. Using multiple OKE node pools can provide more flexibility and control over your Kubernetes cluster, allowing you to optimize resources, improve security, increase availability, and scale your applications more efficiently. Specifically:

- **Resource requirements:** Each node pool can be configured with a specific worker node's shape, depending on the needs of your workloads. For example, if you have some workloads that require GPU resources and others that require high memory resources, you might create two separate node pools, each with the shape optimized for the specific use case.
- **Availability:** Each node pool can be configured with placement configurations that control the distribution of nodes across availability domains (ADs) and fault domains (FDs). By creating multiple node pools with worker nodes in different ADs and/or FDs, you can ensure that your cluster is more resilient to failures. If one AD or FD goes down, your workloads can still run on the nodes in the other pools.

- **Cost optimization:** You might use multiple node pools to optimize the cost of running your cluster. By using different types of worker nodes with different prices, you can save money by paying for only the resources that you actually need. For example, you could use nodes backed by low-cost preemptible instances for fault-tolerant or development workloads and then use higher-cost nodes for production workloads that require higher performance.
- **Security and isolation:** You might also use multiple node pools to improve the security of your cluster. For example, you could create a dedicated node pool for workloads that need to be isolated from other workloads for security reasons. This can be achieved by running the workload on a separate set of nodes with stricter access controls.

Scheduling Workloads on Specific Nodes

Under most circumstances when using Kubernetes, you should let the Kubernetes scheduler manage which nodes in the cluster are chosen for your workloads. The Kubernetes scheduler examines your pod resource requests and matches them with nodes that can satisfy those resource requests. This also allows the control plane to reschedule workloads onto available capacity when failures are detected. This automated and hands-off approach to workload management is one of the major advantages of using Kubernetes. However, in some scenarios, you need to exert control over what nodes your workload can be scheduled on. For instance, if your workload requires access to specialized hardware on specific nodes, you want to make this known to the Kubernetes control plane so that the scheduler can take this into consideration when making scheduling decisions. To schedule your workloads to specific Kubernetes node pools in OKE, you can use node selectors or node affinity, taints and tolerations, and other Kubernetes constructs, such as topology spread constraints.

Node selectors enable you to specify a label on a node pool and then use that label in your pod specification to select the node pool where you want to schedule your workload. For example, if you have a node pool labeled as gpu with GPU shapes selected, you can use the following node selector in your pod specification:

```
spec:
  nodeSelector:
    nodepool: gpu
```

This ensures that your pod is scheduled on a node in the gpu node pool. The same approach can be used with other node shapes, such as ARM.

Node affinity enables you to specify more complex rules to match nodes based on labels or other attributes. For example, Listing 4-7 demonstrates using node affinity to match nodes with a specific label and not match nodes with another label.

Listing 4-7   A Manifest File That Includes a Node Affinity and Expression to Match the Pod to a Node with the gpu Node Selector

```
spec:
 affinity:
  nodeAffinity:
   requiredDuringSchedulingIgnoredDuringExecution:
    nodeSelectorTerms:
    - matchExpressions:
     - key: nodepool
       operator: In
       values:
       - gpu
     - key: nodepool-type
       operator: NotIn
       values:
       - preemptible
```

This ensures that your pod is scheduled on a node in the gpu node pool that is not labeled as preemptible.

Taints and tolerations are a way for you to influence the scheduler and make sure that pods are not placed on nodes that need to be reserved for more critical workloads. For instance, if you have GPU nodes in your cluster, you likely want to deploy workloads that take advantage of those GPUs onto those nodes. A pod that selects a GPU node with a node selector will be assigned to an available GPU node, but this does not prevent other workloads that do not leverage or need the GPUs from being scheduled on the GPU node as well. For instance, a MySQL pod that does not use the GPU can also be scheduled on the GPU node. This can potentially lead to resource exhaustion because the MySQL pod has been allocated CPU resources, and it does not consume GPUs. If a few of these pods are allocated to the GPU node, when a real GPU workload is deployed, it could fail to schedule because there are no available CPUs on the GPU node, even though all the GPUs might be free. In these cases, you need a way for these specific nodes (such as the GPU node) to reject or repel a pod (such as the MySQL pod) unless the pod is specifically designed to use the node, like an actual GPU workload. This is exactly what taints and tolerations do.

Taints are added to nodes, and tolerations are defined in the pod specification. When you taint a node, it will repel all the pods except those that have a toleration for that taint. A node can have one or many taints associated with it.

Pod topology spread constraints offer you a declarative way to configure pod scheduling that is based on some topology key. This is done by grouping the nodes into "domains," on the basis of having the same node label and value. In the example in Listing 4-8, the topology key used is kubernets.io/arch. This is a well-known label that kubelet sets based on the CPU architecture of the node. If the cluster had both x86- and ARM-based nodes, the x86 nodes could have the value amd64 and the ARM nodes could have the value arm64 for the same node label. Pod topology spread constraints use this to split the nodes into two groups or domains, the x86 nodes and the Arm nodes. The scheduler tries to achieve balance among all the groups, so in the example, a similar number of pods will be allocated across each group. Similarly, by choosing another key, such as the availability domain or the fault domain, you can spread your pods across these groups, to prevent pods from being co-scheduled and potentially leading to a larger impact in case of a disruption.

Listing 4-8   Manifest File That Includes a Topology Spread Constraint, a Topology Key, and the Action to Take Depending on Whether the Key Is Present

```
spec:
  topologySpreadConstraints:
  - maxSkew: 1
    topologyKey: kubernetes.io/arch
    whenUnsatisfiable: DoNotSchedule
    labelSelector:
      matchLabels:
        app: wordpress
```

Kubernetes Networking

OKE relies on Oracle Cloud Infrastructure (OCI) virtual cloud networks (VCN). These are virtual versions of traditional network architectures that enable you to connect your OCI resources, such as compute instances and storage volumes, to each other and to the Internet. VCNs provide a logically isolated network environment in the cloud that you can customize to meet your needs. VCNs allow you to define the IP address range for your network, create subnets, and specify security rules to control inbound and outbound traffic.

OKE uses VCNs to provide a secure, isolated networking environment for Kubernetes clusters. When you create a Kubernetes cluster using OKE, you can choose to create a new VCN through the cluster Quick Create workflow or use an existing one through the Custom Create workflow. If you choose to create a new VCN, OKE creates a new VCN with a default set of subnets, security lists, and routing tables. If you choose to bring your own VCN, it is important to make sure that the rules are set up correctly, to ensure proper communication throughout your cluster.

Each node in the cluster is launched in a subnet. OKE supports network security policies, which allow you to define fine-grained rules to control traffic between pods in your Kubernetes cluster. These policies are enforced by the Kubernetes network plug-in running on each node in the cluster.

Container Network Interface (CNI)

The Kubernetes networking model assumes that pods have unique and routable IP addresses within a cluster. In the Kubernetes networking model, pods use those

IP addresses to communicate with each other, the cluster control plane, other resources (for example, storage), and the Internet. Kubernetes clusters use Container Network Interface (CNI) plug-ins for network resource management, such as to implement network connectivity for pods running on worker nodes. The CNI consists of a specification and libraries for writing plug-ins to configure network interfaces in Linux containers, along with a number of supported plug-ins. CNI plug-ins configure network interfaces, provision IP addresses, and maintain connectivity. All the node pools in a cluster use the same CNI plug-in.

OKE supports two types of pod networking out of the box: VCN-native pod networking and Flannel overlay (see Figure 4-12). When creating a Kubernetes cluster with OKE, the network type you select for the cluster determines the CNI plug-in that is used for pod networking.

- Choosing VCN-native pod networking as the network type deploys the OCI VCN-Native Pod Networking CNI plug-in to your nodes.
- Choosing the Flannel overlay network type deploys the flannel CNI plug-in to your nodes.

Note
You can use the OCI VCN-Native Pod Networking CNI plug-in with both virtual node pools and managed node pools. You can use the Flannel CNI plug-in with managed node pools.

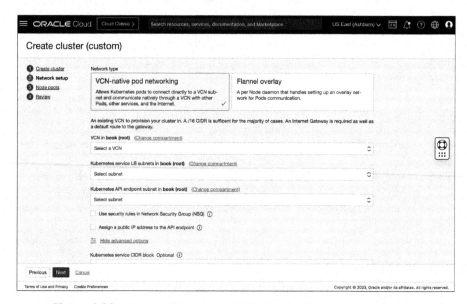

Figure 4-12   Process of Choosing a CNI During the Cluster Creation Process

OCI VCN-Native Pod Networking CNI

The OCI VCN-Native Pod Networking CNI plug-in uses the VCN's CIDR block to provide IP addresses to pods and enables other resources within the same subnet (or a different subnet) to communicate directly with pods in a Kubernetes cluster. Pod IP addresses are directly routable from other VCNs connected to that VCN, from on-premises networks, and from the public Internet.

Because pods are directly routable, you can use *native* VCN functionality to control access to and from pods using security rules defined as part of network security groups or security lists. The security rules apply to all pods in all the worker nodes connected to the pod subnet specified for a node pool. You can also use VCN flow logs to observe the traffic to, from, and between pods, which is useful for troubleshooting and compliance auditing purposes. This also enables you to use route tables and routing rules to route incoming requests to pods based on routing policies. Apart from these management features, because pods are directly connected to the virtual cloud network, no encapsulation is involved in packet transmission; this generally offers consistent performance for workloads that are sensitive to small amounts of latency.

Worker nodes running in clusters using the OCI VCN-Native Pod Networking CNI plug-in are connected to two subnets specified for the node pool: a *worker node subnet* and a *pod subnet*. The worker node subnet supports communication between processes running on the cluster control plane (such as kube-apiserver, kube-controller-manager, and kube-scheduler) and processes running on the worker node (such as kubelet and kube-proxy). The worker node subnet can be private or public and can be a regional subnet or an AD-specific subnet. The pod subnet supports communication between pods and direct access to individual pods using private pod IP addresses. The pod subnet can be private or public, and it must be a regional subnet. The pod subnet enables communication between pods on the same worker node or on other worker nodes, with OCI services (through a service gateway), and with the Internet (through a NAT gateway). You specify a single pod subnet for all the pods running on worker nodes in a node pool. You can specify the same pod subnet or different pod subnets for different node pools in a cluster. You can specify the same pod subnet for node pools in different clusters. The worker node subnet and the pod subnet must be in the same VCN and can be the same subnet. If they are in the same subnet, you should define security rules in network security groups to route network traffic to worker nodes and pods.

Something important to note about VCN-Native Pod Networking is that you might find yourself limited by the number of VNICs available to your chosen worker node shape. A minimum of two VNICs are attached to each worker node: One is connected to the worker node subnet, and the other is connected to the pod subnet. By default, 31 IP addresses are assigned to the VNIC for use by pods running on the worker node. These IP addresses are preallocated in the pod subnet before pods are created in the cluster. If you want more than 31 pods on a single worker node, the shape you specify for the node pool must support more than the minimum two VNICs. The additional VNICs can be connected to the pod subnet, to provide further IP addresses to support more pods. Similarly, VCN-Native Pod Networking consumes IP addresses from the virtual cloud network, which can pose challenges when working in an environment with a constrained IP space.

> ## Note
> Regardless of whether you are using the add-on API, a feature used to gain control over operational software deployed to OKE clusters, Oracle is responsible for deploying updates to the OCI VCN-Native Pod Networking CNI plug-in. The updates are applied only when worker nodes are next rebooted.

Flannel CNI

The Flannel overlay network is a simple private overlay virtual network that attaches IP addresses to containers. The Flannel overlay network uses its own CIDR block to provision pods and worker nodes with IP addresses instead of using IP addresses from a VCN's CIDR block. Because the pods in the private overlay network are accessible only from other pods in the same cluster, you can specify the same Flannel CIDR block for multiple clusters.

Because Flannel provides overlay network, it can be advantageous when you have a lot of pods, each of which requires an IP address, and your network has limited IP space in your cloud network. In these cases, Flannel creates the pods on its own overlay network, and your IP space is left untouched. In other words, if the density of pods per node presents an obstacle using the OCI VCN-Native Pod Networking CNI, consider using the Flannel CNI plug-in because the number of pods per worker node is not determined by the node shape. The disadvantage of using Flannel is that it can involve packet encapsulation, which incurs a performance hit and might not be appropriate for workloads with a high sensitivity to the network performance.

Kubernetes Storage

When a container is deleted or re-created, data stored inside the root file system can disappear. You can use persistent volumes (PVs) to store data outside containers to prevent data loss. PVs are simply storage in the cluster provisioned either dynamically using storage classes or by an administrator. You can think of it as a resource in a cluster just like a node is a resource in a cluster. Persistent volumes provide a mechanism for keeping your stored data intact even when the containers using the storage are terminated. To request persistent storage, you create a persistent volume claim (PVC), which is then bound to a persistent volume. Whereas a pod is a request by a user to consume node resources, a PVC is a request by a user to consume storage resources in the form of persistent volumes. Just as users can request specific levels of CPU and memory resources through pods, users can request specific size and access modes, including `ReadWriteOnce`, `ReadOnlyMany`, and `ReadWriteMany`, through persistent volume claims.

OKE provides two options for provisioning PVCs for OCI resources:

- The Oracle Cloud Infrastructure Block Volume service, which uses either the FlexVolume or CSI (Container Storage Interface) volume plug-ins to connect to OKE clusters
- The Oracle Cloud Infrastructure File Storage service, which uses the CSI volume plug-in to connect to OKE clusters

This section discusses the various storage options available to OKE, including their pros and cons and ways to use these storage options effectively for your workloads. Because OKE has the capability to create and manage these storage resources on your behalf, you need to configure OCI IAM policies to work with storage services. The policies that are required can vary, depending on the topology that you set up; see the official product documentation.

StorageClass: Flex Volume and CSI Plug-ins

A `StorageClass` provides a way for cloud providers or administrators to describe the "classes" of storage that they offer. The `StorageClass` specified for a PVC controls which volume plug-in to use to connect to Block Volume service volumes. Two storage classes are defined by default, `oci-bv` for the CSI volume plug-in and `oci` for the FlexVolume plug-in. If you don't explicitly specify a value for `storageClassName` in the YAML file that defines the PVC, the cluster's default storage class is used. The cluster's default storage class is initially set according to the Kubernetes version that was specified when the cluster was created. Before Kubernetes 1.24, this was the `oci` `StorageClass` used for the FlexVolume plug-in. For Kubernetes 1.24 and onward, this is `oci-bv` `StorageClass` for the CSI volume plug-in. OKE adds new functionality only to the CSI volume plug-in. The CSI plug-in comes with benefits, including the CSI topology feature, which ensures that worker nodes and volumes are colocated in the same availability domain, and the CSI volume plug-in does not require access to underlying operating system and root file system dependencies.

Updating the Default Storage Class

For clusters created on Kubernetes version 1.23 and earlier, and subsequently upgraded to Kubernetes version 1.24 or later, the default storage class is not changed during the upgrade process. This means that unless you manually update your default storage class, it remains `oci`. To shift from `oci` to `oci-bv` as the default storage class, perform the following steps.

This removes `oci` as the default storage class:

```
kubectl patch storageclass oci -p '{"metadata": {"annotations": {"storageclass.
  beta.kubernetes.io/is-default-class":"false"}}}'
```

This adds `oci-bv` as the default storage class:

```
kubectl patch storageclass oci-bv -p '{"metadata": {"annotations":
  {"storageclass.kubernetes.io/is-default-class":"true"}}}'
```

When provisioning a persistent volume claim, you can explicitly specify the volume plug-in to use to connect to the Block Volume service. This is done by specifying a value for `storageClassName` in the YAML file that defines the PVC:

- Specify `storageClassName: "oci-bv"` to use the CSI volume plug-in.
- Specify `storageClassName: "oci"` to use the FlexVolume volume plug-in.

If the cluster administrator has not created any suitable PVs that match the PVC request, you can dynamically provision a block volume using the CSI plug-in specified by the `oci-bv` storage class's definition (`provisioner: blockvolume.csi.oraclecloud.com`). For example, you can define a PVC in a file called `example-csi-pvc.yaml`, as demonstrated in Listing 4-9.

Listing 4-9   Manifest File Used to Create a Persistent Volume Claim

```
apiVersion: v1
kind: PersistentVolumeClaim
metadata:
  name: exampleclaim
spec:
  storageClassName: "oci-bv"
  accessModes:
    - ReadWriteOnce
  resources:
    requests:
      storage: 50Gi
```

Then you can create the PV:

```
kubectl create -f example-csi-pvc.yaml
```

You can verify that the PVC was created by running the following:

```
kubectl get pvc
```

You can use this PVC when creating other Kubernetes objects, such as pods. For example, you can use the pod definition in Listing 4-10 to create a pod that uses the `exampleclaim` PVC as the volume, which is mounted at `/data` by the pod.

Listing 4-10   Example Manifest File Used to Create a Pod That Uses the Previously Created Persistent Volume Claim

```
apiVersion: v1
kind: Pod
metadata:
  name: example
spec:
  containers:
    - name: example
```

```
    image: example:latest
    ports:
      - name: http
        containerPort: 80
    volumeMounts:
      - name: data
        mountPath: /usr/share/example/html
volumes:
  - name: data
    persistentVolumeClaim:
      claimName: exampleclaim
```

You can verify that the pod is using the new persistent volume claim by entering the following command:

```
kubectl describe pod example
```

File System Storage

The Oracle Cloud Infrastructure File Storage Service (FSS) provides a scalable and distributed network file system that uses the NFS v3 protocol. This makes FSS ideal for Kubernetes use cases in which shared storage is required. FSS also scales dynamically without any upfront provisioning, making it simple to use and scale. The CSI volume plug-in that is included with OKE provides support for Kubernetes Persistent Volumes that are backed by the FSS. These persistent volumes can be shared by pods that simultaneously call all reads and writes to the volume, otherwise known as the ReadWriteMany (RWX) access mode.

Before you can successfully leverage FSS storage in your Kubernetes cluster, it is important to understand FSS-specific terminology. Because FSS is an NFS V3 file system, you need an IP address or a DNS name that you can use to mount the file system. This is provided by a *mount target* in OCI. A mount target can be used to make multiple file systems available to users. An NFS client connects to the mount target to access a file system. An *export* controls how an NFS client accesses the file system when connecting to a mount target. Exporting is the act of making a file system available through a mount target. A file system must have at least one export in a mount target for instances to access and mount that file system. When you export a file system, a path to uniquely identify the file system within the mount target is specified. You can associate multiple file systems to a single mount target; this path is called the export path.

You can use the CSI volume plug-in to connect clusters to file systems created by the File Storage service. The CSI volume plug-in supports dynamic provisioning to dynamically create the required resources, such as the mount target and the file system itself, when a persistent volume claim is presented to the cluster. Although this dynamic provisioning capability is handy, FSS file systems are usually long-lived storage solutions that are used by multiple pods as durable shared storage. For this typical use case, it is more desirable to mount and use an existing file system than to create new file systems in an ephemeral fashion. The CSI volume plug-in also supports this model of using a preexisting file system and mount target.

To work with the File Storage service using the CSI volume plug-in, you need to define a storage class that sets up the parameters required when creating and managing file systems and mount targets. The StorageClass definition provides a template for creating the underlying resources. Consider the StorageClass definition in Listing 4-11.

Listing 4-11   Manifest Used to Define a StorageClass for Managing FSS File Systems

```
kind: StorageClass
apiVersion: storage.k8s.io/v1
metadata:
  name: oci-fss
provisioner: fss.csi.oraclecloud.com
parameters:
  availabilityDomain: US-ASHBURN-AD-1
  mountTargetOcid: …
  compartmentOcid: …
  kmsKeyOcid: …
  exportPath: /shared
  exportOptions: [ { "source" : "0.0.0.0/0", "requirePrivilegedSourcePort" :
  false, "access" : "READ_WRITE", "identitySquash" : "ROOT" } ]
  encryptInTransit: "false"
```

This storage class can create new persistent volumes backed by the file system service. The file systems are created in the availability domain specified in the configuration. The `mountTargetOcid` specifies the amount target to use for the file systems created by this storage class. Instead of providing the `mountTargetOcid`, you can also provide a `mountTargetSubnetOcid`. If the `mountTargetSubnetOcid` is provided instead of the `mountTargetOcid`, a new mount target is created in the given subnet. Note that, under most circumstances, you want to use a `mountTargetOcid`. The number of mount targets can be limited, and you typically want to associate multiple file systems to a single mount target. The `kmsKeyOcid` specifies the OCID for your own encryption key that is managed in the OCI vault, for encrypting the data stored on the volume. Data in the file system service is always encrypted, and this option replaces the Oracle managed key that is used by default to encrypt your data in the file system service with your own key. The `exportPath` and the `exportOptions` determine how the file system is made available through the mount target.

With the storage class created, you can now use a persistent volume claim that refers to this storage class to dynamically create the file system, export it, and attach it to your workload. Consider the persistent volume claim definition in Listing 4-12.

Listing 4-12   Manifest Used to Define a Persistent Volume Claim for an FSS File System

```
apiVersion: v1
kind: PersistentVolumeClaim
```

```
metadata:
  name: fss-claim
spec:
  accessModes:
    - ReadWriteMany
  storageClassName: "oci-fss"
  resources:
    requests:
      storage: 100Gi
```

This volume claim specifies a storage class name but not a persistent volume name. This means that the CSI volume driver uses dynamic provisioning to create the required resources, such as the file system. The example references the storage class OCI FSS shown in the prior listing, which specifies a mount target OCID. If the storage class is configured with a `mountTargetSubnetOcid`, the CSI volume driver also creates a mount target in the given subnet as part of the dynamic provisioning process, to satisfy this volume claim.

It is worthwhile to note that, although you need to set a storage size that is required by the `PersistentVolumeClaim` object, this size has no effect on the file system. This is because the OCI file system service transparently scales on demand as more data is written to the file system.

When using dynamic provisioning as shown in Listing 4-11, the export path configured on the storage class is used for exporting the file system that is created. The export path determines the path under the mount point where the file system will be made available. Therefore, when using this approach, you are usually limited to creating only a single file system with a given storage class object. This is because the export path for each file system has to be unique within a mount target, and the storage class sets this statically. This means that there can be only one volume claim referring to this storage class for dynamic provisioning; a second volume claim using this storage class for dynamic provisioning will create a file system and would attempt to use the same export path, which would result in an error. If you used the `mountTargetSubnetOcid` as well, you can create a new mount target each time you use dynamic provisioning; however, you might hit the tenancy limit for the number of mount targets you can have.

For these reasons, in most cases, you typically will want to pre-create a mount target and reference that in the storage class. You can also leave out the `exportPath` parameter from the storage class, which will result in a new PV and file system being generated dynamically each time a PVC is created. The new file system will be exposed by the mount target with a default export path that corresponds to the display name of the file system generated by the CSI volume plugin. Under most circumstances, this will be the behavior you need.

You could also exert more control by provisioning all persistent volumes beforehand. The following example shows how to create a persistent volume object and reference it from your persistent volume claim to get more control over the resources.

To use an existing mount target and a file system, you must create a persistent volume definition that refers to these existing resources. Consider the example in Listing 4-13.

Listing 4-13   Manifest Used to Define a Persistent Volume Backed by an FSS File System

```
apiVersion: v1
kind: PersistentVolume
metadata:
  name: fss-volume
spec:
  capacity:
    storage: 100Gi
  volumeMode: Filesystem
  accessModes:
    - ReadWriteMany
  persistentVolumeReclaimPolicy: Retain
  csi:
    driver: fss.csi.oraclecloud.com
    volumeHandle: ocid1.filesystem.xxx:10.0.0.1:/shared
```

The persistent volume definition describes a volume that can be used by many pods as shared storage due to the ReadWriteMany access mode. The CSI section of the definition specifies the driver to be used and the volume handle. The volume handle points to the existing resources to be used for this volume. It has three elements to it: the OCID of the file system, the IP address of the mount target, and the export path. Once a persistent volume representing an existing file system and the options for accessing it has been created, you can use a persistent volume claim to bind to this volume. Consider the example in Listing 4-14, which demonstrates using a persistent volume claim that refers to this persistent volume.

Listing 4-14   Manifest Used to Create a Persistent Volume Claim Bound to an Existing Persistent Volume Backed by an FSS File System

```
apiVersion: v1
kind: PersistentVolumeClaim
metadata:
  name: fss-claim
spec:
  accessModes:
    - ReadWriteMany
  storageClassName: ""
  resources:
    requests:
      storage: 100Gi
  volumeName: fss-volume
```

This volume claim is similar to the one used for dynamic provisioning, with a few notable differences. The first obvious difference is that the volume name attribute is set; it directly refers to the persistent volume that has been created to interact with the preexisting file system. This binds the persistent volume to this claim after verifying the storage class and the storage requirements. The second difference is that the storage class name has been set to an empty string. This explicitly disables dynamic provisioning for this volume claim. Note that omitting the storage class from the configuration is not the same as setting it to an empty string. This is because, when the storage class is omitted, the default storage class is used, if one is configured. Setting the storage class to the empty string requires the persistent volume claim to be bound to a persistent volume that has no storage class. As before, the storage request does not have any impact on the actual file system; the storage request is considered when binding the persistent volume to the persistent volume claim. If the volume specifies a storage capacity that is lower than the requested capacity in the claim, the volume claim will not be bound to the volume. Therefore, it is best to use the same storage capacity values for both the volume and the volume claim when using FSS with your Kubernetes cluster.

Kubernetes Load Balancer Support

When you create a service that has its `type` set to `LoadBalancer`, Kubernetes attempts to create a load balancer to expose the service. When running on a cloud provider, the Cloud Controller Manager (CCM) is responsible for calling the appropriate APIs on the cloud provider to create and wire the load balancer to the underlying pods. The OCI CCM performs this task on OKE and enables you to manage traffic and the properties of the load balancers. The OCI CCM runs on the OKE control plane and is present on all OKE clusters.

OCI offers two types of load balancers: the standard Load Balancer service, which offers Layer 7 capabilities, and a network load balancer, which offers Layer 4 (TCP/UDP) level load balancing. When creating Service objects, you can add *annotations* to the Service definition's metadata that tell the CCM to create and set up the load balancer in a certain way. Annotations are additional name-value elements in the spec that are read by the CCM that control its behavior. The complete list of annotations and configuration parameters is provided in the CCM documentation.[6] The annotations for the Layer 7 Load Balancer service are with either `service.beta.Kubernetes.io` or `oci.oraclecloud.com` (for OCI-specific features), and the annotations for network load balancers are prefixed with `oci-network-load-balancer.oraclecloud.com`.

Working with the OCI Load Balancer Service

The OCI Load Balancer service is the default choice used by the OCI CCM when creating service objects that are of type `LoadBalancer`. This OCI service offers a highly available and fault-tolerant proxy that can be located across multiple availability domains. Because this is a Layer 7 load balancer service, it can support advanced HTTP routing policies, and it has additional features, such as SSL termination. This is a flexible infrastructure service, meaning that the service automatically scales between a minimum bandwidth value that is always guaranteed and an optional maximum bandwidth value as required by actual real-time traffic, without any intervention. It offers you a choice of public or private IP addresses and is appropriate for load balancing most applications.

When a cluster is created, the user is prompted to allocate a subnet for placing load balancers. The user also has the choice of configuring the subnets for the node pools. When a service of type `LoadBalancer` is created, the CCM creates a load balancer within the subnet and wires them to the pods located on the compute nodes within the node pools. The traffic flow among these various subnets is governed by the VCN's network security groups and security lists. Traffic from external sources such as clients and users outside the OKE cluster, or even the network, is managed and routed by the various configurations for the NSGs and security lists. In OKE, you can decide whether to let the CCM automatically configure these elements for you so that, as you deploy a service, the associated network configuration is updated to route traffic to it by opening the required ports and adding the required access rules. Alternatively, you can manage this yourself if you want a more predictable configuration and you do not want to provide access to the service to make changes to your network's traffic and security settings. The configuration choices are controlled by a set of annotations that you can provide in the *ServiceSpec* or the YAML that defines the service.

To understand the various annotations, their effects, and how best to use them, consider Listing 4-15, which is the most basic service definition for a Kubernetes service, along with a pod that it can point to.

Listing 4-15   Manifest Used to Create an NGINX Pod, Along with a Service of Type LoadBalancer, Backed by the OCI Load Balancer Service

```
apiVersion: v1
kind: Pod
metadata:
  name: nginx
  labels:
    app.kubernetes.io/name: proxy
spec:
  containers:
  - name: nginx
    image: nginx:stable
    ports:
      - containerPort: 80
        name: http-web-svc
---
apiVersion: v1
kind: Service
metadata:
  name: nginx-service
spec:
  type: LoadBalancer
  selector:
    app.kubernetes.io/name: proxy
```

```
ports:
- name: http
  protocol: TCP
  port: 80
  targetPort: http-web-svc
```

This creates a single pod that runs nginx, pulling the image tagged `stable`. The pod is labeled with `app.kubernetes.io/name: proxy`. Next, the Service definition or the ServiceSpec defines the service as `type: LoadBalancer`. The `selector` causes the service to route traffic to pods with the label `app.kubernetes.io/name: proxy`. Port 80 on the Service (load balancer) is exposed, and it points to the port named `http-web-svc` exposed by the pod (also port 80). So much is clear from the definition. When OKE encounters this service spec, it sets up the required infrastructure resources, such as the actual load balancer, listeners, health checks, security rules, and more. Because you did not specify any annotations, the CCM uses the default values for its configuration and sets up the following resources:

- A Layer 7 load balancer, 100Mbps
- An ephemeral public IP, if the load balancer subnet is a public subnet (chosen at cluster creation)
- Instructions to round-robin among all back ends (this example has just a single one)
- Updates to security lists for both the load balancer and the node subnets
  - On the node subnet's security list, an ingress rule is added to allow for ingress on the host port that is opened for pod traffic.
  - On the load balancer subnet, an ingress rule for port 80 is added where the service is exposed externally, and egress rules are added to enable egress from the load balancer to the node subnet on the host port for pod traffic.

Although OKE offers some secure and sensible defaults, in most circumstances, you need to exert some control over these defaults or be explicit in these configurations, for better visibility and predictability with the configuration in a production setting. The previous service spec can be rewritten explicitly as shown in Listing 4-16.

Listing 4-16 How to Add Annotations to the Load Balancer Manifest to Configure Your LoadBalancer Service

```
... Pod Spec Truncated ...
---
apiVersion: v1
kind: Service
metadata:
  name: nginx-service
  annotations:
    oci.oraclecloud.com/load-balancer-type: "lb"
```

```
    service.beta.kubernetes.io/oci-load-balancer-security-list-management-mode :
    "All"
    service.beta.kubernetes.io/oci-load-balancer-shape: "flexible"
    service.beta.kubernetes.io/oci-load-balancer-shape-flex-min: "100"
    service.beta.kubernetes.io/oci-load-balancer-shape-flex-max: "100"
    oci.oraclecloud.com/loadbalancer-policy:"ROUND_ROBIN"
spec:
  type: LoadBalancer
  selector:
    app.kubernetes.io/name: proxy
  ports:
  - name: http
    protocol: TCP
    port: 80
    targetPort: http-web-svc
```

Note

The annotation `service.beta.kubernetes.io/oci-load-balancer-shape` can select a fixed shape, such as 100Mbps. However, Oracle plans to deprecate these fixed shapes in the future. Using flexible load balancers with the upper and lower bounds set to the same number is a way to achieve a similar configuration.

SSL Termination with OCI Load Balancer

The OCI Load Balancer service supports SSL termination at the load balancer. When using Kubernetes services, you can configure and manage this directly from the Kubernetes cluster using standard Kubernetes tooling. To set this up, you need to leverage the following two annotations:

- `service.beta.kubernetes.io/oci-load-balancer-ssl-ports`   This annotation configures the ports to enable SSL termination on the corresponding load balancer listener.
- `service.beta.kubernetes.io/oci-load-balancer-tls-secret`   This annotation references a TLS secret, which is a built-in secret type in Kubernetes for storing certificates and their associated keys. You need to create a Kubernetes secret of type `kubernetes.io/tls` and populate it with the certificate and the private key. Then refer to the secret object by its name in this annotation to install the certificate on the load balancer listeners and have SSL enabled.

To examine this in action, consider the example in Listing 4-17.

Listing 4-17   The Same Manifest Previously Used to Define the LoadBalancer Service, but Now with Additional Annotations and an HTTPS Port

```
... Pod Spec Truncated ...
---
apiVersion: v1
kind: Service
metadata:
  name: nginx-service
  annotations:
    oci.oraclecloud.com/load-balancer-type: "lb"
    service.beta.kubernetes.io/oci-load-balancer-security-list-management-mode :
  "All"
    service.beta.kubernetes.io/oci-load-balancer-shape: "flexible"
    service.beta.kubernetes.io/oci-load-balancer-shape-flex-min: "100"
    service.beta.kubernetes.io/oci-load-balancer-shape-flex-max: "100"
    oci.oraclecloud.com/loadbalancer-policy:"ROUND_ROBIN"
    service.beta.kubernetes.io/oci-load-balancer-ssl-ports: "443"
    service.beta.kubernetes.io/oci-load-balancer-tls-secret: ssl-certificate-
  secret
spec:
  type: LoadBalancer
  selector:
    app.kubernetes.io/name: proxy
  ports:
  - name: http
    protocol: TCP
    port: 80
    targetPort: http-web-svc
  - name: https
    port: 443
    targetPort: http-web-svc
```

This is the same service definition as in the earlier example, with the two new added annotations and an added port for HTTPS. Configuring SSL termination requires that you configure the SSL certificate on the load balancer. When configuring SSL termination at the load balancer for a Kubernetes service, Kubernetes can configure the SSL certificate for the load balancer. The expectation here is that the required SSL certificate and private key is provided to the CCM as a Kubernetes secret of type TLS. Kubernetes provides a built-in secret type `kubernetes.io/tls` for storing a certificate and its associated keys that are typically used for TLS. The annotation `service.beta.kubernetes.io/oci-load-balancer-tls-secret` should point to this secret, and you can see this referencing `ssl-certificate-secret` in Listing 4-17. The secret itself should have a key and a certificate that contains the private key and the certificate that you want to use. This can be created with the `--key` and the `--cert` flags for `kubectl create`. For example, if there were a certificate and key named `tls.crt` and `tls.key` in the current directory, you could use the following command to create the secret of type `kubernetes.io/tls`:

```
kubectl create secret tls ssl-certificate-secret --key tls.key --cert tls.crt
```

Working with the OCI Network Load Balancer Service

The network load balancer is a nonproxy load balancer in OCI that performs pass-through load balancing of Layer 4 (TCP/UDP/ICMP) traffic. It is a highly available load balancer that provides a regional virtual IP (VIP) address. The load balancer can elastically scale without requiring a minimum or maximum bandwidth configuration. It also provides the benefits of flow logs and source and destination IP address preservation. The network load balancer does not directly respond to a client ICMP or TCP/UDP ping packet. Instead, the network load balancer directs the packet to a back-end server in accordance with the load balancing policy. The back-end server then returns a response to the client. The primary advantages of the network load balancer are its capability to preserve source and destination IP addresses, low latency and high throughput load balancing, and the ability to handle UDP traffic. To choose network load balancer when creating a Kubernetes service, you can set the annotation `oci.oraclecloud.com/load-balancer-type: nlb` on your service definition, as shown in Listing 4-18.

Exposing UDP Applications and Preserving IP Addresses

If you choose the network load balancer to expose a UDP application or to preserve IP addresses, you need additional configuration to support these use cases. For exposing UDP applications, you need to set the `protocol` field in the service definition's port configuration. The default value for protocol is `TCP`.

Similarly, to preserve source IP addresses, you need to configure the `externalTrafficPolicy` parameter for the service and set up your security lists to allow traffic from the source IP range. Although enabled by default, you use the annotation `oci-network-load-balancer.oraclecloud.com/is-preserve-source: "true"` to explicitly enable source IP preservation. The `externalTrafficPolicy` is set to `Local` to ensure that Kubernetes does not relay the request through other nodes, which is the default behavior. Services that want to have the source IP preserved should always include this parameter and set `externalTrafficPolicy: Local` in the service definition. Additionally, the security list or the NSG rules for the nodes also need to allow traffic from these original sources to reach the nodes. This is different than with the Layer 7 load balancer because, in that case, the clients communicate with the load balancer, which then proxies the requests to the nodes. The nodes thus would be receiving traffic from the load balancer, and the security lists or NSG rules for the nodes could be configured to accept traffic from the load balancer. When preserving client IP, the nodes' security list or NSG rules need to be configured to allow traffic from the clients directly because the load balancer is not proxying the requests. Table 4-1 outlines an example security list rule.

Table 4-1 Example Security List Rule

State	Source	Protocol/ Destination Port	Description
Stateful	0.0.0.0/0 or subnet CIDR	ALL/30000-32767	Allows worker nodes to receive connections through the OCI network load balancer with the source IP preserved

If the client IPs are known (or are from an internal/known subnet), the security list rule or NSG rule can restrict the source to the known CIDR block for the source. If the service is exposed publicly, the source CIDR needs to be set to 0.0.0.0/0 for allowing traffic from anywhere.

Listing 4-18 shows these configurations in an example.

Listing 4-18 Manifest Used to Create a Network Load Balancer

```
... POD SPEC TRUNCATED ...
---
apiVersion: v1
kind: Service
metadata:
  name: nginx-service
  annotations:
    oci.oraclecloud.com/load-balancer-type: "nlb"
    oci-network-load-balancer.oraclecloud.com/is-preserve-source: "true"
spec:
  type: LoadBalancer
  externalTrafficPolicy: Local
  selector:
    app.kubernetes.io/name: proxy
  ports:
  - port: 80
    protocol: UDP
    targetPort: 80
```

This listing shows the nginx service example, as shown earlier; however, this time the configuration explicitly requests a network load balancer instead of the standard (Layer 7) load balancer by setting the annotation oci.oraclecloud.com/load-balancer-type: "nlb". By setting the protocol:UDP in the port configuration, OKE ensures that the listener created for the network load balancer is configured to accept UDP. Additionally, the configuration to preserve source IPs is enabled by providing the annotation oci-network-load-balancer.oraclecloud.com/is-preserve-source: "true" and setting the parameter externalTrafficPolicy: Local. It is assumed that the NSG rule or the security list rule to allow traffic from the source IPs to the nodes has been created.

Specifying Reserved Public IP Addresses

When you create a public load balancer or network load balancer with OKE, an ephemeral public IP address is assigned to that load balancer. In many circumstances, you might want to have a predefined and known IP address for your service. OCI allows you to reserve public IP addresses. When you create a public load balancer or network load balancer with OKE, you can choose to assign one of your reserved public IP addresses to that load balancer. To configure a public IP address for your load balancer, you need to specify the IP address field in your service definition, and your load balancer must be created in a public subnet. Suppose that 150.136.125.124 is one of your reserved IP addresses. To assign that IP to a load balancer created by the OKE, consider the example in Listing 4-19.

Listing 4-19   Manifest Used to Create a LoadBalancer Service with a Reserved Public IP Address

```
apiVersion: v1
kind: Service
metadata:
  name: nginx-service
spec:
  type: LoadBalancer
  loadBalancerIP: 150.136.125.124
  selector:
    app.kubernetes.io/name: proxy
  ports:
  - name: http
    protocol: TCP
    port: 80
    targetPort: http-web-svc
```

Commonly Used Annotations

The complete list of annotations is documented on the GitHub page for the Cloud Controller Manager; however, this section and the list herein covers the most common and frequently used annotations. Note the prefixes to the various annotations. Certain OCI-specific annotations and those that are common to both load balancers and network load balancers are prefixed with oci.oraclecloud.com. Load balancers use a mix of service.beta.kubernetes.io and oci.oraclecloud.com prefixes, while network load balancer–specific annotations are prefixed with oci-network-load-balancer.oraclecloud.com.

- oci.oraclecloud.com/load-balancer-type   This annotation is used to switch between the type of load balancer. The possible values are lb for the OCI load balancer (Layer 7) or nlb for the OCI network load balancer (Layer 4).
- service.beta.kubernetes.io/oci-load-balancer-shape   This template determines the load balancer's capacity (bandwidth) for ingress and egress traffic.

It should be set to `flexible`. Fixed-bandwidth shapes such as 100Mbps, 400Mbps, and 8000Mbps are now deprecated. This should be used in conjunction with `service.beta.kubernetes.io/oci-load-balancer-shape-flex-min`, which sets the minimum guaranteed bandwidth, and the optional `service.beta.kubernetes.io/oci-load-balancer-shape-flex-max`, which sets the load balancer's maximum capacity that it will scale to.

- `service.beta.kubernetes.io/oci-load-balancer-subnet1` This is the OCID of a subnet to attach the load balancer to when the default choice selected at cluster creation needs to be overridden for a specific service. If the subnet provided is regional, only a single subnet needs to be configured. When using AD-specific subnets, a value also needs to be provided for `service.beta.kubernetes.io/oci-load-balancer-subnet2` to maintain high availability of the load balancer.

- `service.beta.kubernetes.io/oci-load-balancer-health-check-timeout` This is the maximum time, in milliseconds, to wait for a reply to a health check. A health check is successful only if a reply returns within this timeout period. By default, this is set to `3000`, or 30 seconds. You should consider increasing this value for services that are backed by pods that can potentially take more time to start and respond to health check requests. You can also use this in conjunction with `service.beta.kubernetes.io/oci-load-balancer-health-check-retries`, which sets the number of times a failed health check is retried before the back-end server is marked as unhealthy, and `service.beta.kubernetes.io/oci-load-balancer-health-check-interval`, which lets you control the interval between health checks.

- `service.beta.kubernetes.io/oci-load-balancer-security-list-management-mode` This annotation determines how the CCM handles security list updates, to allow traffic among multiple components as services are exposed. This is a crucial setting in most cases, and is covered in detail in the next section. The permissible values for it are `All` (the default), `Frontend`, and `None`.

- `oci.oraclecloud.com/oci-network-security-groups` When using network security groups (NSGs) to manage and secure traffic flow, this annotation is used to designate the newly created load balancer for the given NSG. The NSG rules that you create and associate with this NSG dictate how traffic flow and security are handled.

- `oci.oraclecloud.com/loadbalancer-policy` This specifies the load balancer algorithm used to distribute traffic to the back-end servers. The default is to use `ROUND_ROBIN`, which treats the back ends as a list, sends each incoming request to the next server in the list, and wraps around to the start of the list after each pass through the list. This type of distribution ensures that all back-end servers get relatively the same number of requests, but it does not account for when the request is a simple one that can be completed quickly or one that can be time-consuming. It also assumes that the back ends are all fairly similar in their capabilities for the load to be well balanced across all back ends. You can choose to use the `LEAST_CONNECTIONS` or `IP_HASH` algorithms. Use `LEAST_CONNECTIONS` to have the service choose a back-end server that has the least active connections at that moment to route the request to. This ensures that there is no imbalance between servers that are handling long-lived requests and servers that are receiving smaller requests. The IP_HASH algorithm uses a hashing function to calculate a hash value from the client's IP address so that requests from the same IP address are always routed to the same back-end server. Although this offers the capability to achieve some level of stickiness, which could be important to some applications, it can also create an imbalance if a large number of clients connect to the service through a proxy. In this case, the proxy's IP would be perceived as the source IP, and the hashing function would always send these requests to the same back-end server. If many clients are behind a proxy, that can cause the load to not be well balanced and can potentially overburden an individual back-end server.

Understanding Security List Management Modes

The annotation `service.beta.kubernetes.io/oci-load-balancer-security-list-management-mode` controls how the CCM manages security lists for the load balancer subnet and the node subnet. Appropriate ingress and egress rules on these subnets are required for traffic flow because the default behavior for subnets is to disallow all traffic. The annotation can have the following values:

- All: When the value is set to All, the CCM manages security lists for both the node subnets and the load balancer subnets. When a pod is started on a node and is exposing a set of container ports, these ports are within the network namespace for the pod. Ports are exposed on the host as well to route traffic from the host namespace to the pod namespace. From a VCN networking perspective that sees the hosts and not the pods or containers running on them, these ports on the host need to have security list rules that allow traffic to them. The CCM looks up the subnets for each of the nodes where the pods are running because each node pool can potentially be located on a different subnet; then the CCM adds security list rules that allow these specific host ports to receive traffic from the load balancer subnet.

  Similarly, the CCM updates the security list rules for the load balancer subnet to send traffic to these ports on the node subnet. Because the load balancer is exposing the application and listening on the configured load balancer port, the CCM also adds a security list rule to allow incoming traffic to the load balancer port.

  In this mode, because the CCM is updating resources such as the security list, it is possible for infrastructure management tools that track resource state, such as Terraform, to flag these modifications as configuration drift.

- Frontend: When the value is set to Frontend, the CCM manages security lists for only the front end, or the ingress for the load balancer subnet. Here, it is assumed that you have already configured security rules that open the node port range for your node subnets to the load balancer subnet, with egress rules on the load balancer subnet and ingress rules on the node subnets.

- **None:** In this mode, the CCM does not do any security list rule management. You need to configure these rules externally, such as with Terraform, using well-known ports on the load balancer ingress side and using the node port range between the load balancer and node subnets.

Using Node Label Selectors

As discussed previously in the chapter, the node label selector annotation in OKE is used to organize a subset of nodes in your cluster. In the context of exposing your application using a service, these label selectors enable you to define a subset of nodes to act as the back end for your service. By default, when you deploy a set of pods and expose it using a service, the pods can be located in any node within your cluster, based on how Kubernetes schedules them. In some cases, however, you might want to exert control over what nodes are chosen to be in the back-end set for a service. This can be useful in scenarios such as node upgrades, during which you want to control when traffic moves to a new set of nodes without impacting your existing workloads.

The key idea with using node label selectors is that you label your nodes first; then you can update your service to include a node label selector, which causes the CCM to update the load balancer and include only nodes that match the label selector in the back-end set for the load balancer listener. Consider the example of updating a set of nodes and wanting to update the service to switch over to the new fleet without impacting the workloads. The example here starts off with the existing service and labeled nodes. For example, consider the following command:

```
kubectl label nodes 10.0.1.2 10.0.1.2 10.0.1.3 app-tier=frontend
```

This gives three nodes the label `app-tier=frontend`. With the nodes labeled, you can deploy a workload that is pinned to these nodes with a definition like the one in Listing 4-20 to ensure that the pods are all created on nodes with the specified node selector.

Listing 4-20   Manifest Used to Define a Deployment That Ensures All Pods It Creates Are Scheduled onto Nodes with the Frontend Selector

```
apiVersion: apps/v1
kind: Deployment
metadata:
  name: frontend-deployment
  labels:
    app: frontend
spec:
  replicas: 3
  selector:
    matchLabels:
      app: frontend
  template:
    metadata:
```

```
        name: frontend
        labels:
          app: frontend
      spec:
        affinity:
          nodeAffinity:
            requiredDuringSchedulingIgnoredDuringExecution:
              nodeSelectorTerms:
              - matchExpressions:
                - key: app-tier
                  operator: In
                  values:
                  - frontend
        containers:
        - name: frontend
          image: frontend:1.0.0
          ports:
          - containerPort: 80
            name: http-web-svc
```

> **Note**
>
> In this example, it is assumed that there are several nodes in the cluster, some of which do not match the label selector used here.

The `nodeAffinity` for this deployment restricts the pods running the `frontend:1.0.0` container image to the three nodes that were labeled with `app-tier=frontend`. A service definition can now use the node label selector annotation to select the specific nodes to be added to the load balancer back-end set, as shown in Listing 4-21.

Listing 4-21   Manifest Used to Define a Service with a Back-End Set That Includes Only Nodes Created with the Frontend Selector

```
apiVersion: v1
kind: Service
metadata:
  name: frontend-service
  annotations:
    oci.oraclecloud.com/node-label-selector: app-tier=frontend
spec:
  type: LoadBalancer
  selector:
    app: frontend
  ports:
```

```
- name: http
  protocol: TCP
  port: 80
  targetPort: http-web-svc
```

The annotation ensures that only nodes that carry the label app-tier=frontend will be included in the back-end set for the load balancer's listener. Label selectors can be in several formats, including exclusions such as app-tier!=database, which selects all that have the key app-tier but whose value is not database.

> **Note**
>
> Kubernetes supports a feature gate named ServiceNodeExclusion to label nodes that should be excluded from a load balancer. OKE enables this feature gate by default. This means that you can label your nodes with node.kubernetes.io/exclude-from-external-load-balancers to keep the node from being added to the back-end set of a service.

Now imagine that you want to cycle the nodes that are running the front-end application, and you create three new nodes. You can label them as app-tier=frontend-v2, as shown here:

```
kubectl label nodes 10.0.1.4 10.0.1.5 10.0.1.6 app-tier=frontend-v2
```

The deployment can now be updated to include the new nodes labeled app-tier=frontend-v2, and the service definition can be updated to include both the new nodes and the old nodes:

```
oci.oraclecloud.com/node-label-selector: app-tier=frontend,app-tier=frontend-v2
```

When you have ensured that the pods are available on the new node pool, you can drop the old node pool from the back-end set for the load balancer by setting the annotation as follows:

```
oci.oraclecloud.com/node-label-selector: app-tier=frontend-v2
```

The old nodes can now be cordoned and drained without impacting traffic because the load balancer directs traffic only to the new nodes.

Security Considerations for Your Cluster

As you deploy your applications into a Kubernetes cluster and operate it, security for your cluster and your application becomes important. Unauthorized access can potentially cause application outages that impact business. Worse, it can lead to data breaches that have long-term impacts. This section helps you understand the various facets of a cluster and its infrastructure that needs to be secured, along with ways to achieve it. A wider discussion of securing both your applications and your infrastructure, understanding attack vectors, considering the cloud native security ecosystem, and developing a system's overall security posture is covered in Chapter 6, "Cloud Native Security."

Security for your cluster can broadly be categorized into securing the runtime infrastructure and securing access to the cluster. Securing the runtime infrastructure refers to how security principles are applied to the cluster infrastructure topology and its configuration. Setting up secure access to the cluster considers the controls and configuration for the access paths, authentication mechanisms, and authorization mechanisms to ensure that users can be provided with only the necessary capabilities. On the other hand, securing access to the cluster and establishing good practices for authorization prevents attack vectors that originate from within an organization. Observability through metrics, log analytics, and auditing is also a key component in having a good security strategy.

Cluster Topology and Configuration Security Considerations

The benefit of having a well-thought-out strategy for infrastructure security is the ability to prevent intrusions into your infrastructure components and data—in other words, the capability to shield yourself from attack vectors that originate from the outside. The following sections look at several considerations from an infrastructure perspective.

Cluster Component Visibility

When you create an OKE cluster, one of your first choices is to select the subnets and visibility for the Kubernetes API endpoint and the worker nodes. When using the Quick Create workflow, you are asked to choose the visibility of your Kubernetes API endpoint and your worker nodes. You can opt to make either component public or private. When you use the Custom Create workflow, you are asked to choose the subnets where you want to place your Kubernetes API endpoint, your load balancers, and your worker nodes. If you choose a public subnet, you can assign public IP addresses for these elements; on the other hand, if you choose a private subnet, these elements remain private. Figure 4-13 shows the choices in the Quick Create workflow.

When you expose the Kubernetes endpoint to be public, your Kubernetes endpoint is available via a public IP. This means that, from a visibility or network reachability standpoint, it is open to the Internet for anyone to realize that a Kubernetes API server exists at this location. Access to the API server's resources is still controlled by the user's authorization credentials, so an unauthorized user will be refused service by the API server itself. A public API endpoint is desirable for ease of use because it allows you to connect directly to the API server over the Internet. On the other hand, for most production applications, a private API endpoint can be considered a better and more secure choice because it limits the visibility and reachability of the API server to locations within the virtual cloud network where your cluster is located. To access the API server and interact with it using a client such as kubectl, users typically need a bastion host (also sometimes called a jump host) from where they can connect to the API server.

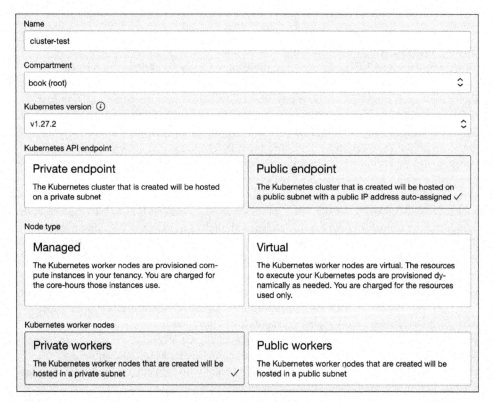

Figure 4-13 Choosing Between Private and Public Endpoints for the Kubernetes API and the Kubernetes Worker Node Subnets

Following similar reasoning, the visibility of the worker nodes should also be limited to be private so that they can be reached only from within the version cloud network. This means that, to access the nodes directly or log into them using SSH, they would need to be within the virtual cloud network, such as on a bastion server. Having private worker nodes does not mean that you cannot expose your workloads externally. A service exposed as a load balancer will cause an OCI load balancer to be created and wired to the pods, and the communication between the load balancer and the private nodes running the pods will be traffic that is private to the virtual cloud network. This will work as long as the load balancer and the worker node subnets are configured to allow communication between each other. If you are using the Quick Create workflow, these security list rules are set up by the service; if you are using the Custom Create workflow, the required rules are documented in the official documentation for a static configuration. It is also worthwhile to note that the OKE CCM (Cloud Controller Manager) is set up by default to update the security lists for the subnets when services are created and destroyed. This ensures that only the required ports are opened, and only while they are needed.

Setting Up NSG Rules and Security List Rules

When you set up an OKE cluster using the Quick Create workflow, the service creates the networking components using a simple dedicated network and configures the components appropriately. In a production scenario, however, you will likely have a different and more complex network topology that is shared with other resources and is perhaps managed by a dedicated team. When you are reusing existing network components, it is important to configure them in a manner that allows the OKE components, especially the control plane and data plane, to effectively communicate with each other. You can perform these configurations using security list rules, NSG rules, or both. Recall that security lists are attached to subnets, and the rules take effect at a subnet level. NSG rules, on the other hand, are applied at a VNIC level. If you use both approaches to control network traffic security, the effect is additive: The effective rule should be the union of the NSG rules and the security list rules. If either of them allows communication between two components, the traffic is allowed.

As a general rule, it is recommended to separately manage the ingress and egress rules for the Kubernetes API endpoint, the load balancers, and the worker nodes. This allows for maximum flexibility without compromising security. When using NSGs, you can have all these elements in the same subnet but still treat the ingress and egress separately by creating NSG rules because NSG rules are applied at a VNIC level. If you are using security list rules, it is important to place these components in separate subnets so that their ingress and egress can be controlled appropriately using security list rules. Consider the diagram in Figure 4-14.

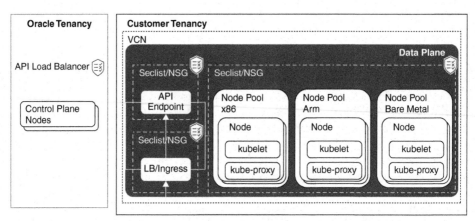

Figure 4-14   Architecture of Network Security Groups and Security Lists

The dashed boundary lines represent security lists or NSGs. Security lists contain rules that govern egress and ingress traffic for the entirety of the subnet. NSGs contain rules that control ingress and egress for traffic on the VNIC for each component, such as the API server endpoint, load balancers, or nodes. In this regard, NSGs offer more fine-grained control at the VNIC level for securing traffic. Regardless of the mechanism used to control ingress and egress traffic, the general recommendation is to use either separate subnets with their own security lists or separate NSGs to secure traffic to the various OKE components. This is because, in most cases, you will need to secure each component differently. For example, you will want to ensure that your public load balancer allows incoming traffic from the Internet, but you wouldn't want to allow external traffic from the Internet to reach your nodes. Having these components in separate subnets or NSGs will make it easy to implement traffic security to meet your needs.

When choosing to place the components in separate subnets, the Kubernetes API endpoint subnet can be small, with room for just three IP addresses. The size of the load balancer subnet depends on how many load balancers you will have within this cluster; this number is generally low, so this subnet can also be relatively small, similar to the Kubernetes APU endpoint subnet. The node subnet, on the other hand, can potentially be large, in case you need to support a fairly large number of nodes within your cluster. You can also have node pools in separate subnets to implement use cases for when you might want isolation at a fundamental level between workloads.

When considering how to set up the ingress and egress rules between these components, the fundamental rules to remember are those outlined in Figure 4-14. They are listed here in a brief form. The complete network ingress and egress rules are detailed in the official documentation.[7]

- The API endpoint should be able to egress to the control plane on port 443, usually over a service gateway.
- The API endpoint should expose 6443 to allow clients to access it. This can be restricted to a specific CIDR or opened to all sources.
- The API endpoint needs to communicate with the worker nodes.
  - TCP ports 6443 and 12250 should be reachable from the nodes or the pod network (when using native pod networking).
  - ICMP 3,4 should be open for ingress and egress between the API endpoint and worker nodes, for path discovery.
- The worker nodes should be able to communicate with the other worker nodes and the pod network (when using native pod networking).
- The worker nodes should also be able to communicate with the control plane and the API endpoint.
- The load balancer should be able to communicate with the worker nodes on the node port range. This rule can be added by the service at runtime when services are annotated to have OKE manage the security list rules on behalf of the application.

Using Compartments to Control Access

OCI compartments can be used effectively to control access to resources. In the case of OKE, you can use compartments to set up various components in separate compartments, to gain fine-grained control over how these resources are accessed and used. For example, you might want to create your network configuration, such as your VCN, subnets, and more, in a specific compartment—for example, a network to which the network engineers have full access but developers have only read access. You might also want to create your nodes in a separate compartment, such as Kubernetes, to which your developers have full access and network engineers have only read access. You can take this concept up a notch by placing each of your node pools into separate compartments. This type of a configuration is particularly attractive for users who run multitenant Software as a Service (SaaS) applications. You can now isolate the workloads of one tenant into a specific node pool and compartment, and create an IAM policy that restricts access to that given compartment—and, thereby, the node pool. You can ensure that pod scheduling respects these boundaries using node taints and tolerations. OCI also offers guidance and automation on bootstrapping environments with predefined and secure isolation models, such as the CIS OCI Landing Zone, which is based on the independent Center for Internet Security (CIS) Foundations Benchmark v1.2 for OCI.

Creating Groups with Limited Access

When starting out with a new service, it is common to rely on superuser privileges. This practice usually gets quicker results because it involves less friction in terms of security controls. However, when teams move from running proof-of-concepts into running production applications, thought should be given to how access control is structured, implemented, and enforced. For instance, consider an organization in which infrastructure management is carried out by a dedicated team and application development is carried out by a development team. When planning access, consider these organizational standards and subdivisions within teams. For example, infrastructure engineers focused on networking require different identity and access than infrastructure engineers focused on image hardening and OS security. Similarly, developers working on the front end of your application don't need the same level of privileges as developers managing your database.

OCI IAM and its policy-driven access model offer several approaches and a flexible way to implement access control, depending on your organizational needs and structure. Access is always denied by default, and policies have an additive effect, making them simple to craft and audit through OCI audit logs and Cloud Guard.

Enabling Image Signature Verification

OKE clusters support image signature verification, which ensures that containers created on the cluster are created from images that have not been tampered with and come unmodified from an authentic source. Images in OCIR can be signed with a master encryption key that you manage. When an image is signed, the signature associates the image to the encryption key used to sign it. You can configure the same encryption key on OKE to verify signatures; during signature verification, OKE uses the key to verify the signature. The signature takes into account the contents of the image and when any of the bits in the image have been manipulated. For example, in a man-in-the-middle attack, signature verification would fail and OKE would refuse to pull the image from OCIR. Image verification includes an additional step of signing the images that you push, but this is a quick and simple operation that can easily be integrated into a build pipeline. Consider the example in Listing 4-22.

Listing 4-22   Example of Using the OCI CLI to Sign and Upload a Container Image to the OCI Registry Service

```
oci artifacts container image-signature sign-upload \
   --compartment-id COMPARTMENT_ID  \
   --kms-key-id KEY_OCID  \
   --kms-key-version-id KEY_VERSION_ID \
   --signing-algorithm ALGORITHM  \ # eg : SHA_224_RSA_PKCS_PSS
   --image-id IMAGE_OCID  \
   --description "Image Signing"
```

This command signs the given image identified by `IMAGE_OCID` with a key and a key version identified by `KEY_OCID` and `KEY_VERSION_OCID`, using the specified algorithm. The algorithm supported by the key is chosen at the time the key is created, and not all algorithms can support a signature. For example, AES keys are symmetric keys that do not support signatures, whereas RSA and ECDSA keys are asymmetric keys that do support it.

With image signature verification enabled, every image that is pulled is then verified for its signature validity. Within your pod spec, you should refer to specific images using their digest value, such as `image_name@sha256:xxxxx`, instead of a transient tag, such as `image_name:latest` or `image_name:1.0.0`. In some emergencies, it might be necessary to "break glass" to deploy an image that would normally fail the signature verification onto a cluster that has the feature enabled. To do this, you use the following policy on the pod spec:

```
oracle.image-policy.k8s.io/break-glass: "true"
```

This allows the cluster to bypass the image verification for this container alone. Needless to say, it is a best practice to have linting enabled for your code repositories and to configure policy check alerts on the audit logs so that the "break glass" function is used only in emergencies and so that alarms are raised when it is.

Encrypting Kubernetes Secrets

A *secret* is an object in Kubernetes that is typically used to store and distribute sensitive data such as passwords, tokens, or configuration information. Secrets are similar to ConfigMaps in how you use them, and they decouple the sensitive information from the application or the container image. Although secrets decouple the application from having to bake sensitive data into the application or the container image, you need to take an informed approach in how your cluster is configured to ensure that secrets are handled and managed safely.

Secrets, like ConfigMaps and most other data that Kubernetes stores, are stored in the *etcd* datastore. etcd runs on the control plane. When you run your own control plane, by default, the data in etcd is stored unencrypted. Anyone with the appropriate API permissions or direct access to etcd can thus access and modify secrets.

When you are using OKE, the control plane is managed by Oracle, and you do not have direct access to it. OKE also manages the etcd datastore for you, and it uses the OCI Block Volume Storage service to persist etcd data. These block volumes are always encrypted, by default, so your secrets, ConfigMaps, and all other Kubernetes objects that are stored in etcd are encrypted at rest. Oracle manages and periodically rotates these encryption keys without any action from you, and this default encryption is always on.

In some scenarios, you might want to bring your own encryption key to encrypt the data in etcd and manage the lifecycle and key rotations yourself. This might be required for compliance reasons or simply because you want to ensure that the data is encrypted with a key that you manage and that Oracle does not have access to. OKE supports this model as well: You can choose to bring your existing keys and store them in the OCI Vault, where you can use them to encrypt the secrets in etcd. This option is available only while creating a cluster, using the Custom Create workflow, and using the APIs and Terraform provider. When you create the cluster, you can choose a Vault and a master encryption key that you have imported to the Vault or generated by yourself. In either case, Oracle does not have access to the key, and you can manage this key.

Note that, when you manage your own keys, if you delete the keys, the secrets encrypted by the key become inaccessible. There is no way to recover the secrets at this point.

When you use your own keys to encrypt secrets in etcd, you might also want to implement key rotation to periodically update the key. When you rotate keys, the key's OCID does not change, but it will have a new value and be considered a new version of the key. Any Kubernetes secret created from that point onward will be encrypted using the new version of the key. Existing secrets will remain encrypted with the old version of the key. This does not introduce any problems, but you have the choice to re-encrypt all the existing secrets as well. For instance, if you suspect that the old key has been compromised, you might want to re-encrypt the existing secrets with the new key. You can re-encrypt the existing secrets in your cluster with the new key using a simple one-line script:

```
kubectl get secrets --all-namespaces -o json | kubectl annotate --overwrite -f
  - encryption-key-rotation-time="<time>"
```

Authorization Using Workload Identity and Instance Principls

When your workload needs to access an OCI API such as read or write from an object storage bucket, you need a way to provide access and permissions to allow this.

This can be achieved using either workload identity or instance principals. These two mechanisms achieve similar goals, but have differences that make them appropriate for specific scenarios. It is important to understand the security implications of choosing one method over the other so that you choose the right approach for any given situation.

Using Instance Principals

Instance principals are a powerful feature in OCI that confers identity and permissions to any compute instance in OCI, including OKE worker nodes. When a compute instance that has been given certain privileges is running a workload, the workload is allowed to interact with the OCI APIs using the credentials and permissions allowed for that instance. In the case of OKE, any of the pods running on such a node can call OCI APIs. Although the scheduler can be influenced to ensure that only selective workloads are running on a node, using this feature with OKE leads to a less than ideal governance model. If a running pod has a vulnerability that lets a malicious user gain access to a workload, the attacker can then leverage the instance principals to perform deeper actions and cause further damage. To use instance principals, you need to create a *dynamic group* that selects a set of compute instances based on *matching criteria*. After the dynamic group is created, you can create an OCI IAM policy that grants permissions to this dynamic group. Consider the following example that defines a dynamic group with a matching criterion:

```
All {instance.compartment.id='<COMPARTMENT_ID>', tag.projectA.env.value='prod'}
```

This dynamic group selects all instances in the compartment with the ID COMPARTMENT_ID and further narrows the instances selected using a tag. Assume that there is a tag namespace of projectA and a tag key named env. The matching rule in the previous example selects all instances that have this tag with the value set to prod. It can be assumed that all nodes that belong to projectA's prod environment may carry this tag. Therefore, the dynamic group would select all of projectA's instances in a given compartment with the projectA.env tag set to prod.

With the dynamic group created, all that remains to be done is to create an IAM policy that gives this dynamic group access to the required OCI resources. Consider the following example:

```
Allow dynamic-group projectA-prod to use buckets in compartment ProjectA
```

This policy allows members of the dynamic group named projectA-prod, which are the instances selected by the matching criteria of the dynamic group, to use object storage buckets that are in the compartment called projectA.

This approach is valid when all the workloads or applications that may run on these instances are trusted. For Kubernetes nodes, this might not be a good general-purpose solution because the applications that are running on this node are not entirely predictable. Take care to ensure that untrusted workloads or applications are not started on nodes because this could abuse the privileges conferred on the nodes. Of course, you can control node scheduling with features such as node affinity, taints and tolerations, or custom schedulers; however, those use cases are generally the exception, not the norm.

Using Workload Identity

For most workloads that need to access OCI APIs, such as to read/write to an object storage bucket, as in the previous example, the preferred approach is to implement workload identity. Workload identity is a feature that enables you to provide access and permissions to your workloads running as pods on OKE. Pods with a specific service account, in a specific cluster, and in a specific Kubernetes namespace are selected and can be given permissions to access OCI APIs. OCI IAM defines a workload resource with this combination of cluster, namespace, and service account. You can write policy statements using these variables to allow a workload access to OCI resources. Applications can then use the OCI SDK and the new OKE authentication provider that authenticates the API calls simply based on the workload's identity, which is defined by service account, namespace, and cluster. Figure 4-15 illustrates the different components of the workload identity architecture, including adding the OCI SDK to customer code that is then deployed to the cluster as a pod.

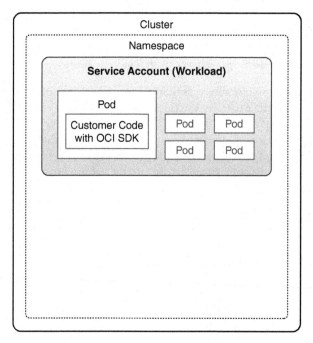

Figure 4-15   Workload Identity Architecture Showing Where a Customer Uses the OCI SDK to Enable Workloads to Authenticate to OCI IAM

This approach considerably narrows the access and ensures that principles of least access are upheld. If Kubernetes moves the pod around multiple nodes in the cluster, access is uninterrupted because the identity rests with the workload (identified by service account, namespace, and cluster), not the instance where the pod runs. This also enables you to control what applications have access to what OCI APIs, unlike with instance principals, which are inherited by any workload that is running on the given instance. Using OCI IAM policies to manage access also ensures a consistent way of managing and auditing access throughout OCI. API requests made using the workload identity are tracked in OCI audit and can be used to satisfy compliance requirements or to monitor for access violations and suspicious activity.

To use workload identity, you need the typical Kubernetes resources, such as namespaces and service accounts.

Create a namespace for your application if one already does not exist. This creates a boundary for your application, and you deploy your pods and other resources within this namespace. Consider the following example that creates a namespace called my-app:

```
kubectl create namespace my-app
```

Create a service account that the pods of the application can use. Pods that are part of your workload will use this service account to run. These service accounts can also be used to enable Kubernetes RBAC for the pod. Consider the following example, which creates a service account named my-app-sa in the namespace my-app:

```
kubectl create serviceaccount my-app-sa \
--namespace my-app
```

The application pods deployed to the my-app namespace should now use this my-app-sa service account when running. This can be set in the pod spec, as demonstrated in Listing 4-23.

Listing 4-23   Manifest Used to Create a Pod That Uses the my-app-sa Service Account

```
apiVersion: v1
kind: Pod
metadata:
  name: my-application
spec:
serviceAccountName: my-app-sa
automountServiceAccountToken: true
containers:
  - name: my-application
    image: my-application:1.0.0
    ports:
    - containerPort: 8080
```

Define an IAM policy to grant the workload resource access to other OCI resources. As with other IAM policies, the policy defines what permissions are granted to the principal. Consider the example in Listing 4-24, which shows a policy that checks the incoming request to ensure that it meets the criteria for the workload identity, the combination of service account, namespace, and cluster ID. Processes that are running in pods with the service account `my-app-sa`, that are running within the `my-app` namespace, and that are in a cluster with a specified `CLUSTER_OCID` are allowed to use object storage buckets in the compartment named `ProjectA`.

Listing 4-24   Example OCI IAM Policy Used to Grant the Target Workload Access to OCI Resources

```
Allow any-user to use buckets in compartment ProjectA where all {
request.principal.type = 'workload',
request.principal.namespace = 'my-app',
request.principal.service_account = 'my-app-sa',
request.principal.cluster_id = 'CLUSTER_OCID'}
```

With the service account and the IAM policy in place, for the workload to access OCI (for example, to use the object storage APIs as indicated in the policy), it needs to use the OKE workload identity provider. Consider the example in Listing 4-25 using the OCI Java SDK.

Listing 4-25   Example of Using the OCI Java SDK to Enable a Workload to Access OCI IAM

```
[...]
final OkeWorkloadIdentityAuthenticationDetailsProvider provider = new
  OkeWorkloadIdentityAuthenticationDetailsProvider
        .OkeWorkloadIdentityAuthenticationDetailsProviderBuilder()
        .build();
    /* create the client using the workload identity provider */
    ObjectStorage osClient =
            ObjectStorageClient.builder().region(Region.US_PHOENIX_1).
  build(provider);
[...]
```

At runtime, when the API call is made, the OKE authentication provider validates the workload identity (service account, namespace, and cluster) and issues a short-lived resource token from the OCI identity service. For most workloads, this approach offers a secure method of accessing OCI APIs without having to grant access too widely or having to manage credentials as secrets that need to be rotated and managed.

Securing Access to the Cluster

Clients interact with Kubernetes through the APIs exposed by the API server. This includes interactions for basic actions such as creating a pod, or more complex ones such as deploying an operator. When a client interacts with the API server, the client is authenticated using the credentials that it provides. On OKE, the default method for a client such as `kubectl` to authenticate with the API server is to use a short-lived token.

Once authenticated, the client credentials are subjected to authorization checks using role-based access control (RBAC). OKE clusters have RBAC enabled by default. RBAC in Kubernetes lets you implement fine-grained access control using the standard Kubernetes roles and RoleBindings. Roles and RoleBindings are bound to namespaces, while `ClusterRoles` and `ClusterRoleBindings` are valid across the cluster. A role represents a set of permissions that allow actions on a set of resources and API groups— for example, allowing the `get` and `list` verbs on the pods resource in the core API group. A set of default Kubernetes `ClusterRole` and `ClusterRoleBinding` objects, such as the `cluster-admin` ClusterRole, is created along with the cluster. Many of the default ClusterRoles and ClusterRoleBindings are prefixed with `system:`, indicating that these are created and managed by the cluster control plane.

OCI IAM and Kubernetes RBAC

OKE comes preconfigured with an authorizer that integrates with OCI IAM. For example, OKE considers anyone in the OCI IAM `Administrators` group to be a Kubernetes `cluster-admin` as well. However, you can—and should—create more fine-grained access policies using `Roles` and `RoleBindings` as a best practice. This way, you can maintain and manage appropriate access while maintaining principles of least access. Because the OKE Authorizer integrates Kubernetes RBAC with OCI IAM, it becomes easy to create and manage `RoleBindings` that associate OCI IAM groups and users to Kubernetes roles.

As an example, consider two users, Bob and Bill. Bob is a member of the `Administrators` group in OCI IAM, and Bill is a member of the `Developers` group in OCI IAM. Bill wants to get full privileges to create and manage Kubernetes resources, but only in the ProjectA namespace. By default, Bob has full access to the cluster, whereas Bill has no access. The first step that you might consider for giving Bill access to the cluster would be to add the group `Developers` to an IAM policy that lets the group members use OKE clusters:

```
Allow group Developers to use clusters in compartment <compartment_name>
```

This grants the members of the `Developers` group, including Bill, the `CLUSTER_USE` permission. Next, you can create a `RoleBinding` in the `ProjectA` namespace that binds the `cluster-admin` ClusterRole to the `Developers` group. This can be done with a `RoleBinding`, as demonstrated in Listing 4-26.

Listing 4-26   Example Manifest Used to Create a Cluster Role Binding That Maps an OCI IAM Group to a Kubernetes Role

```
apiVersion: rbac.authorization.k8s.io/v1
kind: RoleBinding
metadata:
  name: namespace-admin
```

```
    namespace: projectA
subjects:
- kind: Group
  name: [OCID_for_the_Developers_IAM_group]
  apiGroup: rbac.authorization.k8s.io
roleRef:
  kind: ClusterRole
  name: cluster-admin
  apiGroup: rbac.authorization.k8s.io
```

By creating this RoleBinding, you have associated or granted the cluster-admin ClusterRole to the Developers IAM group by providing the group's OCID. Because you created a RoleBinding and not a ClusterRoleBinding, it grants the cluster-admin privileges to the Developers group only in the ProjectA namespace, not across the cluster. With the RoleBinding in place, and because Bill is a member of the Developers group, when he tries to perform an operation such as creating a pod, he is able to do so because the authorizer will allow this request based on his IAM group memberships. Similar to the example here, you can also create a ClusterRoleBinding instead of a RoleBinding, and you can replace the subjects.kind: Group with a subjects.kind: User to bind the role to a single IAM user instead of a group.

Federation with an IDP

The integration between OCI IAM and Kubernetes RBAC can extend to federated identities and groups as well. OCI IAM supports federation with identity providers that adhere to the Security Assertion Markup Language (SAML) 2.0 protocol. Federation enables enterprises to integrate their existing identity provider (IdP) with OCI. Once configured, users can log into OCI and use their existing enterprise usernames and passwords through their familiar single sign-on (SSO) login page. When administrators set up federation in OCI IAM with an IdP, they map the existing groups from the IdP to OCI IAM groups. When creating RoleBinding and ClusterRoleBindings, you can continue to use the OCID for the OCI IAM group to which the IdP group has been mapped. When changes to group memberships occur on the IdP—for example, Bob moved from the Developers group to the SiteReliability group—these changes are synchronized to the mapped groups as well and will correctly reflect the access given to the users by virtue of their group memberships.

Summary

This chapter introduced Container Engine for Kubernetes (OKE). You looked at the basic terminology for the service, including what constitutes the control plane and data plane, and you examined ways to create a new cluster and automate that process. This chapter also introduced the various Kubernetes networking models that are available for use with OKE and storage features that are integrated with various OCI storage services through the Kubernetes persistent volume mechanism. This was followed by a discussion on load balancer support and various configurations to support a wide array of workload types. Additionally, you examined the cluster topology configurations and security considerations, including setting up security rules for various methods of access control. Finally, the chapter discussed ways to secure access to the cluster, including integrating Kubernetes RBAC with OCI IAM and configuring identity federation with an external identity provider (IdP).

References

1 All Image Families: https://docs.oracle.com/en-us/iaas/images/
2 oci_containerengine_cluster: https://registry.terraform.io/providers/oracle/oci/latest/docs/resources/containerengine_cluster
3 oci_containerengine_node_pool: https://registry.terraform.io/providers/oracle/oci/latest/docs/resources/containerengine_node_pool
4 Data source: oci_containerengine_clusters: https://registry.terraform.io/providers/oracle/oci/latest/docs/data-sources/containerengine_clusters
5 Terraform OKE for Oracle Cloud Infrastructure: https://registry.terraform.io/modules/oracle-terraform-modules/oke/oci/latest
6 Load balancer annotations: https://github.com/oracle/oci-cloud-controller-manager/blob/master/docs/load-balancer-annotations.md
7 Security Rule Configuration in Network Security Groups and/or Security Lists: https://docs.oracle.com/en-us/iaas/Content/ContEng/Concepts/contengnetworkconfig.htm#securitylistconfig

Container Engine for Kubernetes in Practice

Container Engine for Kubernetes in OCI enables you to quickly get started with Kubernetes. However, managing a fleet of clusters or a large cluster with several node pools and multitenant workloads running on it can be a bigger challenge than getting started. Owning a cluster also involves planning for and executing routine activities such as patching and upgrading. The burden imposed by these activities also varies by the node pool type. For instance, when using a managed node pool, you have direct control over the underlying node operating system and are responsible for keeping the operating system up to date. On the other hand, when using virtual nodes, the infrastructure is fully managed by Oracle; the user simply triggers an upgrade process at a desired time. Your runbooks for managing cluster components therefore will vary, depending on the specific configuration of your cluster. You might also need to leverage third-party software and use custom configurations to go beyond the defaults provided by the service. This chapter examines the processes and best practices for managing your clusters, integrating with third-party products and services, and using customized infrastructure configurations for your cluster components.

You can view the clusters created in your tenancy by opening the navigation menu in the console and clicking **Developer Services**. Under **Containers & Artifacts**, click **Kubernetes Clusters (OKE)**. Then choose a compartment. You will see the names, statuses, number of node pools, VCN, Kubernetes version, and creation date of all clusters in that compartment and region, as illustrated in Figure 5-1. This overview page is useful for keeping track of the high-level status of your clusters. Clusters running Kubernetes versions earlier than the latest available version display a warning indicating that upgrading to the latest version is recommended. From this page, you can jump directly to the Cluster Details page of a specific cluster by clicking the name of the cluster in the **Name** column. Similarly, you can jump directly to the node pool and VCN pages by clicking on the name in the **Node Pool** and **VCN** columns, respectively.

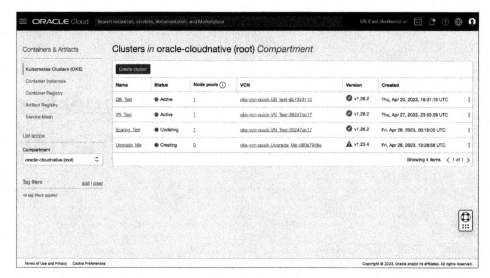

Figure 5-1   Clusters of Varying Statuses and Kubernetes Versions on the Clusters Page of the OCI Console

Kubernetes Version Support

The upstream Kubernetes project is constantly evolving. Changes made to the project are referred to as *enhancements*. The Kubernetes project loosely defines enhancements as a change that a blog would be written about, that needs significant effort or changes Kubernetes in a significant way, or that users will notice or come to rely on. Enhancements are introduced in new minor versions that are typically released every four months. Patches to address bugs are released monthly or, if needed, more frequently, and are cut from the most recent three minor release branches maintained by the upstream Kubernetes project. Kubernetes versions are expressed as $x.y.z$, where x is the major version, y is the minor version, and z is the patch version.

Oracle Container Engine for Kubernetes (OKE) generally supports three versions of Kubernetes at a given time. For a minimum of 30 days after the announcement of support for a new Kubernetes version, OKE continues to support the oldest of the three Kubernetes versions that were previously available. After that time, the oldest Kubernetes version ceases to be supported. When creating a new OKE cluster, it is recommended that you use the most recent Kubernetes version available. When OKE supports a new Kubernetes version, it is recommended that you upgrade existing clusters to use that new Kubernetes version as soon as possible. OKE will not forcibly upgrade clusters if they become unsupported. If your clusters are running an unsupported version, you will be able to upgrade both the control plane and the data plane through unsupported versions to reach a supported one.

Because Kubernetes includes a control plane and a data plane, upgrading a cluster must be done in two parts. The control plane nodes and worker nodes that comprise the cluster can run different versions of Kubernetes, provided that you follow the Kubernetes version skew support policy detailing the maximum supported difference in versions between each component of a cluster. For example, kubectl is supported within one minor version, either older or newer, of the Kubernetes API server. The Kubernetes control plane must be upgraded before the data plane.

Upgrading the Control Plane

You upgrade control plane nodes by upgrading the cluster and specifying a more recent Kubernetes version for the cluster. Control plane nodes running older versions of Kubernetes are upgraded. Because Container Engine for Kubernetes distributes the Kubernetes control plane on multiple Oracle-managed control plane nodes to ensure high availability (distributed across different availability domains in multi-AD regions where this is possible), you're able to upgrade the Kubernetes version running on control plane nodes with zero downtime to the Kubernetes API. The steps for upgrading the control plane are as follows:

Step 1. In the OCI Console, open the navigation menu and click **Developer Services**.

Step 2. Under Containers & Artifacts, click **Kubernetes Clusters (OKE)**.

Step 3. From the Compartment drop-down menu, choose a compartment that contains a cluster you have permission to upgrade.

Step 4. The Version column displays the Kubernetes version of each cluster. Clusters running older versions display a warning stating, "Upgrading to the latest version is recommended." Click the name of the cluster you want to upgrade.

Step 5. On the Cluster Details page, if a newer Kubernetes version than the one running on the control plane nodes in the cluster is available (see Figure 5-2), the Upgrade Available button is enabled at the top of the page.

Step 6. Click **Upgrade Available** and select the Kubernetes version to which you want to upgrade the control plane nodes (see Figure 5-3). Keep in mind that, after you upgrade your cluster control plane, it cannot be downgraded.

Step 7. Click **Upgrade** to apply the update to your cluster.

Step 8. After you click Upgrade, you will see the status of the cluster change to Updating. You can track the status of the upgrade by clicking the **Work Requests** tab and then clicking the work request to open the Work Requests Details page. When the process is complete, the work request status moves from In Progress to Succeeded and the control plane nodes will be running the newer Kubernetes version. From that point on, the new Kubernetes version will appear as an option when defining node pools parameters.

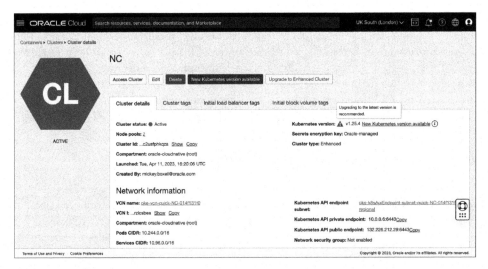

Figure 5-2 Cluster Details Page with a Recommendation to Upgrade to the Latest Available Kubernetes Version

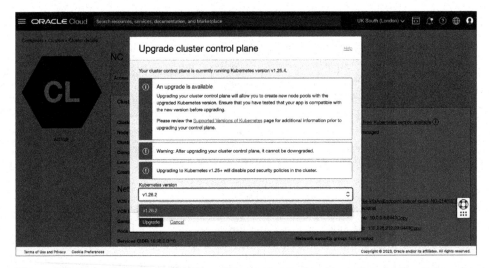

Figure 5-3 Upgrade Cluster Control Plane Window That Enables You to Select a New Kubernetes Version for Your Control Plane

You can update the cluster control plane using the CLI by passing in the OCID of the cluster you want to upgrade and the Kubernetes version you want to upgrade to:

```
oci ce cluster update --cluster-id <cluster-ocid> --kubernetes-version
  <kubernetes-version-number>
```

If you want to upgrade to a version of Kubernetes that is more than one version ahead of the version currently running on the control plane nodes, you *must* upgrade to each intermediate version in sequence, without skipping versions. Skipping minor versions while upgrading a control plane is not supported by OKE or the upstream Kubernetes project.

Upgrading the Data Plane

Following the upgrade of your control plane to a new version of Kubernetes, you can create worker nodes running the newer version as well. Alternatively, you can continue to create nodes running older versions of Kubernetes, as long as the older versions are compatible with the control plane Kubernetes version. As long as you follow the Kubernetes version skew support policy described in the Kubernetes documentation, the control plane nodes and worker nodes that comprise the cluster can run different versions of Kubernetes. Each component of a cluster has its own skew policy, and the official Kubernetes documentation should be treated as the ultimate source of truth when it comes to compatibility. Generally, worker nodes are expected to function without issue as long as their kubelet version is within two minor versions of the control plane. For example, the worker node version for a 1.26 control plane should be 1.26, 1.25, or 1.24.

When it comes to upgrading worker nodes, OKE recommends following the approach of the upstream Kubernetes project by treating nodes as "cattle, not pets." For those unfamiliar, this phrase is used to describe an environment in which you should consider your resources as easily replaceable as opposed to something you would feel distressed about losing. In this context, that means that rather than updating the kubelet on existing worker node hosts, you should terminate the instance and replace it with one running the updated Kubernetes version. This approach applies to the host OS version and other node pool properties as well. Given this recommendation, you can choose one of two paths: upgrading an existing node pool or creating a new node pool.

OKE enables you to define the properties of a node pool, including Kubernetes version, host image, shape, and more, which are then passed down to all the nodes in a pool. This also allows you to update the properties of a node pool. Any node created after the properties are updated will come online with the updated properties. For example, if you change the node pool's Kubernetes version to the latest available Kubernetes version, only nodes created after the change is made will come online with the new version. Existing nodes will continue to run the previous Kubernetes version. The same is true for the other properties of the node pool. The question becomes, how do you move workloads from nodes running the old properties to nodes running the new ones: little by little or all at once?

Upgrading an Existing Node Pool

Upgrading an existing node pool provides you with a mechanism for moving workloads little by little. The approach is useful for users who lack extra capacity or prefer to keep costs low. This approach enables you to sequentially replace as few as one node at a time by adding nodes to a node pool or taking existing nodes offline as you incrementally move work to newly created ones that possess new parameters. You begin by specifying a more recent Kubernetes version for the existing node pool. Then you delete each worker node. OKE allows you to select cordon and drain options, which prevents new pods from starting on the target node or nodes and deleting existing pods, respectively. You can specify to have a new worker node be created to take the place of each worker node that you delete, to ensure that the node pool matches the desired node pool size. All new worker nodes starting in the pool will be running the more recent Kubernetes version you specified. Depending on your availability requirements, you can choose to scale the desired size of the node pool before you terminate nodes, to limit service disruptions. A larger capacity of nodes to run your workloads means more space for pods to be scheduled, as well as a lower likelihood of pods left unscheduled. We recommend leveraging pod disruption budgets for your application to ensure that a sufficient number of replica pods is running throughout the deletion operation. Pod disruption budgets limit the number of instances of your application that can be down at the same time because of a voluntary disruption. The steps for upgrading an existing node pool are as follows:

Step 1. In the OCI Console, open the navigation menu and click **Developer Services**. Under Containers & Artifacts, click **Kubernetes Clusters (OKE)**.

Step 2. On the Cluster List page, choose a compartment and click the name of the cluster where you want to change the Kubernetes version of the worker nodes.

Step 3. On the Cluster Details page, select the **Node Pools** tab. This tab shows the current Kubernetes version of the node pool(s). Click the name of the node pool whose nodes you want to upgrade.

Step 4. On the Node Pool Details page, click **Edit** and, in the Version field, specify the Kubernetes version required for your worker nodes (see Figure 5-4). Keep in mind that the Kubernetes version you specify must be compatible with the version that is running on the control plane nodes. In the case of OKE images (a worker node image type optimized for use with OKE clusters), under Image, you need to click **Change Image** and, with **OKE Worker Node Images** selected as your Image Source, choose an image that matches the updated Kubernetes version. Click **Select Image**.

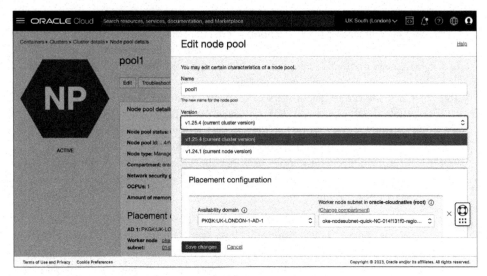

Figure 5-4   Edit Node Pool Panel, Which Enables You to Modify the Properties of an Existing Node Pool—in This Case, by Selecting a New Kubernetes Version

Step 5.   Click **Save Changes** to save the change.

Step 6.   You must now delete existing worker nodes so that new worker nodes are started with the new Kubernetes version. For the first worker node in the node pool, on the Node Pool page, display the Nodes tab and select **Delete Node** from the Actions menu beside the node you want to delete. Either accept the defaults for advanced options or click **Show Advanced Options** and specify the alternatives, as follows:

- **Eviction Grace Period (Mins):** The length of time allowed for nodes to be cordoned and drained before termination. Either accept the default of 60 minutes or specify an alternative value between 0 and 60. To skip cordoning and draining worker nodes, specify 0 minutes.

- **Force Terminate After Grace Period:** The instruction on whether to terminate worker nodes at the end of the specified eviction grace period, even if they have not been successfully cordoned and drained. Select this option if you want worker nodes terminated at the end of the eviction grace period, regardless of whether they have been successfully cordoned and drained. Deselect this option if you want to preserve worker nodes that have not been successfully cordoned and drained by the end of the eviction grace period. Node pools containing worker nodes that fail to be terminated within the specified eviction grace period have the Needs Attention status. The status of the work request that initiated the termination operation will be set to Failed, and the termination operation will be cancelled.

- **Do Not Decrease Node Pool Size:** The option to maintain the current size of the node pool. By default, the size of the node pool will be decremented by one after a node is terminated, and a new node will not come online. To ensure that a new node running the updated Kubernetes version comes online, select this option.

Step 7.   Click **Delete** to delete the worker node. A work request is launched to delete the worker node. You can track the status of the work request by navigating to the Work Requests tab of the Node Pool Details page and choosing the appropriate work request from the Work Requests table.

Step 8.   Repeat the previous step for each remaining worker node in the node pool until all worker nodes in the node pool are running the desired Kubernetes version.

As an alternative to steps 6–8, you can use the OKE on-demand node cycling feature. This feature provides a one-click operation to replace existing nodes with updated nodes. To minimize service disruption, you can specify a maximum number of additional nodes that can be added to the node pool during an upgrade, referred to as `max-surge`. Increasing `max-surge` raises the number of nodes that can be upgraded simultaneously. To account for budget and capacity constraints, you specify a maximum number of nodes that can become unavailable at a given time during an upgrade. Increasing the `max-unavailable` value raises the number of nodes that can be upgraded in parallel in a single node pool. When using `max-unavailable`, nodes will be cordoned/drained based on the node pool's `evictionGracePeriod` and terminated before a new node comes online, to avoid extra costs.

Step 6.   After you save the changes to the node pool parameters in step 5, navigate to the Node Pool Details page and click **Cycle Nodes**.

Step 7.   On the page shown in Figure 5-5, specify a value for **Maximum Surge**, the number of nodes that can be upgraded simultaneously. This value can be an integer or a percentage. This value cannot be greater than the total number of nodes currently running in the pool.

Step 8.   Specify a value for **Maximum Unavailable**, the number of nodes that can simultaneously become unavailable. This value can be an integer or a percentage. This value cannot be greater than the total number of nodes currently running in the pool.

Step 9.   Click **Cycle Nodes** to replace all the nodes in your node pool. A work request is launched to cycle the worker nodes. You can track the status of the work request by navigating to the Work Requests tab of the Node Pool Details page and choosing the appropriate work request from the Work Requests table.

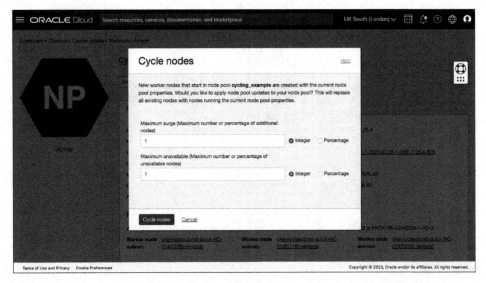

Figure 5-5   The Cycle Nodes Window on the Node Pool Details Page Gives You the Ability to
Cycle the Nodes in Your Node Pool

Upgrading by Adding a Node Pool

Another option for updating nodes in your cluster is to create an additional node pool
and move workloads from your existing pool to the newly created one. This approach
requires capacity to create a second node pool of the same size as your original node
pool. The steps to do this are as follows:

Step 1.   In the OCI console, open the navigation menu and click **Developer
Services**. Under Containers & Artifacts, click **Kubernetes Clusters
(OKE)**.

Step 2.   On the Cluster List page, choose a compartment and click the name of the
cluster where you want to change the Kubernetes version of the worker
nodes.

Step 3.   On the Cluster Details page, select the **Node Pools** tab. This tab shows the
current Kubernetes version of the node pool(s). Click **Add Node Pool** to
create a new node pool with your desired parameters.

Step 4.   On the Add Node Pool panel (see Figure 5-6), in the Version field, specify
the Kubernetes version required for your worker nodes. Keep in mind that
the Kubernetes version you specify must be compatible with the version that
is running on the control plane nodes. In the case of OKE images, a worker
node image type optimized for use with OKE clusters, under Image, you

need to click **Change Image** and then, with OKE Worker Node Images selected as your image source, choose an image that matches the updated Kubernetes version. Click **Select Image**. Fill out the rest of the node pool parameters with your desired values.

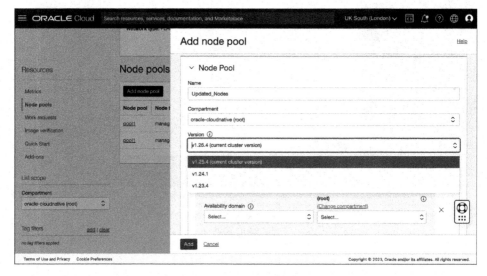

Figure 5-6   The Add Node Pool Panel, Which Enables You to Add a New Node Pool with Your Chosen Options to Your Existing Cluster

Step 5.   Click **Add** to create the new node pool.

Step 6.   A work request is launched to delete the worker node. You can track the status of the work request by navigating to the Work Requests tab of the Node Pool Details page and choosing the appropriate work request from the Work Requests table.

Step 7.   After the new node pool becomes active and the nodes in the new node pool become ready, you can begin to shift work from one pool to the other. To do so, for the first worker node in the original node pool, prevent new pods from starting on a node by entering **kubectl cordon <*node_name*>**. You can do this for multiple nodes in parallel using a label selector. To do so, label the nodes in your node pool and then enter **kubectl drain --selector <*your_node_pool_label*>**. After cordoning your nodes, you can delete pods running on those nodes by entering **kubectl drain <*node_name*>**. This can also be done in parallel by entering: **kubectl drain --selector <*your_node_ pool_label*>**.

Step 8.   When you have drained all the worker nodes from the original node pool and pods are running on worker nodes in the new node pool, you can delete the original node pool. On the Cluster Details page, click the **Node Pools** tab and then select **Delete Node Pool** from the Actions menu beside the original node pool.

Step 9.   A work request is launched to delete the node pool. You can track the status of the work request by navigating to the Work Requests tab of the Node Pool Details page and choosing the appropriate work request from the Work Requests table.

Alternative Host OS (Not Kubernetes Version) Upgrade Options

Although we advocate for an immutable infrastructure approach in which nodes are terminated and re-created instead of being updated in place, it is possible to update existing nodes in place. This approach might be preferred for stateful workloads that are complicated or time-consuming to reschedule.

One option is to connect to your worker nodes using SSH and run a YUM update as you would with any OS to ensure that it is patched. If a reboot is required, drain your pods off that node while rebooting (or just let Kubernetes [k8s] reschedule them—no additional capacity is needed during upgrade).

Run the os-updater tool on your worker nodes. If a reboot is required, drain your pods off that node while rebooting (or just let Kubernetes reschedule them). No additional capacity is needed during an upgrade.

Scaling a Cluster

Scaling OKE clusters occurs differently for the control plane and the data plane. The OKE platform scales the control plane nodes without the need for you to intervene.

Manual Scaling

The number of virtual nodes and managed nodes in a cluster can be scaled manually by specifying a new value for the node count property of the node pool or by adding more node pools with nodes to the cluster. When you increase or decrease the node count in the node pool, the service creates or destroys the required number of nodes to converge onto the new node count set on the node pool. When performing scale-up operations, the service respects the placement configuration provided on the node pool, and the nodes that are created have the most up-to-date configuration of that node pool. For instance, if you updated any of the node pool properties (for example, the cloud-init script), the updated configuration is applied to the new nodes that are created. Manual scaling can be performed using the OCI console, Terraform automation, the OCI CLI, or the APIs directly. You can scale applications manually by updating manifest files. Figure 5-7 shows the window in the Node Pool Details page that can be used to specify a new desired size for your node pool, as well as to define placement configurations used to control the distribution of nodes across availability domains and fault domains.

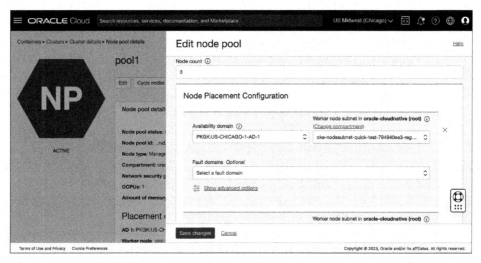

Figure 5-7   Use the Edit Node Pool Page to Specify a New Desired Size for Your Node Pool and Define Placement Configurations Used to Control the Distribution of Nodes Across Availability Domains and Fault Domains

Autoscaling

To optimize resources, you can automatically scale at the node and pod levels of your cluster. Autoscaling at the node level is accomplished by deploying the Kubernetes Cluster Autoscaler. Autoscaling at the pod level is accomplished by deploying the Kubernetes Metrics Server to collect resource metrics from each worker node in the cluster and then deploying either the Kubernetes HorizontalPodAutoscaler (HPA), which is used to adjust the number of pods in a deployment, or the Kubernetes Vertical Pod Autoscaler (VPA), which is used to adjust the resource requests and limits for containers running in a deployment's pods. Kubernetes resource requests are values specified when creating pods to control the resources (for example CPU and memory) guaranteed for a given container. The scheduler takes these values into account when deciding which node to schedule your workloads onto. Kubernetes resource limits are also specified when creating pods and are used to ensure a cap on the resources used by a given container. You will see examples of both resource management tools when we discuss VPA in the "Vertical Pod Autoscaler" section of this chapter.

Autoscaling the data plane depends on the type of nodes chosen for your node pools. In the case of virtual nodes, scaling data plane capacity based on workload demands is largely done for you. Infrastructure-level scaling of a virtual node pool is managed by OKE, which means that the underlying infrastructure capacity is scaled automatically and there is no need to use the Kubernetes Cluster Autoscaler. You can use the Kubernetes

Cluster Autoscaler and the Kubernetes Vertical Pod Autoscaler with managed node pools only. You can use the Kubernetes Metrics Server and the Kubernetes HorizontalPodAutoscaler with both virtual node pools and managed node pools.

Cluster Autoscaler

You can use the Kubernetes Cluster Autoscaler to automatically resize the number of nodes in managed node pools based on workload demands. Resizing enables you to ensure the availability of your application and optimize costs. The Kubernetes Cluster Autoscaler adds worker nodes to a node pool when a pod cannot be scheduled in the cluster because of resource constraints; it removes worker nodes from a node pool when nodes have been underutilized for a given period of time and when pods can be rescheduled on other nodes.

Note

The Cluster Autoscaler scales the number of nodes in a node pool based on resource requests instead of the resource utilization of nodes in the node pool.

The Kubernetes Cluster Autoscaler is configured per node pool using a configuration file that specifies the node pools to target for expansion and contraction. The Cluster Autoscaler manages only node pools referenced in the configuration file. The file also enables you to specify the minimum and maximum sizes for each node pool, in addition to other settings. Because the Cluster Autoscaler itself runs on nodes in your cluster, it is important to ensure that at least one node pool in a cluster is not managed by the Kubernetes Cluster Autoscaler, to avoid a situation in which all Cluster Autoscaler nodes are evicted and cannot be rescheduled. This is also a good reason to ensure that you configure the Cluster Autoscaler deployment to have multiple replicas.

Keep in mind that although the Cluster Autoscaler is managing the capacity of your node pools, you should avoid manually changing the size of node pools or managing them using another tool, such as Terraform; the different capacity management systems will conflict as they try to reconcile one another's changes to reach different desired states.

Using the Cluster Autoscaler

Before using the Cluster Autoscaler, you must configure the identity and access management policies to allow the Cluster Autoscaler to add and remove nodes from your node pools. To do so, follow these steps:

Step 1.   Create a dynamic group to contain the node pools that you want to manage with the Cluster Autoscaler, and add a rule to the group that includes all instances in the compartment that you plan to manage with the Cluster Autoscaler: `ALL {instance.compartment.id = '<compartment-ocid>'}`.

Step 2. Next, create a policy to allow worker nodes to manage node pools:

```
Allow dynamic-group acme-oke-cluster-autoscaler-dyn-grp to manage
cluster-node-pools in compartment <compartment-name>

Allow dynamic-group acme-oke-cluster-autoscaler-dyn-grp to manage
instance-family in compartment <compartment-name>

Allow dynamic-group acme-oke-cluster-autoscaler-dyn-grp to use subnets
in compartment <compartment-name>

Allow dynamic-group acme-oke-cluster-autoscaler-dyn-grp to read
virtual-network-family in compartment <compartment-name>

Allow dynamic-group acme-oke-cluster-autoscaler-dyn-grp to use vnics in
compartment <compartment-name>

Allow dynamic-group acme-oke-cluster-autoscaler-dyn-grp to inspect
compartments in compartment <compartment-name>
```

Replace `<dynamic-group-name>` with the name of the dynamic group you created earlier, and replace `<compartment-name>` with the name of the compartment in which the cluster belongs.

Step 3. Copy the Cluster Autoscaler configuration file, and edit it to apply to your node pools.

Step 4. Create a file called `cluster-autoscaler.yaml` with the following contents:

```
---
apiVersion: v1
kind: ServiceAccount
metadata:
  labels:
    k8s-addon: cluster-autoscaler.addons.k8s.io
    k8s-app: cluster-autoscaler
  name: cluster-autoscaler
  namespace: kube-system
---
apiVersion: rbac.authorization.k8s.io/v1
kind: ClusterRole
metadata:
  name: cluster-autoscaler
  labels:
    k8s-addon: cluster-autoscaler.addons.k8s.io
    k8s-app: cluster-autoscaler
rules:
  - apiGroups: [""]
    resources: ["events", "endpoints"]
    verbs: ["create", "patch"]
```

```
- apiGroups: [""]
  resources: ["pods/eviction"]
  verbs: ["create"]
- apiGroups: [""]
  resources: ["pods/status"]
  verbs: ["update"]
- apiGroups: [""]
  resources: ["endpoints"]
  resourceNames: ["cluster-autoscaler"]
  verbs: ["get", "update"]
- apiGroups: [""]
  resources: ["nodes"]
  verbs: ["watch", "list", "get", "patch", "update"]
- apiGroups: [""]
  resources:
    - "pods"
    - "services"
    - "replicationcontrollers"
    - "persistentvolumeclaims"
    - "persistentvolumes"
  verbs: ["watch", "list", "get"]
- apiGroups: ["extensions"]
  resources: ["replicasets", "daemonsets"]
  verbs: ["watch", "list", "get"]
- apiGroups: ["policy"]
  resources: ["poddisruptionbudgets"]
  verbs: ["watch", "list"]
- apiGroups: ["apps"]
  resources: ["statefulsets", "replicasets", "daemonsets"]
  verbs: ["watch", "list", "get"]
- apiGroups: ["storage.k8s.io"]
  resources: ["storageclasses", "csinodes"]
  verbs: ["watch", "list", "get"]
- apiGroups: ["batch", "extensions"]
  resources: ["jobs"]
  verbs: ["get", "list", "watch", "patch"]
- apiGroups: ["coordination.k8s.io"]
  resources: ["leases"]
```

```
        verbs: ["create"]
    - apiGroups: ["coordination.k8s.io"]
      resourceNames: ["cluster-autoscaler"]
      resources: ["leases"]
      verbs: ["get", "update"]
---
apiVersion: rbac.authorization.k8s.io/v1
kind: Role
metadata:
  name: cluster-autoscaler
  namespace: kube-system
  labels:
    k8s-addon: cluster-autoscaler.addons.k8s.io
    k8s-app: cluster-autoscaler
rules:
  - apiGroups: [""]
    resources: ["configmaps"]
    verbs: ["create","list","watch"]
  - apiGroups: [""]
    resources: ["configmaps"]
    resourceNames: ["cluster-autoscaler-status", "cluster-autoscaler-
priority-expander"]
    verbs: ["delete", "get", "update", "watch"]


---
apiVersion: rbac.authorization.k8s.io/v1
kind: ClusterRoleBinding
metadata:
  name: cluster-autoscaler
  labels:
    k8s-addon: cluster-autoscaler.addons.k8s.io
    k8s-app: cluster-autoscaler
roleRef:
  apiGroup: rbac.authorization.k8s.io
  kind: ClusterRole
  name: cluster-autoscaler
subjects:
  - kind: ServiceAccount
```

```
    name: cluster-autoscaler
    namespace: kube-system


---
apiVersion: rbac.authorization.k8s.io/v1
kind: RoleBinding
metadata:
  name: cluster-autoscaler
  namespace: kube-system
  labels:
    k8s-addon: cluster-autoscaler.addons.k8s.io
    k8s-app: cluster-autoscaler
roleRef:
  apiGroup: rbac.authorization.k8s.io
  kind: Role
  name: cluster-autoscaler
subjects:
  - kind: ServiceAccount
    name: cluster-autoscaler
    namespace: kube-system


---
apiVersion: apps/v1
kind: Deployment
metadata:
  name: cluster-autoscaler
  namespace: kube-system
  labels:
    app: cluster-autoscaler
spec:
  replicas: 3
  selector:
    matchLabels:
      app: cluster-autoscaler
  template:
    metadata:
      labels:
        app: cluster-autoscaler
```

```
        annotations:
          prometheus.io/scrape: 'true'
          prometheus.io/port: '8085'
      spec:
        serviceAccountName: cluster-autoscaler
        containers:
          - image: iad.ocir.io/oracle/oci-cluster-autoscaler:{{ image tag
}}
            name: cluster-autoscaler
            resources:
              limits:
                cpu: 100m
                memory: 300Mi
              requests:
                cpu: 100m
                memory: 300Mi
            command:
              - ./cluster-autoscaler
              - --v=4
              - --stderrthreshold=info
              - --cloud-provider=oci-oke
              - --max-node-provision-time=25m
              - --nodes=1:5:{{ node pool ocid 1 }}
              - --nodes=1:5:{{ node pool ocid 2 }}
              - --scale-down-delay-after-add=10m
              - --scale-down-unneeded-time=10m
              - --unremovable-node-recheck-timeout=5m
              - --balance-similar-node-groups
              - --balancing-ignore-label=displayName
              - --balancing-ignore-label=hostname
              - --balancing-ignore-label=internal_addr
              - --balancing-ignore-label=oci.oraclecloud.com/fault-domain
            imagePullPolicy: "Always"
            env:
              - name: OKE_USE_INSTANCE_PRINCIPAL
                value: "true"
              - name: OCI_SDK_APPEND_USER_AGENT
                value: "oci-oke-cluster-autoscaler"
```

Step 5. Change the image path of the Kubernetes Cluster Autoscaler image in the `cluster-autoscaler.yaml` file to an image stored in the OCIR Registry. Images are available in a number of regions:

a. Find the following line: `- image: iad.ocir.io/oracle/oci-cluster-autoscaler:{{ image tag }}`

b. Update it to the appropriate region and Kubernetes version: `- image: phx.ocir.io/oracle/oci-cluster-autoscaler:1.25.0-6`. This image is from the Phoenix region and was built to run on Kubernetes 1.25.

Step 6. Specify the node pools that you want the Cluster Autoscaler to manage. You can specify multiple node pools:

a. Find the following line: `- --nodes=1:5:{{ node pool ocid 2 }}`. This line is formatted as `--nodes=<min-nodes>:<max-nodes>:<nodepool-ocid>`. `<min-nodes>` and is used to define the minimum number of nodes allowed in the node pool. The number of nodes will not drop below this number. `<max-nodes>` is used to define the maximum number of nodes allowed in the node pool. The number of nodes will not increase above this number. `<nodepool-ocid>` is used to define the node pools you want to manage by the Cluster Autoscaler.

b. You can specify other supported Cluster Autoscaler parameters at this time.

c. Save the `cluster-autoscaler.yaml` file.

Step 7. Deploy the Kubernetes Cluster Autoscaler to the cluster:

```
kubectl apply -f cluster-autoscaler.yaml
```

Step 8. View the Kubernetes Cluster Autoscaler logs to confirm a successful deployment. These logs also indicate whether the workload of node pools in the cluster is currently being monitored:

```
kubectl -n kube-system logs -f deployment.apps/cluster-autoscaler
```

Metrics Server

The Kubernetes Metrics Server is a set of Kubernetes resources that you can deploy to your cluster that collects resource metrics from the kubelet processes running on the data plane nodes in your cluster. Metrics Server collects these metrics and exposes them through the Kubernetes API, using custom resources that represent metric readings. To deploy the Kubernetes Metrics Server to a cluster with managed node pools, use the following command:

```
kubectl apply -f https://github.com/kubernetes-sigs/metrics-server/releases/
   download/<version-number>/components.yaml
```

Update `<version-number>` with the Kubernetes Metrics Server version that you want to deploy (for example, `v0.6.3`). Because the Kubernetes Metrics Server is being actively developed, the version number will change over time.

To deploy the Kubernetes Metrics Server to a cluster with virtual node pools, you need to first disable the liveness and readiness checks for the metric server because virtual nodes do not expose these URLs for the metric server. To make this change, download the manifest file `components.yaml` to a local directory from https://github.com/kubernetes-sigs/metrics-server/releases/download/<version-number>/components.yaml. Ensure that the URL is updated with the latest version number, as in the previous example.

Open the `components.yaml` file in a text editor of your choice, and remove the `livenessProbe` and `readinessProbe` sections (see Listings 5-1 and 5-2) from the manifest of the metrics-server deployment.

Listing 5-1   `livenessProbe` Section

```
livenessProbe:
        failureThreshold: 3
        httpGet:
          path: /livez
          port: https
          scheme: HTTPS
        periodSeconds: 10
```

Listing 5-2   `readinessProbe` Section

```
readinessProbe:
        failureThreshold: 3
        httpGet:
          path: /readyz
          port: https
          scheme: HTTPS
        initialDelaySeconds: 20
        periodSeconds: 10
```

Deploy the Kubernetes Metrics Server by entering this line:

```
kubectl apply -f <local-location>/components.yaml
```

Update with the local directory containing the `components.yaml` file that you just modified.

Confirm that the Kubernetes Metrics Server has been deployed successfully and is available by entering this line:

```
kubectl get deployment metrics-server -n kube-system
```

HorizontalPodAutoscaler

You can use the Kubernetes HorizontalPodAutoscaler to automatically scale a workload resource, such as the number of pods in a deployment, a replica set, or a stateful set, based on that resource's CPU or memory utilization. The HorizontalPodAutoscaler can help applications scale out to meet increased demand or scale when demand decreases. You can set a target metric percentage to meet when scaling applications.

The HorizontalPodAutoscaler does not need to be manually installed into a cluster because it is a standard API resource in Kubernetes. However, it does require the installation of a metrics source, such as the Kubernetes Metrics Server. The Metrics Server is used to collect resource metrics directly from the kubelets running in your cluster. It exposes those metrics through the Kubernetes API. You can use the Kubernetes HorizontalPodAutoscaler with both managed node pools and virtual node pools.

To use the HorizontalPodAutoscaler, if you have not already done so, follow the steps to deploy the Kubernetes Metric Server.

Next, create a HorizontalPodAutoscaler Resource. In this example, the resource will maintain a minimum of one and a maximum of five replicas and will aim for an average CPU utilization of 50%:

```
kubectl autoscale deployment example --cpu-percent=50 --min=1 --max=5
```

This will maintain a minimum of one and a maximum of five replicas of the pods controlled by the example deployment. It will also increase and decrease the number of replicas of the deployment to maintain an average CPU utilization of 50% across all pods. If the average CPU utilization falls below 50%, the HorizontalPodAutoscaler will reduce the number of pods in the deployment to the minimum of 1 that you specified. If the average CPU utilization goes above 50%, the HorizontalPodAutoscaler will increase the number of pods in the deployment to the maximum of 5 that you specified.

You can confirm the current status of the HorizontalPodAutoscaler by entering this line:

```
kubectl get hpa
```

The output from the `kubectl get hpa` command shows the current status, including the deployments, target percentages, minimum and maximum pods, replicas, and age of the resource:

```
NAME        REFERENCE                   TARGET     MINPODS  MAXPODS  REPLICAS  AGE
php-apache  Deployment/php-apache/scale 0% / 50%   1        10       1         30s
```

You can try out the HorizontalPodAutoscaler by deploying a sample application and then generating load against the application in reaction to the load. This sample application includes a container called `hpa-example` that is exposed using a service:

```
apiVersion: apps/v1
kind: Deployment
metadata:
  name: php-apache
```

```
spec:
  selector:
    matchLabels:
      run: php-apache
  template:
    metadata:
      labels:
        run: php-apache
  spec:
    containers:
    - name: php-apache
      image: registry.k8s.io/hpa-example
      ports:
        - containerPort: 80
      resources:
        limits:
          cpu: 500m
        requests:
          cpu: 200m
---
apiVersion: v1
kind: Service
metadata:
  name: php-apache
  labels:
    run: php-apache
spec:
  ports:
    - port: 80
  selector:
    run: php-apache
```

To deploy the sample application, follow these steps:

Step 1.   Enter this line:

```
kubectl apply -f https://k8s.io/examples/application/php-apache.yaml
```

Step 2.   Create an autoscaler, which can be accomplished using the `kubectl`
          `autoscale` command. To match a target CPU utilization across all pods,
          HorizontalPodAutoscaler dynamically increases and decreases the number of
          replicas of a given deployment. In this case, you set a target CPU utilization
          of 50%. You can also set a floor and a ceiling for the number of replicas,
          to ensure that the number of replicas does not drop below a minimum or
          increase beyond a maximum. In this case, you set a minimum of 1 and a
          maximum of 10 replicas. To create the HorizontalPodAutoscaler for the
          `php-apache` application, enter this line:

```
kubectl autoscale deployment php-apache --cpu-percent=50 --min=1
--max=10
```

Step 3. To check the current status of HorizontalPodAutoscaler, enter the following:
`kubectl get hpa`

You will see an output similar to this:

NAME	REFERENCE	TARGET	MINPODS	MAXPODS	REPLICAS	AGE
php-apache	Deployment/php-apache/scale	0% / 50%	1	10	1	30s

In this example, you can see in the TARGET column that the current CPU utilization is 0%. This is because there is currently no load on the application.

Step 4. To see HorizontalPodAutoscaler in action, you can generate load against the application. To do so, you create an additional pod to send a loop of requests to the php-apache application. In your terminal, enter the following:

```
kubectl get hpa php-apache --watch
```

Open a second terminal to ensure that load generation continues, and enter the following:

```
kubectl run -i --tty load-generator --rm --image=busybox:1.28
--restart=Never -- /bin/sh -c "while sleep 0.01; do wget -q -O-
http://php-apache; done"
```

After allowing time for the load generation pod to come online, you will begin to see a higher CPU utilization—for example:

NAME	REFERENCE	TARGET	MINPODS	MAXPODS	REPLICAS	AGE
php-apache	Deployment/php-apache/scale	300% / 50%	1	10	1	2m

Next, you will see additional replicas created to reach the target of 50% utilization across all pods:

NAME	REFERENCE	TARGET	MINPODS	MAXPODS	REPLICAS	AGE
php-apache	Deployment/php-apache/scale	300% / 50%	1	10	7	4m

In this example, CPU utilization increased to 300% of the original value specified in the resource request. Consequently, the HorizontalPodAutoscaler resized the deployment to seven replicas. If you generate even more load against the application, you will see HorizontalPodAutoscaler scale up to the maximum number of replicas, which you set as 10.

Step 5. You can see the resized replica count in the deployment itself by entering this line:

```
kubectl get deployment php-apache
```

You will see an output similar to this:

```
NAME         READY    UP-TO-DATE    AVAILABLE    AGE
php-apache   7/7      7             7            30s
```

After a few minutes, you will see the CPU utilization approximately reach the target utilization value:

```
NAME        REFERENCE                     TARGET    MINPODS MAXPODS  REPLICAS AGE
php-apache Deployment/php-apache/scale   45% / 50% 1         10       7        8m
```

Step 6. To stop generating load, navigate to the terminal where you created the **busybox** pod and enter the following:

```
<Ctrl> + C
```

After a few minutes, you will see the utilization drop down to 0% and HorizontalPodAutoscaler will scale down the replicas to the minimum of one:

```
NAME        REFERENCE                     TARGET    MINPODS  MAXPODS  REPLICAS AGE
php-apache Deployment/php-apache/scale   0% / 50% 1          10       1        11m
```

Step 7. To delete the HorizontalPodAutoscaler, enter the following:

```
kubectl delete horizontalpodautoscaler.autoscaling/php-apache
```

To remove the sample application, enter this:

```
kubectl delete deployment.apps/php-apache service/php-apache
```

Vertical Pod Autoscaler

The Kubernetes Vertical Pod Autoscaler (VPA) can improve cluster resource utilization by automatically adjusting the resource requests and limits for containers running in a deployment's pods. The Vertical Pod Autoscaler can update resource requests automatically based on usage to right-size the resources available for each pod while maintaining ratios between limits and requests specified in the initial container's configuration. This applies to pods that are over-requesting resources and under-requesting resources based on their usage over time. The Vertical Pod Autoscaler has three components:

- The **Recommender** monitors resource consumption and provides recommended CPU and memory request values for a container.
- The **Admission plug-in** configures new pods to use the recommended resource requests on new pods that are created or re-created because of changes made by the Updater.
- The **Updater** checks for pods with incorrect resources and terminates them so that they can be re-created with the updated request values.

Unlike the HorizontalPodAutoscaler, which is already present on clusters, the Vertical Pod Autoscaler must be deployed to your cluster. As with the HorizontalPodAutoscaler, the Vertical Pod Autoscaler requires the installation of a metrics source, such as the Kubernetes Metrics Server, in the cluster.

To use the HorizontalPodAutoscaler, if you have not already done so, first follow the steps to deploy the Kubernetes Metric Server. Then deploy the Vertical Pod Autoscaler as follows:

Step 1.   Download the Vertical Pod Autoscaler source code from GitHub:

```
git clone https://github.com/kubernetes/autoscaler.git
```

Step 2.   Change to the `vertical-pod-autoscaler` directory:

```
cd autoscaler/vertical-pod-autoscaler
```

Step 3.   Deploy the Vertical Pod Autoscaler:

```
./hack/vpa-up.sh
```

Step 4.   Verify that the Vertical Pod Autoscaler pods have been created successfully:

```
kubectl get pods -n kube-system
```

The output from this command shows the `vpa-admission-controller`, `vpa-recommender`, and `vpa-updater` pods:

```
vpa-admission-controller-7c7666f6cd-lcjzn   1/1      Running   0      8s vpa-
recommender-786476d7cc-7qk7k                1/1      Running   0      11s vpa-
updater-79d74db98b-f2zv7                    1/1      Running   0      13s
```

After deploying the Vertical Pod Autoscaler pods, you can use them to recommend and set resource requests for resources in your cluster. To do so, you must create a VPA config for the resource for which you want to receive recommendations or to autoscale. When it comes to the manner in which resources are managed, VPA offers the choice of these modes:

- In **Auto** mode, VPA assigns resource requests at pod creation time and updates resource requests of existing pods.

- In **Recreate** mode, VPA assigns resource requests at pod creation time and updates resource requests of existing pods. Recreate differs from Auto because, with Recreate, pods are evicted when updates to requested resources differ significantly from the original recommendation. This is used when you must ensure that pods are restarted when resource requests change.
- In **Initial** mode, VPA assigns resource requests only at pod creation time and does not update resource requests at any other time.
- In **Off** mode, VPA does not automatically assign resource requests for pods. Recommendations are still calculated and are available for you to review in the VPA object. This mode essentially allows you to audit the values that VPA recommends instead of having them actively applied.

Note

In the example in Listing 5-3, the update mode is not specified. By default, the mode is set to Auto.

You can try out the Vertical Pod Autoscaler by deploying a sample application and then generating load against the application in reaction to the load. This sample application includes a container called `hamster` and a VPA config, as demonstrated in Listing 5-3.

Listing 5-3   Sample Application and VPA Configuration to Scale the Application

```
# This config creates a deployment with two pods, each requesting 100 millicores
# and trying to utilize slightly above 500 millicores (repeatedly using CPU for
# 0.5s and sleeping 0.5s).
# It also creates a corresponding Vertical Pod Autoscaler that adjusts the
# requests.
# Note that the update mode is left unset, so it defaults to "Auto" mode.
---
apiVersion: "autoscaling.k8s.io/v1"
kind: VerticalPodAutoscaler
metadata:
  name: hamster-vpa
spec:
  # recommenders field can be unset when using the default recommender.
  # When using an alternative recommender, the alternative recommender's name
  # can be specified as the following in a list.
  # recommenders:
  #   - name: 'alternative'
  targetRef:
    apiVersion: "apps/v1"
    kind: Deployment
```

```
name: hamster
  resourcePolicy:
    containerPolicies:
      - containerName: '*'
        minAllowed:
          cpu: 100m
          memory: 50Mi
        maxAllowed:
          cpu: 1
          memory: 500Mi
        controlledResources: ["cpu", "memory"]
---
apiVersion: apps/v1
kind: Deployment
metadata:
  name: hamster
spec:
  selector:
    matchLabels:
      app: hamster
  replicas: 2
  template:
    metadata:
      labels:
        app: hamster
    spec:
      securityContext:
        runAsNonRoot: true
        runAsUser: 65534 # nobody
      containers:
        - name: hamster
          image: registry.k8s.io/ubuntu-slim:0.1
          resources:
            requests:
              cpu: 100m
              memory: 50Mi
          command: ["/bin/sh"]
          args:
            - "-c"
            - "while true; do timeout 0.5s yes >/dev/null; sleep 0.5s; done"
```

To create the deployment and config, enter this line:

```
kubectl create -f examples/hamster.yaml
```

Deploying the hamster application creates a deployment with two pods and a Vertical Pod Autoscaler pointing at the deployment. Similar to HorizontalPodAutoscaler, VPA enables you to specify minimum and maximum values for the target resources using `minAllowed` and `maxAllowed`. You can verify that the application is deployed using the following command:

```
$ kubectl get pods -l app=hamster

NAME                         READY  STATUS  RESTARTS  AGE
hamster-65cd4dd797-8vglx 1/1     Running 0         43s
hamster-65cd4dd797-pcwpf 1/1     Running 0         44s
```

Describing one of the pods in the application shows the resource requests for that pod. Replace the pod name with one of the pods running in your cluster, and navigate to the requests section of the output to see the current request values, as demonstrated in Listing 5-4.

Listing 5-4   Current Requested CPU and Memory Values from the Sample Application Pod

```
kubectl describe pod hamster-65cd4dd797-pcwpf

[… output truncated…]
requests:
    cpu:        100m
    memory:      50Mi
[… output truncated…]
```

Each of the pods in the `hamster` application runs a container that tries to utilize more cores and memory than requested. VPA watches these pods and, after a few minutes, updates the CPU and memory request to match the needs of the application. To see this happen in real time, watch the pods running in the application and wait for VPA to start a new pod with updated request values:

```
kubectl get --watch pods -l app=hamster
```

When you see a new pod come online, describe the pod and navigate to the requests section of the output to see the current request values, as demonstrated in Listing 5-5.

Listing 5-5   Updated Requested CPU and Memory Values from the Sample Application Pod

```
kubectl describe pod hamster-7cbfd64f57-wmg4

[… output truncated…]

requests:
    cpu:        587m
```

```
   memory:      262144k
```

[… output truncated…]

You can also view the recommendations made by VPA for the `hamster` application. To do so, enter the following:

```
kubectl describe vpa/hamster-vpa
```

The Recommendation section of the output shows the recommendations:

```
Name:       hamster-vpa
Namespace:  default
Labels:     <none>
Annotations: <none>
API Version: autoscaling.k8s.io/v1
Kind:       VerticalPodAutoscaler
Metadata:
Creation Timestamp: 2023-06-07T22:56:14Z
Generation:      4
Resource Version: 25877689
UID:             07e060c6-b46d-407c-961a-df92bcb6c6b6
Spec:
Resource Policy:
  Container Policies:
    Container Name: *
    Controlled Resources:
      cpu
      memory
    Max Allowed:
      Cpu:    1
      Memory: 500Mi
    Min Allowed:
      Cpu:    100m
      Memory: 50Mi
Target Ref:
  API Version: apps/v1
  Kind:       Deployment
  Name:       hamster
Update Policy:
  Update Mode: Auto
Status:
Conditions:
  Last Transition Time: 2023-06-07T22:57:03Z
  Status:              True
  Type:                RecommendationProvided
Recommendation:
```

```
Container Recommendations:
  Container Name: hamster
  Lower Bound:
    Cpu:     203m
    Memory: 262144k
  Target:
    Cpu:     587m
    Memory: 262144k
  Uncapped Target:
    Cpu:     587m
    Memory: 262144k
  Upper Bound:
    Cpu:     1
    Memory: 500Mi
Events:          <none>
```

To remove the sample application, use the following command:

```
kubectl delete -f examples/hamster.yaml
```

To remove the Vertical Pod Autoscaler, navigate to the directory into which it was downloaded, and use the following command:

```
./hack/vpa-down.sh
```

Scaling Workloads and Infrastructure Together

The Cluster Autoscaler scales nodes based on the resource requests made by pods, not the actual utilization of resources or performance characteristics of your workload. In most situations, you need a way to automatically detect degraded performance from your application and to automatically take actions to mitigate this. For instance, if your application receives more than an average amount of traffic, you might need to scale out to better serve the requests. This workload-level scaling is typically accomplished by using the HorizontalPodAutoscaler or the Vertical Pod Autoscaler.

Therefore, it is common practice to combine the Cluster Autoscaler and the HorizontalPodAutoscaler to automate the process of workload and infrastructure scaling, based on metrics. Continuing the example, if your pods are constantly hitting a high CPU utilization rate, the HorizontalPodAutoscaler can create new pods to spread the load, in order. This can create new resource requests from the new pods that are created, which might not be satisfied by the existing nodes. Once the existing resources in the cluster are exhausted, these pods are unschedulable because there are not enough resources to be allocated; then the Cluster Autoscaler kicks into action and creates new nodes to satisfy the updated resource requests. In this manner, you can scale both your workload and the infrastructure required to run the workload, based on the operational characteristics and metrics from your workload.

Autoscaler Best Practices

It is a best practice to design applications running on node pools managed by the Cluster Autoscaler to be disruption tolerant—for example, by means of pod disruption budgets. The Cluster Autoscaler automatically and dynamically adds and removes worker nodes. In the process, pods are moved from one worker node to another, which can cause disruptions if not properly accounted for. The Kubernetes Cluster Autoscaler respects pod scheduling and eviction rules, including the eviction grace period configured for your node pool. These rules might prevent the Cluster Autoscaler from being able to terminate a worker node.

When deploying workloads across availability domains, we recommend that you create one node pool per availability domain. For instance, when working with a region that has three availability domains, you can create three node pools: one for each availability domain. Now you can configure the Cluster Autoscaler to scale each of those node pools independently. Node pools in Container Engine for Kubernetes use a placement configuration to determine the spread of nodes across availability domains and fault domains. The node pool always tries to balance the number of nodes across its placement configuration. Consider this scenario when you have hit your soft resource limit for the specific CPU type or compute shape that you are using for your nodes in one of the availability domains. The shapes are available in the other availability domains; however, the single node pool with a placement configuration that spreads the nodes across all the three availability domains might not create new nodes because the spread of nodes would no longer be balanced. On the other hand, instead of creating a single node pool, if you configure separate node pools for each of the availability domains, you do not encounter this imbalance. This is because each node pool is restricted to a single availability domain and can scale independently of each other. Even if you hit a soft resource limit in a single availability domain, only that node pool is prevented from scaling, whereas the others can still provide new capacity for your workloads.

Because the Cluster Autoscaler itself is a set of pods that you deploy onto your cluster, you should ensure that you deploy multiple replicas for the autoscaler into your cluster. If the autoscaler itself is evicted for a higher-priority workload during a scaling event, the cluster no longer has the capability to scale. You should also ensure that multiple replicas of the autoscaler are deployed across multiple nodes.

Caution

When you use the Cluster Autoscaler to manage a node pool, you should *not* manually update or scale this node pool. The autoscaler will notice this change and could override your manual changes with the autoscaler's configuration.

The Cluster Autoscaler and the HorizontalPodAutoscaler are often used in conjunction with each other. It is therefore important to understand the interactions between these two mechanisms and know how to control their behavior. For instance, setting an appropriate stabilization window in the HorizontalPodAutoscaler for either the scale-up or the scale-down events can control how aggressively new pods are created or destroyed. Transitively, this also impacts the frequency with which the Cluster Autoscaler creates and destroys new nodes. Misconfigurations with these interactions could potentially lead to race conditions or aggressive node scale-up or scale-down events that might not be productive.

Cluster Access and Token Generation

You can use the Kubernetes command-line tool, kubectl, to perform operations on clusters created with Container Engine for Kubernetes. kubectl is used to communicate with a Kubernetes cluster's control plane using the Kubernetes API, for example, to create, get, describe, and delete resources in your cluster. Your version of kubectl must be compatible with the Kubernetes version of your OKE control plane. To be compatible, Kubectl must be either the same version as your control plane or one version ahead or behind your control plane. kubectl uses a configuration file, or kubeconfig, stored in the $HOME/.kube directory.

To access a cluster configured with a private Kubernetes API endpoint, you must configure your virtual cloud network for access or configure a bastion using the Oracle Cloud Infrastructure Bastion service.

Step 1. Install kubectl following the upstream Kubernetes documentation, if you have not already done so.

Step 2. Set up the kubeconfig file.

　　　　a. Generate an API signing key pair. Navigate to the Profile menu in the console, and click **User Settings**. Click the **API Keys** tab and then click **Add API Key**. Either use OCI to generate an API key pair or upload a PEM format key pair generated yourself, paste the contents of the public key, and click **Add**.

　　　　b. If you have not already done so, install and configure the Oracle Cloud Infrastructure CLI.

　　　　c. Set up the kubeconfig file by navigating to the Cluster Details page of the Kubernetes cluster you want to access and clicking **Access Cluster**, as shown in Figure 5-8. These instructions include the capability to connect using Cloud Shell, the command line built directly into the OCI console, or using local access.

　　　　　Clicking the **Local Access** option opens the steps for how to create a /.kube directory to store the kubeconfig file and how to access the kubeconfig for your cluster via the VCN-Native public or private endpoint. Choose the appropriate options, and then set your kubeconfig variable with export KUBECONFIG=$HOME/.kube/config. If a kubeconfig file already exists in the specified location, details for the new cluster are added as a new context to the existing kubeconfig file, and the current context element in the kubeconfig file is updated to point to the newly created cluster context.

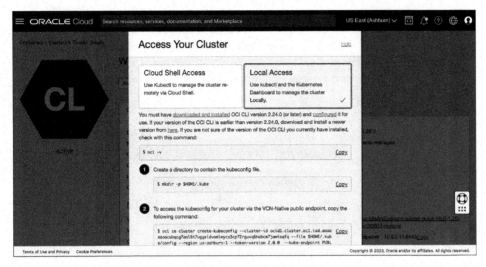

Figure 5-8   Steps for Configuring Cluster Access on the Cluster Details Page of the OCI Console

In your terminal, enter `kubectl`, followed by the command for the operation you want to perform on the cluster—for example, `kubectl get pods`.

A single kubeconfig file can include the details for multiple Kubernetes clusters. Each cluster is referred to as a *context*. The cluster specified by the current context in the kubeconfig file is the cluster on which operations will be performed. The kubeconfig file generated by OKE includes an OCI CLI command that dynamically generates an authentication token and inserts it when you run a kubectl command. For this to function correctly, the OCI CLI must also be available on your shell's executable path. The authentication tokens generated by the OCI CLI command in the kubeconfig file are short lived and specific to individual users, which means they cannot be shared between users to access a Kubernetes cluster.

Service Account Authentication

In addition to authenticating access to a Kubernetes cluster by means of an automatically generated OCI CLI command, users can authenticate by means of a Kubernetes service account. In some situations, automatically generated authentication tokens might be impractical. For example, you might be leveraging tools such as continuous integration and continuous delivery (CI/CD) pipelines that require long-lived authentication tokens. One solution is to use a Kubernetes service account:

Step 1.   Begin by creating a service account: `kubectl -n kube-system create serviceaccount <service account name>`.

Step 2. Create a new `clusterrolebinding` with permissions appropriate for your
use case, and bind it to the service account you just created. For example,
this is how to create a `clusterrolebinding` with administrative access:
`kubectl create clusterrolebinding --clusterrole=cluster-admin`
`--serviceaccount=kube-system: <service account name>`.

> ## Note
>
> It is important to properly scope the permissions of roles in your cluster. The cluster
> admin role has every permission for every resource in the cluster, which is most
> likely too wide a scope for any one user in your organization.

Step 3. Next, create a Kubernetes secret that stores the authentication token for the
service account.

a. To do so, create a `kubeconfig-secret.yaml` file with the following
content:

```
apiVersion: v1
kind: Secret
metadata:
  name: kubeconfig-secret
  namespace: kube-system
  annotations:
    kubernetes.io/service-account.name: kubeconfig-sa
type: kubernetes.io/service-account-token
```

b. Create the token with `kubect apply -f kubeconfig-secret.yaml`.

c. View the details of the secret by describing the secret you just created:
`kubectl describe secrets kubeconfig-secret -n kube-system`.

d. The output from the preceding command includes a Base64-encoded
authentication token as a value of the token element. Obtain the value
of the service account authentication token, and assign its value to an
environment variable after decoding it from Base64: `TOKEN=kubectl -n`
`kube-system get secret oke-kubeconfig-sa-token -o jsonpath='{.`
`data.token}' | base64 --decode`.

Step 4. You can then add the service account and the associated service account
authentication token as a user in the kubeconfig file. Add the service account
(and its authentication token) as a new user definition in the kubeconfig
file by entering the following kubectl command: `kubectl config set-`
`credentials --token=$TOKEN`.

Step 5.   Set the user in the kubeconfig file for the current cluster context to be the new service account user you created: `kubectl config set-context --current --user=<service-account-name>`.

Step 6.   After doing so, other tools may use the service account authentication token when accessing the cluster.

This kubeconfig file can be used across processes and tools to access the cluster.

Configuring DNS

Kubernetes uses DNS records pervasively for services and pods so that they can be discovered and communicated with using DNS names instead of IP addresses. When Kubernetes creates pods and services, it publishes information that the kubelet uses to configure DNS entries for them. OKE clusters use CoreDNS, a general-purpose DNS server that also supports plug-ins, as its DNS server, which you will see running as a pod in the `kube-system` namespace of your cluster.

CoreDNS maintains its configuration properties in a configuration file referred to as a Corefile. When deployed on Kubernetes, the Corefile is maintained as a Kubernetes ConfigMap that is provided to the CoreDNS pods when they are launched. You can view the default CoreDNS settings by using the command demonstrated in Listing 5-6.

Listing 5-6   Default CoreDNS Settings of an OKE Cluster

```
kubectl get cm coredns -n kube-system -o yaml

apiVersion: v1
data:
  Corefile: |-
    .:53 {
      errors
      health {
        lameduck 5s
      }
      ready
      kubernetes cluster.local in-addr.arpa ip6.arpa {
        pods insecure
        fallthrough in-addr.arpa ip6.arpa
      }
      prometheus :9153
      forward . /etc/resolv.conf
      cache 30
      loop
      reload
      loadbalance
    }
```

```
    import custom/*.server
kind: ConfigMap
metadata:
  name: coredns
  namespace: kube-system
...TRUNCATED...
```

The default configuration includes several plug-ins, such as `loadbalance` and `health`, as in the example in Listing 5-6. Of these, the `import` plug-in is noteworthy and provides the mechanism for you to safely extend and customize the configuration. The default Corefile's import plug-in is set up to import other configurations by looking for and importing config files that have the extension `.server` from the `custom` directory. The location of the `custom` directory is relative to the location of the Corefile.

When you need to customize CoreDNS behavior, such as when specifying a forwarding server for your network traffic, enabling logging for debugging DNS queries, or configuring your environment's custom domains and upstream nameservers, you can override the default configuration by creating your own Corefile as a ConfigMap named `coredns-custom`. Because the default Corefile imports everything with a `.server` extension, all you have to do is make sure that the configmap you create has a key that ends in `.server`. Consider the example in Listing 5-7.

Listing 5-7   Corefile, a configmap Used to Customize CoreDNS

```
apiVersion: v1
kind: ConfigMap
metadata:
  name: coredns-custom
  namespace: kube-system
data:
  custom.server: |
    corp.local {
      cache
      forward . _IP_ADDRESS_OF_YOUR_RESOLVER_
    }
```

This ConfigMap defines a custom Corefile named `custom.server` that sends all requests within the *corp.local* domain to the nameserver whose IP address is provided to the forward plug-in. When the custom Corefile is created as a ConfigMap, as in Listing 5-7, the CoreDNS pods can be restarted to load the new config. Because CoreDNS runs as a DaemonSet, you can simply delete the pods to have Kubernetes re-create them with the updated configuration. The default pod definition for the CoreDNS pods loads the default Corefile from the ConfigMap and mounts it at `/etc/coredns` within the coreDNS container. The default pod definition also mounts an optional config volume from a ConfigMap named `coredns-custom` at `/etc/coredns/`

custom. The customized Corefile, custom.server in Listing 5-7 is visible to the pod at /etc/coredns/custom/custom.server. The import plug-in from the default Corefile loads and merges this custom configuration because it meets the import pattern of ending in .server and is located in a directory named custom that is relative to the location of the default Corefile.

OKE also offers a way to customize and control the default Corefile contained in the configmap coredns, which is useful when you want to update the configuration and, say, remove plug-ins from the default plug-in chain. This can be done using the Add-Ons feature. CoreDNS is deployed as a cluster add-on, so it can be configured through the add-on setup process as well. To do this, follow these steps:

Step 1. Navigate to your cluster and the Add-ons section under Resources.

Step 2. Choose the CoreDNS add-on (see Figure 5-9).

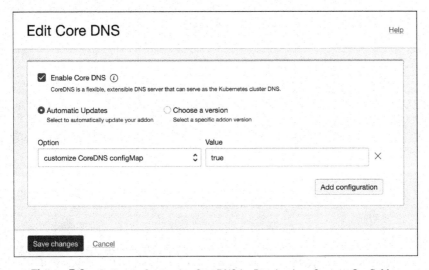

Figure 5-9   Option to Customize CoreDNS by Passing in a Custom ConfigMap

Step 3. In the Options drop-down, choose **Customize CoreDNS ConfigMap**.

Step 4. In the value section, provide the value **true**.

With the CoreDNS add-on customized, you can provide your own default ConfigMap named coredns. During upgrades, OKE will not replace this customized configuration.

Configuring Node Local DNS Cache

Typically, pods that run with the dnsPolicy: ClusterFirst perform DNS queries using the kube-dns service. The service might be running on another node, and this can introduce latency for DNS lookups. The kube-dns service's clusterIP is translated to the

DNS server endpoint using IP tables rules. This can involve connection tracking, and when there are a lot of UDP DNS lookups, the conntrack table sometimes can fill up (usually because UDP entries have to time out in the conntrack table, unlike with TCP). To avoid these issues and improve performance, NodeLocal DNSCache runs a DNS caching agent on cluster nodes as a DaemonSet. Pods reach out to the DNS caching agent running on the same node always (because it is a DaemonSet) and thus can avoid iptables DNAT rules and connection tracking. If the local cache experiences a cache miss, it still queries `kube-dns`; however, the number of these queries that have to go through iptables rules DNAT and conntrack is significantly reduced.

Note

CoreDNS also runs its service under the name `kube-dns` to ensure compatibility with applications and systems that rely on that common name without having a dependency on the DNS server implementation.

The steps to set up the NodeLocal DNS cache are described in Kubernetes documentation[1]; however, this process involves setting a kubelet flag named `--cluster-dns` to override the default. To add this kubelet flag in OKE, you can use the Custom Cloud-Init feature described in Chapter 4, "Understanding Container Engine for Kubernetes," which allows you to pass in these kubelet flags. Consider the following example cloud-init script:

```
#!/bin/bash
curl --fail -H "Authorization: Bearer Oracle" -LO http://169.254.169.254/opc/v2/
  instance/metadata/oke_init_script | base64 --decode >/var/run/oke-init.sh
bash /var/run/oke-init.sh --cluster-dns "CLUSTER_DNS"
```

This simple script does not actually modify the cloud-init script itself. Instead, it downloads the default startup script and runs it with the `--cluster-dns` flag. The value of `CLUSTER_DNS` should be set to something that does not collide with anything else on the cluster. For this reason, it is recommended that you use an address in the link local range of `169.254.0.0/16`, such as `169.254.0.10`.

Configuring ExternalDNS

When building public applications and services, you often expose your application using a Kubernetes service of type load balancer. A public load balancer is allocated a public IP address as well, but you then need to update the DNS entries for your application so that the domain name, such as `https://api.my-app.com`, can now point at your newly created load balancer's IP address, making the application available over it. ExternalDNS is an add-on to Kubernetes that can create these DNS records for services in ExternalDNS providers, including OCI DNS. It eliminates the manual work of setting up DNS records in your DNS provider and makes Kubernetes services seamlessly discoverable. Note that ExternalDNS is not a DNS server such as CoreDNS. It does not perform the functions of DNS; instead, it automates the task of creating and updating DNS configuration in an ExternalDNS provider. The ExternalDNS provider supports OCI DNS, among several other DNS providers. The process of setting up and configuring ExternalDNS depends on the provider you want to use and is documented on the project's GitHub page.[2]

Cluster Add-ons

In the context of Kubernetes, the term *add-ons* refers to operational tools and features used to support and extend the functionality of Kubernetes clusters. This area includes software essential to the proper functioning of a cluster, such as CoreDNS, kube-proxy, and a container network interface (CNI) such as Flannel or Oracle Cloud Infrastructure (OCI) native pod networking. It also includes a growing portfolio of optional add-on software used to extend core Kubernetes functionality and improve cluster manageability and performance, such as the Kubernetes Dashboard, Oracle Database Operator, and WebLogic Kubernetes Operator. In a more concrete sense, add-ons include the software deployed to the kube-system namespace that is present by default when you create a cluster.

The OKE add-on feature gives you the capability to control add-ons deployed to your clusters. You can choose to disable or opt out of using a specific add-on altogether. For example, you can choose to disable the OCI native pod networking CNI and bring your own alternative CNI, such as Calico. If you have specific compliance or audit requirements, you can choose to pin to an add-on version and control when to update the add-on. Alternatively, you can choose to have Oracle fully manage your add-ons, including enabling automatic updates.

Each add-on comes with a set of customizable options. For example, CoreDNS, a general-purpose authoritative DNS server commonly found in Kubernetes environments, comes with the option to bring your own Kubernetes ConfigMap, with a Corefile section that defines CoreDNS behavior. This Corefile configuration includes several CoreDNS plug-ins with different DNS functions to extend the basic functionality. These supported customizations enable you to tailor your add-ons to your specific use cases while still benefitting from lifecycle management by Oracle.

Configuring Add-ons

You can configure add-ons either during the cluster creation process or after you create your cluster. To configure add-ons during cluster creation in the Console, click **Show Advanced Options** on the first page of the custom cluster creation flow, scroll down to the Configure Cluster Add-ons panel, and click the add-on you want to customize. For example, to use the optional Kubernetes dashboard add-on, you can click on the Kubernetes dashboard add-on to open a panel that enables you to choose whether you want to enable or disable the add-on. Enabling the add-on deploys the Kubernetes dashboard as a pod to your cluster. The same panel also allows you to choose to have Oracle automatically manage the lifecycle of the add-on, including updating the add-on as new versions are released over time, or to pin your add-on version and meet internal security and compliance requirements.

Each add-on comes with several configuration options. Some options are common to all add-ons; others are add-on specific. In the case of the Kubernetes dashboard, you can specify the number of replicas you want to make of the Kubernetes dashboard pod and then use node selectors and tolerations to control onto which nodes Kubernetes schedules a given add-on. For the complete list of key/value pairs used to pass on add-on specific arguments to the cluster, consult the Oracle documentation.

After you create your clusters, you can view your deployed add-ons by navigating to the Add-ons tab on the Clusters Details page. Here, you can see a list of deployed add-ons, details on whether they're automatically updated, the status, and the add-on version (see Figure 5-10).

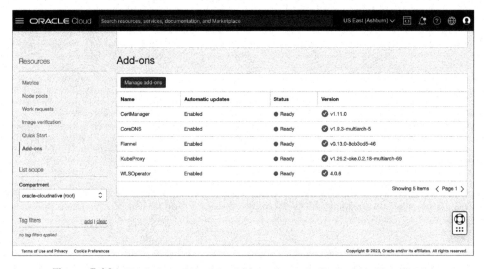

Figure 5-10   Displaying a List of the Add-ons Currently Deployed to Your Cluster

You can also configure add-ons after you create a cluster. To do so, click **Manage Add-ons**. This selection opens a panel showing all available add-ons. Clicking into an add-on gives you the capability to update the configuration. To apply the updates, click **Save Changes**. To track the changes in real time, navigate to the Work Requests tab and click the appropriate work request.

Not all add-ons can be deployed to all node types. For example, the Kubernetes dashboard runs on managed nodes but not virtual nodes.

Disabling Add-ons

Two options are available if you want to remove an add-on from your cluster: You can remove it, which actively deletes it from your cluster, or you can disable it, which leaves the pods running in your cluster. If you disable an essential cluster add-on, a warning indicates that you have taken responsibility for deploying and configuring an alternative add-on to provide equivalent functionality.

Observability: Prometheus and Grafana

Prometheus and Grafana are some of the most commonly used tools for metrics and monitoring with Kubernetes. The kube-prometheus project offers a "batteries included" experience to get started with Prometheus and Grafana on Kubernetes. It is built on top of the Prometheus Operator for Kubernetes that implements the operator pattern to manage Prometheus deployments on Kubernetes. The project also includes prebuilt Grafana dashboards and Prometheus rules to create an end-to-end solution for monitoring Kubernetes clusters. This project offers a good starting point for most Kubernetes users.

The kube-prometheus project can be deployed in two ways: directly using the manifests provided or using the Helm chart. Deploying from the manifest files is the simplest way to get started, but the kube-prometheus project uses Jsonnet to customize the manifests, if customization is desired. If you are new to Jsonnet, the Helm chart offers a simpler and more widely used method to customize the manifests before deployment. In this document, we use the Helm chart to deploy the kube-prometheus-stack.

Monitoring Stack Components

Several CNCF projects are used in combination to create this monitoring stack. These include the Prometheus Monitoring system and time series database; Alertmanager, which can deliver rule base alerts in response to events; and Grafana, for visualizing the monitoring data and interacting with it. The next sections look at each of these in detail.

Installing the kube-prometheus-stack

You can install the kube-prometheus-stack using Helm. The default installation does not use persistent storage, so the collected metrics will be lost if the pods are restarted. To overcome this, you can customize the `values.yaml` passed to the Helm chart, with added storage configuration. Create a new file named `values-oci.yaml` (see Listing 5-8).

Listing 5-8   File Used to Configure Default Values for the Prometheus Stack

```
cat <<EOF > values-oci.yaml
prometheus:
  prometheusSpec:
    storageSpec:
     volumeClaimTemplate:
       spec:
         storageClassName: oci-bv
         accessModes: ["ReadWriteOnce"]
         resources:
           requests:
             storage: 50Gi
EOF
```

> **Note**
>
> This is a minimal configuration of the default values, and the charts offer a lot more configuration options. Notably, this setup does not cover the creation of an ingress resource for Grafana or Prometheus, so these services will be accessed later using a port-forward. If you want to configure a LoadBalancer or an ingress for the components, you can customize this through the Helm chart.

Now add the Helm repo and update the charts:

```
helm repo add prometheus-community https://prometheus-community.github.io/
  helm-charts
helm repo update
```

Install the chart, providing the `values-oci.yaml` with overrides for the default chart values.

```
helm install kube-prometheus-stack \
  --namespace monitoring \
  --create-namespace \
  -f values-oci.yaml \
prometheus-community/kube-prometheus-stack
```

In a few moments, the Kubernetes resources are provisioned and the monitoring stack then is operational. To track the progress of the deployment, use the following command and ensure that all resources are ready:

```
kubectl get statefulsets,deploy,svc,po  -n monitoring
```

Note

You might have to run this command repeatedly, or you could prepend the command with watch -n5 to execute the command every 5 seconds until all resources are ready. This requires you to have the watch utility installed.

When all resources are ready, you can get the default password for the Grafana UI from the Kubernetes secret that was created during the deployment:

```
kubectl get secret kube-prometheus-stack-grafana -o jsonpath="{.data.admin-
    password}" -n monitoring | base64 --decode;echo
```

To log into the Grafana UI, you need to expose the service for Grafana. You can use a port-forward for this. The service that is created for Grafana is listening on port 80, by default. To create a port-forward, you can use the following command, which forwards port 3000 on the host to the service's port 80:

```
kubectl --namespace monitoring port-forward svc/kube-prometheus-stack-grafana
    3000:80
```

You can now access the Grafana UI at http://localhost:3000.

The kube-prometheus-stack [https://github.com/prometheus-community/helm-charts/tree/main/charts/kube-prometheus-stack#kube-prometheus-stack] comes bundled with a set of dashboards. These dashboards provide commonly used metrics and serve as examples of creating your own dashboards.

The bundled dashboards are grouped into the General folder. You can navigate to the list of dashboards through **Dashboards > Browse > General**, as shown in Figure 5-11.

Figure 5-11 Set of Default Dashboards Available Through Grafana

From here, clicking any of the dashboards opens it and displays the metrics, as illustrated in Figure 5-12. Most dashboards are parametrized, meaning that you can specify the scope of the data displayed by narrowing the data to a specific cluster, namespace, and even resources within a namespace.

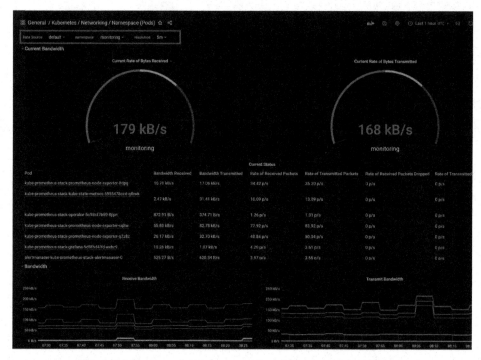

Figure 5-12   Example Grafana Dashboard Monitoring Pod Bandwidth

Operators and OCI Service Operator for Kubernetes

Operators in Kubernetes are a way to package, run, and manage the entire lifecycle of a Kubernetes-native application, including actions such as upgrades. Any application that is built to rely on and take advantage of the Kubernetes features and tools for its operation and management can be called a Kubernetes-native application.

By itself, Kubernetes provides many features and capabilities to manage applications as pods, make them resilient to failures, and scale them up or down, based on need. However it also typically relies on the assumption that pods are arbitrarily replaceable. This model works well for stateless applications, and modern distributed application design practices promote this approach of preferring stateless services that inherently have properties such as better scalability. However, most applications require you to manage state; this state can be pushed down and consolidated further down the stack, but this still requires a workload-specific approach for handling replication of the state and for managing failover scenarios. For instance, how a sharded database is managed differs from how MySQL is managed, and Kubernetes would not be expected to know these differences. Similarly, some software components, such as a distributed cache, often have their own notion of what a "cluster" means, how to join and maintain membership in the cluster, and elect a leader among members of those specific components. Complex software systems can also have dependencies among their components, startup ordering requirements, specialized initialization and termination handling across dependent components, and more.

When the requirements of specialized stateful workloads go beyond the level of capabilities that Kubernetes offers as a general-purpose platform for all types of workloads, you need a way to manage that in a Kubernetes environment. When these applications operate outside Kubernetes, they often require the help of human actors to perform the required orchestration and to effectively *operate* the stack. If you move away from these manual operations and apply modern principles such as building software to automate the management of systems to this problem of managing complex and customized workflows for stateful applications in Kubernetes, you approach the notion of *operators*. For example, the Oracle database operator for Kubernetes knows the details of how to manage multiple types of databases, such as a sharded database on Kubernetes. In addition to making the process of setting up the workload easier, an operator also continuously monitors the workload and performs actions such as routine upgrades, data backups, and failover. Operators and the operator framework make use of the standard Kubernetes extension mechanisms. This means that operators work with the existing tooling for Kubernetes. Operators bring a custom resource definition (CRD) and the operator code that monitors for changes to the CRD and takes appropriate action.

Although operators make it easy to manage complex applications on top of Kubernetes, writing an operator can be challenging. The Operator SDK is a framework that uses the Kubernetes controller-runtime library to make writing operators easier. The Operator SDK provides high-level APIs and tools such as the `operator-sdk` CLI to make it easier to develop and work with operators.

Another component of the operator framework is the Operator Lifecycle Manager (OLM). The OLM provides an easy way for users to manage operators themselves. The process of installing, upgrading, and keeping operators up-to-date is made easier by using the OLM. For those developing operators, the OLM offers a model to package operators with declarative dependencies and offers discoverability for operators.

Getting Started with Operators on OKE

To install operators and work with them, the first step is to install the operator framework and tooling. The installation for the operator framework is documented in the official Operator Framework page.[3] The following command showcases the installation on macOS:

```
brew install operator-sdk
```

This installs the `operator-sdk` CLI tool, which offers a streamlined way to install the OLM. The OLM is installed into a target Kubernetes cluster, such as an OKE cluster:

```
$ operator-sdk olm install --version 0.20.0
...

...
INFO[0079] Successfully installed OLM version "latest"
```

This installs the OLM and its required components into your cluster. It also creates a dedicated namespace named `olm` for these components. When OLM is installed on the cluster, you can use it to install and manage community operators. To list the operators available, use the following command:

```
kubectl get packagemanifest -n olm
```

Operators for OCI, Oracle Database, and Oracle WebLogic

Oracle offers several operators that can help you manage and operate Oracle products and services directly from your Kubernetes cluster using familiar Kubernetes tooling. These range from operators that help you deploy and manage a sharded Oracle database on your Kubernetes cluster to the OCI Service Operator for Kubernetes (OSOK), which helps you create and manage OCI services such as the MySQL database or Object Storage buckets. It also includes operators that can manage WebLogic server clusters deployed on top of Kubernetes.

The OCI Service Operator for Kubernetes (OSOK)[4] makes it easy to create, manage, and connect to OCI resources from a Kubernetes environment. OSOK supports the following services at the time of writing:

- Autonomous Database Service
- Oracle Streaming Service
- MySQL DB System Service
- Service Mesh Service

The operator enables you to manage these services as if they were part of your application. When the operator is installed,[5] it sets up the custom resources that represent these resources in OCI. The operator also installs the controllers that react to these resource definitions by invoking the OCI APIs on your behalf to manage the service. This effectively allows you to manage OCI services using Kubernetes tooling and a Kubernetes resource definition in YAML. Consider the example in Listing 5-9.

Listing 5-9 Managing OCI Services

```
apiVersion: oci.oracle.com/v1beta1
kind: MySqlDbSystem
metadata:
```

```
  name: mysql_db
spec:
  compartmentId: ...compartment.ocid...
  displayName: ApplicationDatabase
  shapeName: MySQL.VM.Standard.E4.8.128GB
  subnetId: ...subnet...
  configuration:
    id: MySQL.VM.Standard.E4.8.128GB.HA
  availabilityDomain: ...avaiability.domain...
  adminUsername:
    secret:
      secretName: ...kubernetes.secret...
  adminPassword:
    secret:
      secretName: ...kubernetes.secret...
```

The manifest represents an object of kind: MySqlDbSystem, which is not a standard Kubernetes object, but a custom resource that is managed by the OSOK operator. When this manifest is deployed alongside the standard Kubernetes pods and services that make up an application, you are effectively creating the application database in OCI. The standard Kubernetes controllers take on the task of creating the pods for the application; the controller that the OSOK operator installed knows how to interpret the resource definition for the MySqlDbSystem and make the appropriate calls to OCI to create this database instance of OCI if it does not exist.

Another operator that is available from Oracle is the Oracle Database Operator. The Oracle Database Operator supports multiple database deployment models that you can directly manage from your Kubernetes cluster. These offer a wide range of configuration options from dedicated autonomous databases on the OCI infrastructure to multitenant databases and containerized sharded databases within the cluster.

The operator itself can be installed by following the documentation, or you can enable it as an add-on for your cluster. To install the operator through OKE add-ons, follow these steps:

Step 1. Navigate to the add-ons section for the cluster.
Step 2. Select **Oracle Database Operator**.
Step 3. Select a version or choose to keep the operator automatically updated.
Step 4. Select the check box to enable the operator add-on.
Step 5. Save your changes.

Figure 5-13 shows configuring the database operator as an add-on.

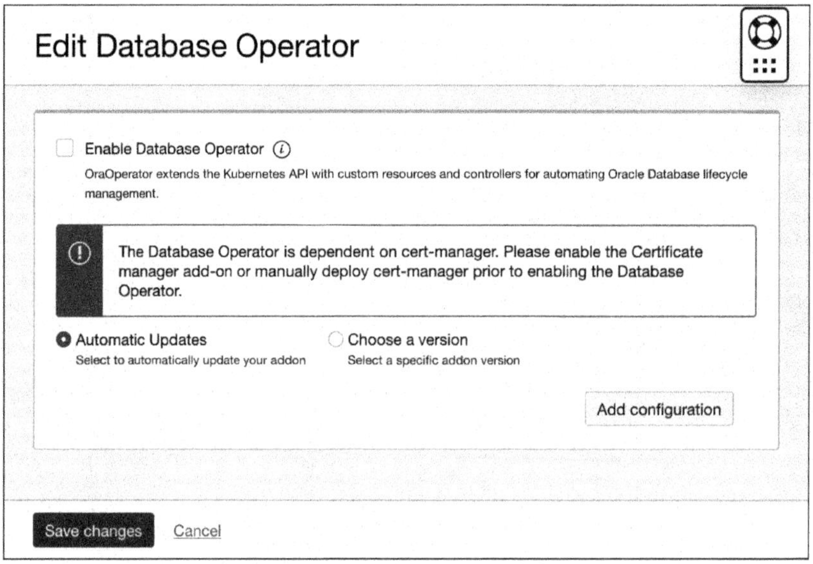

Figure 5-13   Oracle Database Operator as a Cluster Add-on

As with any operator, you can use the CRDs that are enabled to describe the database and configuration you need; the operator then can create and help you operate the database. Listing 5-10 showcases the CRD for an Oracle sharded database.

Listing 5-10   CRD for an Oracle Sharded Database

```
apiVersion: database.oracle.com/v1alpha1
kind: ShardingDatabase
metadata:
  name: shardingdatabase-sample
  namespace: shns
spec:
 shard:
    - name: shard1
      storageSizeInGb: 50
    - name: shard2
      storageSizeInGb: 50
 catalog:
    - name: catalog
      storageSizeInGb: 50
...TRUNCATED ...
```

Oracle sharding distributes segments of a data set across many databases (shards), which can be distributed across multiple systems or locations. When combined together, the individual shards make up a single logical database. This greatly improves the scalability of the database while still maintaining Oracle database features, such as powerful SQL and strong consistency guarantees. The Sharding Database controller that is installed to your cluster with the Oracle Database Operator deploys Oracle sharding topology as a stateful set when it encounters a CRD such as the one shown in Listing 5-10. The Sharding Database controller also manages the typical lifecycle of Oracle sharding topology in the Kubernetes cluster.

Additionally, Oracle offers a WebLogic Kubernetes Operator that can be used to create and manage WebLogic clusters and applications on Kubernetes. The WebLogic Kubernetes Operator is highly flexible and can be configured in a multitude of ways. These include the capability to configure WebLogic domains as Kubernetes resources (using CRDs), manage multiple WebLogic domains across namespaces, scale domains by adding or removing managed servers, integrate the operations with HorizontalPodAutoscaler, and more. Consider the partial example in Listing 5-11.

Listing 5-11 Manifest Used to Create the WebLogic Kubernetes Operator

```
apiVersion: "weblogic.oracle/v1"
kind: Cluster
metadata:
  name: sample-domain1-cluster-1
  namespace: sample-domain1-ns
  labels:
    weblogic.domainUID: sample-domain1
spec:
  replicas: 2
  clusterName: cluster-1

---
apiVersion: "weblogic.oracle/v9"
kind: Domain
metadata:
  name: sample-domain1
  namespace: sample-domain1-ns
  labels:
    weblogic.domainUID: sample-domain1

spec:
  configuration:
    model:
      auxiliaryImages:
      - image: "phx.ocir.io/weblogick8s/quick-start-aux-image:v1"
  domainHomeSourceType: FromModel
  domainHome: /u01/domains/sample-domain1
  image: "container-registry.oracle.com/middleware/weblogic:12.2.1.4"
  serverStartPolicy: IfNeeded
```

```
serverPod:
  resources:
    requests:
      cpu: "250m"
      memory: "768Mi"
replicas: 1
clusters:
- name: sample-domain1-cluster-1

...TRUNCATED ...
```

In the partial example in Listing 5-11, the CRDs describe both a `Cluster` resource and a `Domain` resource. The `Domain` resource is a way to provide the WebLogic domain configuration, a WebLogic install, and other components and configurations to run the domain. A `Cluster` resource models a WebLogic cluster within a given WebLogic domain. Because WebLogic has its own notion of what a "cluster" is and how cluster operations such as scaling function, the `Cluster` resource bridges Kubernetes to the WebLogic notion of a cluster. This makes operations such as scaling a WebLogic cluster possible through Kubernetes tooling and integrates it with typical Kubernetes scaling processes such as the HorizontalPodAutoscaler. The `Domain` resource and `Cluster` resource do not replace the traditional WebLogic configuration files; instead, they cooperate with those files to describe the Kubernetes artifacts of the corresponding domain.

Troubleshooting Nodes with Node Doctor

As with most software systems, you will occasionally encounter issues with your cluster that you need to troubleshoot. With a managed Kubernetes service such as OKE, the control plane is fully managed by the cloud provider and the data plane is managed by the user. This means that most issues that require you to gather data and analyze will be related to the data plane. These issues can range from infrastructure and OS-level issues with the data plane nodes, to problems with components such as the kubelet, the CNI, or other system pods and DaemonSets that run on the data plane. Troubleshooting these components can usually be done with some common diagnostic commands; however, a deep knowledge of Kubernetes is usually required to do this. When using OKE, users have access to additional tooling provided by OCI, called Node Doctor. Node Doctor helps users gather diagnostic data, provides suggestions, and troubleshoots data plane–related issues without requiring users to have a deep knowledge of Kubernetes- or Linux-based systems. The tool can also create support bundles that users can provide to Oracle support, avoiding time-consuming back-and-forth communications as support engineers ask for diagnostic data.

Node Doctor is a script that is preinstalled on the data plane nodes for OKE clusters; it is available in the location `/usr/local/bin/node-doctor.sh`. You can run Node

Doctor by executing the script after logging into the data plane node using SSH, or you can execute it using the OCI Run-Command feature. The OCI console also includes a useful step-by-step guide that walks you through the process, regardless of how you want to run the Node Doctor tool. The guide can be accessed by navigating to the Node Pool Details page and then clicking the **Troubleshoot Nodes** button. Figure 5-14 shows the guide that provides you with specific instructions for the selected cluster and node pool.

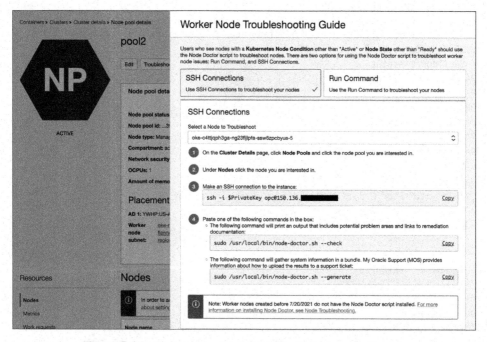

Figure 5-14   Steps to Run Node Doctor Available from the Console

When you run Node Doctor, you can choose to use the `--check` flag to get a health report for the node, with a summary of the checks performed and the issues identified, along with suggested actions to resolve the issues (see Listing 5-12).

Listing 5-12   Getting a Health Report for a Node

```
$ sudo /usr/local/bin/node-doctor.sh --check

INFO: /usr/local/bin/oke-node-doctor.tar.gz already exists and MD5 match.
pip requires Python '>=3.7' but the running Python is 3.6.8
Running node doctor...
PASS node health...
PASS DNS lookup...
```

```
PASS kubelet cert rotation flag...
PASS kubelet logs...
PASS iscsi health...
PASS service health...
PASS instance metadata...
WARN cloud-init version...
SKIP cloud-init status...
SKIP chef onboard status...
PASS image and instance info...
Command line error: one of the following arguments is required: --save --add-repo
  --dump --dump-variables --set-enabled --enable --set-disabled --disable
SKIP yum status...
PASS flannel status...
PASS coredns status...
PASS proxymux-client status...
PASS kube-proxy status...
PASS pods in ImagePullBackOff...
PASS pods failed mounting volume...
FAIL proxymux client registration status...
PASS runc version...
PASS pod usage...
PASS br_netfilter module availability...


NODE DOCTOR REPORT
------------------
17/19 checks passed
2 Signal(s) generated

Signal 1: CLOUD_INIT_CUSTOMIZED
Description:
Instance user_data is different from OKE native cloud init


Signal 2: PROXYMUX_CLIENT_REGISTRATION_FAILURE
Description:
Proxymux client is not able to register with proxymux server




Resolution 1: CHECK_VCN_K8S_ENDPOINT
Description: Network related failures have been detected. Please validate the
  network settings. Most likely, port 12250 in the security list of the k8s api
  endpoint VCN is misconfigured.
Useful links: ['https://docs.oracle.com/en-us/iaas/Content/ContEng/Concepts/
  contengnetworkconfig.htm', 'https://docs.oracle.com/en-us/iaas/Content/ContEng/
  Concepts/contengnetworkconfigexample.htm']
```

```
Related Signals:
PROXYMUX_CLIENT_REGISTRATION_FAILURE: Proxymux client is not able to register with
  proxymux server
```

```
Node doctor scan is complete. Report has been saved at /var/log/oke-node-doctor/
  oke-node-doctor-2092328.log
```

Alternatively, if you are working with support, you can use the --generate flag to generate a TAR file that collects multiple log files, diagnostic command output, and other data that helps you or the support team quickly analyze the state of the node from multiple fronts. Contained in the data collected as a bundle is information and output from diagnostic commands, including VNIC details, iptables rules, and storage information. The tools try to limit the data collected, with a goal to keep the bundle's size less than 10MB; however, this might mean that log files with critical data must be truncated. To prevent this, you can combine the --generate flag with the --large flag to avoid a size goal for the generated bundle or combine the --since and --until flags to restrict the data collected within a time boundary. Listing 5-13 shows Node Doctor usage for generating a support bundle and some of the logs and diagnostics that are included in the bundle.

Listing 5-13   Generating a Support Bundle Using Node Doctor

```
[opc@oke-c4ttjqph3ga-ng23fijlpfa-ssw6zpcbyua-5 ~]$ sudo /usr/local/bin/node-
  doctor.sh --generate --large

--- TRUNCATED ---

Generating node doctor bundle...
Generated /tmp/oke-support-bundle-2023-04-19T19-17-08.tar

[opc@oke-c4ttjqph3ga-ng23fijlpfa-ssw6zpcbyua-5 ~]$ tar -tf /tmp/oke-support-
  bundle-2023-04-19T19-17-08.tar

--- TRUNCATED ---

home/opc/TEMP_DIR/tmpypxxadi7/system/iptables_filter
home/opc/TEMP_DIR/tmpypxxadi7/system/iptables_nat
home/opc/TEMP_DIR/tmpypxxadi7/system/crictl_pods
home/opc/TEMP_DIR/tmpypxxadi7/system/crictl_images
home/opc/TEMP_DIR/tmpypxxadi7/logs/
home/opc/TEMP_DIR/tmpypxxadi7/logs/kubelet.gz
home/opc/TEMP_DIR/tmpypxxadi7/logs/containers/kube-flannel-ds-zb9zm_kube-system_
  install-cni.log.gz
home/opc/TEMP_DIR/tmpypxxadi7/logs/containers/proxymux-client-dgbcn_kube-system_
  proxymux-client.log.gz
```

```
home/opc/TEMP_DIR/tmpypxxadi7/logs/containers/csi-oci-node-sncjp_kube-system_csi-
   node-driver.log.gz
```

--- TRUNCATED ---

Configuring SR-IOV Interfaces for Pods on OKE Using Multus

When highly network-oriented workloads require setting up secondary network interfaces within pods, you can use a meta CNI such as Multus[6] to achieve this. The secondary network interfaces that are usually attached in these cases have specialized networking capabilities or properties, such as single root IO virtualization (SR-IOV).

SR-IOV is a specification that allows a single PCIe device to appear to be multiple separate physical PCIe devices. SR-IOV works by introducing the idea of physical functions (PFs) and virtual functions (VFs). A PF is used by the host and usually represents a single NIC port. VF is a lightweight version of that PF. With appropriate support, SR-IOV presents a way for the physical hardware (such as a SmartNIC) to present itself as several distinct (network interface) devices. With containers, you can then move one of these interfaces (a VF) from the host into the network namespace for a container or a pod so that the container can now directly access the interface. The advantage this offers is that you get none of the overhead with virt-io and you get native device performance.

Significant differences exist between how the interfaces are created and managed when using bare metal nodes (you have full control over the hardware) and VM-based nodes (a hypervisor abstracts your access to the underlying hardware and you do not have as much control over it). Specifically, when using VMs, you do not typically have access to the PF. In both cases, however, Multus is used to provide additional network interfaces to pods. The sections that follow look at how these secondary network interfaces are created and examine the different plug-ins used to manage them.

Using Bare Metal Nodes

When running on bare metal nodes, you can leverage the SR-IOV CNI plug-in to manage SR-IOV virtual functions as resources that can be allocated on a node and use the Multus meta CNI to add network interfaces to pods. The approach has several layers and components. At its crux, a Kubernetes device plug-in manages a set of virtual functions and publishes it as an allocatable resource on the node. When a pod requests such a resource, the pod can be assigned to a node where the resource is available and an SR-IOV CNI can plumb the virtual function into the pod's network namespace. A CNI meta plug-in such as Multus handles multiple network attachments to the pod so that the pod can communicate over both the SR-IOV and the overlay networks.

You first set up a number of VFs on the SR-IOV-capable smartNICs, which then present themselves as individual NICs. You then configure these VFs with MAC addresses that OCI recognizes. These VFs are created outside Multus, either manually (as described in this tutorial) or using a script that can be invoked at node creation time. At this point, you have a pool of VFs, each identified by the host as a separate NIC, and an OCI MAC address. The Kubernetes network plumbing working group maintains a special-purpose network device plug-in that discovers and publishes VFs as allocatable node resources. The SR-IOV CNI (also from the Kubernetes network plumbing working group) works alongside the device plug-in and manages the assignment of these virtual functions to the pod based on the pod lifecycle.

Now you have one or more nodes with a pool of VFs that are recognized and managed by the SR-IOV device plug-in as allocatable node resources. These can be requested by pods. The SR-IOV CNI plumbs (moves) the VF into the pod's network namespace upon pod creation and releases the VF (moves it back to the root namespace) upon pod deletion. This makes the VF available to be allocated for another pod. A meta plug-in such as Multus can provide the VF information to the CNI and manage multiple network attachments on the pod. Figure 5-15 illustrates a pod with three network interfaces attached, with the first interface eth0 being used for liveness and readiness probes, as well as kubelet and Kubernetes API server communications. The two other interfaces are connected to two separate networks, and the workload is assumed to be able to make use of these interfaces to communicate with them individually.

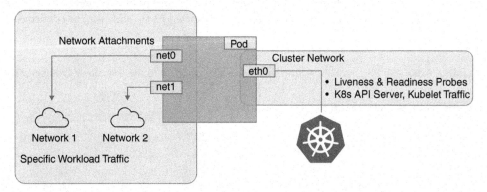

Figure 5-15   Pod with Multiple Network Interfaces Providing Connectivity to Multiple Networks

The first task is to set up the bare metal hosts by creating the VFs on the PCIe device. This can be done by setting the number of desired VFs in /sys/class/net/${PHYSICAL_ DEVICE}/device/sriov_numvfs. The ${PHYSICAL_DEVICE} can be identified by running ip addr show and looking for the primary interface. These steps can be condensed into a simple script, as provided in Listing 5-14.

Listing 5-14   Script to Create and Verify the VFs

```
# Gets the physical device. Alternatively, just run `ip addr show` and look at the
  primary iface to set $PHYSDEV
URL=http://169.254.169.254/opc/v1/vnics/
baseAddress=`curl -s ${URL} | jq -r '.[0] | .privateIp'`
PHYSDEV=`ip -o -4 addr show | grep ${baseAddress} | awk -F: '{gsub(/^[ \t]|[
  \t]$/,"",$2);split($2,out,/[ \t]+/);print out[1]}'`

# Add two VFs
echo "2" > /sys/class/net/${PHYSDEV}/device/sriov_numvfs

# Verify the VFs
ip link show ${PHYSDEV}
```

Next, you need to assign OCI MAC addresses to the VFs. These VFs that were just created have autogenerated MAC addresses to begin with (or 000). For the traffic from these VFs to be permissible on the OCI network, you need to set MAC addresses that OCI provides. These can be generated by creating VNIC attachments or using the API for it. From the OCI console, create the same number of VNIC attachments on the host as the number of VFs created. Note the MAC addresses of each VNIC attachment. Now these MAC addresses that are recognized by OCI can be assigned to each of these VFs that was created earlier. This completes the host setup. At this point, you have a bare metal instance with multiple VFs that have OCI-generated MAC addresses, as confirmed in Listing 5-15.

Listing 5-15   Setting the MAC Addresses and Assigning Them to the Previously Created VFs

```
...
# For each MAC address from the VNIC attachments

ip link set ${PHYSDEV} vf <n= 0..numVFs> mac <MAC Address from VNIC attachment>
  spoofchk off

# verify all VFs have Mac addresses from OCI
ip link show ${PHYSDEV}

...
```

With the host setup completed, the next step is to install the SR-IOV CNI and device plug-in. The SR-IOV CNI enables the configuration and use of SR-IOV VF networks from within pods; the device plug-in discovers and advertises the SR-IOV capable network devices on the node. This makes these SR-IOV devices allocatable resources on the node that pods can request, just as a pod requests CPU and memory.

This SR-IOV CNI can be installed on any Kubernetes cluster that is running Kubernetes version 1.16 or later. The CNI runs on the cluster as a daemon set. Because it is common for only some nodes in the cluster to have SR-IOV, nodes without SR-IOV devices are handled gracefully by the device plug-in itself:

```
git clone https://github.com/k8snetworkplumbingwg/sriov-cni.git && cd
  sriov-cni
kubectl apply -f images/k8s-v1.16/sriov-cni-daemonset.yaml && cd..
```

The primary purpose of the device plug-in is to discover, advertise, and track the usage of the SR-IOV-capable network devices on the node, so a configuration (expressed as a ConfigMap) is required to enable it to create the device plug-in endpoints. The configuration is specific to the NIC hardware and identifies the devices and the drivers used. To create this configuration, you need to know the vendor ID, device ID, and driver used by the device. This can be done with standard tools such as `lspci`. Listing 5-16 shows how to find the vendor ID and device ID.

Listing 5-16   How to Find the Vendor and Device IDs

```
lspci -nn|grep Virtual

31:02.0 Ethernet controller [0200]: Broadcom Inc. and subsidiaries NetXtreme-E
  Ethernet Virtual Function [14e4:16dc]
31:02.1 Ethernet controller [0200]: Broadcom Inc. and subsidiaries NetXtreme-E
  Ethernet Virtual Function [14e4:16dc]
```

The example in Listing 5-16 shows two VFs because we filtered the output of `lspci` with the keyword `Virtual`. `lspci` reads through the `sysfs` entries and presents the information in an easy-to-understand (and easy-to-parse) manner. In the example here, `31:02.0` represents the bus number (31), device number (02), and function (0). `lspci` uses `libpci`, which uses the PCI identification data in `/usr/share/hwdata/pci.ids` to decode information such as vendor and device numbers; it then uses that information here to identify the device class (`0200`) as an Ethernet controller and present the vendor information (Broadcom). The last bit of information provides the vendor ID (`14e4`) and device ID (`16dc`). You can cross-check this with the `hwdata` that `lspci` uses. The output shows that it is indeed an Ethernet virtual function from the vendor:

```
cat /usr/share/hwdata/pci.ids|grep 16dc

  16dc  NetXtreme-E Ethernet Virtual Function
```

With the device ID and vendor ID identified, you now need to find the drivers used. You can do this by searching `/sys` for the driver user on the PCI bus number, device number, and function. In the example here, the PCI bus, device, and function can be seen from the previous `lspci` output: `31:02.0`. Searching `sysfs` for this device reveals the driver name to be `bnxt_en`, as shown in Listing 5-17.

Listing 5-17   How to Find the Drivers Used

```
# filtering based on the PCIe slots.
Find /sys | grep drivers.*31:02.0|awk -F/ '{print $6}'

bnxt_en
```

Now you have the information to set up the configuration for the SR-IOV device plug-in. Create a configMap; it should be named `sriovdp-config` and should have a key `config.json`. Listing 5-18 shows an example of how this configMap should look.

Listing 5-18   Example configMap

```
cat << EOF > sriovdp-config.yaml
apiVersion: v1
kind: ConfigMap
metadata:
  name: sriovdp-config
  namespace: kube-system
data:
  config.json: |
    {
      "resourceList": [
        {
            "resourceName": "netxtreme_sriov_rdma",
            "resourcePrefix": "broadcom.com",
            "selectors": {
              "vendors": ["14e4"],
              "devices": ["16dc"],
              "drivers": ["bnxt_en"],
              "isRdma": false
            }
        }
      ]
    }
EOF

kubectl create -f sriovdp-config.yaml
```

This configuration lets the device plug-in look for PCIe devices that match the `selectors` in the configuration and advertise that the node has this type of resource. Pods then can request these by the `resourceName` in the configuration. An example of how a pod requests these resources is presented later in the chapter, in Listing 5-21.

With the config map created, the device plug-in can be installed as a DaemonSet:

```
git clone https://github.com/k8snetworkplumbingwg/sriov-network-device-plugin.git
  && cd sriov-network-device-plugin
kubectl create -f deployments/k8s-v1.16/sriovdp-daemonset.yaml && cd ..
```

With the DaemonSets deployed, you can check the container logs for troubleshooting. After a successful deployment, the node should list the virtual functions as allocatable resources. In this example, because you created two VFs and configured them with resourceName: netxtreme_sriov_rdma and resourcePrefix: broadcom. com, you see that the node now has two of these broadcom.com/netxtreme_sriov_rdma resources that can be requested by pods, along with the CPU, memory, and other resources on the node (see Listing 5-19).

Listing 5-19 Output of Running kubectl get nodes to See VFs as Allocatable Node Resources

```
```
kubectl get node <node_name> -o json | jq '.status.allocatable'

{
  "broadcom.com/netxtreme_sriov_rdma": "2",
  "cpu": "128",
  "ephemeral-storage": "37070025462",
  "hugepages-1Gi": "0",
  "hugepages-2Mi": "0",
  "memory": "527632840Ki",
  "pods": "110"
}
```
```

With the SR-IOV CNI and device plug-in set up, pods can now request these resources. However, you still need a way to plumb multiple network interfaces to a pod. This can be done by Multus, so the next task is to install Multus.

Multus is a meta plug-in that can chain multiple CNI plug-ins such as the SR-IOV CNI plug-in and the Flannel CNI plug-in, to support "multi-homed" pods or pods with multiple network interfaces. Installing Multus is done by simply applying the Multus DaemonSet:

```
git clone https://github.com/k8snetworkplumbingwg/multus-cni.git && cd multus-cni
kubectl apply -f images/multus-daemonset.yml && cd ..
```

To attach additional interfaces to the pods, you need a configuration for the interface to be attached. This is encapsulated in the custom resource of kind: NetworkAttachmentDefinition. This CRD is created when Multus is installed. This configuration is essentially a CNI configuration packaged as a custom resource. Listing 5-20 shows a NetworkAttachmentDefinition that uses the VFs created earlier.

Listing 5-20   Example Manifest Used to Create a `NetworkAttachmentDefinition` Custom Resource

```
cat << EOF > sriov-net1.yaml
apiVersion: k8s.cni.cncf.io/v1
kind: NetworkAttachmentDefinition
metadata:
  name: sriov-net1
  annotations:
    k8s.v1.cni.cncf.io/resourceName: broadcom.com/netxtreme_sriov_rdma
spec:
  config: '{
  "type": "sriov",
  "cniVersion": "0.3.1",
  "name": "sriov-network",
  "ipam": {
    "type": "host-local",
    "subnet": "10.20.30.0/25",
    "routes": [{
      "dst": "0.0.0.0/0"
    }],
    "gateway": "10.20.10.1"
  }
}'
EOF

kubectl apply -f sriov-net1.yaml
```

Pods can now request additional interfaces using an annotation and resource request. The resource request helps the scheduler assign the pod based on VF availability on nodes, and the annotation lets the meta plug-in (Multus) know which `NetworkAttachmentDefinition` (CNI Config) to use. Listing 5-21 shows an example with a test pod.

Listing 5-21   Example Manifest Used to Create Pods That Will Be Scheduled Based on the Availability of VFs on Nodes

```
## Create the first pod
cat << EOF | kubectl create -f -
apiVersion: v1
kind: Pod
metadata:
  name: testpod1
  annotations:
    k8s.v1.cni.cncf.io/networks: sriov-net1
spec:
  containers:
```

```
    - name: appcntr1
      image: centos/tools
      imagePullPolicy: IfNotPresent
      command: [ "/bin/bash", "-c", "--" ]
      args: [ "while true; do sleep 300000; done;" ]
      resources:
        requests:
          broadcom.com/netxtreme_sriov_rdma: '1'
        limits:
          broadcom.com/netxtreme_sriov_rdma: '1'
EOF

## Create a second pod
cat << EOF | kubectl create -f -
apiVersion: v1
kind: Pod
metadata:
  name: testpod2
  annotations:
    k8s.v1.cni.cncf.io/networks: sriov-net1
spec:
  containers:
  - name: appcntr1
    image: centos/tools
    imagePullPolicy: IfNotPresent
    command: [ "/bin/bash", "-c", "--" ]
    args: [ "while true; do sleep 300000; done;" ]
    resources:
      requests:
        broadcom.com/netxtreme_sriov_rdma: '1'
      limits:
        broadcom.com/netxtreme_sriov_rdma: '1'
EOF
```

With two pods created, you should be able to see that they are both running. Each pod is annotated with the k8s.v1.cni.cncf.io/networks: sriov-net1 annotation, which tells Multus that this pod needs to be attached to the network whose configuration is defined in the NetworkAttachmentDefinition named sriov-net1. Of course, this is the CNI configuration, and it establishes the default routes and IP address management. Additionally, the pod is making a resource request for the resource broadcom.com/netxtreme_sriov_rdma and is requesting a count of 1 of these resources. This effectively tells the Kubernetes scheduler that this pod needs to be allocated to a node that has at least one of these VFs available. When the network attachment has been made, the device plug-in updates the node and decrements the number of available VFs by one. When this pod is terminated, the VF that it has been using is released, and the device plug-in updates the node and increments the number of available VFs by one.

After the pods have been deployed, you can check that they both have multiple interfaces. You also can check the communication between the pods over the SR-IOV devices, as demonstrated in Listing 5-22.

Listing 5-22   Verifying That the Deployed Pods Have Multiple Interfaces and Can Communicate over SR-IOV

```
## Verify that both pods have two interfaces. An `eth0` on the overlay and a
## `net1` which is the VF.
kubectl exec -it testpod1 -- ip addr show
kubectl exec -it testpod2 -- ip addr show

## Checkout the routes
kubectl exec -it testpod1 -- route -n
kubectl exec -it testpod2 -- route -n

## test communication
kubectl exec -it testpod1 -- ping <IP for net1 on pod2>
```

Using Virtual Machine Nodes

Significant differences exist in how the interfaces are created and managed between bare metal and virtual machines. On a VM, you do not have access to the physical functions (PFs) on a PCIe device, so you must instead use the cloud provider APIs to interact with the PCIe device in order to create and manage the SR-IOV virtual functions (VFs) on them.

On VMs, you still use Multus to provide multiple interfaces to a pod; however, the SR-IOV CNI and the associated device plug-in are not used. This is because the SR-IOV CNI requires direct access to the underlying hardware. To overcome this challenge, you can use the OCI networking APIs for VNICs, to create a VF on the PF as in the bare metal scenario and give the VM direct and unobstructed access to this VF. These VFs now can be attached to a compute instance, including OKE nodes, as network interfaces. These interfaces/VFs can be moved to the network namespaces for pods, which allow the pod to use the VF directly and exclusively as a network interface. From the perspective of the pods, they are not able to distinguish between the two and, in both cases, have access to a VF that they can directly use.

To give a VM direct access to a VF, you need to launch the VM with the VFIO network attachment mode instead of the default *paravirtualized* mode. This choice is controlled by the launch mode for the compute instance. When the network attachment mode is set as VFIO, you can create network attachments using the OCI APIs, which creates VFs on the underlying PF and provides the VF directly to the VM. The OS on the host recognizes these as network interfaces. When the VF is available to the VM, it can be moved to the pod namespace. In this model, the VFs are created using OCI APIs instead of system commands in the bare-metal scenario. Figure 5-16 shows the VFs (ens5 and ens6) being moved into the pod namespace as net0 and net1.

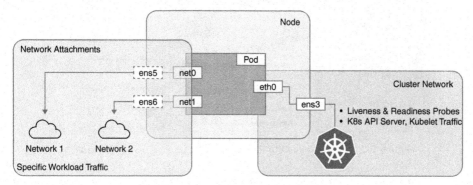

Figure 5-16 A Pod with Multiple Network Interfaces—Additional Interfaces Are Made Available to the Pod by Moving Them from the Host's Network Namespace to the Pod's Network Namespace

The first task in setting up SR-IOV-based secondary interfaces for pods is to prepare the nodes in a manner similar to the bare metal servers. In the case of VMs, each node that requires access to SR-IOV interfaces must be prepared for hardware-assisted network attachments before it can be used by pods. This is done by editing the nodes and updating their network attachment type.

Note

The method described here can be performed through the OCI console, which makes it easier to comprehend; however, this method is limited to clusters that operate using the Flannel CNI. The goal of updating the launch options is to essentially launch these nodes in the hardware-assisted (SR-IOV) mode, which creates a VF on the underlying PF and provides that to the VM when a network attachment is made. An alternate way to accomplish this, which also is applicable for clusters using the OCI native CNI, is to create a custom image based on the standard OKE image; edit the image capabilities and set the image to launch instances using the hardware-assisted (SR-IOV) mode; and then use this custom image for your node pools.

To update the nodes to use the hardware-assisted (SR-IOV) mode, edit the instance properties of the node as shown in Figure 5-17.

On the instance properties, click **Show Advanced Options** to view the additional properties. On the **Launch Options** tab, choose **Hardware-Assisted (SR-IOV) Networking** for the networking type, as illustrated in Figure 5-18.

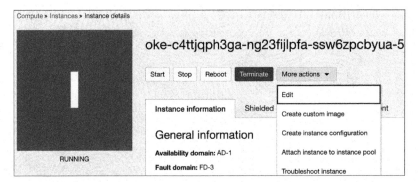

Figure 5-17   How to Edit the Properties of an Existing Compute Instance

> ## Note
> After an instance has been switched from *paravirtualized* network attachment to hardware-assisted (SR-IOV or VFIO) mode, it is no longer eligible for live migration for infrastructure maintenance.

The update workflow prompts you to reboot the instance. After the reboot, the instance has VFIO network attachments. This can be verified on the console, as Figure 5-19 illustrates.

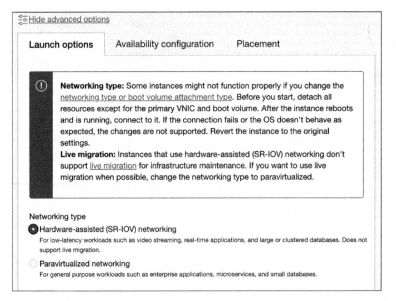

Figure 5-18   Updating the Networking Type of an Instance to Use Hardware-Assisted (SR-IOV) Networking

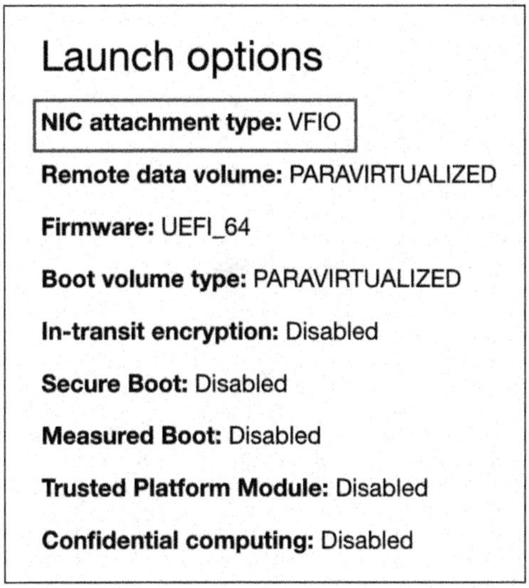

```
Launch options

NIC attachment type: VFIO

Remote data volume: PARAVIRTUALIZED

Firmware: UEFI_64

Boot volume type: PARAVIRTUALIZED

In-transit encryption: Disabled

Secure Boot: Disabled

Measured Boot: Disabled

Trusted Platform Module: Disabled

Confidential computing: Disabled
```

Figure 5-19   Current Launch Options for the Instance, Including the VFIO Network Attachment

Additionally, you can verify that your instances are using SR-IOV network attachments to connect to a node using SSH and use lspci to list the PCI devices on the VM. You should be able to see the underlying virtual function directly on the VM instead of a device using a virtio driver (such as the storage controller in Listing 5-23.

Listing 5-23   Using lspci to Verify That the Virtual Function Is Directly Visible from the VM

```
$ lspci
00:00.0 Host bridge: Intel Corporation 440FX - 82441FX PM [Natoma] (rev 02)
00:01.0 ISA bridge: Intel Corporation 82371SB PIIX3 ISA [Natoma/Triton II]
00:01.1 IDE interface: Intel Corporation 82371SB PIIX3 IDE [Natoma/Triton II]
00:01.2 USB controller: Intel Corporation 82371SB PIIX3 USB [Natoma/Triton II]
  (rev 01)
C00:01.3 Bridge: Intel Corporation 82371AB/EB/MB PIIX4 ACPI (rev 03)
00:02.0 VGA compatible controller: Device 1234:1111 (rev 02)
00:03.0. Ethernet controller: Mellanox Technologies MT28800 Family [Connect-5 Ex
  Virtual Function]
00:04.0 SCSI storage controller: Red Hat, Inc. Virtio SCSI
```

At this point, the node has a single VNIC attachment, which is the primary VNIC used for all communications to the node. Because the instance is using hardware-assisted network attachments, the network attachment is visible to the node as a virtual function on the underlying hardware. For pods to have exclusive use of a virtual function (VF), you need additional VFs on the VM. This can be provided using the console or API to add VNIC attachments to the instance. These VNIC attachments are VFs on the underlying PF. They can be verified with lspci.

To add VNIC attachments, from the instance page, choose **Attached VNICs** and click **Create VNIC**, as shown in Figure 5-20.

Figure 5-20   Creating a VNIC in the Console

On this page, you can configure the VNIC using the VCN and subnet that is needed, as demonstrated in Figure 5-21.

Figure 5-21   Selecting the VCN and Subnet for Use with Your VNIC

When this is configured, you should verify that the VNIC can be seen on the host as a virtual function (as before) by connecting to the node using SSH and running `lspci`, as demonstrated in Figure 5-22.

```
[opc@oke-c4ttjqph3ga-ng23fijlpfa-ssw6zpcbyua-5 ~]$ lspci
00:00.0 Host bridge: Intel Corporation 440FX - 82441FX PMC [Natoma] (rev 02)
00:01.0 ISA bridge: Intel Corporation 82371SB PIIX3 ISA [Natoma/Triton II]
00:01.1 IDE interface: Intel Corporation 82371SB PIIX3 IDE [Natoma/Triton II]
00:01.2 USB controller: Intel Corporation 82371SB PIIX3 USB [Natoma/Triton II] (rev 01)
00:01.3 Bridge: Intel Corporation 82371AB/EB/MB PIIX4 ACPI (rev 03)
00:02.0 VGA compatible controller: Device 1234:1111 (rev 02)
00:03.0 Ethernet controller: Mellanox Technologies MT28800 Family [ConnectX-5 Ex Virtual Function]
00:04.0 SCSI storage controller: Red Hat, Inc. Virtio SCSI
[opc@oke-c4ttjqph3ga-ng23fijlpfa-ssw6zpcbyua-5 ~]$ lspci
00:00.0 Host bridge: Intel Corporation 440FX - 82441FX PMC [Natoma] (rev 02)
00:01.0 ISA bridge: Intel Corporation 82371SB PIIX3 ISA [Natoma/Triton II]
00:01.1 IDE interface: Intel Corporation 82371SB PIIX3 IDE [Natoma/Triton II]
00:01.2 USB controller: Intel Corporation 82371SB PIIX3 USB [Natoma/Triton II] (rev 01)
00:01.3 Bridge: Intel Corporation 82371AB/EB/MB PIIX4 ACPI (rev 03)
00:02.0 VGA compatible controller: Device 1234:1111 (rev 02)
00:03.0 Ethernet controller: Mellanox Technologies MT28800 Family [ConnectX-5 Ex Virtual Function]
00:04.0 SCSI storage controller: Red Hat, Inc. Virtio SCSI
00:05.0 Ethernet controller: Mellanox Technologies MT28800 Family [ConnectX-5 Ex Virtual Function]
[opc@oke-c4ttjqph3ga-ng23fijlpfa-ssw6zpcbyua-5 ~]$ []
```

Figure 5-22   Displaying the VNIC on the Host as a VF

When you add a secondary VNIC to a Linux VM instance, a new interface (that is, an Ethernet device) is added to the instance and automatically recognized by the OS. However, DHCP is not active for the secondary VNIC, and you must configure the interface with the static IP address and default route. The next step is to configure the OS for secondary VNICs. OCI provides documentation and a script for configuring the OS for secondary VNICs. To configure the secondary VNIC, download the script on the node and run it based on the instructions provided in the OCI documentation.

After the script for configuring the secondary VNICs has been run, you should verify that the interface is now connected, with its IP address and default route. To check that this has been configured, use the command `ip addr` as shown in Figure 5-23 or a similar tool like `nmcli`.

```
[opc@oke-c4ttjqph3ga-ng23fijlpfa-ssw6zpcbyua-5 ~]$ ip addr
1: lo: <LOOPBACK,UP,LOWER_UP> mtu 65536 qdisc noqueue state UNKNOWN group default qlen 1000
    link/loopback 00:00:00:00:00:00 brd 00:00:00:00:00:00
    inet 127.0.0.1/8 scope host lo
       valid_lft forever preferred_lft forever
    inet6 ::1/128 scope host
       valid_lft forever preferred_lft forever
2: ens3: <BROADCAST,MULTICAST,UP,LOWER_UP> mtu 9000 qdisc mq state UP group default qlen 1000
    link/ether 00:00:17:01:01:e8 brd ff:ff:ff:ff:ff:ff
    altname enp0s3
    inet 10.0.10.188/24 brd 10.0.10.255 scope global dynamic ens3
       valid_lft 76585sec preferred_lft 76585sec
    inet6 fe80::200:17ff:fe01:1e8/64 scope link
       valid_lft forever preferred_lft forever
3: ens5: <BROADCAST,MULTICAST,UP,LOWER_UP> mtu 9000 qdisc mq state UP group default qlen 1000
    link/ether 02:00:17:16:45:16 brd ff:ff:ff:ff:ff:ff
    altname enp0s5
    inet 10.0.10.93/24 scope global ens5
       valid_lft forever preferred_lft forever
```

Figure 5-23   Verifying Whether the Interface Is Now Connected

Optionally, it would be a good practice to verify the routing using a ping to reach the secondary IP addresses from each other. In Figure 5-24 and Figure 5-25, 10.0.10.238 is the secondary IP on a second node in the cluster. This completes the host setup for the nodes.

```
[opc@oke-c4ttjqph3ga-ng23fijlpfa-ssw6zpcbyua-5 ~]$ ping -S 10.0.10.93 10.0.10.238
PING 10.0.10.238 (10.0.10.238) 56(84) bytes of data.
64 bytes from 10.0.10.238: icmp_seq=1 ttl=64 time=0.873 ms
64 bytes from 10.0.10.238: icmp_seq=2 ttl=64 time=0.759 ms
64 bytes from 10.0.10.238: icmp_seq=3 ttl=64 time=1.41 ms
64 bytes from 10.0.10.238: icmp_seq=4 ttl=64 time=0.787 ms
64 bytes from 10.0.10.238: icmp_seq=5 ttl=64 time=0.817 ms
64 bytes from 10.0.10.238: icmp_seq=6 ttl=64 time=0.806 ms
^C
--- 10.0.10.238 ping statistics ---
6 packets transmitted, 6 received, 0% packet loss, time 5116ms
rtt min/avg/max/mdev = 0.759/0.908/1.409/0.228 ms
[opc@oke-c4ttjqph3ga-ng23fijlpfa-ssw6zpcbyua-5 ~]$ ▮
```

Figure 5-24   Verifying Connectivity Between the Secondary VNICs

```
[opc@oke-c4ttjqph3ga-ng23fijlpfa-ssw6zpcbyua-0 ~]$ ping -S 10.0.10.238 10.0.10.93
PING 10.0.10.93 (10.0.10.93) 56(84) bytes of data.
64 bytes from 10.0.10.93: icmp_seq=1 ttl=64 time=0.909 ms
64 bytes from 10.0.10.93: icmp_seq=2 ttl=64 time=0.780 ms
64 bytes from 10.0.10.93: icmp_seq=3 ttl=64 time=0.842 ms
64 bytes from 10.0.10.93: icmp_seq=4 ttl=64 time=0.784 ms
64 bytes from 10.0.10.93: icmp_seq=5 ttl=64 time=0.831 ms
64 bytes from 10.0.10.93: icmp_seq=6 ttl=64 time=0.814 ms
^C
--- 10.0.10.93 ping statistics ---
6 packets transmitted, 6 received, 0% packet loss, time 5106ms
rtt min/avg/max/mdev = 0.780/0.826/0.909/0.054 ms
[opc@oke-c4ttjqph3ga-ng23fijlpfa-ssw6zpcbyua-0 ~]$ ▮
```

Figure 5-25   Verifying Connectivity Between the Secondary VNICs from the Other Direction

With the host setup completed, you can now install Multus on the cluster. The installation of Multus follows the exact same steps as for the bare metal nodes. This is because Multus is just software that runs on the cluster and does not care about the node types.

With Multus installed on the cluster, you are ready to attach multiple interfaces to pods. To do this, you need a configuration for the interface to be attached, which is expressed as a NetworkAttachmentDefinition just as before, for bare metal nodes. This configuration is essentially a CNI configuration packaged as a custom resource. When using VMs, there is no access to the underlying hardware, and the VM is directly given access to one or more virtual functions on the physical NIC. The goal for the NetworkAttachmentDefinition is to provide an SR-IOV virtual function that has already been created for the exclusive use of a single pod so that the pod can take advantage of the capabilities without interference of any layers in between. To grant a pod exclusive access to the VF, you can leverage the host device plug-in that enables you to move the interface from the default or the root namespace into the pod's namespace so that it has exclusive access to it.

The examples in Listing 5-24 show `NetworkAttachmentDefinition` objects that configure the secondary `ens5` interface that was added to the nodes. The `ipam` plug-in configuration determines how IP addresses are managed for these interfaces. In this example, because you want to use the same IP addresses that were assigned to the secondary interfaces by OCI, you use the static `ipam` configuration with the appropriate routes. `ipam` configuration also supports other methods, such as `host-local` or `dhcp`, for more flexible configurations.

Listing 5-24   Creating the Objects Used to Configure the Secondary ens5 Interface Added to the Nodes

```
## network attachment for the first node. Note the IPaddress assignment in the
## `ipam` configuration.

cat << EOF | kubectl create -f -
apiVersion: "k8s.cni.cncf.io/v1"
kind: NetworkAttachmentDefinition
metadata:
  name: sriov-vnic-1
spec:
  config: '{
        "cniVersion": "0.3.1",
        "type": "host-device",
        "device": "ens5",
        "ipam": {
                "type": "static",
                "addresses": [
                    {
                        "address": "10.0.10.93/24",
                        "gateway": "0.0.0.0"
                    }
                ],
                "routes": [
                    { "dst": "10.0.10.0/24", "gw": "0.0.0.0" }
                ]
            }
        }'
EOF

## network attachment for the second node. Note the IPaddress assignment in the
## `ipam` configuration.

cat << EOF | kubectl create -f -
```

```
apiVersion: "k8s.cni.cncf.io/v1"
kind: NetworkAttachmentDefinition
metadata:
  name: sriov-vnic-2
spec:
  config: '{
        "cniVersion": "0.3.1",
        "type": "host-device",
        "device": "ens5",
        "ipam": {
                "type": "static",
                "addresses": [
                    {
                        "address": "10.0.10.238/24",
                        "gateway": "0.0.0.0"
                    }
                ],
                "routes": [
                    { "dst": "10.0.10.0/24", "gw": "0.0.0.0" }
                ]
            }
        }'
EOF
```

With Multus configured with these additional network attachment definitions, pods can now request additional interfaces using an annotation. The annotation lets the meta plug-in (Multus) know what NetworkAttachmentDefinition (CNI Config) to use to provide additional interfaces when the pod is created.

Note

When using a static configuration like the one shown in Listing 5-24, the pods need to have node affinity set so that the pod is scheduled on the node where the desired host device is available. This differs from the approach when using bare metal nodes: In that case, you can use the SR-IOV device plug-in that keeps track of the VFs that are available on the node.

Listing 5-25 shows an example with a test pod.

Listing 5-25   Creating a Test Pod That Requests Additional Interfaces

```
## Create the first pod
cat << EOF | kubectl create -f -
apiVersion: v1
kind: Pod
metadata:
  name: testpod1
```

```
    annotations:
      k8s.v1.cni.cncf.io/networks: sriov-vnic-1
  spec:
    containers:
    - name: appcntr1
      image: centos/tools
      imagePullPolicy: IfNotPresent
      command: [ "/bin/bash", "-c", "--" ]
      args: [ "while true; do sleep 300000; done;" ]

EOF

## Create a second pod
cat << EOF | kubectl create -f -
apiVersion: v1
kind: Pod
metadata:
  name: testpod2
  annotations:
    k8s.v1.cni.cncf.io/networks: sriov-vnic-2
spec:
  containers:
  - name: appcntr1
    image: centos/tools
    imagePullPolicy: IfNotPresent
    command: [ "/bin/bash", "-c", "--" ]
    args: [ "while true; do sleep 300000; done;" ]

EOF
```

With two pods created and in the running state, you should be able to see that additional network interfaces were created during the creation of the pods. Multus provides the eth0 interface that is backed by the default CNI (Flannel, in this example) and an additional net1 interface that is the SR-IOV virtual function. You can describe the pods and observe the Events section of the output to see the various events, including the interfaces attached to the pod (see Figure 5-26).

```
Events:
  Type    Reason          Age   From               Message
  ----    ------          ---   ----               -------
  Normal  Scheduled       99s   default-scheduler  Successfully assigned default/testpod1 to 10.0.10.188
  Normal  AddedInterface  99s   multus             Add eth0 [10.244.4.32/25] from cbr0
  Normal  AddedInterface  99s   multus             Add net1 [10.0.10.93/24] from default/sriov-vnic-1
  Normal  Pulling         99s   kubelet            Pulling image "centos/tools"
  Normal  Pulled          68s   kubelet            Successfully pulled image "centos/tools" in 30.536042966s
  Normal  Created         68s   kubelet            Created container appcntr1
  Normal  Started         68s   kubelet            Started container appcntr1
```

Figure 5-26   Events Associated with Creating Additional Network Interfaces When the Pods Were Started

After the pods have started, you can perform a quick test (see Listing 5-26) to verify that the pods have multiple network interfaces attached to them.

Listing 5-26   Verifying That the Pods Have Multiple Network Interfaces Attached to Them

```
## Verify that both pods have two interfaces. An `eth0` on the overlay and a
## `net1` which is the VF, along with the IP address for the secondary VNIC.
kubectl exec -it testpod1 -- ip addr show
kubectl exec -it testpod2 -- ip addr show
```

The output should be similar to Figure 5-27 and Figure 5-28.

```
> kubectl exec -it testpod1 -- ip addr show
1: lo: <LOOPBACK,UP,LOWER_UP> mtu 65536 qdisc noqueue state UNKNOWN group default qlen 1000
    link/loopback 00:00:00:00:00:00 brd 00:00:00:00:00:00
    inet 127.0.0.1/8 scope host lo
       valid_lft forever preferred_lft forever
    inet6 ::1/128 scope host
       valid_lft forever preferred_lft forever
3: eth0@if37: <BROADCAST,MULTICAST,UP,LOWER_UP> mtu 8950 qdisc noqueue state UP group default
    link/ether 2a:11:96:ce:5d:7c brd ff:ff:ff:ff:ff:ff link-netnsid 0
    inet 10.244.4.32/25 brd 10.244.4.127 scope global eth0
       valid_lft forever preferred_lft forever
    inet6 fe80::2811:96ff:fece:5d7c/64 scope link
       valid_lft forever preferred_lft forever
14: net1: <BROADCAST,MULTICAST,UP,LOWER_UP> mtu 9000 qdisc mq state UP group default qlen 1000
    link/ether 02:00:17:16:45:16 brd ff:ff:ff:ff:ff:ff
    inet 10.0.10.93/24 brd 10.0.10.255 scope global net1
       valid_lft forever preferred_lft forever
    inet6 fe80::17ff:fe16:4516/64 scope link
       valid_lft forever preferred_lft forever
```

Figure 5-27   Output for the First Pod of the Test to Verify That Pods Have Multiple Network Interfaces Attached to Them

```
> kubectl exec -it testpod2 -- ip addr show
1: lo: <LOOPBACK,UP,LOWER_UP> mtu 65536 qdisc noqueue state UNKNOWN group default qlen 1000
    link/loopback 00:00:00:00:00:00 brd 00:00:00:00:00:00
    inet 127.0.0.1/8 scope host lo
       valid_lft forever preferred_lft forever
    inet6 ::1/128 scope host
       valid_lft forever preferred_lft forever
3: eth0@if50: <BROADCAST,MULTICAST,UP,LOWER_UP> mtu 8950 qdisc noqueue state UP group default
    link/ether de:ee:ab:3e:19:e3 brd ff:ff:ff:ff:ff:ff link-netnsid 0
    inet 10.244.4.174/25 brd 10.244.4.255 scope global eth0
       valid_lft forever preferred_lft forever
    inet6 fe80::dcee:abff:fe3e:19e3/64 scope link
       valid_lft forever preferred_lft forever
18: net1: <BROADCAST,MULTICAST,UP,LOWER_UP> mtu 9000 qdisc mq state UP group default qlen 1000
    link/ether 02:00:17:14:28:b9 brd ff:ff:ff:ff:ff:ff
    inet 10.0.10.238/24 brd 10.0.10.255 scope global net1
       valid_lft forever preferred_lft forever
    inet6 fe80::17ff:fe14:28b9/64 scope link
```

Figure 5-28   Output for the Second Pod of the Test to Verify That Pods Have Multiple Network Interfaces Attached to Them

After you have verified that the pods have the SR-IOV interfaces attached to them in addition to the primary interface, you can verify the communication between the two pods over these secondary (SR-IOV) interfaces using the commands in Listing 5-27.

Listing 5-27 Testing Connectivity Between the Two Pods over the Secondary Interfaces

```
## test communication
kubectl exec -it testpod1 -- ping -I net1  <ip address for secondary vnic on the
   other pod/node>
kubectl exec -it testpod2 -- ping -I net1  <ip address for secondary vnic on the
   other pod/node>
```

The output should be similar to Figure 5-29 and Figure 5-30.

```
) kubectl exec -it testpod1 -- ping -I net1 10.0.10.238
PING 10.0.10.238 (10.0.10.238) from 10.0.10.93 net1: 56(84) bytes of data.
64 bytes from 10.0.10.238: icmp_seq=1 ttl=64 time=0.815 ms
64 bytes from 10.0.10.238: icmp_seq=2 ttl=64 time=0.764 ms
64 bytes from 10.0.10.238: icmp_seq=3 ttl=64 time=0.778 ms
64 bytes from 10.0.10.238: icmp_seq=4 ttl=64 time=0.747 ms
64 bytes from 10.0.10.238: icmp_seq=5 ttl=64 time=0.820 ms
64 bytes from 10.0.10.238: icmp_seq=6 ttl=64 time=0.765 ms
^C
--- 10.0.10.238 ping statistics ---
6 packets transmitted, 6 received, 0% packet loss, time 5102ms
rtt min/avg/max/mdev = 0.747/0.781/0.820/0.038 ms
```

Figure 5-29 Output of the Connectivity Test for the First Pod

```
) kubectl exec -it testpod2 -- ping -I net1 10.0.10.93
PING 10.0.10.93 (10.0.10.93) from 10.0.10.238 net1: 56(84) bytes of data.
64 bytes from 10.0.10.93: icmp_seq=1 ttl=64 time=0.768 ms
64 bytes from 10.0.10.93: icmp_seq=2 ttl=64 time=0.730 ms
64 bytes from 10.0.10.93: icmp_seq=3 ttl=64 time=0.795 ms
64 bytes from 10.0.10.93: icmp_seq=4 ttl=64 time=0.743 ms
64 bytes from 10.0.10.93: icmp_seq=5 ttl=64 time=0.788 ms
64 bytes from 10.0.10.93: icmp_seq=6 ttl=64 time=0.760 ms
^C
--- 10.0.10.93 ping statistics ---
6 packets transmitted, 6 received, 0% packet loss, time 5152ms
rtt min/avg/max/mdev = 0.730/0.764/0.795/0.022 ms
```

Figure 5-30 Output of the Connectivity Test for the Second Pod

Optionally, you can validate that the pods are routable using their network attachments by trying to reach them from the VMs or any other source within the VCN using the commands in Listing 5-28.

Listing 5-28   Verifying Whether the Pods Are Routable from Another Source Within the VCN, Such as a VM

```
## Test that the pod is routable from outside Kubernetes. This is executed from
   node1.
ping 10.0.10.238

## similarly, from node 2
ping 10.0.10.93
```

The output should resemble Figure 5-31 and Figure 5-32.

```
[opc@oke-c4ttjqph3ga-ng23fijlpfa-ssw6zpcbyua-5 ~]$ ping 10.0.10.238
PING 10.0.10.238 (10.0.10.238) 56(84) bytes of data.
64 bytes from 10.0.10.238: icmp_seq=1 ttl=64 time=0.863 ms
64 bytes from 10.0.10.238: icmp_seq=2 ttl=64 time=0.804 ms
64 bytes from 10.0.10.238: icmp_seq=3 ttl=64 time=0.779 ms
64 bytes from 10.0.10.238: icmp_seq=4 ttl=64 time=0.836 ms
^C
--- 10.0.10.238 ping statistics ---
4 packets transmitted, 4 received, 0% packet loss, time 3071ms
rtt min/avg/max/mdev = 0.779/0.820/0.863/0.042 ms
```

Figure 5-31   Output of the Routability Test for the First Pod

```
[opc@oke-c4ttjqph3ga-ng23fijlpfa-ssw6zpcbyua-0 ~]$ ping 10.0.10.93
PING 10.0.10.93 (10.0.10.93) 56(84) bytes of data.
64 bytes from 10.0.10.93: icmp_seq=1 ttl=64 time=0.831 ms
64 bytes from 10.0.10.93: icmp_seq=2 ttl=64 time=0.784 ms
64 bytes from 10.0.10.93: icmp_seq=3 ttl=64 time=1.41 ms
64 bytes from 10.0.10.93: icmp_seq=4 ttl=64 time=0.830 ms
64 bytes from 10.0.10.93: icmp_seq=5 ttl=64 time=0.805 ms
^C
--- 10.0.10.93 ping statistics ---
5 packets transmitted, 5 received, 0% packet loss, time 4114ms
rtt min/avg/max/mdev = 0.784/0.932/1.412/0.241 ms
```

Figure 5-32   Output of the Routability Test for the Second Pod

Summary

This chapter examined what it is like to own and operate a Kubernetes cluster with Container Engine for Kubernetes. The chapter started with the most common and most frequent task that Kubernetes operators perform: upgrades. You examined upgrades for your control plane and looked at several strategies for upgrading your data plane or nodes. Then you delved into strategies for scaling a cluster to meet the demands of workloads—after all, workloads and their characteristics change. The chapter discussed various autoscaling mechanisms, including the HorizontalPodAutoscaler (HPA), the Vertical Pod Autoscaler (VPA,) and the Kubernetes Cluster Autoscaler, which scales the cluster infrastructure. You also looked at some autoscaler best practices and the interactions between the HPA and the Cluster Autoscaler, which are commonly used together to orchestrate and automate cluster scaling operations and to optimize cost. Additionally, you examined other day 2 operational concerns, such as service account authentication, client token generation, and DNS configuration both within the cluster and using ExternalDNS.

The chapter moved on to look at extending cluster functionality with cluster add-ons and did a deep dive on setting up a monitoring stack based on Prometheus and Grafana. You also looked at operators for Kubernetes, including the operators for OCI, Oracle Database, and Oracle WebLogic. A critical aspect of managing your own cluster is troubleshooting it when you encounter issues. You saw how Node Doctor from OCI helps you diagnose and troubleshoot issues with your cluster nodes.

Finally, you looked at an advanced configuration that showcases several techniques for cluster configuration and customization by deploying a meta CNI and additional device plug-ins on both bare metal and virtual machine nodes, to grant additional networking capabilities for your pods.

References

1 Setting up a NodeLocal DNS cache: https://kubernetes.io/docs/tasks/administer-cluster/nodelocaldns/#configuration

2 Setting up ExternalDNS for Oracle Cloud Infrastructure (OCI): https://github.com/kubernetes-sigs/external-dns/blob/master/docs/tutorials/oracle.md

3 OKE Operator Framework page: https://sdk.operatorframework.io/docs/installation/

4 OCI Service Operator for Kubernetes (OSOK): https://github.com/oracle/oci-service-operator

5 Installing the Operator SDK: https://github.com/oracle/oci-service-operator/blob/main/docs/installation.md#install-operator-sdk

6 Multus CNI: https://github.com/k8snetworkplumbingwg/multus-cni

6

Securing Your Workloads
and Infrastructure

"Kubernetes has become the de-facto standard for managing containerized applications. It is used by many organizations to deploy, scale, and manage their applications in a distributed environment. However, with the rise of Kubernetes, there has been an increased focus on Kubernetes security. Security is essential to any infrastructure, and Kubernetes is no exception."

—Anonymous

Securing workloads on Kubernetes and the connected infrastructure is one of the most important—and, at the same time, one of the most forgotten and procrastinated— steps in deployments. The goal of this chapter is to highlight the various security aspects of running Kubernetes in production. These sections look at the various facets of security related to Kubernetes and dive deeper into some of the more common tools and practices of securing workloads and infrastructure when using Kubernetes.

Kubernetes Security Challenges

A Kubernetes cluster is a complex system made up of a large number of moving parts, ranging from the core Kubernetes components and controllers to third-party and open-source software add-ons. Moreover, Kubernetes is a distributed system that uses networks to communicate and orchestrate work. It also relies on more fundamental building blocks, such as a container runtime and operating system features. This means that the security challenges of running Kubernetes are distributed across several strata:

- **Access control:** Kubernetes provides several access control mechanisms, such as role-based access control (RBAC) and network policies, to control access to the Kubernetes application programming interface (API) and resources. Misconfigurations or incorrect use of these mechanisms can lead to unauthorized access.
- **Network security:** Kubernetes is designed to run containerized applications in a networked environment; however, this introduces several challenges, such as handling network segmentation, securing the network, and managing network policies.

- **Container security:** Kubernetes uses containers to run applications, which means that the security of the containers is critical. Vulnerabilities in the containers can be exploited to gain unauthorized access to the Kubernetes environment.
- **Supply chain security:** The container image supply chain involves several parties, including developers, maintainers, and third-party software vendors. Any of these parties can introduce vulnerabilities into the container images, which can then be exploited to gain unauthorized access.

Concepts of Kubernetes Security

With the expansive nature of Kubernetes security, it is often easier to think about security pillars for your Kubernetes cluster instead of the nebulous concept of securing your cluster as a whole. With this view you can identify and segregate some of the primary security pillars, as follows:

- **Authentication:** The process of verifying the identity of a user or process. Kubernetes supports several authentication mechanisms, such as X.509 client certificates, static token files, bootstrap tokens, and OpenID Connect tokens.
- **Network security:** The process of protecting the network and its resources from unauthorized access, misuse, modification, and denial. Kubernetes supports several network security mechanisms, such as network policies and network segmentation.
- **Container security:** The process of protecting the container and its resources from unauthorized access, misuse, modification, and denial. Kubernetes supports several container security mechanisms, such as container vulnerability scanning, image signing, and least privilege.
- **Threat modeling:** The process of identifying, understanding, and mitigating the security risks to a system or application. Threat modeling is a critical step in the software development lifecycle.

4Cs of Kubernetes Security

The Kubernetes project promotes a layered view for cloud native security that is complementary to the defense-in-depth approach to security. The four layers of security, proposed by the Kubernetes project, is the recommendation to secure the cloud, clusters, containers, and code. In most cases, this model cuts down on cross-team dependencies to implement security because each layer is owned and managed by an individual team. Furthermore, this layered view of securing your workloads can make it easy to keep a tight focus on the individual areas or layers. Figure 6-1 illustrates the 4Cs of Kubernetes security.

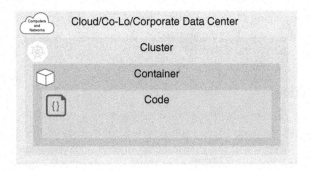

Figure 6-1   4Cs of Kubernetes Security

It is important to note that vulnerabilities at the cluster layer can significantly affect the layers within, including the code layer. This means that even if you try to protect your code layer, it might still be vulnerable if there are issues with the cluster layer.

Each component of a cluster has its own potential security concerns, which the next section explores. Container security relies on trusted code. By combining container vulnerability scanning and image signing, you can ensure that nothing has been modified, thus preventing any malicious activity that could bypass the least privileges required.

Numerous cloud providers exist, each with their own security best practices and settings. Although most are secure, it's always a good idea to research the settings yourself instead of relying solely on the provider's security measures. This is especially important if you are using a multicloud strategy with different security configurations. The next section covers Oracle Cloud Infrastructure Container Engine for Kubernetes (OKE) and the supporting infrastructure.

Securing Oracle Cloud Infrastructure Container Engine for Kubernetes (OKE)

Securing the cloud infrastructure for the managed Kubernetes is the first C of the 4Cs of Kubernetes security, and this is the first layer to secure your workloads.

Oracle Cloud Infrastructure is a security-focused cloud provider that offers a highly secure computing environment. It starts with off-box virtualization and is complemented by secure defaults for all infrastructure components at every level. This focus on security extends to the Kubernetes clusters created by OKE. These clusters have secure configurations with minimal access, by default, and feature different options and configurations to accommodate corporate policies and methodologies.

With Oracle managing the Kubernetes Control Plane, the security implementations remain on the cloud layer, allowing abstraction for the cluster to use standard Kubernetes security features—the second C layer.

Private Clusters

Creating a private cluster is an option when provisioning a new OKE cluster, making the Kubernetes API endpoint private and accessible only from within the cluster's virtual cloud network (VCN). Using this option, you can have a private cluster with no public IP address. To access Kubernetes APIs from tools such as kubectl, you need to use a bastion host or a connection that has access to the private network.

The section "Creating a Cluster" in Chapter 4, "Understanding Container Engine for Kubernetes," covers the creation of a private cluster using the OCI console, CLI, and Terraform.

Using a private endpoint and private workers, you isolate the nodes and pods from the Internet, by default, for either managed or virtual node pools.

Other extra measures to guarantee that your cluster will stay private include using security zones with the Maximum-Security Recipe, which prevents any user, including administrators, from exposing the cluster to the Internet. In this case, if you need to create Load Balancers that expose services to the Internet, you need to use a subnet that is not part of the security zone or use a subnet from a different VCN and configure the peering. Figure 6-2 illustrates the separation of resources on a private cluster.

For an extra level of security for a private cluster, you can consider limiting the images used by the deployments by using a private registry, such as Oracle Cloud Infrastructure Registry (OCIR), or a private repository, such as Harbor, to ensure that only trusted images are used.

Accessing Private Clusters

Bastion hosts (also known as jump boxes) are the most common way to access private clusters. Bastion hosts are virtual machines that are deployed in the same VCN as the cluster. Bastion hosts are used to access the cluster's Kubernetes API endpoint. Bastion hosts are not part of the cluster and are not managed by Kubernetes. Bastion hosts are not required to be running at all times; they can be started and stopped as needed. To create a new bastion host, you can use the OCI Console, OCI CLI, or OCI Terraform Provider to create a new compute instance that is either in the same VCN as the cluster or that has connectivity to the cluster's VCN.

Another option for accessing private clusters is Bastion Service, a service that runs in the cluster and provides access to the cluster's Kubernetes API endpoint. Different from the Bastion Host, the Bastion Service does not need a compute instance to run and does not need to be in the cluster's VCN. As with the other resources, you can create the Bastion Service with any OCI tool.

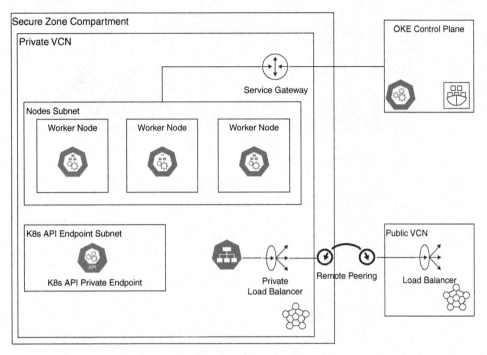

Figure 6-2 Private Cluster Diagram

Another powerful tool to access private clusters is the OCI Cloud Shell, a browser-based shell that you can use to access OCI resources. OCI Cloud Shell is a fully managed service that runs in the cloud and provides access to OCI resources without the need to install and configure any software on your local machine. After configuring the kubeconfig file, you can change the OCI Cloud Shell network to be the same VCN as the Cluster, selecting a subnet that has access to the cluster's Kubernetes API endpoint. Figure 6-3 illustrates the OCI Cloud Shell option to access a private network.

In some cases, you might not want to use bastion hosts or jump boxes to access your private clusters. Instead, you can use a VPN connection to access the cluster's Kubernetes API endpoint. To create a VPN connection or a remote peering connection with access to a different cloud or on-premises network, you need to configure the connection according to your network topology. Figure 6-4 illustrates different options to access and maintain OKE private clusters.

When deploying apps to private clusters and using tools such as Terraform (using the Terraform Kubernetes/Helm providers) or OCI Ansible modules, you can use the OCI Bastion Service or OCI Cloud Shell to access the cluster's Kubernetes API endpoint. When using OCI Resource Manager, you can create a private endpoint and configure the Terraform Kubernetes Provider to use the private endpoint.

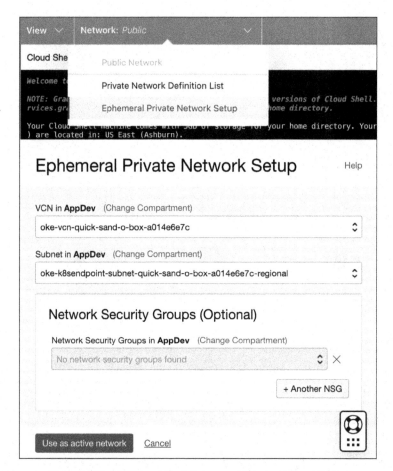

Figure 6-3   OCI Cloud Shell Ephemeral Private Network Setup

Listing 6-1 provides an example of a Terraform Kubernetes Provider configuration using the OCI Resource Manager private endpoint.

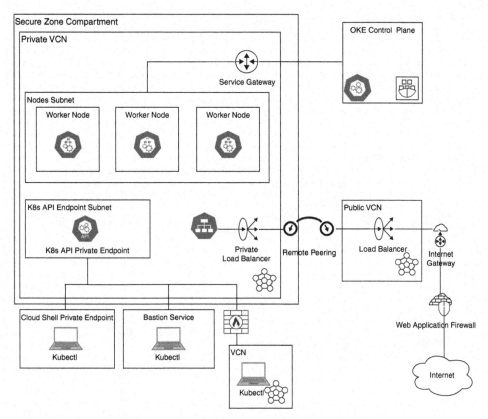

Figure 6-4   Different Access Options for OKE Private Clusters

Listing 6-1   OCI Resource Manager Private Endpoint Terraform HCL Script
_____
```
...
resource "oci_resourcemanager_private_endpoint" "private_kubernetes_endpoint" {
    compartment_id = local.oke_compartment_ocid
    display_name   = "Private Endpoint for OKE"
    description    = "Resource Manager Private Endpoint for OKE"
    vcn_id         = var.vcn_id
    subnet_id      = var.k8s_endpoint_subnet_id
    freeform_tags  = var.cluster_tags.freeformTags
    defined_tags   = var.cluster_tags.definedTags
}
```

```
# Resolves the private IP of the customer's private endpoint to a NAT IP.
data "oci_resourcemanager_private_endpoint_reachable_ip" "private_kubernetes_
  endpoint" {
    private_endpoint_id = var.create_new_oke_cluster ? oci_resourcemanager_
    private_endpoint.private_kubernetes_endpoint.id : var.existent_oke_cluster_
    private_endpoint
    private_ip          = trimsuffix(oci_containerengine_cluster.oke_cluster[0].
    endpoints.0.private_endpoint, ":6443")
}
...
provider "kubernetes" {
host                    = (var.cluster_endpoint_visibility == "Private") ?
  ("https://${data.oci_resourcemanager_private_endpoint_reachable_ip.private_
  kubernetes_endpoint.ip_address}:6443") : (yamldecode(module.oke.kubeconfig)
  ["clusters"][0]["cluster"]["server"])
cluster_ca_certificate = base64decode(yamldecode(module.oke-quickstart.kubeconfig)
  ["clusters"][0]["cluster"]["certificate-authority-data"])
insecure                = (var.cluster_endpoint_visibility == "Private") ? true :
  false
exec {
    api_version = "client.authentication.k8s.io/v1beta1"
    args        = ["ce", "cluster", "generate-token", "--cluster-id",
    yamldecode(module.oke-quickstart.kubeconfig)["users"][0]["user"]["exec"]["args"]
    [4], "--region", yamldecode(module.oke-quickstart.kubeconfig)["users"][0]
    ["user"]["exec"]["args"][6]]
    command     = "oci"
    }
}
```

Kubernetes Role-Based Access Control (RBAC) with OCI IAM Groups

Kubernetes offers different ways to manage access to the cluster. The most common way is to use Kubernetes RBAC, a method of regulating access to computer or network resources based on the roles of individual users within an enterprise. RBAC enables you to define roles and assign them to users or groups. You can then use these roles to control access to Kubernetes resources. Figure 6-5 illustrates the Kubernetes RBAC relationship.

OKE natively integrates the clusters with the OCI Identity and Access Management (IAM) service. OCI IAM provides strong user authentication to access your clusters and gives you authorization to use the OKE API so that you can define cluster administrators and cluster users.

Chapter 4 covers the integration between OCI IAM and Kubernetes RBAC in detail, including identity federation.

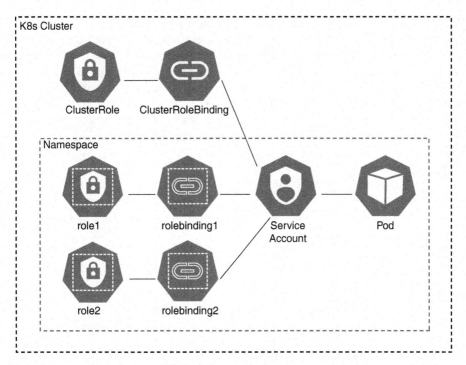

Figure 6-5 Kubernetes RBAC

Following the principle of least privilege, your users can access only the Kubernetes resources that they're authorized to. Kubernetes RBAC is aware of OCI user identities and can bind Kubernetes roles to OCI users. To streamline the configuration of Kubernetes RBAC, OKE added support for binding Kubernetes roles to OCI IAM groups. As a result, the Kubernetes RBAC configuration is greatly simplified. Moreover, you can apply the Kubernetes role definition and the binding to OCI groups across multiple clusters.

Consider the example of a product inventory application. This application runs in the Kubernetes namespace inventory. An OCI group named inventory-app-admin includes OCI users responsible for the lifecycle of the inventory application. A Kubernetes role allows full access to the namespace inventory. This role is bound to the OCI group inventory-app-admin. As a result, all users in the OCI group inventory-app-admin can create and delete any applications in the namespace inventory, but not in any other namespaces.

Administrators can simply add or remove members to or from groups using the Oracle Cloud Console or API.

OCI IAM Multifactor Authentication (MFA) for Kubernetes API

The authentication of a user who makes Kubernetes API requests through the kubectl CLI relies on an RSA public key in PEM format (minimum 2,048 bits). Although this authentication method is strong, you might want to add a second factor to complete the authentication. OKE supports OCI IAM MFA. With MFA enabled in the IAM service, when a user connects to a cluster Kubernetes API, the RSA key is checked, which is the first factor. The user is then prompted to provide a second verification code from a registered MFA device, such as a phone, as the second factor. The two factors work together, offering an extra layer of security to verify the user's identity and complete the authentication process.

Note that, to use MFA, you must have a registered MFA device and the OCI policies to enforce the security. You also need to update the kubeconfig file to use the MFA token. For more information, see the OCI documentation.

Data Encryption and Key Management Service

By default, OCI provides data encryption for all data stored in the cloud. This includes block volumes, boot volumes, file storage, volume backups, and other services. OKE consumes these services transparently to Kubernetes, including encryption at rest.

You might want to manage the encryption keys for some use cases. For example, you can use OCI Vault, a Key Management Service (KMS), to create, manage, and use encryption keys to encrypt and decrypt data. You can also use the OCI KMS service to manage the lifecycle of the encryption keys. OCI Vault offers keys in highly available and durable hardware security modules (HSMs) that meet Federal Information Processing Standards (FIPS) 140-2 Security Level 3 security certification.

Using customer-managed encryption keys (CMEK) for OKE with OCI Vault, you first need to create a vault and a key in OCI Vault. Then you enter the OCID of the key on the OKE cluster provisioning for each component that you want to use with CMEK instead of Oracle-managed keys, as illustrated in Figure 6-6.

After creating the vault and key, you can enable them on different parts of your Kubernetes cluster. You can reuse the same vault/key for all resources or select a different one for each resource. Figure 6-7 illustrates the resources where you can use customer-managed encryption keys.

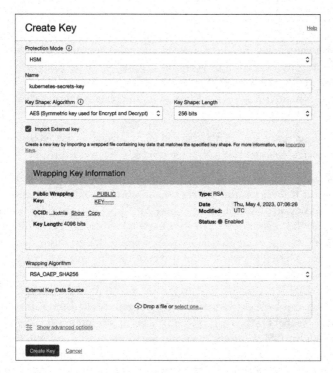

Figure 6-6   OCI Vault Create Key Example

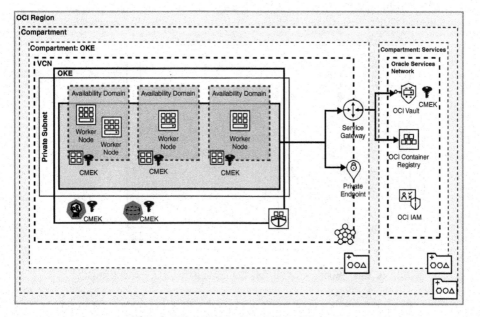

Figure 6-7   Resources That Can Use CMEK

Managing Secrets

In Kubernetes, secrets are used to securely store and manage sensitive information. Secrets can store credentials, API keys, tokens, and other sensitive data that applications require for secure communication or access to external services. Kubernetes secrets are Base64 encoded and stored as an API resource within the cluster.

When using Container Engine for Kubernetes to create Kubernetes clusters, you have two options for storing application secrets:

- Kubernetes secret objects that are stored and managed inside etcd
- External secrets that use the Kubernetes Secrets Store CSI driver

Kubernetes secret objects can be stored and managed in etcd, an open-source distributed key-value store that Kubernetes uses for cluster coordination and state management. In Kubernetes clusters created by Container Engine for Kubernetes, etcd writes data to and reads data from block storage volumes in the Oracle Cloud Infrastructure Block Volume service. By default, Oracle encrypts data in block volumes at rest; this includes etcd and Kubernetes secrets. This encryption is managed by Oracle using a master encryption key, meaning that no action is required on your part. You can also bring your own encryption keys through the OCI Vault service to encypt these secrets in etcd as well.

External secrets can be securely stored and managed through the Kubernetes Secrets Store CSI driver (`secrets-store.csi.k8s.io`). This driver integrates secrets stores with Kubernetes clusters as CSI volumes, to enable the mounting of multiple secrets, keys, and certificates stored externally into pods. When this driver is attached, the data in the volume is mounted into the application container's file system. OCI Vault is an example of an external secrets store. Oracle offers the open-source OCI Secrets Store CSI Driver Provider to enable Kubernetes clusters to access secrets in Vault. Figure 6-8 illustrates the interaction of Kubernetes secrets with the OCI Vault using the Kubernetes CSI.

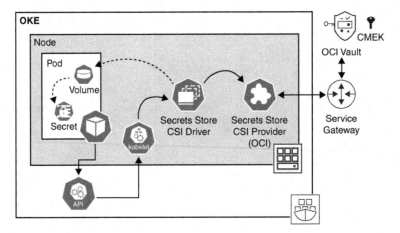

Figure 6-8   Kubernetes Secrets Connecting to the OCI Vault Using CSI

In this model, the Kubernetes Secrets Store CSI Driver Provider is deployed to the Kubernetes cluster as a `DaemonSet`. The `DaemonSet` ensures that a CSI driver pod is running on each node in the cluster. The Kubernetes Secrets Store CSI Driver Provider communicates with the Vault service to retrieve secrets. The Kubernetes Secrets Store CSI Driver Provider mounts the secrets as a volume in the pod. Now the application running in the pod can access the secrets as files in the volume. The Kubernetes Secrets Store CSI Driver Provider can also be configured to renew and rotate the secrets before they expire automatically.

To configure this in your cluster, you need to create the appropriate OCI policies and decide whether you will use user principals or instance principals to access the OCI Vault. You can then install the CSI driver and create a Kubernetes resource of the kind `SecretProviderClass` to link the secret volume to the OCI Vault secret. The specific steps for configuring the OCI secret store driver can be found at the oci-secrets-store-csi-driver GitHub repository.[1]

Both aforementioned options enable you to use master encryption keys from other tenancies. You simply need to include the appropriate policies to authorize the tenancy running OKE to use keys from other tenancies. The OCI documentation[2] covers the specific policies required and the detailed steps for configuration.

Audit Logging

Audit logging plays a crucial role in maintaining the security, compliance, and operational integrity of Kubernetes clusters. It provides a detailed record of all activities within the cluster, including API calls, configuration changes, and resource access. Audit logs enable organizations to do the following:

- **Identify and investigate security incidents:** Audit logs provide a valuable source of information for detecting and investigating potential security breaches or unauthorized access attempts.
- **Ensure compliance:** Many industry regulations and standards, such as PCI-DSS and HIPAA, require organizations to maintain comprehensive audit logs to demonstrate compliance with security and privacy requirements.
- **Support incident response and forensics:** If a security incident occurs, audit logs serve as a valuable resource for understanding the sequence of events, identifying the root cause, and conducting forensic analysis.

On OKE, all Kubernetes audit events are made available in the OCI Audit service. It's crucial to monitor user and application activity on your Kubernetes cluster, to detect any unusual behavior or security breaches. This service provides a unified overview of all user activity across your applications on OCI. You can easily spot security incidents by monitoring successful and unsuccessful login attempts, such as identifying whether your cluster is under attack. Additionally, you can link Kubernetes audit events to other audit events in your OCI tenancy, such as updates to your clusters or resources.

To visualize the logs, you have two standard interfaces on the OCI console: Audit Events,[3] shown in Figure 6-9, and Audit Logs,[4] shown in Figure 6-10. The information is also available for other tools, including OCI Logging Analytics and third-party tools such as Datadog.

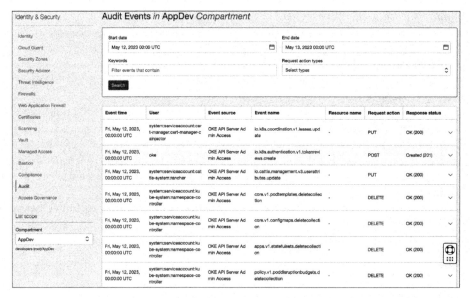

Figure 6-9   Example of Audit Events from OKE API Server Audit Logs

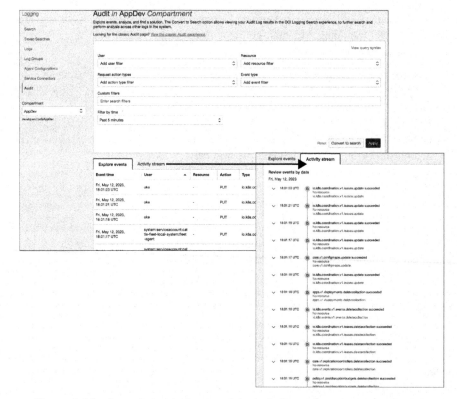

Figure 6-10   Example Activity Stream of the Audit Events from the Kubernetes API

More information on the OCI Audit service can be found in Chapter 8, "Observability."

Security Zones

Oracle Cloud Infrastructure (OCI) security zones offer a comprehensive approach to securing workloads and data in the cloud. A security zone is a logically isolated and self-contained compartment within OCI that provides enhanced security and regulatory compliance capabilities. The following list describes the benefits of using OCI security zones:

- **Enhanced security isolation:** OCI security zones provide a high level of security isolation between different compartments within an OCI tenancy. Each security zone operates as an independent security boundary, allowing organizations to isolate sensitive workloads and data from other parts of their cloud infrastructure. This isolation helps mitigate the risk of lateral movement and unauthorized access, protecting critical assets from potential security threats.
- **Regulatory compliance:** Security and compliance are top priorities for many organizations. OCI security zones are designed to meet the stringent security and regulatory requirements of various industries, such as finance, healthcare, and government. These zones incorporate security controls and practices that align with industry standards, including data sovereignty, data residency, and compliance certifications. By leveraging security zones, organizations can address specific regulatory requirements and confidently deploy workloads that require adherence to strict compliance frameworks.
- **Network segmentation:** Network segmentation is a crucial aspect of cloud security. OCI security zones offer granular control over network traffic flow, allowing organizations to define and enforce access policies between different security zones. This segmentation helps limit the lateral movement of threats within the cloud environment, minimizing the impact of potential security breaches. Administrators can define security rules and access controls specific to each security zone, ensuring that only authorized traffic is allowed to enter or leave the zone.
- **Enhanced access control:** OCI security zones provide fine-grained access controls, enabling organizations to enforce strict permissions and privileges within each zone. Administrators can define security policies and identity and access management (IAM) rules tailored to the specific requirements of each security zone. This level of access control ensures that only authorized users and applications have the necessary permissions to interact with resources within a given zone, reducing the risk of unauthorized access and data breaches.
- **Monitoring and logging:** Visibility into security events and activities is crucial for maintaining a secure cloud environment. OCI security zones offer robust

monitoring and logging capabilities, providing organizations with detailed visibility into the security posture of each zone. Administrators can monitor network traffic, access logs, and security events within security zones, enabling them to promptly detect and respond to potential security incidents. OCI's Logging Service and other monitoring tools can be integrated with security zones to provide real-time insights and proactive threat detection.

- **Disaster recovery and business continuity:** OCI security zones support disaster recovery and business continuity strategies by providing isolation and redundancy across different zones. Organizations can deploy resources and replicate data across multiple security zones within the same region or different regions. This redundancy ensures that, if a localized failure or disaster occurs, critical workloads and data will remain accessible and operational in a separate security zone, minimizing downtime and preserving business continuity.

Network Security Groups (NSGs)

Network security groups (NSGs) are essential components of the overall network security architecture within the Oracle Cloud ecosystem. They play a vital role in safeguarding cloud resources and protecting critical workloads from unauthorized access, network threats, and potential vulnerabilities. NSGs provide several benefits and features to secure your network infrastructure:

- **Network segmentation and isolation:** NSGs enable network segmentation by allowing administrators to define security rules at the subnet level. Administrators can restrict traffic flow between subnets or between on-premises networks and the cloud by specifying ingress and egress rules. This segmentation enhances security by isolating different components of an application, preventing unauthorized lateral movement within the network, and limiting the potential impact of security breaches.

- **Access control and allowlisting:** NSGs provide fine-grained control over network traffic by allowing administrators to define specific rules to allow or deny access based on IP addresses, ports, and protocols. This capability enables administrators to create allowlists of trusted sources, effectively blocking traffic from unknown or untrusted sources. By implementing access control policies through NSGs, organizations can enforce the principle of least privilege and reduce the attack surface.

- **Defense against external threats:** NSGs act as a first line of defense against external threats by filtering and blocking malicious traffic at the network level. Administrators can define rules to block common attack vectors, such as denial-of-service (DoS) attacks, port scanning, or brute-force attempts. By proactively preventing such attacks, NSGs contribute to maintaining the availability, integrity, and confidentiality of cloud resources.

- **Traffic monitoring and logging:** NSGs offer comprehensive logging and monitoring capabilities. They allow administrators to track network traffic patterns, monitor access attempts, and identify potential security incidents or anomalies. By analyzing NSG logs and leveraging security monitoring tools, organizations can proactively detect and respond to security threats, ensuring timely incident response and minimizing the impact of potential breaches.
- **Compliance and regulatory requirements:** Many industries and organizations have specific compliance and regulatory requirements concerning data protection, privacy, and security. NSGs can help meet these requirements by implementing security controls and enforcing network policies aligned with industry standards. They enable organizations to demonstrate due diligence and adherence to security best practices, facilitating compliance audits and ensuring a solid security posture.
- **Dynamic and scalable security:** OCI network security groups provide flexibility and scalability in managing security policies. Administrators can easily modify security rules to accommodate changing business needs, add or remove rules to reflect application updates, and scale security configurations alongside resource scaling. This dynamic nature of NSGs ensures that security measures remain effective even in dynamic cloud environments with evolving requirements.

NSGs are essential for Kubernetes deployments on OKE. They provide critical security capabilities, such as pod-to-pod communication security, protection against external threats, access control and segmentation, compliance adherence, monitoring and auditing capabilities, and dynamic scalability. By leveraging NSGs effectively, organizations can enhance the overall security posture of their OKE clusters and protect critical workloads and data.

The section "Setting Up NSG Rules and Security List Rules," in Chapter 4, covers how to configure NSG rules and security list rules to secure OKE.

Web Application Firewall (WAF)

The OCI Web Application Firewall (WAF) can help secure web applications deployed on Oracle Kubernetes Engine (OKE) on first-mile security, offering robust protection against web-based attacks (including attacks to REST APIs), mitigating vulnerabilities, and enhancing the overall security posture of web applications.

WAF operates at the application layer (Layer 7) of the network stack, enabling it to inspect and filter HTTP/S traffic directed at web applications running on OKE. By analyzing the content of web requests and responses, WAF can detect and prevent a wide range of common web-based attacks, such as cross-site scripting (XSS), SQL injection, and malicious file uploads. WAF also provides Layer 7 DDoS mitigation provided by Specialists in Oracle Cloud customer support. To use the mitigation service, you must allow the specialists to access your tenancy using IAM service policies. Layer 3/4 (L3/4) DDoS attack mitigation is part of the regular infrastructure service.

WAF also provides intelligent threat detection and prevention by using sophisticated threat-detection algorithms and security rules to identify and block malicious traffic. It leverages machine learning and behavioral analytics to detect anomalies, including advanced threats that traditional signature-based security mechanisms might not recognize. This proactive approach helps protect web applications from evolving attack techniques and zero-day vulnerabilities. It allows administrators to define and enforce custom security policies tailored to the specific needs of their web applications. These policies include rulesets, allowlist/blocklist configurations, and rate-limiting thresholds. By customizing the security policies, organizations can strike a balance between application security and legitimate traffic, ensuring protection without impacting the functionality and performance of the web application. WAF also provides a built-in set of security rules that cover common vulnerabilities and attack patterns. Oracle security experts regularly update and maintain these rules to address emerging threats. With automatic rule updates, organizations can protect their web applications against the latest attack vectors without manual intervention. Figure 6-11 illustrates the recommended and preset WAF rules, with the option to turn them on or off.

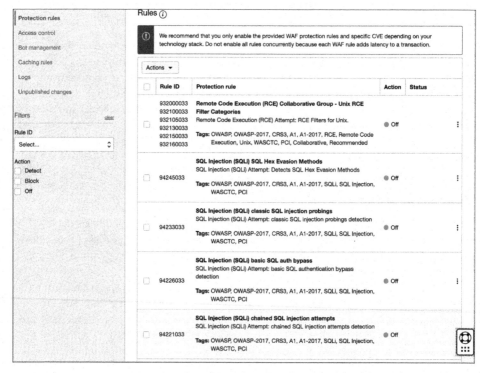

Figure 6-11   Predefined WAF Rules Available to Activate

OCI WAF offers access rules (see Figure 6-12) that can intercept inbound web traffic before it reaches the OKE cluster. These rules can be applied to a specific Kubernetes workload with HTTP metadata (such as HTTP header, method, user agent, and URL with particular content) or a geographical location. The actions on the access rule include Log and Allow, Detect Only, Block, Redirect, Bypass, and Show CAPTCHA. This integration ensures that web application traffic is inspected and protected at the edge, reducing the risk of attacks reaching the underlying applications and infrastructure.

OCI WAF offers comprehensive monitoring capabilities, providing real-time visibility into web traffic and security events. Administrators can access detailed logs, metrics, and reports to gain insights into web application traffic patterns, attack attempts, and overall security posture. Additionally, OCI WAF can generate alerts and notifications when suspicious activity or potential security incidents are detected, enabling timely response and mitigation. It is also designed to handle high volumes of web traffic, and it can scale dynamically to meet application demands. OCI WAF operates across multiple availability domains within OCI, providing high availability and fault tolerance. This ensures that web applications are protected even during periods of high traffic or when infrastructure failures occur.

You can provision WAF in two different ways. One way, you can create a Load Balancer that is not managed by Kubernetes, enable the web application firewall under the Security tab, and configure it to be in front of the LoadBalancer[5] managed by a Kubernetes resource (Ingress Controller or Service Type LoadBalancer). Figure 6-13 illustrates the option for the WAF as a Service (WaaS) configured directly on the Load Balancer.

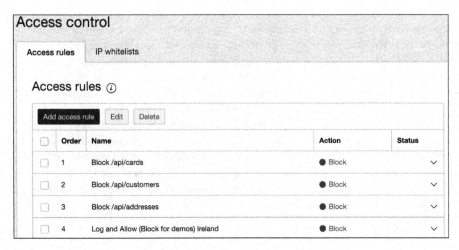

Figure 6-12   WAF Access Rules

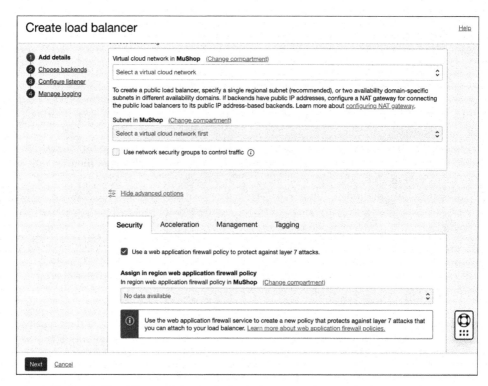

Figure 6-13   OCI Load Balancer Creation UI, with the Option to Enable WAF Policy

Alternatively, you can create a new WAF edge policy[6] and configure the DNS to point to the endpoints you want to protect on Kubernetes, as illustrated in Figure 6-14. This is the recommended option if you want full control on the rules and configurations.

The architecture diagram in Figure 6-15 shows an application that is protected by the Web Application Firewall. The diagram shows that the microservices within Kubernetes continue to function seamlessly despite the addition of the WAF. When a request is made, the DNS routes it to the WAF for validation before being directed to the Load Balancer managed by Kubernetes' Ingress Controller. In a multicluster setting (not depicted), the OCI Traffic Manager's Global Load Balancer collaborates with the WAF without any impact on Kubernetes cluster workloads. This means that the WAF can be added to any existing application and can be removed from the architecture without any code changes or deployments.

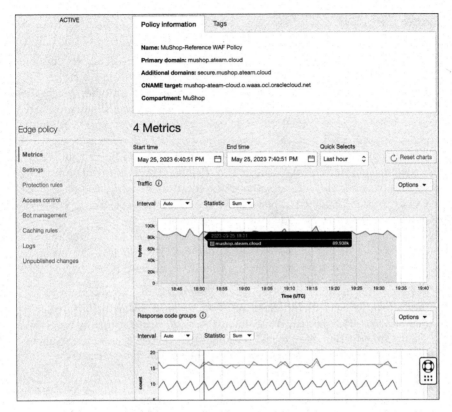

Figure 6-14   Example WAF Edge Policy

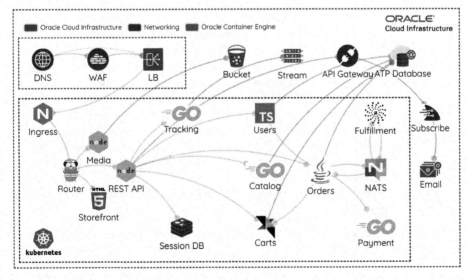

Figure 6-15   Ecommerce App (MuShop) Diagram Example Showing Multiple OCI Services, Including WAF

Network Firewall

Network Firewall is a cloud-based network security service that allows customers to filter traffic based on IP addresses, ports, and protocols. A stateful firewall enables customers to define rules to allow or deny traffic to and from their resources in the cloud. Network Firewall is a fully managed service that is integrated with other Oracle Cloud Infrastructure services, such as the Compute, Load Balancing, and Kubernetes Engine services. It is combined with the OCI Logging service to give customers visibility into their network traffic. OCI Network Firewall is powered by Palo Alto Networks.

Network Firewall acts as a security control point between the Internet and the resources within an OCI virtual cloud network (VCN). The network firewall allows organizations to define and enforce granular access control policies based on source IP addresses, destination IP addresses, ports, and protocols. It helps protect applications and data from unauthorized access and network-based threats.

By combining the capabilities of OCI Network Firewall and OKE, organizations can establish a secure environment for their Kubernetes deployments. The integration between these services enables the following security measures:

- **Network segmentation:** OCI Network Firewall allows organizations to define security rules that control traffic flow between different VCNs, subnets, and resources. Administrators can enforce network segmentation by properly configuring the firewall rules and isolating OKE clusters from other resources within the VCN. This ensures that only authorized traffic can reach the Kubernetes clusters.
- **Access control policies:** OCI Network Firewall provides fine-grained access control policies that can be applied to inbound and outbound traffic. By defining firewall rules based on source IP addresses, destination IP addresses, ports, and protocols, organizations can restrict access to OKE clusters, allowing only trusted sources to communicate with the Kubernetes API server and worker nodes. This helps prevent unauthorized access and protects against potential attacks.
- **Application layer security:** Beyond network-level security, OCI Network Firewall allows organizations to define rules based on specific application protocols and payloads. This enables deep packet inspection and the capability to detect and block malicious activities at the application layer. Organizations can identify and block any unauthorized or suspicious activities by defining rules that match the traffic patterns of Kubernetes API calls and container communications.
- **Logging and monitoring:** OCI Network Firewall provides detailed logging and monitoring capabilities, allowing organizations to track and analyze network traffic. By integrating with OCI logging and monitoring services, administrators can gain visibility into network activities, detect anomalies, and respond to security incidents promptly.

Figure 6-16 illustrates an example production architecture using the OCI Network Firewall service to manage all traffic into and out of a multicluster deployment.

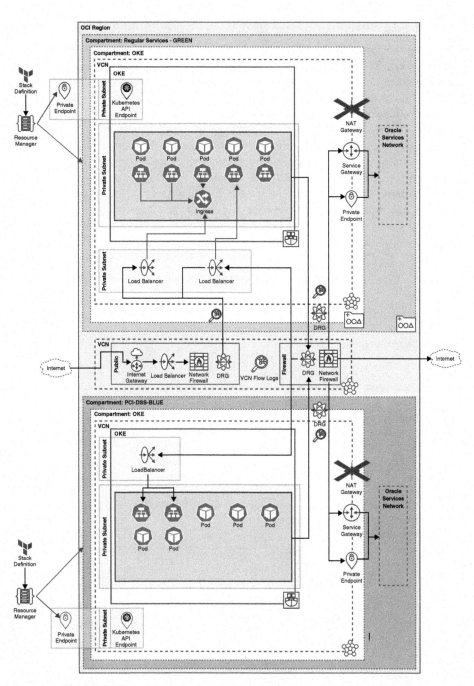

Figure 6-16   Multicluster Deployment with Network Firewall Architecture

Allowed Registries

Allowed registries refer to the container image registries that are permitted to be used within a cluster. These registries are the trusted sources from which Kubernetes nodes can pull container images for deploying and running applications. Using allowed registries alone does not ensure that only approved images can be used. To accomplish this, you need controllers acting on Kubernetes.

Controlling the allowed registries helps enforce security and compliance policies, ensuring that only approved and verified images are used in the cluster. To enforce allowed registries, you can use admission controllers that intercept registry requests for validation before the Kubernetes API Server commits them.

One recommended option is to use the Open Policy Agent (OPA) to create a policy that denies resources to container registries that do not match specific registries.

Listing 6-2 shows an example of OPA configuration using Rego to deny pods in a specific namespace from using container registries that do not match a specific registry.

Listing 6-2   Example of OPA Policy Written in Rego, Allowing Only ocir.io Registries on the Cluster

```
package admission

import data.k8s.matches

deny[{
    "id": "container-image-allowlist",
    "resource": {
        "kind": "pods",
        "namespace": namespace,
        "name": name
    },
    "resolution": {"message": msg},
}] {
    matches[["pods", namespace, name, matched_pod]]
    container = matched_pod.spec.containers[_]
    not re_match("^ocir.io/.+$", container.image) # The actual validation
    msg := sprintf("invalid container registry image %q", [container.image])
}
```

The Rego Policy file can be directly loaded into OPA Gatekeeper as a configmap or as a ConstraintTemplate, illustrated in Listing 6-3.

Listing 6-3   OPA Gatekeeper Manifest with Rego Policies

```
apiVersion: templates.gatekeeper.sh/v1
kind: ConstraintTemplate
metadata:
name: k8sallowedrepos
```

```
spec:
crd:
    spec:
    names:
        kind: K8sAllowedRepos
    validation:
        openAPIV3Schema:
        type: object
        properties:
            repos:
            type: array
            items:
                type: string
targets:
    - target: admission.k8s.gatekeeper.sh
    rego: |
        package k8sallowedrepos
        violation[{"msg": msg}] {
        container := input.review.object.spec.containers[_]
        satisfied := [good | repo = input.parameters.repos[_] ; good =
startswith(container.image, repo)]
        not any(satisfied)
        msg := sprintf("container <%v> has an invalid image repo <%v>, allowed
repos are %v", [container.name, container.image, input.parameters.repos])
        }
        violation[{"msg": msg}] {
        container := input.review.object.spec.initContainers[_]
        satisfied := [good | repo = input.parameters.repos[_] ; good =
startswith(container.image, repo)]
        not any(satisfied)
        msg := sprintf("container <%v> has an invalid image repo <%v>, allowed
repos are %v", [container.name, container.image, input.parameters.repos])
        }
```

After the new ConstraintTemplate creation, the new constraint can be consumed and configured, as illustrated in Listing 6-4.

Listing 6-4   Example of yaml manifest to consume the Gatekeeper manifest ConstraintTemplate

```
apiVersion: constraints.gatekeeper.sh/v1beta1
kind: K8sAllowedRepos
metadata:
name: allowed-container-registries
spec:
match:
    kinds:
    - apiGroups: [""]
        kinds: ["Pod"]
```

```
    namespaces:
    - "production"
parameters:
    repos:
    - "ocir.io/tenancy/namespace/*"
    - "ghcr.io/account/*"
```

The section "Open Policy Agent (OPA)," later in this chapter, provides more information about OPA, OPA gatekeeper, and OPA Rules/Rego.

Controlling the allowed registries on OKE ensures that container images used within the cluster come from trusted and approved sources. This is one step in enforcing security and compliance, preventing unapproved sources, promoting standardization, optimizing resources, and offering configuration flexibility for a secure and controlled deployment environment for containerized applications.

Cloud Guard

OCI Cloud Guard is a comprehensive, unified security and compliance monitoring service. It helps organizations proactively identify, prioritize, and resolve security issues across their OCI environments, including OKE. By leveraging machine learning and AI technologies, Cloud Guard continuously analyzes telemetry data and configuration settings to detect potential security risks, threats, misconfigurations, and compliance violations. Cloud Guard is always active and evaluating the default rules. You can add detectors and responder recipes to extend the feature set for Cloud Guard to have custom notifications and monitor your own custom conditions for your infrastructure security posture. The key features of OCI Cloud Guard include the following:

- **Security monitoring:** Cloud Guard continuously monitors the security posture of OCI resources, including compute instances, storage, networks, and databases, to identify security vulnerabilities and threats.
- **Automated security policies:** Predefined security policies are provided, based on industry best practices and regulatory standards. These policies can be customized or extended to align with specific security requirements.
- **Real-time notifications:** Cloud Guard sends real-time alerts and notifications when security incidents are detected, enabling prompt action and mitigation.
- **Threat intelligence integration:** This feature integrates with Oracle's Threat Intelligence service, which offers up-to-date threat intelligence feeds, enhancing the detection and response capabilities of Cloud Guard.
- **Compliance monitoring:** This feature provides built-in compliance frameworks and checks, such as CIS benchmarks, to ensure adherence to security standards and regulatory requirements.
- **Security recommendations:** Cloud Guard provides actionable recommendations to address security issues and guides users on best practices for securing their OCI resources.

Figure 6-17 shows Cloud Guard in action, with its dashboard showing the security score, the risk score, and an overview of the security posture for the entire tenancy. Administrators can use this reporting to examine and analyze the data, to quickly zone in on the resources that are security threats and/or challenges. Administrators then can create detector and responder recipes to automate how certain conditions are detected and addressed.

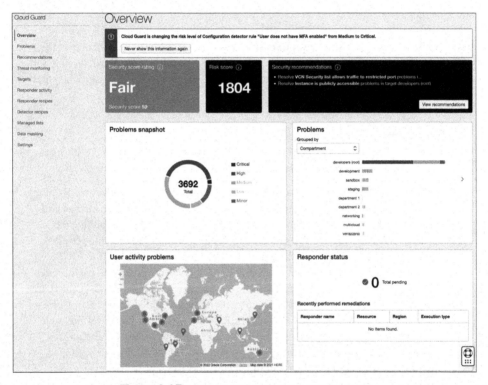

Figure 6-17   OCI Cloud Guard Dashboard Overview

Hardening Containers and OKE Worker Nodes

Containers and OKE worker nodes are critical components of a Kubernetes cluster that attackers frequently target. Containers are designed to be lightweight and portable, but they can also introduce security risks if they are not properly secured. Kubernetes worker nodes are the compute instances in a cluster that are responsible for running containers; if these nodes are compromised, an attacker can gain access to the entire cluster.

Hardening measures, such as limiting container privileges, implementing RBAC, configuring network security, and monitoring Kubernetes cluster activity, can help prevent attacks and detect malicious activity.

Container Scanning

Containers are essential to modern application development because they provide a lightweight, scalable, and portable way to package and deploy applications. However, container images can also contain security vulnerabilities that attackers can exploit. In a Kubernetes environment, where containers are managed and orchestrated by Kubernetes, it is critical to scan container images before deployment, to identify any security vulnerabilities.

Container scanning tools can detect various security issues, including known vulnerabilities in the software components and libraries used in the container image, misconfigurations in the container, and other security-related issues. By detecting and addressing these issues, container scanning can significantly reduce the risk of security breaches in Kubernetes environments.

How to Implement Container Scanning on OKE

Container scanning can be implemented on OKE using various tools and techniques. These are some of the popular approaches:

- **OCIR container image scanning:** The Oracle Cloud Infrastructure Registry (OCIR) enables users or systems to push container images to repositories and enable the scanning of container images stored in the OCIR for published security vulnerabilities in the publicly available Common Vulnerabilities and Exposures (CVE) database. When repository scanning is enabled, the OCI Vulnerability Scanning service scans any images that you push into the repository and any images that are already present. Repositories with scanning enabled are automatically rescanned when new vulnerabilities are added to the list of threats. For every scanned image you can view the scan results, the risk level for each scan, the description of each vulnerability, and the link to the CVE database. Figure 6-18 illustrates the creation of a target for Container Image Scanning, with the option to select the scanning recipe and the repositories that will be automatically scanned.

- **External container image scanning for container repositories:** Kubernetes can integrate with container image scanning tools such as Aqua Security, Twistlock, NeuVector, and Alcide, which scan container images for security vulnerabilities before they are deployed. This is important if you are not using OCIR or if you want to check for container image vulnerabilities from external repositories.

- **Kubernetes resources image scanning:** Some tools integrate into OKE to check for vulnerabilities on the container images defined on Kubernetes resources such as deployments, StatefulSets, and DaemonSets. Tools such as Snyk and Sysdig provide this kind of service. Quickstarts to deploy these solutions are available on the Oracle Quickstarts repo. Here are some examples:
  - Snyk.io (https://snyk.io/)[7]
  - Sysdig.com (https://sysdig.com/)[8]

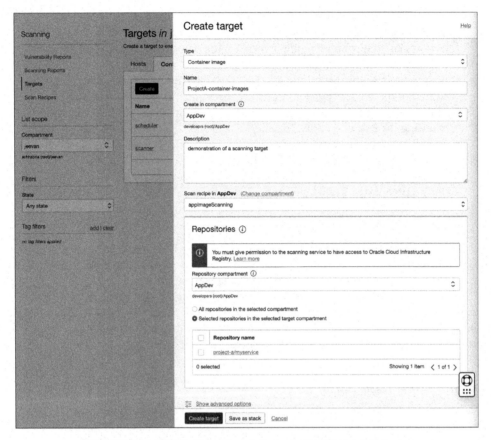

Figure 6-18   OCIR Container Image Scanning Target Creation Screen

- **Continuous integration/continuous deployment (CI/CD) pipelines:**
  CI/CD pipelines can include container scanning as part of the automated build
  process, to ensure that container images are scanned before deployment.
- **Kubernetes admission controllers:** Admission controllers enforce policies
  on Kubernetes objects before they are created or modified. By using admission
  controllers, organizations can implement policies that require container images to
  be scanned before deployment. OKE supports the use of the ImagePolicyWebhook
  admission controllers, to allow only images that pass the enforced rule.

Best Practices for Kubernetes Container Scanning

The following are some best practices to follow when implementing container scanning
on OKE:

- **Enable OCIR image scanning:** Enabling image scanning for container
  images hosted on the ocir.io is the first step, allowing better control on the same
  infrastructure that is running the OKE.

- **Use multiple scanning tools:** Running multiple container scanning tools increases the likelihood of detecting security vulnerabilities. Each tool has strengths and weaknesses, so using multiple tools can provide a comprehensive scan of container images.
- **Implement scanning in the CI/CD pipeline:** Implement container scanning as part of the CI/CD pipeline to ensure that container images are scanned before deployment. This helps catch vulnerabilities early in the development process, reducing the risk of security breaches.
- **Monitor scanning results:** Monitor the results of container scanning to identify trends and patterns. This helps identify potential risk areas and allows organizations to take appropriate measures to address them.
- **Stay up to date:** Keep scanning tools and libraries up to date, to ensure that they can detect the latest security vulnerabilities. Container scanning tools should be updated regularly to ensure that they can detect newly discovered vulnerabilities.

Container scanning is an essential security practice for Kubernetes environments. By implementing container scanning on OKE, organizations can identify and mitigate potential security vulnerabilities in container images before deployment. Container scanning tools can detect various security issues, including known vulnerabilities, misconfigurations, and other security-related issues. By following best practices, organizations can ensure that container scanning is implemented effectively and efficiently in Kubernetes environments, reducing the risk of security breaches.

Container Image Signing

To enhance your runtime security, you can also sign your container images with cryptograph keys. You can configure OKE to pull container images that are signed and its signature verified. This ensures that only signed images that have not been tampered with can be deployed to OKE. The section "Enabling Image Signature Verification," in Chapter 4, has more details on container image signing.

Center for Internet Security (CIS) Kubernetes Benchmarks

The Center for Internet Security (CIS) is a community-driven nonprofit organization that provides many free and paid resources to improve IT security. The CIS Kubernetes Benchmark is a set of security recommendations designed to help organizations secure their Kubernetes deployments. This section provides an overview of the CIS Kubernetes Benchmark and shows how to implement its recommendations to secure an OKE cluster. You also see practical examples and best practices to help organizations comply with the CIS Kubernetes Benchmark. A free downloadable benchmark can be found at www.cisecurity.org/benchmark/kubernetes.[9] For OKE, the benchmark is named Oracle Cloud Infrastructure Container Engine for Kubernetes (OKE). On this benchmark, you will find a comprehensive set of best practices and security controls designed to help organizations secure their Kubernetes deployments; it also provides guidelines for securing the Kubernetes worker nodes and some Kubernetes control plane components. The benchmark covers a wide range of security controls, including these:

- Cluster configuration
- Network security
- Authentication and authorization
- Cluster hardening
- Logging and auditing
- Secure communication between Kubernetes components
- Pod security
- Node security

The benchmark can be consumed as a reading guide or can be made available for tools such as CIS-CAT Pro and Kube-bench to automate security checks and remediations. References on both tools can be found in the "Supporting Tools" section.

The CIS Benchmark has two levels for OKE. Level 1 has practical recommendations, and the OKE Control Plane follows what is most beneficial. The minimum recommendations necessary for the worker nodes is applied for a secure node without impeding the usage and performance. The customer is responsible for hardening the worker nodes to the next level. Level 2 extends Level 1 and is intended for environments or use cases in which security is the most important concern. Applying Level 2 recommendations can affect the Kubernetes functionality and performance.

One of the primary and most basic purposes of the CIS Kubernetes Benchmark is to ensure that your cluster is configured with secure settings. This includes enforcing TLS communication for all components, disabling insecure communication protocols, and disabling anonymous access. Similarly, the benchmark evaluates the network security aspects of your cluster. Kubernetes provides a rich set of network security features that can be leveraged to secure your cluster. For example, you can configure network policies to control traffic between pods, implement network segmentation, and enforce secure communication over the network. The benchmark can provide feedback on the current networking configuration in your cluster and best-practice suggestions to improve it. It also evaluates the security for the communication between Kubernetes components. Kubernetes components communicate with each other using various protocols, and it is important to ensure that these communications are secure. The CIS Kubernetes Benchmark provides recommendations for securing communication between Kubernetes components, including configuring Transport Layer Security (TLS) and using secure communication protocols.

The benchmark also evaluates the Kubernetes authentication and authorization configuration. Kubernetes provides several authentication and authorization mechanisms, such as role-based access control (RBAC), that can be used to control access to the Kubernetes API server and other cluster components. The CIS Kubernetes Benchmark provides recommendations for implementing secure authentication and authorization practices.

Logging and auditing are critical for detecting and investigating security incidents in your Kubernetes cluster. The CIS Kubernetes Benchmark provides recommendations for configuring Kubernetes logging and auditing to ensure that all security-related events are captured.

The best practices for implementing the CIS Kubernetes Benchmark are as follows:

1. Regularly review and update your Kubernetes cluster configuration to ensure that it remains compliant with the CIS Kubernetes Benchmark.
2. Automate as much of the benchmark implementation as possible using tools such as Kubernetes manifests and configuration management tools.
3. Regularly review Kubernetes logs and audit logs to detect and investigate potential security incidents.
4. Use RBAC to control access to Kubernetes components and resources.
5. Use network segmentation to limit the impact of potential security breaches.

Using SELinux with OKE

SELinux is a Linux kernel security module that provides a mechanism for enforcing mandatory access control policies. This section covers how SELinux can be used with Kubernetes to enhance the security of your Kubernetes environment. SELinux is based on the principle of mandatory access control (MAC), which means that every process and user on the system is assigned a security context that determines its level of access to system resources. SELinux defines security contexts for files, processes, sockets, and other system resources. Each security context is associated with a set of rules that governs the interactions between processes and system resources.

SELinux has three modes of operation:

- **Enforcing:** SELinux enforces the security policies defined in the security context. Any attempt to violate the security policies results in an access denial.
- **Permissive:** SELinux logs all the security violations but does not enforce the policies.
- **Disabled:** SELinux is disabled, and no security policies are enforced.

By default, SELinux is enabled on OKE worker nodes and is set to run in permissive mode. When run in permissive mode, SELinux does not enforce access rules; it only performs logging. To enforce access rules, set SELinux to run in enforcing mode. When run in enforcing mode, SELinux blocks actions that are contrary to the policy and logs a corresponding event in the audit log. To set SELinux to run in enforcing mode, you must set a custom cloud-init for your worker nodes, as discussed in Chapter 4.

Consider the cloud-init script in Listing 6-5, which sets the SELinux policy on OKE nodes to enforcing mode.

Listing 6-5   Setting the SELinux Policy on OKE Nodes to Enforcing

```
#!/bin/bash
curl --fail -H "Authorization: Bearer Oracle" -LO http://169.254.169.254/opc/v2/
  instance/metadata/oke_init_script | base64 --decode >/var/run/oke-init.sh
bash /var/run/oke-init.sh
setenforce 1
sed -i 's/^SELINUX=.*/SELINUX=enforcing/' /etc/selinux/config
```

When SELinux is running in enforcing mode, you can define security contexts for Kubernetes objects such as pods, containers, and volumes. You can use the `securityContext` field in the pod specification to define the security context for a pod. The security context can include the SELinux options field, which allows you to specify the SELinux security context for the pod.

Consider the example in Listing 6-6.

Listing 6-6   SELinux Configuration in a Pod YAML Manifest

```
apiVersion: v1
kind: Pod
metadata:
name: nginx-pod
spec:
  containers:
  - name: nginx
    image: nginx
    securityContext:
    seLinuxOptions:
        level: s0
        categories: c123,c456
```

In this example, you define a pod named `nginx-pod` and set the security context for the `nginx` container using the `seLinuxOptions` field. The level option sets the SELinux security level to `s0`, and the category options `c123` and `c456` define the SELinux categories.

Patching Worker Nodes

OKE provides a managed control plane where the CVEs and other security tasks are done regularly and automated. Kubernetes version updates can be requested by customers and done through a button on the OCI Console, as illustrated in Figure 6-19.

For the customer-managed worker nodes, the Kubernetes version updates are also done at the customer's convenience. Still, the customer manages the operating system, and major upgrades need to be planned. OCI provides tools and agents to scan and report CVEs and other possible vulnerabilities. Figure 6-20 illustrates the version upgrade lifecycle of the worker nodes on the same node pool.

Figure 6-19   Upgrading the Kubernetes Version

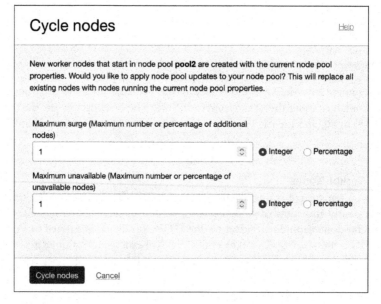

Figure 6-20   Worker Node Cycling for a Node Pool Can Safely Update Worker Nodes

The importance of regularly updating Kubernetes worker nodes and patching vulnerabilities to maintain security cannot be understated. New vulnerabilities are constantly being discovered, and attackers are always developing new methods of attack.

If the workload needs public worker nodes, monitoring and constant patching need to be mandatory and must be part of the organization's DevSecOps strategy.

Worker Nodes Limited Access

Regarding security, limiting external access to the production environment is crucial. It is essential to strike a balance between granting end users appropriate access and avoiding unnecessary access. This involves several layers of protection, with the number of layers and their complexity varying, based on the sensitivity of the information being safeguarded.

Securing network traffic requires more than just making edge decisions. A series of firewalls working together must protect every connection between nodes, as well as intranode communication.

A dynamic CI/CD environment presents unique security challenges because of its constantly changing nature. To address this, scanning and verification tools should be integrated into the pipeline, with ongoing assessments carried out to quickly identify and resolve issues.

In addition to using container-specific security tools, such as SELinux, Kerberos, and SAML, noncontainer specific tools should be utilized to manage access at each layer, from the hardware to the application.

Securing Your Workloads

This section emphasizes the need for robust security measures, to protect Kubernetes workloads from potential vulnerabilities and attacks.

Security Context

Container security at scale can be challenging: The annual CNCF survey consistently ranks security as one of the top challenges for organizations that have adopted containers for most of their workloads. One particular aspect might contribute to this complexity: When you run containers, Linux operating system security concepts can bleed into the developer realm, whereas it previously existed only on the infrastructure and DevOps realms. This means that the change in the developer workflow, with developers now delivering an application container instead of an application package, is not just a packaging change. The new packaging format, containers, also needs to account for the security of the container environment. Thus, it is essential for developers who build and package their code to do so while still paying attention to the security posture. It is equally important for administrators to understand container settings and PodSpecs, to identify potentially misconfigured workloads that could pose a security risk.

Container runtimes and the underlying Linux features they are built upon, such as cgroups and namespaces, expose a plethora of options. For example, to run the processes inside a container as a specific user, Docker provides the `--user` flag. Within Kubernetes, the `securityContext` for a container or a pod determines how these are configured. Effectively using the features provided by the `securityContext` is an essential but often overlooked aspect. This could be because the options on offer are often unfamiliar to application developers, who largely focus on the app development stack, not on the Linux security best practices. This section describes the most common configuration options for `securityContext`; the Kubernetes documentation covers all the allowed configuration parameters.[10]

Kubernetes `securityContext` settings can be defined in both the `spec.pod` and `spec.containers` portions of the resource manifest (PodSpec and ContainerSpec APIs). Formally, the `securityContext` set at the PodSpec is called the `PodSecurityContext`, and the term `SecurityContext` refers to the configuration in the ContainerSpec. However, these are always applied at a container level, and specifying `PodSecurityContext` is a quick way to uniformly apply the same `securityContext` configuration to all containers running within the pod. If the `securityContext` setting is configured for both the PodSpec and the ContainerSpec, the configuration at the ContainerSpec takes precedence; you can think of this as the `PodSecurityContext` configuration being overridden by the `SecurityContext` configuration.

runAsNonRoot

As the name indicates, the `runAsNonRoot` setting set to `true` tells the kubelet to validate that the container is not running as root. Processes inside containers are run as `root` by default when no alternatives are provided. Because containers share a kernel, this also means that the process has the same access as the `root` account on the host. Containers use Linux features such as cgroups and namespaces to isolate the container; however, vulnerability exploits and misconfigurations can potentially give an attacker a path for escaping the container. As a general rule, there should be no reason for the vast majority of workloads to run as root. The `runAsNonRoot` configuration provides a mechanism to enforce this for your workloads.

As a best practice, your Dockerfile should create a user and set the default user as well, as shown in Listing 6-7.

Listing 6-7   Example Dockerfile Not Using Root User To Be Able To Be Deployed as runAsNonRoot on Kubernetes

```
RUN groupadd -g 10001 myapp && \
useradd -u 10000 -g myapp \
&& chown -R myapp:myapp /app

USER myapp:myapp
```

Note

The UID and GID specified are larger numbers, to avoid the possibility of these UIDs and GIDs existing on the host and inheriting privileges. Using a larger number—say, 10,000 or higher—reduces the chance of a user or group existing on the host with the same UID/GID.

Occasionally, the image you are running might not define a nonroot user, and you might not have direct control over the Dockerfile. This can often happen when the image comes from a vendor that no longer exists or that is refusing to add and set a default nonroot user. In these cases, as a last resort, you can create your own image based on the original by extending the Dockerfile, adding the new UID/GID, and setting those as the default.

To maintain a good security posture for the cluster, you set `runAsNonRoot: true` for your workloads. This ensures that the processes inside the container cannot use UID 0. If the `runAsNonRoot` is omitted, it has the same effect as setting it to `false`. If possible, you should always set `runAsNonRoot` explicitly, even if it is set to `false` for a workload that absolutely must run as root. This clearly communicates the intention and ensures that changes to the values can easily be audited.

runAsUser and runAsGroup

These configurations are used to run containers using the provided values for the UID and GID. They override the default UID and GID set within the container image and are often used in conjunction with the `runAsNonRoot` option. It is common for developers to provide an image with a nonroot user created but not set as the default. In this case, you can easily use the `runAsUser` and `runAsGroup` attributes to configure the included users. Specifying these values explicitly, even if they are set as the default in the image, makes them more visible and easier to track changes. These options should be used with care, and the values should not be set randomly. Many workloads have specific requirements on the UID and GID for the processes. For example, a container might need access to files that are accessible only by the user or group set by default in the image. In such cases, overriding these values could cause the application to malfunction.

As a best practice, do not rely on the `runAsUser` or `runAsGroup` settings to set the container processes' UID and GID: They could cause incompatibilities or could potentially be removed later. Instead, the user and group should be created within the container image, and `runAsUser` or `runAsGroup` should be used to explicitly state the UID and GIDs, along with setting `runAsNonRoot` to `true`.

readOnlyRootFilesystem

If you have a stateful workload that needs to write data, you can take advantage of the storage mechanisms in Kubernetes, including ephemeral volumes and persistent volumes. Alternatively, your application might store state in a database. Writes to the container's filesystem are made to the container's top writable layer. The data is ephemeral and is not easily portable across nodes; any data written locally on the container will not persist when the pod is restarted. For this reason, containers in your workload generally do not need the capability to write to the container filesystem. However, the container filesystem opens some security concerns. If attackers are able to gain access to the container, they can update the configuration of the container when the container filesystem is writable. For example, an attacker could install new software packages within the container and open up new attack vectors. To avoid this, you can set the container's root filesystem to be read-only. Note that this attribute is available only on the `SecurityContext`, not on the `PodSecurityContext`.

privileged

Setting the `privileged` attribute to `true` runs the container in privileged mode, which is essentially equivalent to running as root on the host. The default value for this attribute is `false`; it is available only on the `SecurityContext`, not on the `PodSecurityContext`. As a best practice, you should consider explicitly setting this to `false` so that the intent of running a container without `privileged` mode is clear and changes can be easily tracked.

capabilities

POSIX capabilities are a kernel feature that allows for granular control over the kernel calls a process can make. The idea is to group all the privileged kernel calls into related categories and then assign processes only to the categories they need. With the `capabilities` attribute, you have the capability to drop or add capabilities to containers. The default set of capabilities that a container gets is determined by the container runtime. Using the `capabilities.add` and `capabilities.drop` attributes, you can provide one or more capabilities as a comma-separated list. You use the `-all` keyword to cover all capabilities. As a best practice, consider dropping all capabilities and adding only the capabilities that your workload actually needs, as shown in Listing 6-8.

Listing 6-8   Example of `SecurityContext.capabilities` on a Deployment YAML Manifest

```
securityContext:
    capabilities:
        drop:
        - all
        add: ["NET_ADMIN", "SYS_TIME"]
```

syscalls and seccomp

System calls are the fundamental interface between user-level programs and the operating system kernel, often abbreviated as syscalls. They provide a means for applications to request services from the operating system, such as file operations, network communication, process management, and more. Every time an application needs to interact with the underlying system, it uses syscalls to perform the necessary operations.

Container Isolation and syscalls

Containerization technologies such as Docker and CRI-O leverage the underlying Linux kernel's features, such as namespaces and cgroups, to provide isolation between containers. syscalls play a crucial role in enabling this isolation by acting as the gatekeepers between the container and the host operating system. When a containerized application makes a syscall, it is intercepted by the container runtime, such as Docker or containerd, before it reaches the underlying kernel. The runtime validates the syscall, ensuring that it complies with the container's defined isolation policies. This validation includes checking whether the syscall is allowed, restricted, or prohibited, based on the container's configuration.

seccomp and syscall Filtering

Kubernetes employs several mechanisms to control and filter syscalls. One such mechanism is seccomp, or secure computing mode, which enables administrators to define a policy for a container that specifies which syscalls are permitted. Restricting the set of allowed syscalls significantly reduces the attack surface of a container and enhances its security. seccomp works by leveraging Linux's seccomp-bpf (Berkeley Packet Filter) mechanism, which filters syscalls using a predefined filter expression. This expression can be customized to allowlist or blocklist specific syscalls, based on the container's requirements. Kubernetes provides a default seccomp profile, but users can also define their own profiles, for fine-grained control.

The example in Listing 6-9 uses a seccomp profile for syscall auditing.

Listing 6-9 Example of a YAML Pod Manifest File Using securityContext.seccompProfile

```
apiVersion: v1
kind: Pod
metadata:
name: audit-pod
labels:
    app: audit-pod
spec:
  securityContext:
    seccompProfile:
      type: Localhost
      localhostProfile: profiles/audit.json
  containers:
  - name: test-container
    image: hashicorp/http-echo:0.2.3
    args:
    - "-text=just made some syscalls!"
    securityContext:
      allowPrivilegeEscalation: false
```

By default, seccomp allows only restricting specific system calls, such as `read()`, `write()`, `exit()`, and `sigreturn()`. All other system calls are prohibited.

Mode 2 enables the utilization of BPF and eBPF filters to determine which system calls are permitted. After the eBPF program is created and installed into the kernel, all system calls pass through the filter. Additional features and generalizations of BPF have been added throughout the years.

Capabilities and Privileged Containers

In addition to seccomp, Kubernetes employs capabilities to further control container permissions. Capabilities allow containers to perform specific privileged operations, such as changing network settings or accessing kernel-level resources. By default, Kubernetes drops most capabilities, ensuring that containers run with the minimum necessary privileges; however, administrators can selectively enable or disable capabilities, based on the requirements of their applications.

Syscall Interception and User-Space Proxies

In some cases, Kubernetes deployments include user-space proxies such as Envoy (used by Istio), for traffic management and observability. These proxies often intercept network-related syscalls to enable advanced networking features such as service discovery, load balancing, and mutual TLS authentication. By intercepting syscalls, these proxies can modify network behavior at runtime, enabling a more flexible and dynamic networking environment for Kubernetes clusters.

Open Policy Agent (OPA)

Open Policy Agent (OPA) is a general-purpose policy engine that provides a flexible and policy-driven approach to enforce rules and regulations in Kubernetes deployments. OPA allows organizations to define and enforce policies such as access control, data filtering, and configuration validation across various domains. OPA relies on the declarative language Rego to express policies. These policies are expressed as rules and can be evaluated against data, to determine compliance.

OPA Integration with Kubernetes

OPA can be integrated with Kubernetes in various ways to enforce policies across different aspects of the cluster:

- **Admission control:** OPA can be integrated with Kubernetes admission controllers to validate and mutate requests made to the cluster. Admission controllers intercept requests for creating or modifying Kubernetes resources and apply policy-based checks before allowing or rejecting them. OPA can evaluate admission policies using Rego and enforce custom policies for resource creation and modification.

- **Policy enforcement:** OPA can be used to enforce policies at runtime by integrating with dynamic admission control in Kubernetes. This enables fine-grained policy enforcement based on real-time data and context. For example, OPA can be used to enforce pod-to-pod communication policies, network policies, or even access control policies based on user roles and permissions.
- **Configuration management:** OPA can be used to manage and enforce configuration policies for Kubernetes resources. With OPA, organizations can define policies for resource configurations, such as ensuring that containers use specific versions, enforcing resource limits, or validating security-related configurations. OPA can evaluate the desired state against defined policies and reject or modify configurations that violate the policies.
- **Governance and compliance:** OPA can help organizations maintain governance and compliance within their Kubernetes environments. By defining policies that align with industry regulations or internal security standards, OPA can ensure that Kubernetes resources adhere to these policies. This includes policies for image scanning, secrets management, auditing, and more.

Deploying OPA on OKE

OPA integrates seamlessly with Kubernetes, enabling administrators to define and enforce policies specific to their Kubernetes deployments. This integration is typically achieved using the Kubernetes admission control mechanism, which intercepts API requests and evaluates them against OPA policies before allowing them to proceed. OPA can be deployed as a standalone service, integrated as a sidecar container alongside other application containers, or used as a library within an application. The chosen deployment method depends on the organization's specific requirements and use cases.

You can deploy OPA to OKE in two ways, as illustrated in Figure 6-21. The first is to use plain OPA and Kube-mgmt, which is enabled as the Kubernetes Admission Controller. This option is more complex and needs to make changes to the ValidationAdmissionController and some mutating controllers; it is not covered in this book. For more information on the supported admission controllers on OKE, check the documentation.[11]

The second approach is to use OPA Gatekeeper, an extension of the Open Policy Agent (OPA) project. OPA Gatekeeper offers a first-class integration between OPA and Kubernetes for policy enforcement.

OPA Gatekeeper includes additional features on top of the basic OPA:

- An extensible, parameterized policy library
- Native Kubernetes CRDs for instantiating the policy library (constraints)
- Native Kubernetes CRDs for extending the policy library (constraint templates)
- Audit functionality

The upcoming section "OPA Gatekeeper" provides additional details.

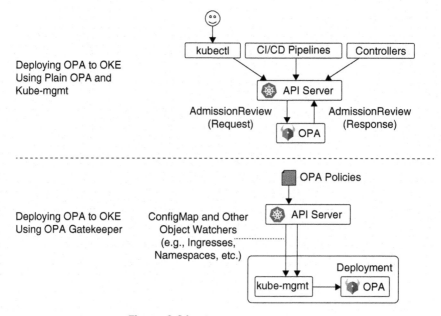

Figure 6-21   OPA Deployment Options

Defining Policies with Rego

Rego is the declarative language used by OPA to express policies. It provides a flexible syntax for defining rules and constraints that govern Kubernetes resources. Rego policies can be written to validate resource configurations, enforce naming conventions, restrict image usage, ensure compliance with security standards, and perform custom checks tailored to the organization's requirements.

Listing 6-10 provides an example of a Rego declarative policy.

Listing 6-10   Example Rego Declarative Policy

```
package kubernetes.admission

import future.keywords

deny contains msg if {
    input.request.kind.kind == "Pod"
    some container in input.request.object.spec.containers
    image := container.image
    not startswith(image, "hooli.com/")
    msg := sprintf("image '%s' comes from untrusted registry", [image])
}
```

Policy Decision and Enforcement

A request to the Kubernetes API server triggers the admission control webhook configured with OPA. The webhook forwards the request to OPA, which evaluates the request against the defined policies in Rego. OPA returns a policy decision to the admission control webhook, indicating whether the request is allowed or denied, based on policy evaluation. The webhook then enforces the decision by either allowing or rejecting the request.

Dynamic Policy Updates and Live Configuration Changes

One of the advantages of using OPA with Kubernetes is its capability to dynamically update policies without requiring a cluster restart. This dynamic behavior enables administrators to make policy changes on the fly and adapt to evolving requirements. OPA can fetch policy updates from external sources or integrate them with configuration management tools, ensuring that policy changes are propagated efficiently throughout the cluster.

Auditing and Compliance Reporting

OPA's policy engine provides organizations with valuable insights into the compliance status of their Kubernetes deployments. Organizations can generate compliance reports and audit trails by logging policy decisions and evaluations. These reports help demonstrate adherence to regulatory standards and provide visibility into any potential policy violations or security gaps.

OPA Gatekeeper

OPA Gatekeeper is an admission controller for Kubernetes that integrates with OPA to enforce policies during resource creation and modification. It enables administrators to define and enforce policies using the Rego language, ensuring that Kubernetes resources comply with specific requirements and constraints (see Figure 6-22).

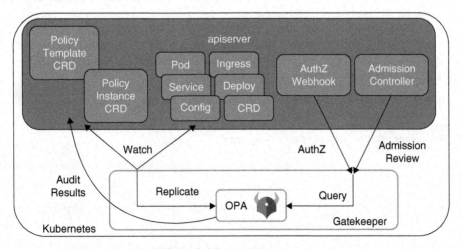

Figure 6-22   OPA Gatekeeper

Benefits of OPA Gatekeeper

OPA Gatekeeper offers several benefits for policy enforcement in Kubernetes deployments:

- **Declarative policy enforcement:** Policies can be defined using the Rego language in a declarative manner, making it easier to express complex constraints and requirements.
- **Kubernetes-native integration:** OPA Gatekeeper is purpose-built for Kubernetes and integrates seamlessly into the admission control workflow, enforcing policies during resource creation and modification.
- **Policy as code:** Policies defined using OPA Gatekeeper are treated as code, allowing for version control, collaboration, and auditability. They can be stored alongside other Kubernetes manifests and managed using standard Git workflows.
- **Dynamic policy evaluation:** OPA Gatekeeper enables dynamic policy evaluation based on real-time data and context. Policies can reference external data sources, making it possible to enforce policies that depend on information from external systems or services.

Deploying OPA Gatekeeper

Deploying OPA Gatekeeper on the OKE cluster requires setting up the following components:

- **OPA Gatekeeper constraint templates:** Constraint templates are used to define the types of policies that OPA Gatekeeper can enforce. These templates specify the structure and parameters of the policies. Organizations can use built-in templates provided by the OPA Gatekeeper project or create custom templates based on their specific needs.
- **Constraints:** Constraints are instances of constraint templates that define specific policy rules. They specify the desired state and properties that Kubernetes resources should adhere to. Constraints are used to evaluate resources against policies during admission control.
- **OPA Gatekeeper controller:** The OPA Gatekeeper controller is responsible for managing constraint templates, constraints, and the policy evaluation process. It communicates with the OPA server to enforce policies and validate resources during admission control.

You can deploy OPA Gatekeeper using the manifest with predefined settings:

```
kubectl apply -f https://raw.githubusercontent.com/open-policy-agent/
  gatekeeper/master/deploy/gatekeeper.yaml
```

Alternately, you can deploy OPA Gatekeeper using the Helm chart, as demonstrated here:

```
helm repo add gatekeeper https://open-policy-agent.github.io/gatekeeper/
  charts
```

```
helm upgrade --install gatekeeper/gatekeeper --name-template=gatekeeper
  --namespace gatekeeper-system --create-namespace
```

Enforcing Policies with OPA Gatekeeper

After you deploy OPA Gatekeeper and set up the necessary components, you can define and enforce policies using constraint templates and constraints. The policy enforcement workflow typically involves the following steps:

Step 1. **Defining constraint templates:** Administrators define constraint templates using the Rego language. These templates specify the structure, parameters, and conditions of the policies to be enforced. The Rego language provides flexibility to express complex policies using logical operators, pattern matching, and iteration.

Step 2. **Creating constraints:** Based on the defined constraint templates, administrators create constraints that apply specific policies to Kubernetes resources. Constraints define the desired state and properties that resources must conform to. They are associated with constraint templates and are evaluated during admission control.

Step 3. **Evaluating admission control:** When a resource creation or modification request is made to the Kubernetes API server, the OPA Gatekeeper controller intercepts the request as part of the admission control process. It evaluates the resource against the defined constraints using the OPA server. If the resource violates any policies, then the request is rejected and the resource is not created or modified.

Step 4. **Continuously enforcing policy:** OPA Gatekeeper provides continuous policy enforcement by ensuring that resources remain compliant even after they are admitted. It periodically reevaluates existing resources against the defined policies, detecting and alerting any policy violations or drifts.

Open Web Application Security Project (OWASP)

The Open Web Application Security Project (OWASP) is a widely recognized nonprofit organization that focuses on improving the security of software applications.

OWASP provides a wealth of knowledge and resources to help organizations identify and address common security vulnerabilities in web applications and APIs. Its flagship project, the OWASP Top Ten, highlights the most critical security risks applications face. The OWASP community actively develops tools, guides, and best practices to help organizations build secure software.

Kubernetes introduces unique security challenges that organizations must address to ensure their containerized applications' integrity and confidentiality. In a cloud native environment powered by Kubernetes, containers themselves must be properly secured. Organizations should ensure that container images are free from vulnerabilities and adhere to secure coding practices. OWASP guides secure container development and the use of secure base images.

Properly configuring Kubernetes clusters is critical for maintaining security as well. Misconfigured clusters can lead to unauthorized access, data breaches, and other security incidents. Organizations should follow Kubernetes security best practices, such as implementing strong authentication and authorization mechanisms, enabling encryption, and restricting access to sensitive resources.

OWASP guidance on secure network design can be applied to Kubernetes environments as well. This is because Kubernetes networking introduces additional challenges in securing communication between pods, services, and external resources. OWASP provides guidance in using network policies, ingress controllers, and secure communication protocols, such as Transport Layer Security (TLS), that are recommended to protect network traffic.

Similarly, OWASP recommendations on secure key management can be applied to Kubernetes secrets and other sensitive data. Managing sensitive information such as API keys, passwords, and certificates is crucial in Kubernetes. Organizations should follow the best secure secret management practices, including proper encryption, restricted access, and secure storage mechanisms.

Leveraging OWASP Best Practices on OKE

Some of the best practices and resources available to leverage OWASP guidance for OKE clusters include the following:

- **OWASP Top Ten:** The OWASP Top Ten list of common vulnerabilities and corresponding mitigation techniques (https://owasp.org/www-project-kubernetes-top-ten/)[12] is a valuable resource in securing web applications. Although Kubernetes is not a web application, many security risks identified by OWASP, such as injection attacks, broken authentication, and insecure access control, are still relevant in Kubernetes deployments. Organizations should review the OWASP Top Ten and apply relevant mitigations to their Kubernetes environments.

- **OWASP Secure Coding Practices:** OWASP provides a comprehensive set of secure coding practices that can be applied to containerized applications running on OKE. These practices cover areas such as input validation, output encoding, access control, and error handling. Adhering to these practices helps reduce the risk of common application-level vulnerabilities. Secure Coding Practices extend to OCI SDK usage with access to the infrastructure services.

- **OWASP tools and libraries:** OWASP offers a range of security tools and libraries that can be integrated into the CI/CD pipeline and runtime environment of Kubernetes applications. For example, tools such as OWASP Zed Attack Proxy (ZAP) can be used to perform security testing on containerized applications during development and deployment.

- **Continuous security testing and monitoring:** In addition to applying OWASP best practices, organizations should implement continuous security testing and monitoring in their Kubernetes environments. This includes vulnerability scanning of container images, runtime monitoring of cluster activities, and regular security assessments. The OWASP toolset provides several resources for security testing, including dependency checkers, vulnerability scanners, and secure code analysis tools. This chapter covered many resources integrated into the OWASP toolset and practices.

Supporting Tools

This section describes tools that were tested on OKE and can support the security activities and your DevSecOps strategy.

External Container Scanning Tools

Several tools are available for Kubernetes container scanning. These are some popular open-source tools:

- **Trivy:** Trivy is an open-source vulnerability scanner for containers. It can scan container images for vulnerabilities and generate a report. Trivy can be integrated with Kubernetes and can scan containers in a Kubernetes cluster.
- **Anchore:** Anchore is an open-source container image analysis tool. It can scan container images for vulnerabilities, configuration issues, and policy violations. Anchore can be integrated with Kubernetes and can be used to scan containers in a Kubernetes cluster.
- **Clair:** Clair is an open-source vulnerability scanner for containers. It can scan container images for vulnerabilities and generate a report. Clair can be integrated with Kubernetes and can be used to scan containers in a Kubernetes cluster.
- **Aqua Security:** Aqua Security provides a comprehensive container security platform, including container scanning, runtime protection, and compliance monitoring. Aqua Security can be integrated with Kubernetes and can be used to scan containers in a Kubernetes cluster.

CIS-CAT Pro Assessor

CIS-CAT Pro Assessor is a tool developed by the Center for Internet Security that automates assessing the security configurations of various technologies, including Kubernetes clusters. It uses CIS Benchmarks, consensus-based guidelines that provide recommendations for secure system configurations. Using CIS-CAT Pro Assessor, organizations can identify vulnerabilities, misconfigurations, and security weaknesses within their Kubernetes environments.

To leverage the advanced capabilities of CIS-CAT Pro Assessor with Kubernetes Benchmarks, follow these steps:

Step 1. **Download CIS-CAT Pro Assessor:** CIS-CAT Pro Assessor is a commercial tool that can be obtained from the Center for Internet Security. After acquiring the tool, follow the installation instructions provided by CIS.

Step 2. **Obtain the Kubernetes Benchmarks:** Download the CIS Kubernetes Benchmarks from the CIS website. The benchmarks are available in various formats, including YAML and JSON. Make sure you obtain the Oracle Cloud Infrastructure Container Engine for Kubernetes (OKE) Benchmark.

Step 3. **Configure CIS-CAT Pro Assessor:** When CIS-CAT Pro Assessor is installed, you need to configure it to work with Kubernetes Benchmarks. This involves specifying the location of the benchmark files and setting up any required parameters or options. The configuration file should contain information about your Kubernetes deployment, such as the API server URL, authentication credentials, and the location of the Kubernetes configuration file. OKE kubeconfig needs the oci-cli to be installed and configured for the same tenancy of the cluster, or using the `--profile` parameter if more than one profile is on the same machine.

Step 4. **Run the assessment:** Launch CIS-CAT Pro Assessor and initiate the assessment process by providing the necessary inputs, such as the target Kubernetes cluster information. The tool automatically evaluates the cluster's security configurations against the CIS Kubernetes Benchmark. You can run the assessment using the command line or the graphical user interface (GUI), as shown in Figure 6-23.

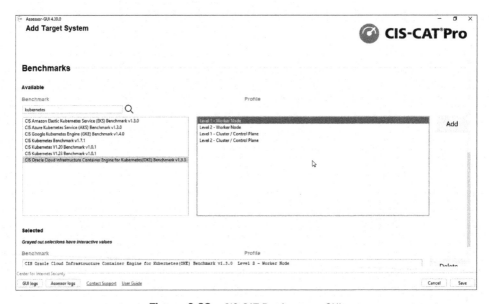

Figure 6-23   CIS-CAT Pro Assessor GUI

Listing 6-11 provides an example of running the assessment using the CIS-CAT CLI using OKE Benchmark.

Listing 6-11 CIS-CAT CLI: Using the OKE Benchmark

```
./Assessor-CLI.sh -b benchmarks/CIS_Oracle_Cloud_Infrastructure_Container_Engine_
    for_Kubernetes(OKE)_Benchmark_v1.3.0-xccdf.xml
```

Listing 6-12 provides an example of running the assessment using the CIS-CAT CLI using a custom configuration file.

Listing 6-12 CIS-CAT: Using Custom Configuration File

```
./Assessor-CLI.sh --config-xml /CIS/kubernetes_assessment-configuration.xml
```

Step 5. **Review the assessment results:** CIS-CAT Pro Assessor generates a comprehensive report highlighting deviations from the recommended configurations outlined in the Kubernetes Benchmark (see Figure 6-24). Carefully review the report to identify areas that require attention or remediation.

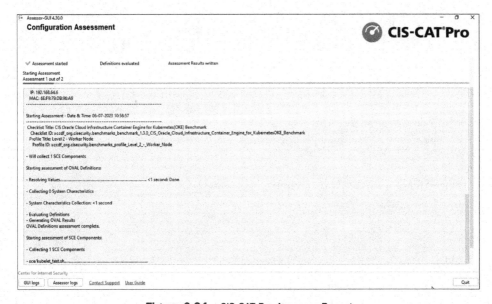

Figure 6-24 CIS-CAT Pro Assessor Report

kube-bench

kube-bench is a security auditing tool developed by Aqua Security. It automates checking Kubernetes configurations against the CIS Kubernetes Benchmark. This benchmark provides a comprehensive set of best practices for securing Kubernetes deployments.

After running all the checks, kube-bench gives you a formatted output of FAIL, WARN, and PASS benchmarks. It supports various output formats, including console, JSON, and JUnit XML, making it easy to integrate with other tools and systems. Figure 6-25 illustrates the log report of the Kubernetes job executed by kube-bench against the OKE.

```
> kubectl logs kube-bench-kxs4j
[INFO] 4 Worker Node Security Configuration
[INFO] 4.1 Worker Node Configuration Files
[FAIL] 4.1.1 Ensure that the kubelet service file permissions are set to 600 or more restrictive (Automated)
[PASS] 4.1.2 Ensure that the kubelet service file ownership is set to root:root (Automated)
[PASS] 4.1.3 If proxy kubeconfig file exists ensure permissions are set to 600 or more restrictive (Manual)
[PASS] 4.1.4 If proxy kubeconfig file exists ensure ownership is set to root:root (Manual)
[PASS] 4.1.5 Ensure that the --kubeconfig kubelet.conf file permissions are set to 600 or more restrictive (Automated)
[PASS] 4.1.6 Ensure that the --kubeconfig kubelet.conf file ownership is set to root:root (Automated)
[WARN] 4.1.7 Ensure that the certificate authorities file permissions are set to 600 or more restrictive (Manual)
[WARN] 4.1.8 Ensure that the client certificate authorities file ownership is set to root:root (Manual)
[WARN] 4.1.9 If the kubelet config.yaml configuration file is being used validate permissions set to 600 or more restrictive (Manual)
[PASS] 4.1.10 If the kubelet config.yaml configuration file is being used validate file ownership is set to root:root (Manual)
[INFO] 4.2 Kubelet
[FAIL] 4.2.1 Ensure that the --anonymous-auth argument is set to false (Automated)
[FAIL] 4.2.2 Ensure that the --authorization-mode argument is not set to AlwaysAllow (Automated)
[FAIL] 4.2.3 Ensure that the --client-ca-file argument is set as appropriate (Automated)
[PASS] 4.2.4 Verify that the --read-only-port argument is set to 0 (Manual)
[PASS] 4.2.5 Ensure that the --streaming-connection-idle-timeout argument is not set to 0 (Manual)
[PASS] 4.2.6 Ensure that the --make-iptables-util-chains argument is set to true (Automated)
[WARN] 4.2.7 Ensure that the --hostname-override argument is not set (Manual)
[PASS] 4.2.8 Ensure that the eventRecordQPS argument is set to a level which ensures appropriate event capture (Manual)
[WARN] 4.2.9 Ensure that the --tls-cert-file and --tls-private-key-file arguments are set as appropriate (Manual)
[PASS] 4.2.10 Ensure that the --rotate-certificates argument is not set to false (Automated)
[PASS] 4.2.11 Verify that the RotateKubeletServerCertificate argument is set to true (Manual)
[PASS] 4.2.12 Ensure that the Kubelet only makes use of Strong Cryptographic Ciphers (Manual)
[WARN] 4.2.13 Ensure that a limit is set on pod PIDs (Manual)

== Remediations node ==
```

Figure 6-25   kube-bench Log Report from the Kubernetes Job Execution

Using kube-bench with OKE requires you to have cluster-admin access; you also must have deployed the provided job.yaml or installed the kube-bench CLI.

To deploy as a job using the generic Kubernetes Benchmark, run the following commands:

```
kubectl apply -f job.yaml
```

You can monitor the job's progress:

```
kubectl logs -f job/kube-bench
```

Additionally, you can retrieve the job's results:

```
kubectl logs job/kube-bench > kube-bench-results.txt
```

Running kube-bench using the CLI is simple as well:

```
kube-bench run --targets node
```

You can find the configurations for OKE in the book's GitHub repository.

```
-- oke-1.4.0
   |-- config.yaml
   |-- controlplane.yaml
```

```
|-- managedservices.yaml
|-- master.yaml
|-- node.yaml
'-- policies.yaml
```

To include an OKE-specific benchmark, download the OKE benchmark from the book's GitHub repository, copy it to the `kube-bench/cfg` directory, and run the following command:

```
kube-bench run --benchmark oke-1.4.0
```

kube-bench provides detailed results indicating the compliance status of each check in the CIS Kubernetes Benchmark. It highlights failed or skipped checks, enabling you to identify potential security vulnerabilities or misconfigurations. Analyze the results carefully, taking appropriate actions to remediate any security issues discovered.

AppArmor

AppArmor is an alternative Linux Security Module (LSM) to SELinux. Support for it has been incorporated in the Linux kernel since 2006. It has been used by Oracle Linux, SUSE, Ubuntu, and other distributions. AppArmor supplements the traditional UNIX discretionary access control (DAC) model by providing mandatory access control (MAC). In addition to manually specifying profiles, AppArmor includes a learning mode, in which violations of the profile are logged but not prevented. This log can then be turned into a profile, based on the program's typical behavior.

Consider some AppArmor facts:

- It allows administrators to associate a security profile to a program that restricts its capabilities
- It is sometimes considered easier to use than SELinux
- It is considered filesystem neutral (no security labels required)

For an AppArmor profile to be used by a pod, it must be available on the node where it is assigned. There is no native process for Kubernetes to load policies. As a result, you need to ensure that policies are loaded on every node where AppArmor-required pods are scheduled and that the scheduler is unaware of which nodes have profiles. Adding profiles can be done during node installation with a tool such as Ansible or Puppet, at least for some of the nodes. If only some nodes will have profiles installed, you can use a NodeSelector or a taint to ensure that the scheduler chooses the appropriate node. Another solution is to deploy a DaemonSet and allow the pod to modify the host and add profiles. This would assign the responsibility to the cluster administrators, if they are different from the administrators responsible for operating system configuration and security. If you need to disable AppArmor on the entire cluster (perhaps to troubleshoot), you pass the `--feature-gates=AppArmor=false` option.

AppArmor has several administrative utilities for monitoring and control (see Table 6-1).

Table 6-1   AppArmor Administrative Utilities

Program	Use
apparmor_status	Shows the status of all profiles and processes with profiles.
apparmor_notify	Shows a summary for AppArmor log messages.
complain	Sets a specified profile to complain mode.
enforce	Sets a specified profile to enforce mode.
disable	Unloads a specified profile from the current kernel and prevents it from being loaded upon system startup.
logprof	Scans the log file and suggests modifications to augment the existing profile if there are new AppArmor events that are not covered by it. If AppArmor is running, the updated profiles are reloaded and processes are set to run under their proper profiles.
easyprof	Helps set up a basic AppArmor profile for a program.

On an Oracle Linux system, AppArmor has the following monitoring and controlling utilities:

```
$ rpm -qil apparmor-utils | grep bin
/usr/bin/aa-easyprof
/usr/sbin/aa-audit
/usr/sbin/aa-autodep
/usr/sbin/aa-cleanprof
/usr/sbin/aa-complain
/usr/sbin/aa-decode
/usr/sbin/aa-disable
/usr/sbin/aa-enforce
/usr/sbin/aa-genprof
/usr/sbin/aa-logprof
/usr/sbin/aa-notify
/usr/sbin/aa-remove-unknown
/usr/sbin/aa-status
...
/usr/sbin/complain
/usr/sbin/decode
/usr/sbin/disable
/usr/sbin/enforce
```

Note that many of these utilities can be invoked with either their short or long names:

```
opc:/etc/apparmor.d > ls -l /usr/sbin/*complain
-rwxr-xr-x 1 root root 1442 Jan 25 07:37 /usr/sbin/aa-complain*
lrwxrwxrwx 1 root root   11 Feb 11 13:02 /usr/sbin/complain -> aa-complain*
```

Falco

Falco is a container runtime security tool that deploys to your cluster and starts gathering data for analysis in real time. Falco runs a set of rules against this constant stream of data and raises alerts when the rules detect an event. Falco is deployed to a Kubernetes cluster as a DaemonSet, ensuring that it runs on all nodes. From here, it can start instrumenting system calls, Kubernetes audit logs, and other data sources. Falco can correlate the data from these multiple sources to create a more complete picture of the events in your environment. The capability to instrument system calls is what makes Falco interesting; the Linux system calls power basically everything from opening a file to sending a packet of data to a network device. This means that malicious attackers have to use system calls even if they manage to circumvent other security precautions. Instrumenting system calls can be challenging because they are so pervasive in the normal functioning of the OS; adding instrumentation can negatively affect the system performance. To instrument system calls efficiently, Falco offers a kernel module that is very performant or an eBPF probe for systems that can use eBPF. Figure 6-26 illustrates the high-level architecture for Falco.

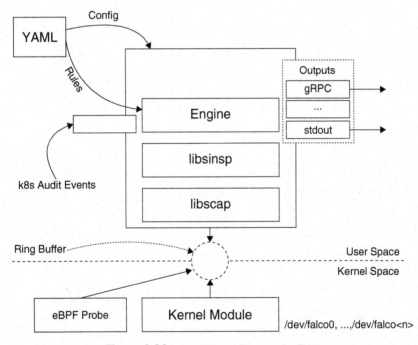

Figure 6-26   Architecture Diagram for Falco

Tracee

Tracee is a tool that allows for the real-time monitoring of system calls and kernel events. Although all actions are traced, you can grep through the output to narrow it to a particular pod. The information shown has a precise time stamp, uts_name, UID,

PID, return code, event, and arguments. For Tracee to run, you need to provide at least three volume locations with the -v option for the kernel information to be pulled (such as /lib/modules/ and /usr/src), as well as ephemeral information such as /tmp/tracee. Many options are available for working with the traced information, such as capturing data that a container writes to disk or memory, for further investigation, as well as extracting binaries from a container. All of these features allow Tracee to provide in-depth tracing of an entire container or pod. Although Clair uses alpine-secdb (which covers back-ported fixes), it is not complete—it might have half as many issues as are currently discovered.

Trivy

Trivy is a simple and comprehensive vulnerability scanner for containers. Each time Trivy is run, it retrieves a more complete list of vulnerabilities (vuln-list) to analyze. Because this list is downloaded from Alpine Linux, it is most complete when analyzing Alpine and RHEL/CentOS. In a large environment, you might want to set up your own server of the vuln-list, and then use Trivy in client mode and pass the address and port of the server. This does not download the database; instead, it references the common one on the server. This approach also helps in an air-gapped environment, where you can download the list on an external system, check the contents, and manually install the list on a protected server. Another reason Trivy might be a more accurate scanner in finding issues is that it checks the middle layers of an image to find the version of the static linking library. Several continuous integration (CI) tools have easy-to-use integration files for using Trivy in a CI/CD pipeline.

National Institute of Standards and Technology (NIST) Kubernetes Benchmarks

The National Institute of Standards and Technology (NIST) has developed Kubernetes Benchmarks, a comprehensive set of guidelines and best practices to ensure the secure deployment and operation of Kubernetes clusters. This section explores the key components of the NIST Kubernetes Benchmarks and discusses how organizations can leverage them to enhance their Kubernetes security posture.

Staying informed about security threats requires reading numerous publications. To start, check out the Federal Information Processing Standard (FIPS) and visit the Computer Security Resource Center Publications web page for standards, special publications, research reports, and more.[13]

The vast amount of information can be overwhelming, so consider using the Cybersecurity Framework (CSF) to organize security into five activities: identify, protect, detect, respond, and recover.

By breaking down cybersecurity into manageable activities and categories, you can focus on the most important information for your current role and expand your knowledge over time.

NIST Kubernetes Benchmarks

The Kubernetes Benchmarks provided by NIST are a valuable resource for organizations looking to secure their Kubernetes deployments. They offer a systematic approach to assess and validate the security configurations and controls within a Kubernetes environment. The benchmarks cover various aspects of Kubernetes security, including authentication, authorization, network policies, and logging. By adhering to these benchmarks, organizations can reduce the risk of security incidents, enhance their ability to detect and respond to threats, and maintain compliance with relevant industry standards and regulations.

- **Configuration and hardening guidelines:** One of the fundamental aspects of Kubernetes security involves ensuring the proper configuration and hardening of the cluster components. The NIST Kubernetes Benchmarks provide detailed recommendations for securing the Kubernetes control plane, worker nodes, and associated resources. These guidelines include recommendations for securing the Kubernetes API server, restricting privileged access, enabling secure communication channels, configuring pod security policies, and implementing network segmentation.
- **Authentication and authorization controls:** Authentication and authorization mechanisms ensure that only authorized entities can access and operate within a Kubernetes cluster. The Kubernetes Benchmarks outline best practices for implementing strong authentication mechanisms, such as mutual TLS authentication, integration with external identity providers, and the enforcement of secure password policies. Additionally, the benchmarks provide guidance on implementing fine-grained authorization controls using Kubernetes role-based access control (RBAC) and other relevant mechanisms.
- **Network policies and segmentation:** Effective network policies and segmentation are essential for isolating workloads, preventing lateral movement within a cluster, and protecting sensitive data. The Kubernetes Benchmarks provide recommendations for defining network policies that restrict traffic flows between pods and namespaces, implementing network segmentation through the use of network plug-ins, and enabling encrypted communication between components using Transport Layer Security (TLS).
- **Logging and monitoring:** Comprehensive logging and monitoring are crucial for detecting and investigating security incidents within a Kubernetes cluster. The benchmarks highlight the importance of configuring centralized logging for Kubernetes components, capturing relevant log events, and retaining logs for an appropriate duration. Additionally, the benchmarks emphasize the implementation of robust monitoring solutions that can provide real-time visibility into the cluster's security posture and facilitate timely incident response.
- **Implementing Kubernetes Benchmarks:** Organizations should adopt a systematic approach to effectively implement the NIST Kubernetes Benchmarks. This involves performing a security assessment of the Kubernetes cluster against the benchmark recommendations, identifying areas of noncompliance or potential

vulnerabilities, and remediating them accordingly. Organizations can leverage various tools and technologies to automate the assessment process and continuously monitor their Kubernetes environment for compliance deviations or security incidents.

National Checklist Program Repository

The National Checklist Program (NCP), defined by the NIST SP 800-70 Rev. 4, is the U.S. government repository of publicly available security checklists (or benchmarks) that provide detailed low-level guidance on setting the security configuration of operating systems and applications.[14] NCP provides guidance on secure configuration and vulnerability assessments for various operating systems and applications, including Kubernetes and operating systems used by the containers.

National Vulnerability Database

The National Vulnerability Database (NVD) is a resource offered by the National Institute of Standards and Technology (NIST), a physical sciences laboratory run by the U.S. government. NIST also manages the Computer Security Resource Center (CSRC), which provides access to documents such as Federal Information Processing Standards (FIPS) and Special Publications (SP). The NVD contains a wealth of information, including checklists for compliance, known issues, and specialized vulnerabilities.[15]

NIST SP 800-190 Application Container Security Guide

The NIST SP 800-190 Application Container Security Guide provides an overview of containers and their security challenges. It also provides recommendations for securing container-based applications throughout the entire application lifecycle.[16]

Summary

Security is such a pervasive and multifaceted topic that entire books have been dedicated to it. This chapter merely scratched the surface of security practices in a cloud native environment. To start, you looked at the 4Cs of cloud native security and examined the various security controls, features, and best practices for securing your workloads and infrastructure. You explored several security controls services and features offered by Oracle Cloud Infrastructure. You worked your way through the various layers, including cluster-level security controls, containers, and container supply chain security, and you looked at best practices and tools to ensure secure coding. You also examined several third-party and open-source tools that are popular in the cloud native community for implementing security best practices and ensuring a good security posture.

References

1 Secrets Store CSI Driver Provider for OCI Vault: https://github.com/oracle/
   oci-secrets-store-csi-driver-provider/blob/main/GettingStarted.md
2 Master Encryption Keys in Other Tenancies: https://docs.oracle.com/
   en-us/iaas/Content/ContEng/Tasks/contengencryptingdata.htm#
   contengencryptingdata_topic_Encryption_keys_in_other_tenancies
3 Audit events: https://cloud.oracle.com/audit/events
4 Audit logs: https://cloud.oracle.com/logging/audit
5 LoadBalancer: https://cloud.oracle.com/load-balancer/load-balancers
6 WAF edge policies: https://cloud.oracle.com/waf/policies
7 Snyk.io (https://snyk.io/): https://github.com/oracle-quickstart/oke-snyk
8 Sysdig.com (https://sysdig.com/)8: https://github.com/oracle-quickstart/
   oke-sysdig
9 Kubernetes CIS Benchmark: https://www.cisecurity.org/benchmark/kubernetes
10 securityContext Options: https://kubernetes.io/docs/reference/kubernetes-api/
   workload-resources/pod-v1/#security-context-1
11 Supported admission controllers: https://docs.oracle.com/en-us/iaas/Content/
   ContEng/Reference/contengadmissioncontrollers.htm
12 OWASP Top Ten reference: https://owasp.org/www-project-kubernetes-top-ten/
13 NIST Computer Security Resource Center: https://csrc.nist.gov/publications
14 National Checklist Program (NCP): https://nvd.nist.gov/ncp/repository
15 National Vulnerability Database (NVD): https://nvd.nist.gov/
16 NIST SP 800-190 Application Container Security Guide: https://nvlpubs.nist.gov/
   nistpubs/SpecialPublications/NIST.SP.800-190.pdf

7

Serverless Platforms and Applications

Serverless platforms enable users to focus more on the applications they build than on infrastructure management. In this sense, the word *serverless* is a misnomer because serverless applications still require a server infrastructure to run. However, the servers on which applications run and the management of these servers generally are abstracted from developers by the cloud infrastructure provider. The rise of serverless platforms can be seen as a direct result of cloud adoption, in many cases. Applications are increasingly adopting cloud native design principles such as automation, immutability, and observability to take advantage of the elasticity, resilience, and cost advantages offered by public cloud providers. Developers thus can offload most of the infrastructure management to the cloud provider itself. This means that challenges that previously required custom solutions, such as scaling a system based on application metrics, can now be fully handed over to a cloud provider. For new applications, this often delivers a significant reduction in the time it takes to bring it to production: Teams no longer need an initial infrastructure setup that can potentially delay the start; the process of owning and operating the application also becomes significantly simpler, with no infrastructure management activity such as patching and updating servers.

The term *serverless* stretches across a wide range of services with varying degrees of capabilities. The term also can vary in meaning depending on how infrastructure is abstracted from developers. Some approaches require developers to use specific libraries and packaging methods; other approaches impose a lesser burden on the application development and packaging. The level of management and control that various platforms offer over the infrastructure can also differ. Some platforms autonomously manage scalability, and others let developers assign a guaranteed set of resources to their applications, with more control over scaling and cost management. Ultimately, these differences offer a choice to developers in building applications so that they can use the tools and processes that offer the right level of control and agility.

Container Instances

Container Instances in Oracle Cloud Infrastructure (OCI) offers a streamlined way of running application containers. At its core, Container Instances offer a simple and secure way to quickly launch containerized workloads on OCI, without the need to plan and manage servers or other infrastructure. The service manages the provisioning, lifecycle, patching, and upgrades for the infrastructure, allowing users to focus on application development. Compared to the alternative (in which a compute instance is spun up, a container runtime is installed, and then its lifecycle is managed through scaling and patching), Container Instances offer a faster path for deploying existing container workloads without modification and then operating them without infrastructure management overhead.

The experience for creating a container instance is simple: The user picks the number of CPU cores and memory, along with the container images that the user wants to run. Advanced controls throttle individual containers within a container instance, manage graceful container termination, provide environment variables, and override start-up parameters for the containers that users want to run. Container images can be pulled from any container image registry, including the OCI Container Image Registry (OCIR), and third-party registries such as ghcr.io, quay.io, and DockerHub, among others. When a container instance is launched, it can be allocated public or private IP addresses, and the application can be exposed to users. The Container Instances service also provides logging and monitoring capabilities out of the box. All infrastructure management, including patching and upgrades, is handled by the service transparently, without any burden on the user or the workload.

Architecture

A container instance is an OCI resource similar to a compute VM that is fine-tuned to run containerized applications. Container instances offer hypervisor-level isolation between each other and can support multiple containers within a given container instance. Within a container instance, the containers can interact with each other, similar to containers in a Kubernetes pod. Containers can communicate with each other over the loopback interface and 127.0.0.1, and they can share ephemeral storage. The strong isolation between container instances that this architecture provides can even protect workloads from being compromised by potential container escape vulnerabilities. A malicious user that escapes a container has visibility to the other containers within the container instance but is isolated from other container instances at the hypervisor level, thus limiting the attack vectors. Figure 7-1 illustrates the architecture for container instances.

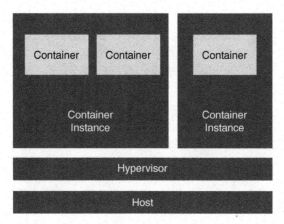

Figure 7-1   Container Instances Offer Strong Isolation Without Infrastructure Overhead

Using Container Instances

When you launch a container instance, you can choose several parameters that control how the container instance behaves and reacts to events. In addition to choosing the name for the container instance, you can choose the number of OCPUs and memory to allocate to the container instance. This compute capacity is shared among all containers in the container instance, but the service also offers the capability to throttle resources allocated to each container so that a single container cannot hog the resource in the container instance. You can also select the networking properties for the container instance, including the subnets, NSGs, and more. If you allocate a public IP address to the container instance, the instance can be reachable from the Internet, as long as the NSG rules or security lists allow traffic and as long as an application within one of the containers in the container instance is listening on an open port.

Container instances support setting a restart policy. This is important because the containers in a container instance are not managed by a container orchestration tool such as Kubernetes. The restart policy for the container instance determines how container exits within the container instance are handled. A restart policy of *Always* restarts an exited container always, and this is a good choice for services that you always want running, such as a web server or a database. On the other hand, a container that just performs some one-time activity is generally expected to exit once the job is done, and these can choose a restart policy of *Never*. The choice of *OnFailure* is appropriate for containers that you expect to exit, but with an exit code of 0; this setting restarts the container if it exits with a nonzero exit code.

Container instances can also be configured with a graceful shutdown timeout. This value determines how long the service will wait for a container inside a container instance to exit before forcibly killing the container after the container instance has received a termination request. This is important for application containers that might be holding external resources, such as database connections, and need to clean up before exiting. When you terminate a container instance, the container instance terminates the containers, which gives containers a way to clean up before exiting. The container instance then waits for the duration set for the *graceful shutdown* before forcibly terminating it. Figure 7-2 shows the restart policy and graceful shutdown time period.

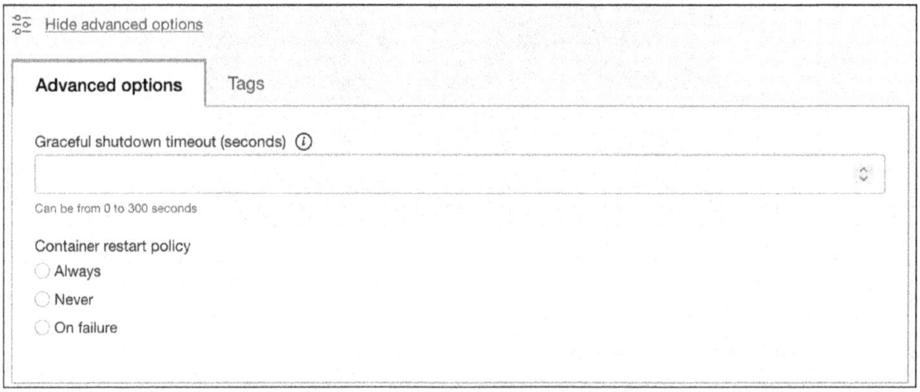

Figure 7-2   Container Instances Offer a Restart Policy That Manages How Containers Within the Container Instance Are Restarted

A container instance can run multiple containers within it, and each of these containers can also be configured independently. These options include the capability to throttle resources per container, overriding the container image's startup options and setting the environment variables for the container. An example can help in examining these settings.

Imagine that you are deploying an application that is accompanied by a sidecar container that exports logs from the application to an external datastore. You assume that the application is following standard best practices for configuring the application using environment variables and externalized configuration. You start by creating the container instance and choosing the desired amount of OCPUs and memory for all containers that you plan to place within the container instance. After you choose the network's configuration and, optionally, the restart policy, you can choose the containers that you want to place in the container instance (see Figure 7-3). The container image for each container can be from a different repository; OCIR is the default option; however, there is support for any external or third-party registry.

After you choose the image, you can configure it. The example in Figure 7-4 uses a Java application, so here you can set some application properties and JVM arguments using the environment variables. Optionally, you can also enable resource throttling on the instance, which limits the amount of resources (such as CPU and memory) that a container can consume from the container instance. Resource limits can be set using absolute units or percentages. In the example in Figure 7-4, the CPU usage for the application container is limited to 75% of what is available to the container instance.

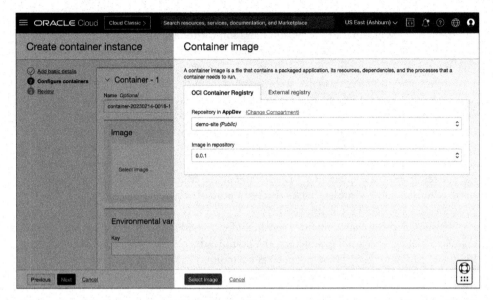

Figure 7-3   Container Images Can Be Sourced from the Oracle Container Image Registry (OCIR)
or Any External Registry

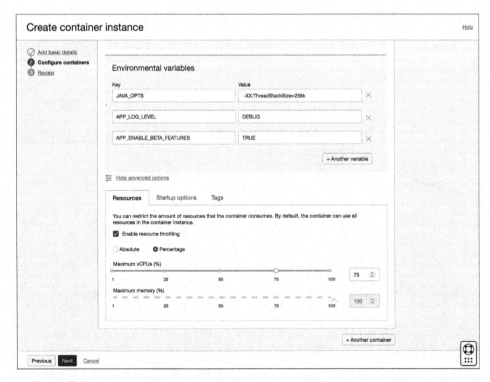

Figure 7-4   Container Instances Can Throttle Resources for Each Container Within It, Giving
Developers Greater Control over How Resources Are Allocated Among Containers

Similarly, you can add a sidecar (say, a fluentd container from DockerHub) and throttle it to 25% of the CPU. This configuration for the resource throttling ensures that the app container does not consume more than 75% of the CPU and that the fluentd container does not consume more than 25%. Assuming that these are the only containers in the container instance, this effectively guarantees up to 25% of the CPU to fluentd and up to 75% of the CPU to the app container. By default, containers can consume as many resources as possible; therefore, you could have resource-throttled only the fluentd container to 25% and left the application container without any limits. Such a configuration would limit the fluentd container from consuming any more than 25% of the CPU, while allowing the app container to use as much CPU as it needs, without guaranteeing any fixed quota of CPU for the fluentd container. Based on application needs, these resource throttles can be used to optimally allocate resources to the containers in your container instance.

Configuration for each container also includes overriding some of the image defaults, such as the working directory, the command, and the entry point arguments, as illustrated in Figure 7-5. These parameters correspond to the respective `WorkingDir`, `Cmd`, and `Entrypoint` configuration properties in the Open Container Initiative Specification.[1]

Figure 7-5   Each Container in a Container Instance Can Be Configured Using Environment Variables and Startup Options

Serverless Functions

Functions-as-a-Service (FaaS) platforms are the ubiquitous serverless computing model in which you develop an application and then deploy and operate it without any infrastructure management. Functions typically use a programming model that leverages a software stack that includes components that are purposely built for integrating the function with a service that manages the infrastructure needs and scaling for the application. This enables you to quickly build highly scalable applications and operate them purely from the application's business functionality and feature needs. This model lets you focus on application development without factoring in infrastructure management and thereby enables a drastically faster time to bring applications to production usage.

As the name indicates, a serverless function typically models a single *action*. Functions can be invoked directly or can be triggered by events. Most cloud platforms have an events service that provides a mechanism for your applications or other services to be notified about actions that occur within a cloud environment. An event service captures metadata about the occurrence of an action in the environment (say, a file being uploaded to an object storage bucket) and delivers the event to any service or application that is subscribing to it. Functions are commonly written to respond to events, as in the aforementioned example in which a file is being uploaded to an object storage bucket and now can be read by the function to perform some data processing. Functions and events can be chained together to create complex flows of data that are triggered by various events. This allows for the creation of an elastic and reactive system that springs into action when it needs to. Because the operational infrastructure for functions is abstracted away from the user and usually managed by a cloud provider, these platforms can optimize the resource usage by automatically scaling the resources for function invocations. Functions can be spun up when they are invoked, scaled up to meet demand peaks, and scaled down when they are no longer being invoked. Therefore, functions do not always need a running process because they are instantiated and scaled based on actual usage or invocations.

Functions also typically enforce the use of a prescriptive programming model, an SDK, or libraries that coordinate and manage the lifecycle of the function from the cloud service. These models can also place requirements and take an opinionated approach to how functions are developed, run, and managed. For instance, because most FaaS platforms abstract infrastructure management, functions are typically charged by the number of invocations instead of the usual infrastructure units of billing, such as CPUs. Functions can use as many CPUs as they need, and scale as they need, and the user pays for only how many times the function is invoked. With models like these, platforms can limit how long a function can run, what programming languages can be used to build functions, and more. These choices can also prevent portability of your functions across cloud providers, causing a gradual vendor lock-in for your applications. Care should be taken to evaluate the functions' platform so that you do not have to sacrifice portability and productivity to gain the features of a serverless FaaS platform.

OCI Functions

Oracle Cloud Infrastructure Functions is a fully managed FaaS platform that is based on the Fn Project open-source engine. Fn Project is an open-source, container-native, serverless platform that can be run anywhere—in any cloud or on-premises. With OCI Functions, you develop your application in Java, Python, Node, Go, Ruby, and C# using the Function Development Kit (FDK) and then deploy it to the platform. Advanced users can also bring their own Dockerfile or use GraalVM. No infrastructure administration or software administration is necessary for you to perform. You do not provision or maintain compute instances, and operating system software patches and upgrades are applied automatically. OCI Functions simply ensures that your app is highly available, scalable, secure, and monitored. You can then deploy your code, call it directly, or trigger it in response to events, and get billed only for the resources consumed during the execution. Figure 7-6 illustrates how the OCI Functions service integrates with other systems and services to provide a model that responds to events and other triggers.

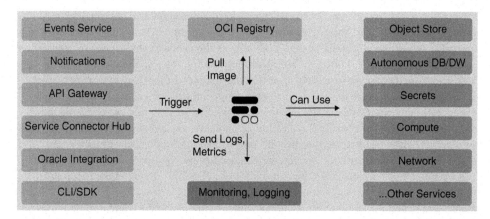

Figure 7-6   The Functions Service Integrates with Other Systems and Can Respond to External Triggers

Using OCI Functions

An *application* is the most fundamental resource you create when you start working with OCI Functions. An application resource can be considered as a logical container for grouping functions. An application can have multiple functions inside it. Functions within an application can share configuration variables and resources, which are allocated to the application. For instance, networking resources, such as subnets to run the functions in, and the logging configurations for functions are configured at the application level when defining the application. When functions from different applications are invoked simultaneously, the application construct acts as the isolation boundary, ensuring that the functions are executed in isolation from each other. Ideally, similar and closely related functions should be grouped into a single application, for better efficiency and performance.

The function itself is a piece of code that you write using the Functions FDK. This code is built and packaged as a container image. When working with the OCI Functions service, developers can use the Fn CLI tool or the OCI Code Editor built into the OCI Console to generate the scaffolding for your functions code, build your function, deploy it to OCI, and manage the lifecycle of the function. The OCI Cloud Shell also comes with the Fn CLI preinstalled, if you need to experience it without installing and setting up a local development environment. Each function is part of an application and contains metadata that is stored on the OCI Functions service that tells the service how to create the execution environment for the function and execute it.

To create an OCI function, you start by creating a new application or choosing an existing application within which to create the new function. Then the function is created using the CLI or the OCI Code Editor. Creating the function includes generating the code scaffolding and the function metadata. Figure 7-7 shows the scaffold generated within the OCI Code Editor.

Figure 7-7   The Code Editor in the OCI Console Comes Preconfigured with Plug-ins for Functions That Can Generate Code Scaffolding and Deploy Functions

The OCI Functions tooling also enables you to customize the scaffolding it creates for you, such as using your own `Dockerfile` to build the final container image or using your own custom image to base the function on. When you have generated the scaffold and written the code to accomplish the task you want your function to perform, you can deploy the function. Deploying the function using the tooling provided by OCI Functions will build your code, package it as a container image, and push the container image to the image repository. This deployment process also pushes the function metadata to the OCI Functions service, which identifies the image to use for the function, and properties for the function, such as the version of the function and the runtime. After the function is deployed, it can be invoked directly or in response to events. In most circumstances, functions are invoked in response to a cloud event. The OCI Functions service manages the lifecycle of the infrastructure used for function invocations and scales it up or down in real time, based on invocations. After a function has been deployed, you can gather metrics and other observability data from it, as well as manage the lifecycle and security controls for it. Figure 7-8 outlines the overall process.

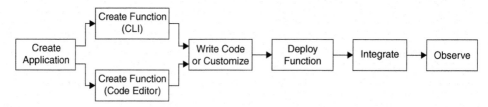

Figure 7-8   The High-Level Developer Workflow for Building and Deploying OCI Functions

Building Your First Function

To get started with OCI Functions, you first create an Application. This is easily done though the console, by choosing a name for your application, the VCN, and the subnet to use for the function (see Figure 7-9). With an Application to group your functions, you can now start with creating your first function.

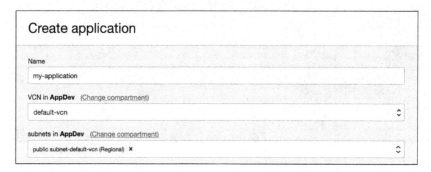

Figure 7-9   The Basic Configuration Elements for Creating an Application

The essential prerequisites are the OCI Functions CLI and a configuration profile for the OCI CLI. The Fn CLI uses the OCI CLI configuration to authenticate itself with the OCI Functions service. The OCI Cloud Shell and the OCI Code Editor both support building functions out of the box; this is the easiest way to get started with OCI Functions.

> **Note**
>
> You can also configure a local development environment to use with OCI Functions. The steps required for this setup are covered in the OCI Functions documentation.[2]

Start by opening the OCI Cloud Shell. When using the OCI Cloud Shell, the Fn CLI is already installed for you. The Fn CLI configuration is grouped into *contexts*. A context specifies the OCI Functions endpoints, the compartment to which deployed functions will belong, and the container image registry to use for the functions you build. The OCI Cloud Shell comes preconfigured with two contexts, a default context and a region-specific one. The regional context should be set as the default, to ensure that this uses the following commands:

```
fn list context            # Shows the contexts that are available.
                           # This should show two contexts, with the
                           # regional context set as the current one.

fn use context <ctx_name>  # Explicitly set the context to the regional context.
```

> **Note**
>
> These commands can be found on the application's Getting Started page, where the relevant OCIDs are prepopulated for you in a manner that is easy to copy and paste into the OCI Cloud Shell.

The preconfigured regional context has already set up the OCI Functions endpoints for the region. You now need to configure the compartment to which the functions will belong, as well as the container image registry. To configure these parameters, use the following commands, substituting the placeholders for the `compartment_ocid` and the image registry prefix:

```
fn update context oracle.compartment-id <compartment_ocid> # sets the compartment
  under which functions will be created.
fn update context registry <region_key>.ocir.io/<tenancy-namespace>/[repo-name-
  prefix]
```

When you deploy a function, the Fn CLI builds a container image and pushes the container image to the registry that is configured. Therefore, you should also log into the registry. For OCIR, you need to generate an Auth token from your User Settings page (which is accessed using your logged-in profile icon on the top right of the screen), which you can use to log in to your registry.

```
docker login -u '<tenancy-namespace>/<username>' <region_key>.ocir.io
```

Note

If you use the Oracle Identity Cloud service to federate your user account, the username is in the form `<tenancy-namespace>/oracleidentitycloudservice/<user name>`.

With the CLI configured, you can now create a function using the OCI Cloud Shell. On the OCI Functions page, choose to create a new function in the OCI Code Editor, as demonstrated in Figure 7-10.

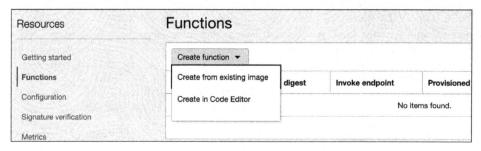

Figure 7-10   Accessing the OCI Code Editor for Creating a Function

When the OCI Code Editor launches, it walks you through creating a scaffold for your application. Alternatively, you can open the OCI Code Editor, navigate to the application object within the OCI Function plug-in, and create a function directly from within the OCI Code Editor, as shown in Figure 7-11.

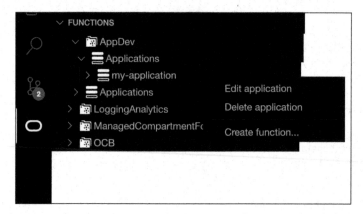

Figure 7-11   The OCI Code Editor Has Built-in Support for Working with OCI Functions

The OCI Code Editor walks you through a workflow to start your function. It offers the capability to start from a template, an existing Git repository, or a sample (see Figure 7-12).

Figure 7-12 The OCI Code Editor Offers Multiple Options to Bootstrap a New Function

For your first function, you can start from a template and choose the language you want to develop your function in. The example in Figure 7-13 shows Python. You are prompted for the function name, and the OCI Code Editor then generates a scaffold for the function that you can expand upon.

Figure 7-13 When Starting from an OCI Functions Template, You Can Build Your Function Using a Wide Range of Languages and SDKs

When the scaffold is created, it will have files named func.yaml, func.py, and requirements.txt. The func.py and the requirements.txt are part of the scaffold, with starting code and dependencies. The func.yaml is the function definition. It looks similar to Listing 7-1.

Listing 7-1 An Example of a Function Definition Generated by the OCI Code Editor

```
schema_version: 20180708
name: myfunction
version: 0.0.1
runtime: python
build_image: fnproject/python:3.9-dev
run_image: fnproject/python:3.9
entrypoint: /python/bin/fdk /function/func.py handler
memory: 256
```

This function definition identifies the function and several of its properties, including the runtime to use, the container images to use for building the function container, and the base image for the runtime. It also shows the entry point to use when the container image is generated and the amount of memory to request for the function. The OCI Functions service uses this definition to set up the runtime environment for the function at execution time.

With the scaffold generated, you can now build and test the function. The OCI Code Editor offers tools to commit the generated resources to a Git repository, including public repositories such as GitHub, and directly use the cloud editor to deploy and invoke the function. You can also use the terminal to quickly deploy and test your function using the Fn CLI. To do this, right-click func.py and choose Open in Terminal. The terminal window opens in the location where your function code is located. From here, you can build and deploy the function to the application in one step using the command in Listing 7-2.

Listing 7-2 An Example Showing a Function Deployment in Progress

```
$ fn deploy --app my-application

Deploying myfunction to app: my-application
Bumped to version 0.0.11
Using Container engine docker to push
Pushing iad.ocir.io/xxxxxxxxx/functions/myfunction:0.0.11 to docker registry...
  The push refers to repository [iad.ocir.io/xxxxxxxxx/functions/myfunction]
466fd30b96ba: Pushed
7464153686f5: Pushed
3ffc4f8259bf: Pushed
7656fdef3d98: Pushed
23ca6a735cc7: Layer already exists
b939f13c738d: Layer already exists
606f5e26329f: Layer already exists
0.0.11: digest: sha256:01e409b27ddb01c810fbe705b541dbfb6142485eabc9607f1a4bcdb0131
  40cc2 size: 1781
Updating function myfunction using image iad.ocir.io/xxxxxxxxx/functions/
  myfunction:0.0.11...
```

When the function is deployed, you can invoke it. On the OCI Functions page in the console, you can see the invoke endpoint (see Figure 7-14).

To invoke a function directly using the invoke endpoint, you need to sign your requests. This authenticates the request with your identity. The most common way to do this is to use the raw-request feature of the OCI CLI. This enables you to use the OCI CLI to directly send requests to OCI resources such as your function, and the OCI CLI will handle the request signing. To use this to invoke the function directly, use the command in Listing 7-3. The example here shows a POST request because the default scaffolding code generated by the OCI Code Editor can parse a JSON request body, if one is provided. Listing 7-3 shows the typical response.

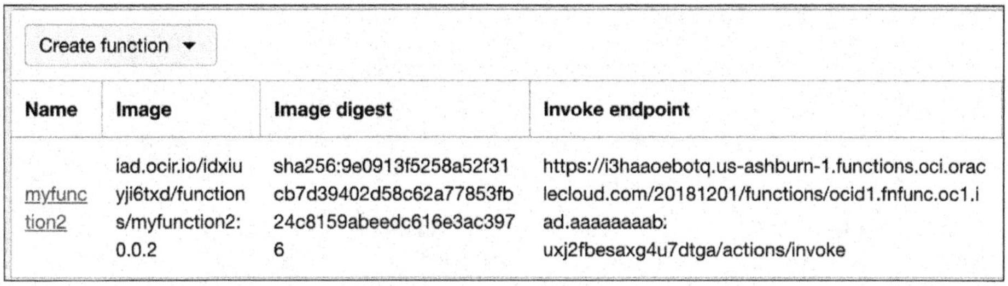

Name	Image	Image digest	Invoke endpoint
myfunc tion2	iad.ocir.io/idxiu yji6txd/function s/myfunction2: 0.0.2	sha256:9e0913f5258a52f31 cb7d39402d58c62a77853fb 24c8159abeedc616e3ac397 6	https://i3haaoebotq.us-ashburn-1.functions.oci.orac lecloud.com/20181201/functions/ocid1.fnfunc.oc1.i ad.aaaaaaaab; uxj2fbesaxg4u7dtga/actions/invoke

Figure 7-14 The OCI Console Displays the Invoke Endpoint for a Function After It Has Been Deployed

Listing 7-3 An Example of How to Invoke a Function Manually Using the OCI CLI

```
$ oci raw-request --http-method POST  --target-uri <invoke_endpoint> --request-
body '{"name":"user"}'

{
  "data": {
    "message": "Hello user"
  },
  "headers": {
    "Content-Length": "25",
    "Content-Type": "application/json",
    "Date": "Tue, 14 Mar 2023 04:53:57 GMT",
    "Fn-Call-Id": "01GVF7FGZB1BT0S38ZJ00E8QXM",
    "Fn-Fdk-Runtime": "python/3.9.13 final",
    "Fn-Fdk-Version": "fdk-python/0.1.51",
    "Opc-Request-Id": "21D2172E020D43EFB212A3EB4B15A02E/xxxxxxxxxxxxxxxx/
xxxxxxxxxxxxxxxx"
  },
  "status": "200 OK"
}
```

When a function is invoked for the first time, the OCI Functions service pulls the function's container image from the specified container registry, runs it as a container, and executes the function. If there are subsequent requests to the same function, OCI Functions directs those requests to the same container. If there are concurrent requests to the function, the OCI Functions service creates more containers, as needed, to scale up; after a period of being idle, the containers are scaled down as well.

To prevent the initial delay in serving a function call, you can also set up provisioned concurrency. Provisioned concurrency is a feature of OCI Functions by which the service always maintains the execution infrastructure for at least a certain minimum number of concurrent function invocations. Enabling provisioned concurrency ensures that your functions will have sub-second latencies from the very first invocation.

Adding an API Gateway

In most situations, the function endpoints are not directly exposed to external users. Instead, the function is wrapped by an API Gateway to provide some API shaping and control. The quickest way to create a gateway is through the OCI console, as shown here:

Step 1. Click **Developer Services -> API Gateway** from the sidebar on the left.

Step 2. Click the **Create Gateway** button.

Step 3. Enter the following values (you can use a different name if you'd like):

- **Name:** function-gateway
- **Type:** Public
- **Virtual Cloud Network:** Pick one from the dropdown
- **Subnet:** Pick the subnet from the dropdown

Step 4. Click **Create**.

Step 5. When the gateway is created, click the **Deployments** link from the sidebar on the left.

Step 6. Under Deployments, click the **Create Deployment** button. Make sure the **From Scratch** option is selected at the top, and enter the following values (you can leave the other values as they are—no need to enable CORS, Authentication, or Rate Limiting):

- **Name:** functions
- **Path prefix:** /functions
- **Compartment:**
- **API Logging Policies:** Information

Step 7. Click **Next** to define authentication, and choose **No Authentication**.

Step 8. Click **Next** to define the route. Enter the following values for Route 1:

- **Path:** /my-function
- **Methods:** POST
- **Type:** Oracle Functions
- **Application:** my-application (or other, if you used a different name)
- **Function name:** myfunction

Step 9. Click **Next** and review the deployment.

Step 10. Click **Create** to create the gateway deployment.

When deployment completes, navigate to it to get the URL for the gateway. Click the Show link next to the Endpoint label to reveal the full URL for the deployment. It should look like this:

```
https://j2fd2x25qkrtupcrtxvienbywy.apigateway.us-ashburn-1.oci.customer-
   oci.com/functions
```

You can now use the following command to test your function through the gateway:

```
curl -X POST -d '{"name": "user"}' https://j2fd2x25qkrtupcrtxvienbywy.
  apigateway.us-ashburn-1.oci.customer-oci.com/functions/myfunction
```

Function Logs and Distributed Tracing

After you have created a function, you want to observe the performance metrics of the function. Occasionally, when a function is not performing or behaving as expected, you also need to troubleshoot and debug it. As a serverless service, this can initially sound challenging because developers will not have access to the "servers" that are running these functions. However, the OCI Functions service provides multiple ways to enable developers to productively troubleshoot their code.

OCI Functions shows information about function invocations in metric charts. These are available on the console, by default, and include several metrics, such as the number of times a function is invoked, the duration for which the function runs, and invocations that resulted in a throttle (HTTP 429, "Too many requests") or an error.

If you notice that your function metrics indicate an error or that the result of an invocation provided an unexpected response, you should enable logging for the function. Enabling logging automatically gathers the logs that a function emits from its code into the OCI Logging service. These log events capture the actual log line and metadata that can be searched through and analyzed further in the Logging service.

Logging can be enabled for an application and all functions within it. The logs are sent to a Log resource in a LogGroup; if these resources do not exist, they are created for you. Figure 7-15 illustrates the logging controls at the application level.

Figure 7-15   Logging Controls for an Application

Consider the code in Listing 7-4 in a function handler.

Listing 7-4   A Function Demonstrating Logging

```
def handler(ctx, data: io.BytesIO=None):
    name = "World"
    logging.getLogger().info("Inside Python function")
    try:
        body = json.loads(data.getvalue())
```

```
    name = body.get("name")
except (Exception, ValueError) as ex:
    logging.getLogger().info('error parsing json payload: ' + str(ex))

return response.Response(
        ctx, response_data=json.dumps(
            {"message": "Hello {0}".format(name)}),
        headers={"Content-Type": "application/json"}
    )
```

As the handler is invoked, the code logs the line `Inside Python Function`. When logging is enabled, these log lines are captured and collected within the Logging service, as demonstrated in Figure 7-16. Developers can add more logs for specific conditions that help follow the code execution path and identify runtime conditions and data to troubleshoot a function.

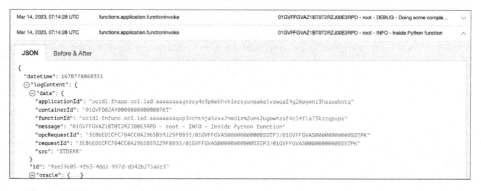

Figure 7-16 Logs from the Function Are Sent to the Logging Service, Where They Can Be Queried, Analyzed, or Exported to Other Systems

Beyond metrics and logging, the OCI Functions service also integrates with the Log Analytics service to provide deep performance analysis and tracing. As with logging, tracing can be enabled for an application; the traces are sent to an application performance monitoring (APM) domain in the Log Analytics service. If an APM domain does not exist, one is created for you.

With tracing enabled, you can add tracing spans directly in your code. Consider the example in Listing 7-5.

The code adds the Zipkin tracing libraries to the application. Using these, every function in the code adds metadata such as `service_name` and `span_name`. The main handler function sets the span name `Function Handler`. From within this function, it invokes two other functions, `do_work` and `do_more_work`. Both these functions add their spans and sleep for a short duration (150ms). Note that the second function, `do_more_work`, also throws an exception.

Listing 7-5   An Example Function Illustrating the Use of Zipkin Libraries for Tracing

```python
import io
import json
import logging
import requests
import time
from collections import namedtuple

from py_zipkin.zipkin import zipkin_span
from py_zipkin.encoding import Encoding
from fdk import response


def handler(ctx, data: io.BytesIO=None):
    tracing_context = ctx.TracingContext()
    with zipkin_span(
        service_name=tracing_context.service_name(),
        span_name="Function Handler",
        transport_handler=(
            lambda encoded_span: transport_handler(
                encoded_span, tracing_context
            )
        ),
        zipkin_attrs=tracing_context.zipkin_attrs(),
        encoding=Encoding.V2_JSON,
        binary_annotations=tracing_context.annotations()
    ):
        name = "World"
        logging.getLogger().info("Inside Python function")
        try:
            body = json.loads(data.getvalue())
            name = body.get("name")
        except (Exception, ValueError) as ex:
            logging.getLogger().info('error parsing json payload: ' + str(ex))


        do_work(ctx)
        do_more_work(ctx)
        return response.Response(
            ctx, response_data=json.dumps(
                {"message": "Hello {0}".format(name)}),
            headers={"Content-Type": "application/json"}
        )

# transport handler, needed by py_zipkin
def transport_handler(encoded_span, tracing_context):
    return requests.post(
```

```
            tracing_context.trace_collector_url(),
            data=encoded_span,
            headers={"Content-Type": "application/json"},
        )


def do_work(ctx):
    with zipkin_span(
        service_name=ctx.TracingContext().service_name(),
        span_name="Doing Error Prone work",
        binary_annotations=ctx.TracingContext().annotations()
    ) as example_span_context:
        try:
            logging.getLogger().debug("Doing some complex task")
            time.sleep(0.15)
        except (Exception, ValueError) as error:
            example_span_context.update_binary_annotations(
                {"Error": True, "errorMessage": str(error)}
            )
        else:
            FakeResponse = namedtuple("FakeResponse", "status, message")
            fakeResponse = FakeResponse(200, "OK")
            # how to update the span dimensions/annotations
            example_span_context.update_binary_annotations(
                {
                    "responseCode": fakeResponse.status,
                    "responseMessage": fakeResponse.message
                }
            )


def do_more_work(ctx):
    with zipkin_span(
        service_name=ctx.TracingContext().service_name(),
        span_name="Do more work",
        binary_annotations=ctx.TracingContext().annotations()
    ) as example_span_context:
        try:
            logging.getLogger().debug("Doing some complex task")
            time.sleep(0.15)
            # throwing an exception to show how to add error messages to spans
            raise Exception('do_more_work - failed. Handling error.')
        except (Exception, ValueError) as error:
            example_span_context.update_binary_annotations(
                {"Error": True, "errorMessage": str(error)}
            )
        else:
            FakeResponse = namedtuple("FakeResponse", "status, message")
            fakeResponse = FakeResponse(200, "OK")
```

```
# how to update the span dimensions/annotations
example_span_context.update_binary_annotations(
    {
        "responseCode": fakeResponse.status,
        "responseMessage": fakeResponse.message
    }
)
```

The trace for a function invocation shows the topology of the calls, as well as the spans, their duration, and their status (see Figure 7-17).

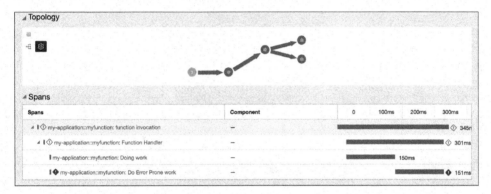

Figure 7-17   Traces Can Be Visualized to Quickly Identify Performance Bottlenecks

Tracing enables developers to visually see the code execution flow and quickly identify where code execution time is spent. This allows developers to identify bottlenecks and address them quickly.

Service Mesh

As application services evolve into smaller and more focused services that scale independently, they get more distributed. This creates a challenge to manage the constantly evolving set of services and the communication between them. Common challenges include securing the communication between the services, managing traffic between services, and implementing observability across a range of services. A service mesh is an infrastructure layer for facilitating these service-to-service communications between services or microservices. A proxy-based model typically is used to accomplish this.

The OCI Service Mesh uses such a proxy-based model based on the Envoy proxy. The proxy runs alongside each microservice, which receives configuration information from a managed control plane. These proxies are separate from the services themselves, so the services and the application code do not need to change or even know about the proxy to use a service mesh. In a Kubernetes environment, these proxies run within the same pod as the application, but as separate containers and separate processes; thus, they are often called sidecars. The service mesh uses the proxies to implement security, observability, and traffic management on behalf of your application because the proxy acts as a facade to the actual application. Figure 7-18 shows how the OCI Service Mesh introduces new resources into an existing application and transparently provides new features and functionality.

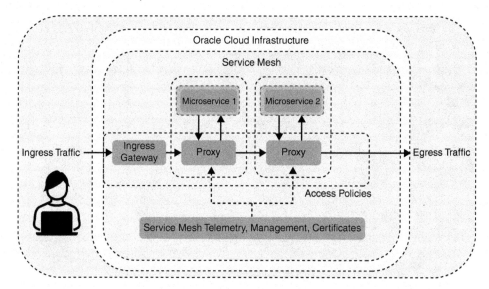

Figure 7-18 The OCI Service Mesh Can Transparently Add New Capabilities and Rules to an Existing Application Without Code Changes, Using Its Proxy-Based Model

Using the Service Mesh

When the service mesh has been installed in your cluster, you can access the OCI Service Mesh using the OCI console, OCI CLI, REST APIs, and the Kubernetes CLI tool kubectl. However, you can manage your mesh resources either through the OCI APIs (Console, CLI, or Terraform) or through Kubernetes. When creating the mesh resources, you need to pick an approach. If you create the mesh resources with the OCI APIs, these resources will exist only on the control plane, with no corresponding resource definitions (CRDs) created in the Kubernetes cluster. However, if you choose to create these resources as CRDs in your Kubernetes cluster, the Kubernetes operator creates their definitions on the mesh control plane. The Kubernetes resources that you create using the CRDs become the source of truth, in this case, and you should continue to use this approach for modifying and managing the resources. Mesh resources managed by the Kubernetes operator cannot be modified using the OCI Console, CLI, or Terraform. In most cases, it might be more natural to manage these resources as Kubernetes resources. Mesh resources are closely associated with your application resources, and this is the most common way users interact with mesh resources.

As Figure 7-18 illustrated, the OCI service mesh consists of resources that are mapped to application components such as *VirtualDeployments*, *VirtualServices*, *IngressGateways*, and more. These resources are instrumental in providing the Service Mesh features. Figure 7-19 shows the various resources that make up the service mesh and how they are related.

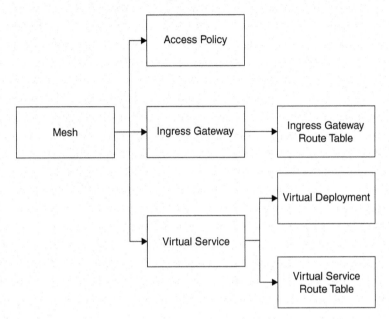

Figure 7-19   The Various Resources That Make Up a Service Mesh

The relationships and interactions between these resources can seem quite daunting at first, but these become easier to understand in the context of an example application.

Adding a Service Mesh to an Application

Consider this simple deployment of nginx in Listing 7-6. This consists of a *Deployment* resource and a *Service* resource, to keep the example simple. The Deployment is backed by a replicas set with two replicas, as indicated by the `replicas` property in the deployment spec. The replicas set creates and manages the two pods of nginx. The pods have the label `app: nginx`, and the service targets all pods with the same label. The service is of type `LoadBalancer`, which indicates that the Kubernetes cluster will create an appropriate load balancer on the cloud provider and wire it to the pods targeted by the service.

Listing 7-6   Kubernetes Resources That Describe an Application Without a Service Mesh

```
apiVersion: v1
kind: Service
metadata:
  name: my-nginx-svc
```

```
    labels:
        app: nginx
spec:
    type: LoadBalancer
    ports:
    - port: 80
    selector:
        app: nginx
---
apiVersion: apps/v1
kind: Deployment
metadata:
  name: my-nginx
  labels:
      app: nginx
spec:
  replicas: 2
  selector:
    matchLabels:
        app: nginx
  template:
    metadata:
      labels:
          app: nginx
    spec:
      containers:
      - name: nginx
        image: nginx:1.14.2
        ports:
        - containerPort: 80
```

To add a service mesh to this application, we can introduce the service mesh resources into the mix that wrap and encapsulate these Kubernetes resources.

The *Mesh* is the top-level resource that includes all mesh resources; it represents the boundary of services and traffic that the service mesh manages. The mesh also identifies a certificate authority that will be used to generate certificates to secure communications among the workloads that are covered by the service mesh. Listing 7-7 shows the definition of a mesh resource.

Listing 7-7   Mesh Resource Definition

```
kind: Mesh
apiVersion: servicemesh.oci.oracle.com/v1beta1
metadata:
  name: nginx
```

```
spec:
  compartmentId: ocid1.compartment.oc1..
  aaaaaaaahgeqvnooufd5efvafgiobngb2xfcih62h3u7o2sq2wfhei5ddgoa
  certificateAuthorities:
    - id: ocid1.certificateauthority.oc1.iad.
  amaaaaaab5uyggqan7pi3iozlv2g7godjk5jclf3tlbrtlfar4c7sk3f72uq
  displayName: nginx-mesh
  mtls:
    minimum: PERMISSIVE
```

IngressGateways are the entry point of traffic into all resources managed by the mesh. All incoming traffic passes through the ingress gateway, so it implements customized security policies on how to manage this ingress and transparently provide observability and traffic shaping for the services within the mesh. For example, the ingress gateway can be configured to enable encryption on all incoming traffic using TLS or to keep track of an access log. An ingress gateway can be configured with a set of DNS hostnames and listener ports that clients use to make their requests to. Clients communicate with the application through the ingress gateway using one of these hostnames and ports where the ingress gateway is listening. The ingress gateway is an optional resource and is not mandatory for all situations. The ingress gateway handles traffic as it enters the application, which provides the capability to track the traffic from the start. Without an ingress gateway, you would not have service mesh control over this segment in the traffic flow. Listing 7-8 shows a typical ingress gateway. Notice that it is associated with a mesh resource.

Listing 7-8   An Example IngressGateway Illustrating Hostnames and Listeners

```
kind: IngressGateway
apiVersion: servicemesh.oci.oracle.com/v1beta1
metadata:
  name: nginx-ingress-gateway
spec:
  compartmentId: ocid1.compartment.oc1..
  aaaaaaaahgeqvnooufd5efvafgiobngb2xfcih62h3u7o2sq2wfhei5ddgoa
  mesh:
    ref:
      name: nginx
  hosts:
    - name: nginxHost
      hostnames:
        - nginx.example.com
      listeners:
        - port: 8080
          protocol: HTTP
          tls:
            mode: DISABLED
  accessLogging:
    isEnabled: true
```

The ingress gateway resource is supported by resources such as an *IngressGatewayDeployment* and an *IngressGatewayRouteTable*. The ingress gateway resource defines the properties and configuration of the ingress gateway, which is an OCI resource. In a Kubernetes cluster, the ingress gateway is manifested as a set of Kubernetes resources, such as pods, that implement the configuration defined in the ingress gateway. This is accomplished by an *IngressGatewayDeployment* resource. This resource exists only on the Kubernetes cluster; it uses the configuration from the ingress gateway it is attached to and configures the Kubernetes resources in the cluster. This can be seen as a manifestation of the ingress gateway resource from the mesh service within a Kubernetes context and is analogous to the Kubernetes *Ingress* resource. When using the service mesh, the *IngressGatewayDeployment* resource replaces the *Ingress* resource. Listing 7-9 shows an example ingress gateway deployment. Notice that the ingress gateway deployment has options to autoscale the number of pods handling the ingress traffic. The ingress gateway deployment creates a Kubernetes service, and the `service.type` can be used to control what type of service is created.

Listing 7-9   An Example IngressGatewayDeployment Resource That Wraps an IngressGateway

```
apiVersion: servicemesh.oci.oracle.com/v1beta1
kind: IngressGatewayDeployment
metadata:
  name: nginx-ingress-gateway-deployment
  labels:
    mesh-ingress: nginx
spec:
  ingressGateway:
    ref:
      name: nginx-ingress-gateway
  deployment:
    autoscaling:
      minPods: 2
      maxPods: 4
  ports:
    - protocol: TCP
      port: 8080
      serviceport: 80
  service:
    type: LoadBalancer
```

An *IngressGatewayRouteTable* defines traffic routing rules that are applied to the traffic that is coming through an ingress gateway. These route rules are applied to the specific ingress gateway hosts and ports. For HTTP requests, the ingress gateway route table has route rules that match an incoming request's path and directs the requests to one of the virtual services. Listing 7-10 shows an ingress gateway route table. It is associated with an ingress gateway, and the `routeRules` determine how traffic arriving on this ingress gateway gets routed to the various downstream virtual services.

Listing 7-10 An IngressGatewayRouteTable Illustrating Various Route Rules to Be Applied

```
apiVersion: servicemesh.oci.oracle.com/v1beta1
kind: IngressGatewayRouteTable
metadata:
  name: nginx-ingress-gateway-route-table
spec:
  compartmentId: ocid1.compartment.oc1..
aaaaaaaahgeqvnooufd5efvafgiobngb2xfcih62h3u7o2sq2wfhei5ddgoa
  ingressGateway:
    ref:
      name: nginx-ingress-gateway
  routeRules:
  - httpRoute:
      destinations:
        - virtualService:
            ref:
              name: mesh-nginx
      ingressGatewayHost:
        name: nginxHost
```

A *VirtualService* is a logical service definition in a service mesh. In a typical Kubernetes application with pods and services, a virtual service represents the service mesh wrapper around multiple versions of a Kubernetes service. It is typically used to implement traffic flow control and management when deploying two versions of the service alongside each other. This makes it easy to implement canary deployments and have a solid rollback strategy in case the new version is deemed unstable. Listing 7-11 shows a virtual service.

Listing 7-11 An Example VirtualService

```
kind: VirtualService
apiVersion: servicemesh.oci.oracle.com/v1beta1
metadata:
  name: mesh-nginx
spec:
  mesh:
    ref:
      name: nginx
  defaultRoutingPolicy:
    type: UNIFORM
```

```
compartmentId: ocid1.compartment.oc1..
aaaaaaaahgeqvnooufd5efvafgiobngb2xfcih62h3u7o2sq2wfhei5ddgoa
hosts:
  - mesh-nginx
```

Virtual services are backed by one or more virtual deployments that represent a single version of the Kubernetes service. In this regard, virtual deployments are associated with individual Kubernetes services. Virtual services and virtual deployments use DNS for service discovery; this allows applications to use consistent DNS names provided by the virtual services, while the service mesh can work with multiple versions of a Kubernetes service and perform traffic management transparently. The virtual service directs traffic to its associated virtual deployment based on a virtual service route table. Listing 7-12 shows a virtual deployment as well as a virtual service route table. Note that the virtual service does not refer to the virtual deployments backing it, but the individual virtual deployments carry a reference to the virtual service. The virtual service route table determines how traffic is distributed to each virtual deployment that is part of the virtual service. To better understand these ServiceMesh objects and their relationships, consider the diagram in Figure 7-20.

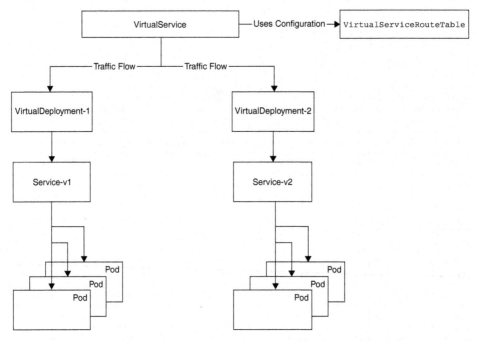

Figure 7-20   Traffic Flow Through VirtualServices and VirtualDeployments, Based on the Configuration Contained in VirtualServiceRouteTables

Listing 7-12   An Example VirtualDeployment

```
kind: VirtualDeployment
apiVersion: servicemesh.oci.oracle.com/v1beta1
metadata:
  name: nginx-v1
spec:
  virtualService:
    ref:
      name: mesh-nginx
  compartmentId: ocid1.compartment.oc1..
  aaaaaaaahgeqvnooufd5efvafgiobngb2xfcih62h3u7o2sq2wfhei5ddgoa
  listener:
    - port: 80
      protocol: HTTP
  accessLogging:
    isEnabled: true
  serviceDiscovery:
    type: DNS
    hostname: nginx-v1
---
apiVersion: servicemesh.oci.oracle.com/v1beta1
kind: VirtualServiceRouteTable
metadata:
  name: nginx-route-table
spec:
  compartmentId: ocid1.compartment.oc1..
  aaaaaaaahgeqvnooufd5efvafgiobngb2xfcih62h3u7o2sq2wfhei5ddgoa
  virtualService:
    ref:
      name: mesh-nginx
  routeRules:
    - httpRoute:
        destinations:
          - virtualDeployment:
              ref:
                name: nginx-v1
            weight: 100
        isGrpc: false
        path: /
        pathType: PREFIX
```

A virtual deployment is a logical resource that is managed by the service mesh control plane. It needs an implementation or a manifestation of that definition on the platform it runs. Within a Kubernetes cluster, this is a *VirtualDeploymentBinding*, which connects the control plane definition of virtual deployment to the pods running on the Kubernetes cluster.

Here you have a typical application made up of several pods that is exposed as a service. Now consider that you deployed a newer version of this application. The diagram in Figure 7-20 shows two versions of this application, v1 and v2, each exposed as its own service that is mapped to its own set of resources. You can use the service mesh features to perform some traffic management so that you can slowly transition users from the older version of the application to the newer version. The new version of the application is represented by the new virtual deployment, VirtualDeployment-2; the old version is represented by the virtual deployment VirtualDeployment-1. The virtual service can now direct traffic to either virtual deployments. This traffic management policy is defined by the virtual service route table associated with the virtual service.

Similar to these resources, the mesh supports access policies that define access rules for communication between virtual services and to external services. Access policies exist for the entire mesh and control whether communication is allowed between any given source and a destination. These sources and destinations can be internal or external. One example of internal communication is the common use case of one virtual service communicating with one or more other virtual services within the mesh boundary. In a microservice architecture, this type of control is helpful if you want to ensure that only a select set of services can communicate with a sensitive service. Examples of external communication include use cases in which clients outside the mesh communicate to virtual services through an ingress gateway where you can allow the ingress gateway to communicate with only a subset of virtual services. Another common example is an access policy that allows a virtual service within the mesh to communicate to a limited set of external destinations. Listing 7-13 shows an access policy resource that is allowing communication from the ingress gateway to a virtual service.

Listing 7-13 An Example Access Policy Controlling Communication Between an IngressGateway and a VirtualService

```
kind: AccessPolicy
apiVersion: servicemesh.oci.oracle.com/v1beta1
metadata:
  name: nginx-policy
spec:
  mesh:
    ref:
      name: nginx
  compartmentId: ocid1.compartment.oc1..
aaaaaaaahgeqvnooufd5efvafgiobngb2xfcih62h3u7o2sq2wfhei5ddgoa
  rules:
    - action: ALLOW
      source:
        ingressGateway:
          ref:
            name: nginx-ingress-gateway
```

```
    destination:
      virtualService:
        ref:
          name: mesh-nginx
```

By default, every mesh is secure and denies all communication, which includes ingress, egress, and communication within the mesh. When the service mesh resources are created, you must create an access policy to enable communication. These policies can be fine-grained, identifying exact sources and destinations, or they can be broader and target multiple virtual services or use wildcards for external hostnames.

With the application and the mesh resources deployed, the CRDs for the mesh jump into action to set up the proxies and implement the mesh. You can check the progress and status for the various resources using the command in Listing 7-14.

Listing 7-14 Interacting with Service MeshResources Using Kubernetes Tooling

```
$ kubectl get meshes,virtualservices,virtualdeployments,virtualserviceroutetabl
  es,ingressgateways,ingressgatewayroutetables,accesspolicies,virtualdeployment
  bindings,ingressgatewaydeployments

NAME                                      ACTIVE   AGE
mesh.servicemesh.oci.oracle.com/nginx     True     5d1h

NAME                                             ACTIVE   AGE
virtualservice.servicemesh.oci.oracle.com/mesh-nginx   True   5d1h

NAME                                               ACTIVE   AGE
virtualdeployment.servicemesh.oci.oracle.com/nginx-v1   True   5d1h

NAME                                                     ACTIVE   AGE
virtualserviceroutetable.servicemesh.oci.oracle.com/nginx-route-table   True
  5d1h

NAME                                                    ACTIVE   AGE
ingressgateway.servicemesh.oci.oracle.com/nginx-ingress-gateway   True   5d1h

NAME                                                    ACTIVE   AGE
ingressgatewayroutetable.servicemesh.oci.oracle.com/nginx-ingress-gateway-route-
  table   True   5d1h

NAME                                             ACTIVE   AGE
accesspolicy.servicemesh.oci.oracle.com/nginx-policy   True   5d1h

NAME                                                       ACTIVE   AGE
virtualdeploymentbinding.servicemesh.oci.oracle.com/nginx-binding   True   5d1h
```

```
NAME                                                               ACTIVE    AGE
ingressgatewaydeployment.servicemesh.oci.oracle.com/nginx-ingress-gateway-
    deployment   True     5d1h
```

The first time you deploy the resources, you might notice a time delay for them to move to the ACTIVE state. This is expected because the resources are created in the control plane and reconciled. To look for potential issues or to check on progress, you can check the logs on the controller manager for the OCI service operator:

```
kubectl logs -n oci-service-operator-system deploy/oci-service-operator-
    controller-manager -f
```

With the service mesh deployed and your application managed by the service mesh, you can now use the mesh resources to implement traffic shaping using virtual service route tables and control both north/south and east/west traffic access using access policies.

Summary

This chapter examined three key serverless platforms for application development on OCI. The main characteristic of all these systems is that they involve no infrastructure management and can automatically scale to meet the rising needs of your application. The three services examined in this chapter are each aimed at a different type of use case. Container Instances makes the process of running containers easy by completely removing infrastructure management and letting you focus on your containers, while still providing features such as resource throttling and configuration. OCI Functions provide an even more agile experience, in which the OCI Functions SDKs and CLI directly work with your code to make them fully managed functions that can scale for full elasticity. They also integrate with multiple OCI services and external triggers to help you create reactive applications. Finally, OCI Service Mesh introduces a method to transparently add new capabilities to your existing Kubernetes-based applications with the help of a fully managed service mesh. The OCI Service Mesh, based on the Envoy proxy, lets you easily add features such as mTLS, traffic shaping, and observability to your applications without requiring any code changes. Serverless platforms and services often act as a way to build scalable integrations among multiple systems or to enhance existing systems with new capabilities in a cloud native manner.

References

1 OCI Image Specification: https://github.com/opencontainers/image-spec/blob/main/config.md
2 Functions QuickStart on Local Host: https://docs.oracle.com/en-us/iaas/Content/Functions/Tasks/functionsquickstartlocalhost.htm

8

Observability

Cloud native architectures and paradigms introduce new challenges and opportunities related to systems management and observation. Monolithic applications are being broken into microservices, applications and their runtime environment and configurations are getting packaged as containers, and infrastructure is becoming ephemeral. Just as these general paradigms are changing, so should the techniques and tools to observe and monitor them. The distributed nature of these application architectures requires the ability to observe a multitude of systems in isolation and correlate these metrics to get a complete view. The polyglot nature of these systems also give us opportunities to gather metrics and performance data from individual systems using tools and techniques that are optimal for each service or unit, without needing to manage dependencies, choosing tools that work across a wide range of technologies, or deal with cascading effects from other systems. The same notions apply to infrastructure. With ephemeral infrastructure, it can be daunting to track infrastructure changes across time and other dimensions, such as the correlated impact on applications, cost, and fault tolerance.

Observability can be defined as the capability to track and trace the happenings within your systems, at both the application and infrastructure levels. This data helps you understand and reason about behaviors you see within the system. In many cases, it is not enough to just observe and reason about observed behavior. You also need to be able to predict future behavior.

Oracle Cloud Infrastructure (OCI) offers several tools and solutions to observe your applications and services. In keeping with OCI's open approach to the platform, you can also bring in your own tools that you might be more comfortable with. These include tools and platforms that gather metrics or logging, use agents or ingest log data, or use tools such as Extended Berkeley Packet Filter (eBPF) to gain insights into your workloads. This chapter takes a look at the various services and some popular open-source tools that you can use to observe your cloud native applications deployed to OCI.

OCI Monitoring

OCI Monitoring is a service that keeps track of your resources across OCI using resource metrics, and then alerts you to various conditions using alarms. A metric is a data point related to the health, capacity, or performance of any resource in OCI.

These data points have time stamps, dimensions, and other metadata. Metric data can originate from OCI services or can be published by your own applications. The most common and trivial example of a metric is the CPU and memory utilization of a compute instance. Metrics can be unique as well, such as the number of unschedulable pods in an OKE cluster or the number of vulnerabilities found by a vulnerability scan. Several OCI services report metrics out of the box; the most common of these are the compute instance metrics. Every compute instance reports metrics such as its own CPU and memory utilization. In this example, the CPU utilization value for an instance is the metric (a measured value); it is accompanied by the time stamp for that measurement. A metric definition adds data to the metric, such as metadata that indicate the unit of measure for the value in the metric, and dimensions that are attributes for that measurement. The compute instance OCID, its availability domain, and its compartment are examples of dimensions that can be added to the metric and its metadata to form a metric definition.

Additionally, a metric definition includes a metric namespace that acts as a grouping construct for identifying and grouping the class of resources where the metric originates. The raw metric data emitted from the various sources, such as the services in OCI and the various applications, is consumed and aggregated by the monitoring service. Figure 8-1 shows how the metric data flows through the monitoring service.

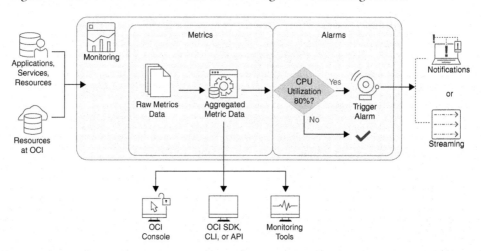

Figure 8-1   Typical Flow of Observability Data in OCI

Once the raw metrics have been ingested by the monitoring service, it can be queried to get the aggregated data. These queries are the primary mechanisms through which data is extracted from the service and are the most fundamental way to monitor your resources in OCI. Metric queries are written in Monitoring Query Language (MQL), an intuitive query language that is similar to natural language. The OCI console includes Metrics Explorer, an intuitive query builder that helps you construct the queries in a visual environment (see Figure 8-2).

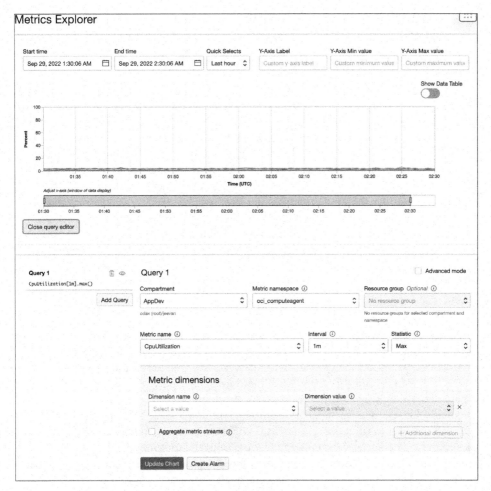

Figure 8-2   The Metrics Explorer in OCI Offers an Intuitive Visual Query Builder for Querying Metrics

The Metrics Explorer can help you construct most common queries visually. Besides the visual query builder, the Metrics Explorer offers an Advanced mode that enables you to write your own MQL queries. Understanding MQL can be useful: With it, you can build advanced queries and use the monitoring service from the CLI, SDKs, and APIs. MQL queries have components such as the metric to be queried (such as CpuUtilization); an interval that determines the aggregation window of the raw metric data (CPU utilization for every 1 minute); and a statistic, which is the aggregation function applied (such as max). Taken together, a query of this nature would be expressing a request to get the mean CpuUtilization in intervals of 1 minute. The monitoring service would aggregate the raw data points for the CpuUtilization metric in windows of 1 minute and get the max value from each 1-minute window. The resulting aggregated data for the metric that is returned from the service is called a metric stream. The MQL syntax for this query follows:

```
CpuUtilization[1m].max()
```

This simple query shows the required parts of an MQL query—the metric, interval, and statistic. Different resources, such as the various OCI service or custom applications, emit different metrics; therefore, the metric you can query from the monitoring service depends on what has been ingested. The OCI documentation[1] covers every metric that is emitted by the various OCI services. The interval can be specified in minutes (as in 1m), hours (as in 2h), or days (as in 5d). The valid intervals in a query also change, depending on the time range for the query. For instance, a query pulling data for the past 30 days requires the minimum interval to be 1d. The service also supports several statistics, including counts, min, max, mean, various percentiles, and rates (rate of an occurrence). Beyond these required components, MQL syntax includes features that are much more powerful in targeting specific resources, grouping them and aggregating metrics. The general form of an MQL query that includes these optional components is as follows:

```
metric[interval]{dimensionname=dimensionvalue}.groupingfunction.statistic
```

As you can see, MQL can include dimensions that you can use as a filter in your queries and grouping functions to determine how the metrics are aggregated. Dimensions are attributes from the metric data that you can use to filter your query and restrict it to certain data points with these attributes. For example, to look at the CpuUtilization in a single region or a single availability domain, you could use the dimension filter to restrict the query. Similarly, you might want to group the data in a way that makes it easy to work with. MQL supports grouping functions such as `groupBy` or `grouping`. The `groupBy` grouping function groups the metrics by one or more attributes, to aggregate them. The `grouping` function, on the other hand, aggregates all the metric streams from the query into a single aggregation.

To understand these components a bit better, let's look at an example. Imagine that you want to track underutilized or abandoned OKE clusters in development environments. Reclaiming underutilized or abandoned cloud resources is a common cost optimization approach. Here, the intent behind the notion of *utilization* is fairly vaguely defined, and it could mean several things. It could refer to the cluster whose nodes exhibit the most/least CPU utilization, but a critical workload that experiences sudden volatility in usage or traffic could lead to false positives. Another way to define *utilization* could be to look for clusters that see very few API server calls. Clusters running production workloads generally see fewer API server calls than clusters running in a development environment. For this example, let's use this metric to identify clusters that see comparatively fewer API server requests. The OKE service exposes a metric named `APIServerRequestCount` that you can use to accomplish this. Consider the following query:

```
APIServerRequestCount[1m].groupBy(clusterId).rate()
```

The query tracks the rate of Kubernetes API server requests in 1-minute intervals. Then it groups the data by cluster ID and produces one metric stream per cluster. On the console, this can appear as shown in Figure 8-3.

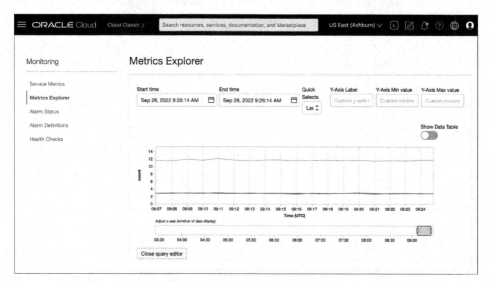

Figure 8-3   The Metrics Explorer Generating a Graph for a Custom Query to Track API Requests Across Multiple Kubernetes Clusters

In this example, you can see three lines, corresponding to the three metric streams. Each metric stream represents a single cluster because the query groups the metrics data by `clusterId`. If there were four clusters, the `groupBy` grouping function would group the data into four metric streams; the console then would show four lines representing the four metric streams. From the figure, it is clear that one cluster is seeing more API server requests than the other two. Having this query on a dashboard can help users and infrastructure admins quickly identify potentially underutilized resources on which to focus cost optimization efforts.

A *dimension* filter can filter the data points based on the dimensions available in the raw data. Consider the following example:

```
APIServerRequestCount[1m]{clusterId = "ocid1.cluster.oc1.iad.
  aaaaaaaadcnof56t6ijrxbzjluujrjlwwvxz7u3guqxi7cyy5cemaalmxtlq"}.rate()
```

The preceding query demonstrates a dimension filter that filters out the metric data for all but one cluster, identified by its OCID, and gets the rate of Kubernetes API server requests. Dimension filters can use fuzzy filters to match multiple filter values and conditions. If you had a set of clusters and you wanted to track the same `APIServerRequestCount` metric across this set of clusters, you could use a fuzzy filter such as the one that follows:

```
APIServerRequestCount[1m]{clusterId =~ "*cemaalmxtlq|*jluujrjlwwv"}.
  groupBy(clusterId).rate()
```

The query has three noteworthy aspects:

1. The =~ comparison operator specifies a fuzzy match.
2. The * wildcard in the dimension filter matches zero or more characters. This wildcard is used to create a match with a partial OCID, much like a regular expression.
3. The | acts as the *OR* operation for the dimension filter values, which causes the dimension filter to do a fuzzy match on either of the two partial values.

The combined effect of this query is that you track the `APIServerRequestCount` metric in 1-minute intervals, and the query uses a dimension filter that uses fuzzy matching to filter the metric data that matches either of the two OCIDs. Then the results are grouped by the `clusterId`. This grouping generates two metric streams because the dimension filter also uses the `clusterId` to filter data that matches either of two clusters. Finally, the rate of requests is the statistic that is reported by the query for both metric streams.

Apart from the metrics that OCI services emit, your own applications can emit metrics to be ingested by the OCI Monitoring service. To use the service from within your applications, the easiest method is to use the OCI SDKs. The SDK includes code examples that demonstrate how this API can be integrated with your applications; it can be found on GitHub.[2] Metrics are secured by IAM, so to use the service, you also need to give access to your applications through policies such as the one that follows:

```
Allow dynamic-group ObservableApps to use metrics in tenancy where target.
  metrics.namespace='AppMetricsNamespace'
```

Here, it is assumed that `ObservableApps` is a dynamic group that includes the instances where your application is running.

Alarms

Closely related to, and often used in conjunction with, metrics, are alarms. Alarms are simply notifications triggered by a specified condition. In the case of OCI, the monitoring service uses the notifications service to send a message when a condition is met. Alarms are also based on the same MQL queries. In addition to the query structure that has been examined so far, an alarm query has a condition. Consider the following example:

```
UnschedulablePods[1m].grouping().max() >= 1
```

This line tracks the number of unschedulable pods across clusters. If there is at least 1 unschedulable pod, it raises an alarm. The MQL syntax is the same as before, except for the addition of a condition, >= 1. This is the condition that the alarm continuously evaluates; if it becomes true, the alarm starts to fire.

Every alarm definition also includes a severity that you can set, based on the criticality you assign to your query. The available severity levels are Critical, Error, Warning, and Info. Severity is an arbitrary value that the user creating an alarm can set, based on the perceived importance of the alarm. For example, an unschedulable pod might be an Info-level alarm in some applications but a Critical-level alarm for other applications. In practice, alarms often require tuning and these severity levels can change over time. For instance, when you start with a new application, you might set the alarms and severity levels based on an educated guess. Over time, however, you might notice that some alarms are noisy and get triggered too often without much impact to the application, so you could then adjust the trigger conditions and severity. You might also notice that you missed creating some alarms, as you find better predictors of trouble for your applications. This makes tuning your alarms an activity worth revisiting periodically.

Much like the Metrics Explorer, the OCI console has a visual interface to define and manage alarms. This interface enables you to create MQL queries both visually and with straight MQL (Advanced mode). Unlike the Metrics Explorer, however, here you can add conditions to the query and specify what actions to take when the alarm is firing. The actions could raise the alarm by using the notifications service or publishing it to the streaming service. Figure 8-4 shows this interface to define alarms that are triggered based on metrics being collected continuously from OCI resources or your own applications.

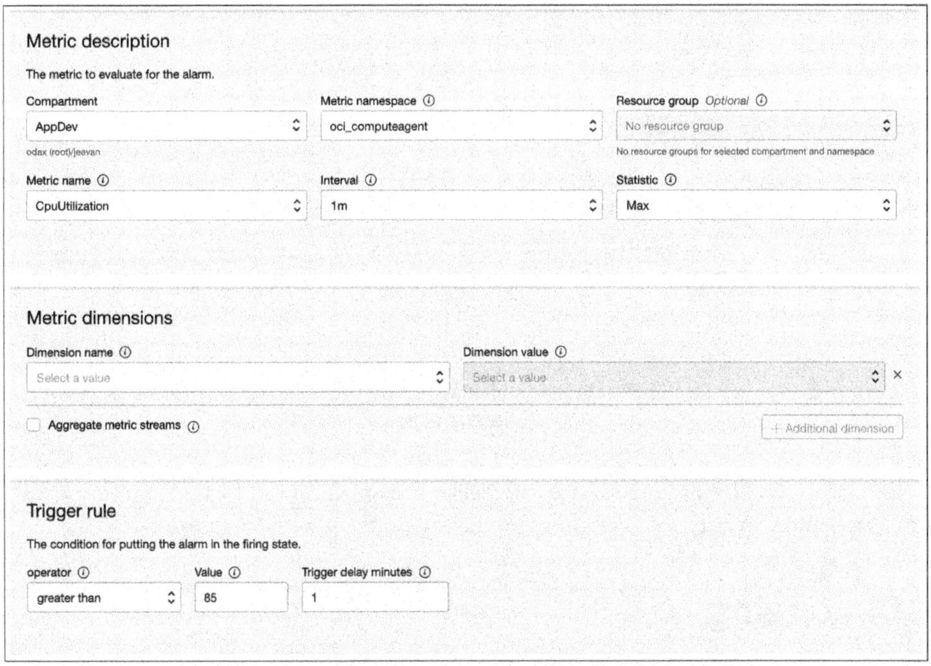

Figure 8-4   Creating Alarms That Are Triggered by Resource Metrics That Meet Desired Conditions

The notification service is a low-latency PubSub messaging service within OCI that supports durable messages with delivery guarantees. It provides topics and subscriptions, in which a service or application can send messages to a topic via the Notifications service. When a message is published to a topic, the Notifications service sends the message to all of the topic's subscriptions. When the alarm destination is the notification service, you can choose to publish formatted text, pretty printed JSON, or raw JSON to the destination, as illustrated in Figure 8-5. The choice depends on how you want to process the notification. For instance, if you want to directly create a PagerDuty subscription, perhaps formatted text is the most appropriate. On the other hand, if you need to send it to a function to perform some action, such as to trigger the creation of a compute instance to automatically resolve an alarm, the JSON-formatted message is likely more appropriate.

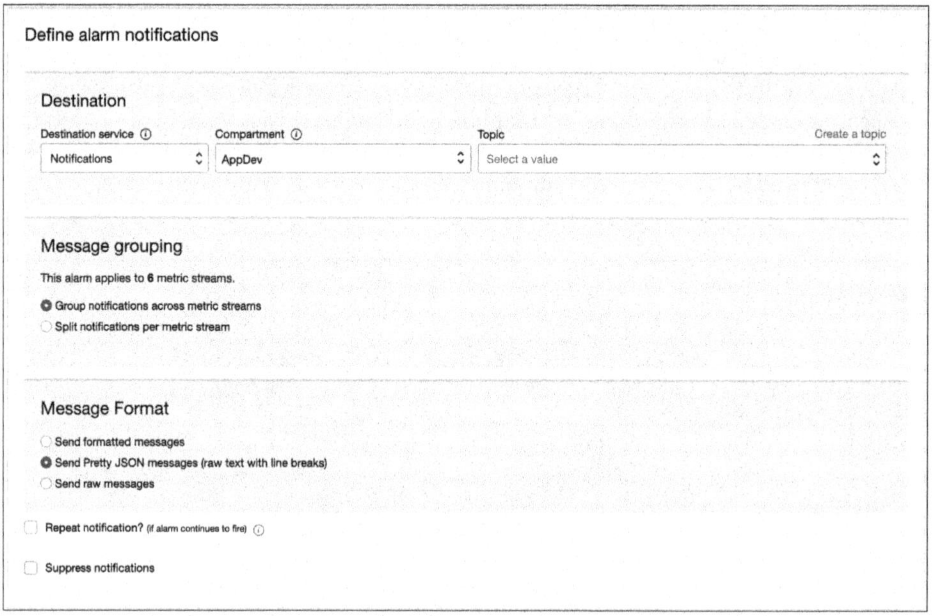

Figure 8-5   Alarms Can Be Sent to the Notifications Service, Which Can Trigger Other Systems for Corrective Actions.

Similar to the Notification service, the delivery destination can be a stream in the OCI Streaming service. The streaming service supports only JSON message format.

OCI Logging

Logs are a fundamental source of insight into your applications and the services you use. Log data often includes diagnostic information that can help you troubleshoot issues and understand the performance characteristics of your application. Logs can also provide intelligence about the security posture of your cloud resources and keep track of changes to your infrastructure, its configuration, and who made them. The OCI Logging service provides a fully managed and scalable way to manage logs across applications and OCI services in your tenancy. The OCI Logging service provides features to store, organize, and search log data. Log data can come from OCI services when you enable them or from your own applications.

The first thing most people think about when hearing about logs is log files. Although the idea of representing and recording an event in an application or service in a file is still relevant, services such as OCI Logging provide a persistence mechanism that is efficient for searching, indexing, and applying data processing techniques. A *log* in this context is an OCI resource with its own OCID. You can think of this resource as a store for event data collected from an OCI service or your own applications. The actual log message that an application or service writes to standard out (STDOUT) is a *log event* that is captured in the log. The logging system captures the entire context of what happens when the service or application emitted the log message; this is why the log entry is called a log event. The information contained in the log event depends on the event type. All OCI services have log events that capture a great deal of contextual data about the event. Logs themselves are organized into *log groups*, logical containers for logs that help you organize similar logs. Log groups also help secure and manage these logs by applying IAM policies to log groups that determine who has access to the logs. For instance, you might want to create log groups based on the sensitivity of the log messages contained within logs. Logs that contain sensitive information can be grouped together into a separate log group. IAM policies can then be set up in such a way that access to this log group requires a specific role. This effectively restricts access to sensitive information and controls access purely through the use of policies. Figure 8-6 shows this hierarchy of logging resources.

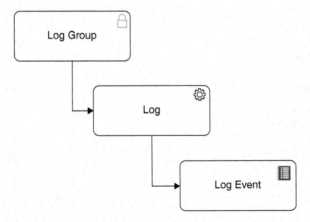

Figure 8-6   Hierarchy of Logging Resources

Service Logs

Service logs are logs from the various OCI services, and they are the most common type of logs in OCI. Service logs provide insight into the utilization, health, and performance of these services. These logs are collected by the OCI Logging service, which is made available to you and can be queried. Service logs are *enabled* in OCI Logging. This is simply because the services themselves emit log events that are discarded if they are not captured by enabling the log for a service. Users can easily enable logs for any service using the console. When you enable a service log, you must add it to a log group (see Figure 8-7); you can select the service and a resource provided by the service when enabling the service log. When the log is enabled, the log events pertaining to the resource are collected and indexed in the log from where it can be queried. Service logs can also be ingested into other services, where they can be combined with other operational data to provide more insight into your business and any applications running on OCI.

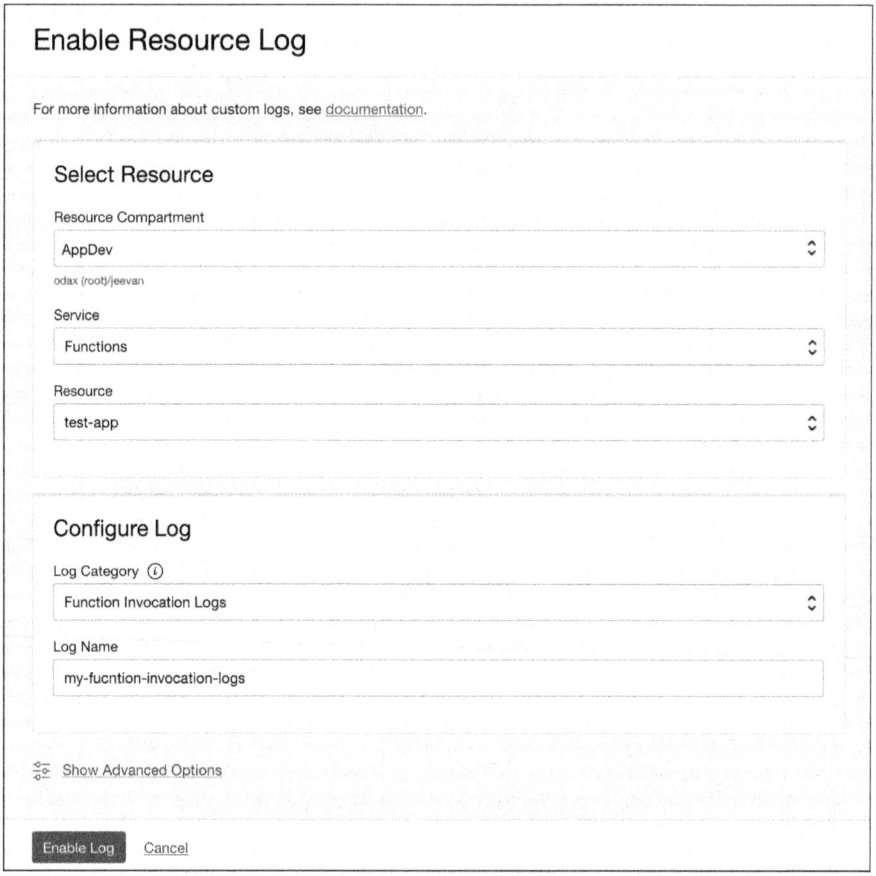

Figure 8-7   Enabling Logging for a Service—in This Case, a Specific OCI Function

Custom Logs

The logs that are created by your applications can be ingested into the OCI Logging service. These are called *custom logs*. The main reason to ingest custom logs is to put your application logs in the same context as the infrastructure logs, to draw correlations between them and derive deeper insights. Unlike service logs that are enabled, custom logs are ingested into the OCI Logging service. The log resource is the same; however, the source behaves differently here. Service logs create high-fidelity log events with detailed contextual information. Custom logs, on the other hand, typically originate from a log file. OCI provides an agent to extract, parse, and ingest directly to the OCI Logging service. Typically, each line in a log file is considered to be a separate log event. Depending on the log format, the information in the log line can be tokenized or parsed to generate the fields of the log event to index it and make it searchable. Some logging formats, such as a web server, might be common, so parsers and tokenizers might exist for these; custom applications, on the other hand, might have a custom log format that requires a custom tokenizer. To set up custom logs, you create an agent configuration, as shown in Figure 8-8.

The agent configuration starts with determining the group of hosts from which to get the logs. This is typically a *dynamic group*. The dynamic groups are listed so that you can easily pick one. In the example shown in Figure 8-8, the agent configuration is set up to ingest container logs from all containers running on a given OKE cluster. For this, the user first defines a dynamic group that contains all nodes that make up the cluster. It is not necessary to keep the granularity at the cluster level: The user could have created a dynamic group that picked a select subset of nodes in the cluster (say, GPU nodes used for a machine-learning workload) or all nodes across an availability domain or region, regardless of whether they were OKE nodes. The dynamic group has to be given access to the OCI Logging service so that the agents running on these hosts can push the log files to the service. Next, you configure the various log sources. These can be one or more paths where the log files of interest to you are located on the hosts. In the example, you see a single path for /var/log/containers/*, which ingests all log files in this location. You can set up multiple paths to ingest from multiple sources simultaneously. For every input, you also set up the parser options to tokenize the log files to convert them into log events. More than 200 predefined parsers that cover popular log file formats such as Kubernetes Audit Logs, etcd logs, Apache logs, and syslog are supported, apart from generic formats such as JSON and XML. You can also create custom parsers used to tokenize your application's log files that use a custom format for log data. Finally, you choose the destination log resource in the OCI Logging service to which the events from the log files should be ingested. After they are ingested, the log events are indexed and become searchable like service logs.

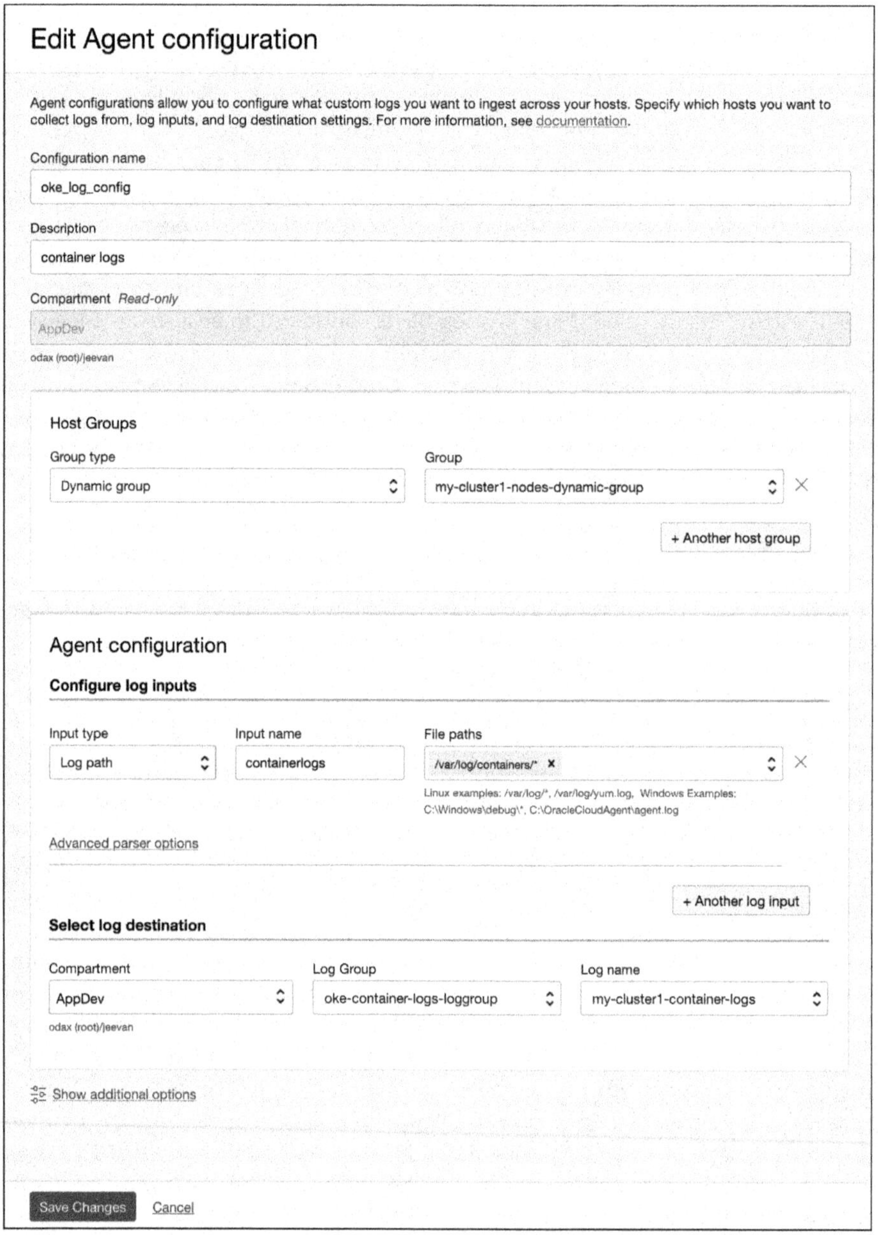

Edit Agent configuration

Agent configurations allow you to configure what custom logs you want to ingest across your hosts. Specify which hosts you want to collect logs from, log inputs, and log destination settings. For more information, see documentation.

Configuration name

oke_log_config

Description

container logs

Compartment *Read-only*

AppDev

odax (root)/jeevan

Host Groups

Group type

Dynamic group ⇕

Group

my-cluster1-nodes-dynamic-group ⇕ ✕

+ Another host group

Agent configuration

Configure log inputs

Input type

Log path ⇕

Input name

containerlogs

File paths

/var/log/containers/* ✕ ⇕ ✕

Linux examples: /var/log/*, /var/log/yum.log. Windows Examples: C:\Windows\debug*, C:\OracleCloudAgent\agent.log

Advanced parser options

+ Another log input

Select log destination

Compartment

AppDev ⇕

odax (root)/jeevan

Log Group

oke-container-logs-loggroup ⇕

Log name

my-cluster1-container-logs ⇕

Show additional options

Save Changes   Cancel

Figure 8-8 Agent Configuration for Custom Logs—the Image Shows the Log Inputs but Does Not Show the Parser Configuration (Which Can Be Selected for Each Log Input)

Audit Logs

OCI also tracks how and when each service is being accessed, and by whom. It captures metadata about the access or action performed to the resource, to provide a complete view into how your resources are being accessed and how. This is called the *audit log* and is separate from service logs. The audit service calls to all OCI API endpoints as log events. Because the service operates at the API level, log events are generated for all operations, regardless of whether they originate from within OCI or externally, and regardless of the clients (such as the CLI, the SDK, or custom applications) used to make the API calls.

The audit event is structured data and uses a well-defined schema called the audit schema to publish audit events. Using the standardized message structure provided by the schema makes it easy for consumers to listen to audit events, process them, and build automation code that can react to certain events. It is also worthwhile to note that OCI offers mechanisms to listen to events and take actions based on those using services, such as Cloud Guard, that do not involve custom code development. Event data in the audit schema is structured into a payload and an envelope. The payload is the data about the specific API call that is provided by the service that was the target of the API call. This can include the OCID for the resource that is targeted by the API call; information about the request, response, and identity of the caller; any resource state changes; and more. This payload is wrapped in an envelope that uses the CNCF CloudEvents[3] standard. Listing 8-1 shows an example audit log event.

Listing 8-1 Example Audit Log Event

```
{
  "datetime": 1667373839959,
  "logContent": {
    "dataschema": "2.0",
    "id": "346d7f82-ea45-48fe-b7b4-a6cb3fb56dad",
    "oracle": {
      "enantednted": "ocid1.compartment.oc1..xxxx",
      "ingestedtime": "2022-11-02T07:24:08.990Z",
      "loggroupid": "_Audit",
      "enanted": "ocid1.tenancy.oc1..xxxx"
    },
    "source": "oke-k8sApiEndpoint-subnet-xxxx",
    "specversion": "1.0",
    "time": "2022-11-02T07:23:59.959Z",
    "type": "com.oraclecloud.virtualNetwork.GetSubnet",
    "data": {
      "additionalDetails": {
        "X-Real-Port": 59226
      },
      "availabilityDomain": "AD2",
```

```
      "compartmentId": "xxxxxxxx",
      "compartmentName": "AppDev",
      "resourceId": "ocid1.subnet.oc1.iad.xxxx",
      "definedTags": {},
      "eventGroupingId": "xxxx/xxxx",
      "eventName": "GetSubnet",
      "freeformTags": {},
      "identity": {
        "authType": null,
        "callerId": null,
        "callerName": null,
        "consoleSessionId": null,
        "credentials": "xxxx,
        "ipAddress": "10.240.2.7",
        "principalId": "xxxx",
        "principalName": "oke",
        "tenantId": "xxxx",
        "userAgent": "Oracle-JavaSDK/2.11.1 (Linux/4.14.35-2047;Java 64-Bit Server
VM GraalVM EE)"
      },
      "message": "oke-k8sApiEndpoint-subnet-xxxx GetSubnet succeeded",
      "request": {
        "action": "GET",
        "headers": {},
        "id": "xxxx/xxxx/xxxx",
        "parameters": {},
        "path": "/20160918/subnets/ocid1.subnet.oc1.iad.xxxx"
      },
      "response": {
        "headers": {},
        "message": null,
        "payload": {},
        "responseTime": "2022-11-02T07:23:59.959Z",
        "status": "200"
      },
      "stateChange": {
        "current": null,
        "previous": null
      }
    }
  }
}
```

The logcontent contains the overall envelope for the event. The data element within the envelope contains the resource-specific audit information. The envelope structure is the same for all events, regardless of the service; however, the payload contained in the data section is dependent on the type of the event.

Auditing OKE Activity

Audit logging captures activity within a service that can be used to create an audit trail of events and occurrences. It can be used to answer questions such as, "Who did what and when?" Audit logging is an important part of several security and compliance programs because it maintains an immutable log of events and changes that occur within the services. In the case of cloud native execution environments such as OKE, these events can occur on two different levels:

- The infrastructure level, where some infrastructure configuration for your cluster is changing, such as the number of nodes in a node pool, the shape of the instances, or the version of Kubernetes being used. These changes are captured by the audit service along with metadata such as who made the change, when the change was made, whether the change was successful, and the previous and current states of the resources affected by the change.
- Within the execution environment itself. In the case of a Kubernetes cluster, these could be changes to the Kubernetes resources or actions and events that are performed on the cluster objects. For instance, if a user deploys a new pod onto the cluster, that event needs to be audited. In fact, for platforms such as OKE, these activities are more common and frequent than infrastructure events.

OKE captures changes to the Kubernetes objects in the audit log to provide a full audit trail of cluster events that occur within the cluster. These include all interactions with the Kubernetes API, including those made by nonhuman users such as service accounts. For example, consider an OKE cluster that deploys its workloads in a GitOps model using ArgoCD. ArgoCD runs as a workload on the cluster and periodically checks a Git repository for changes to the application deployment YAMLs. When a change is detected, ArgoCD deploys the change and updates the Kubernetes objects. This is an example of when there is no human interaction in the deployment process; the Kubernetes objects are updated by an automated system that identifies itself with a service account. Listing 8-2 shows a PATCH event in which a change is deployed to the cluster.

Listing 8-2 Example PATCH Event: Change Deployed to Cluster

```
{
  "datetime": 1667528786186,
  "logContent": {
    "data": {
      "additionalDetails": null,
      "availabilityDomain": null,
      "compartmentId": "ocid1.compartment.oc1..
aaaaaaaagup7orev5wck2z3nh5hd6kgoaubksrundbrndocucev5dzct7wsq",
      "compartmentName": "AppDev",
      "definedTags": null,
      "eventGroupingId": "c45ef9f5-5ec2-4dc8-a83b-2f9f2ba3ab64",
      "eventName": "io.argoproj.v1alpha1.applications.patch",
      "freeformTags": null,
      "identity": {
```

```
      "authType": "Native",
      "callerId": null,
      "callerName": null,
      "consoleSessionId": null,
      "credentials": "",
      "ipAddress": null,
      "principalId": null,
      "principalName": "system:serviceaccount:argocd:argocd-application-
controller",
      "tenantId": "",
      "userAgent": "Go-http-client/2.0"
    },
    "message": "io.argoproj.v1alpha1.applications.patch succeeded",
    "request": {
      "action": "PATCH",
      "headers": null,
      "id": "c45ef9f5-5ec2-4dc8-a83b-2f9f2ba3ab64",
      "parameters": null,
      "path": "/apis/argoproj.io/v1alpha1/namespaces/argocd/applications/
wordpress"
    },
    "resourceId": "ocid1.cluster.oc1.iad.
aaaaaaaadcnof56t6ijrxbzjluujrjlwwvxz7u3guqxi7cyy5cemaalmxtlq",
    "response": {
      "headers": null,
      "message": null,
      "payload": null,
      "responseTime": "2022-11-04T02:26:26.201Z",
      "status": "200"
    },
    "stateChange": {
      "current": {
        "responseObject": null
      },
      "previous": {
        "requestObject": null
      }
    }
  },
  "dataschema": "2.0",
  "id": "c45ef9f5-5ec2-4dc8-a83b-2f9f2ba3ab64",
  "oracle": {
    "compartmentid": "ocid1.compartment.oc1..
aaaaaaaagup7orev5wck2z3nh5hd6kgoaubksrundbrndocucev5dzct7wsq",
    "ingestedtime": "2022-11-04T02:26:35.914Z",
    "loggroupid": "_Audit",
    "tenantid": ""
  },
  "source": "",
```

```
    "specversion": "1.0",
    "time": "2022-11-04T02:26:26.186Z",
    "type": "io.argoproj.v1alpha1.applications.patch"
  }
}
```

Advanced Observability in OCI

Advanced observability in OCI refers to a set of services that provide observability across several services and correlate information across structured and unstructured data. This includes, for example, the capability to derive insights by correlating data across logs and metrics from various services to form a more complete view of the systems and processes that are under observation. The advantage of using this set of advanced observability tools is that users can derive deep business insights and drive root cause analysis instead of focusing on surface-level problems. As an example, consider a scenario in which the metrics from an application indicate degraded performance for one of its service endpoints. The metrics from the application can point to the endpoint that is performing poorly and help you identify the issue. However, this issue could have been occurring in some other component, and that component might have been logging warnings about degraded performance for a while. In this instance, the capability to correlate the performance degradation on the service with the logs that described a potential warning on another service could have helped you to find the root cause for this issue and address it more quickly. In practice, however, the root cause for an issue could be a result of multiple separate systems interacting with each other in unexpected ways, with several smaller inefficiencies having a cumulative effect. The advanced tools in OCI are designed to observe a wide range of systems, from databases and file systems to Kubernetes clusters and application logs. This gives the advanced tools in OCI the capability to correlate metrics and log data across several layers in the stack, to create a complete 360-degree view of your workloads across applications, infrastructure, and external systems.

Logging Analytics

The biggest challenge with observability when operating at scale is the sheer amount of noise that it generates under normal operating conditions. Millions of events can be happening every second in a large enough set of distributed applications. Sifting through the noise to identify real events and signals and then correlate them to form insightful and actionable information is a real challenge. For instance, it would be trivial to monitor the network latencies and set up an alarm. This might be useful with a single application, but an application development team is less likely to be taking on infrastructure or network management responsibilities so that it can remediate a problem. An infrastructure or network team, on the other hand, would have multiple applications to service; when operating at scale, these alarms and events simply become noise. Another common example involves a security team. Security events can include file access, network connections, and process spawning, all of which can lead to a lot of noise in the raw data.

When discussing observability in this context, a common phrase used is "single pane of glass" for monitoring and observing systems and processes. The true intention of this phrase is to indicate visibility into all aspects of a system so that you can fully visualize and observe it from all angles and vantage points. In practice, however, this is harder to define (not implement) than it looks. This is because, as you saw in the earlier example, the view that is relevant to an operations and site reliability engineer might be very different from what is relevant to a developer or a penetration tester. Medium and large organizations have various personas, ranging from DevOps teams, to DBAs, to developers, to security teams. When you need observability in a "single pane of glass" across these teams, you need observability across your IT landscape, not just a few applications. It is also desirable to limit the number of tools used, to keep maintenance and dependencies in check. Log analytics is the general approach to solving this at scale. Industry solutions include Splunk and App Dynamics, among others.

OCI Logging Analytics is an OCI native service that provides these advanced analytic capabilities so that you can derive insights from across your entire IT landscape. OCI Logging Analytics can ingest data from various sources and correlate this to automatically generate complete application topologies and other visualizations. This makes it easy for every persona to have a relevant view, without having to invest time in capturing every metric and building every possible visualization. Figure 8-9 shows an example in which OCI Logging Analytics has constructed a topology diagram for an application based on the log analysis.

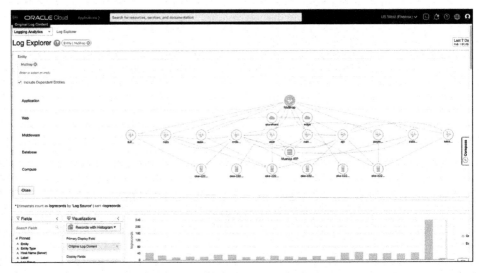

Figure 8-9 Logging Analytics Can Create Visual Representations of Applications and Systems, Along with How They Communicate, Based on Logs from the Various Systems—the Image Shows the Microservices That Make Up the MuShop Application Being Visualized, Based on the Logs Each Service Generates

These advanced analytical abilities can automatically learn patterns from the constant flow of metric and log data and can be used to identify unusual usage patterns that might indicate a security event or predict problems. These tools can be customized with additional log parsers as well.

Enabling and Using Logging Analytics

Logging Analytics works with OCI Logging and uses OCI IAM to control access, as with other services. The process of configuring the service includes setting up relevant IAM policies, followed by configuring how data is ingested into the Logging Analytics service. Log ingestion can ingest logs from both your tenancy and your on-premises resources. Additionally, the service can be configured to ingest audit logs from OCI, for added fidelity. Logs from compute instances and on-premises servers are collected by the compute management agent and sent over to the log group that is created for it. Although this host-level data is necessary, in the case of cloud native applications deployed to a Kubernetes cluster, you also need cluster-level metrics and logs to fully analyze the state of your workloads. To enable this, Logging Analytics uses fluentD to collect Kubernetes system/service logs, Linux system logs, and application pod/container logs. A preconfigured fluentD container can be deployed to your Kubernetes cluster as a DaemonSet, which continually collects data and ingests it into Log Analytics.

OCI Logging Analytics also includes built-in knowledge about well-known large-scale enterprise systems such as EBS. This is particularly useful when Oracle E-Business Suite (EBS) or a similar enterprise application suite is extended with custom bespoke applications that are now moving into a cloud native model. In these scenarios, Log Analytics can automatically discover your EBS or similar enterprise application deployment, including all its components and layers, and correlate it with systems that interact with it, such as a microservice running on a Kubernetes cluster.

Prometheus and Grafana with OKE

Prometheus and Grafana are some of the most widely used tools for monitoring metrics in Kubernetes. The kube-prometheus project provides a comprehensive experience for deploying Prometheus and Grafana on Kubernetes. It is based on the Prometheus Operator for Kubernetes, which uses the operator pattern to manage Prometheus deployments. The project provides pre-built Grafana dashboards and Prometheus rules, making it a complete monitoring solution for Kubernetes clusters. This project is an ideal starting point for most Kubernetes users. Chapter 5 includes the complete steps to deploy and manage this stack on OKE.

Using the OCI DataSource Plug-ins for Grafana

OCI provides data source plug-ins for Grafana that enable you to create panels and dashboards that query OCI directly. Data sources for both OCI Logging[4] and OCI

Metrics[5] are available. The capabilities and query methods of each data source are different; in the case of the OCI plug-ins, you construct queries based on the region, compartment, metric namespace, and other OCI-specific dimensions. The OCI data source plug-in for Grafana has a customized Query Editor UI that is tuned for the features and capabilities that the plug-in exposes. In Grafana, you can combine data from multiple data sources onto a single dashboard, but each panel is tied to a specific data source. You can also create alerts based on OCI metrics using Alertmanager. You can download and install these plug-ins from the Grafana marketplace (see the "Resources" section at the end of the chapter).

eBPF-Based Monitoring with Tetragon on OKE

Security applications often have requirements and scenarios that are very broad in nature, such as being able to watch for all programs that are opening a sensitive file and perhaps even terminating programs that are exhibiting behaviors you are not expecting. The deepest you can get is down to the operating system kernel itself because very little activity in the OS escapes the kernel. Implementing these security protocols broadly across a system often leads to performance degradation of unacceptable levels because the tools typically run outside the kernel's privileged execution context. This leads most users to settle for monitoring specific applications or smaller parts of a system. Building this functionality directly into the kernel or as kernel modules that execute within the kernel space often lets a program have very low overhead, but traditionally this comes at the cost of security and maintenance of these kernel modules. eBPF fundamentally changes this equation by providing a method of introducing new functionality that can execute in a sandboxed and privileged context without changing kernel source code or loading a kernel module. It essentially functions by creating a paradigm similar to a programming language virtual machine, such as Java. Modern Java programs are compiled into platform agnostic bytecode. This bytecode is consumed by the Java Virtual Machine (JVM), which uses a built-in Just-In-Time (JIT) compiler to convert the bytecode into native machine code to get native performance. Similarly, eBPF programs have a bytecode representation. BPF is deeply tied to the Linux kernel and can be considered a virtual machine inside the kernel. The in-kernel JIT compiler consumes an eBPF program in the eBPF bytecode and compiles it into native code that can execute in the kernel space.

eBPF uses an event-based model to load programs, and eBPF programs are written to "hook" into network events, systems calls, and more. When an event that an eBPF program hooks into is called, the eBPF program is loaded into the kernel after verification and JIT compilation. The verification step ensures that the program is safe to run, has the right privileges, and can run to completion; the JIT compilation ensures native performance. In many cases, eBPF programs are written in higher-level languages and compiled into the bytecode representation. These are then loaded into a running kernel after JIT compilation, based on the events that the programs are hooked into.

Tetragon: eBPF-Based Security Observability and Enforcement

Tetragon is a cloud native eBPF-based tool that performs security observability and enforcement. It is a component of the Cilium project. Using eBPF, Tetragon filters and observes events and applies policies in real time without sending events to an agent that is running outside the kernel. Tetragon can address numerous security and observability use cases by filtering for events such as a workload opening a network connection, accessing a file, or even starting a process inside a container. For instance, a shell process being started inside an application container could be considered a security event. Someone could be trying to troubleshoot an issue, or this could be some malicious activity—either way, it should trigger a security check to rule out an attack on the system. The same could be said about network connections being opened or files being read. Tetragon can trace and filter these activities while introducing little to no overhead, usually at the earliest stage that these events can be detected in software.

Tetragon is ideally suited for all Kubernetes workloads, and it runs as a DaemonSet in each node on the cluster. Tetragon can then pull metadata from the Kubernetes API server and correlate that metadata with the events observed within the kernel of each node. Tetragon makes it easy to set up real-time filters for these activities and more using TracingPolicies. A TracingPolicy is a custom resource created by Tetragon that enables admins and DevSecOps teams to create and deploy filters for kernel events as Kubernetes resources. A TracingPolicy can match system calls, process attributes and arguments, and also trigger an action on matches.

Running Tetragon on Oracle Container Engine for Kubernetes (OKE)

Tetragon can be deployed to Kubernetes clusters on OKE using the Helm chart published by the Tetragon project. After it is installed, the TracingPolicy Custom Resource Definition (CRD) is created and Tetragon runs on the cluster nodes as a DaemonSet.

Prerequisites for Oracle Linux

OKE uses Oracle Linux, and Tetragon relies on having the BPF Type Format (BTF) support in the kernel. Recent Oracle Linux kernels include this out of the box. For this reason, users should use a kernel that is 5.4.17-2136.305.3.el7uek or newer. Tetragon also does not provide support for ARM (linux/arm64) architecture; at the time of writing, it provides only x86 (linux/amd64) support. If you have ARM nodes in your OKE cluster, the DaemonSet will stay in the `Init:CrashLoopBackOff` status.

Recent versions of the OKE node images are based on kernels that include BTF support. This caveat for BTF support is applicable only for clusters in which the node OS has not been updated in a while, not for newly created clusters. If you are unsure, the best way to check whether you have BTF support is to log in to the node using SSH and run `ls /sys/kernel/btf`. You should see the kernel (vmlinux) and modules listed here.

To check the version of the kernel that your nodes are using, run `uname -a` on the node. If you are running an older version of the kernel, you can upgrade the version on the node pool configuration. However, this affects only newly created nodes; existing nodes are not upgraded automatically to ensure continuity for the workloads that might be running on them. You can follow the node pool upgrade process to bring your existing nodes up to the newer kernel versions.

When you have ensured that you are running on a recent version of the kernel on your nodes, you can get started with Tetragon installation using the Tetragon Helm chart. You can follow the instructions from the Tetragon GitHub page as well. To use the Helm chart Tetragon, follow these instructions:

```
helm repo add cilium https://helm.cilium.io
helm repo update
helm install tetragon cilium/tetragon -n kube-system
kubectl rollout status -n kube-system ds/tetragon -w
```

If you see that Tetragon pods are in a `CrashLoopBackOff` state, this could be caused by one of two reasons. The most likely reason is that this is occurring on ARM-based nodes, if you have them in your cluster. Tetragon does not yet run on ARM as of the time of writing. To confirm that this is the case, use the following line:

```
kubectl describe pod
```

You will then see the init container named tetragon-operator. This is likely failing and in a terminated state, with an exit code of 1. You can use the following line to view the init container logs:

```
kubectl logs <pod_name> -c tetragon-operator -n kube-system
```

You might see the reason for the init container to terminate as `standard_init_linux.go:228: exec user process caused: exec format error`, indicating that the binary is not meant for use on ARM CPU architecture.

The second reason Tetragon pods are in a `CrashLoopBackOff` state could be that you have an older kernel on your node, and BTF support is not included in it. To verify this, get the container logs for the failing container in the pod, as described previously. If the lack of BTF support in the kernel is the issue, you will see an error message similar to the following:

```
aborting kernel autodiscovery failed: Kernel version BTF search failed kernel is
    not included in supported list.
Use --btf option to specify BTF path and/or '--kernel' to specify kernel version
```

This is expected on nodes that have not had their OS updated for a while. To resolve this, the node pool configuration needs to be updated and the nodes need to be upgraded, following the standard node pool upgrade process.

When the DaemonSet is ready and the Tetragon pods are in the `Running` state, you can start listening to events on your nodes. Out of the box, Tetragon can monitor process execution. Tetragon emits the events it matches in JSON format, and the logs can be observed with the following command (assuming that you have jq installed):

```
kubectl logs -n kube-system -l app.kubernetes.io/name=tetragon -c export-stdout
  -f | jq
```

Depending on what activity is occurring on your cluster, you will see a stream of JSON objects that represent these events. Listing 8-4 shows sample output from a cluster that was running ArgoCD, where it was cloning a Git repository.

Listing 8-4 Example Logs from Tetragon Showing Activities That It Is Tracking

```
{
  "process_exec": {
    "process": {
      "exec_id": "MTAuMC4xMC4yMTg6OTE0MTQ2NjAzODUOMDcwOjEwNDA4Ng==",
      "pid": 104086,
      "uid": 999,
      "cwd": "/tmp/_argocd-repo/83c509d8-f9ba-48c3-a217-a9278134963e/",
      "binary": "/usr/bin/git",
      "arguments": "rev-parse HEAD",
      "flags": "execve clone",
      "start_time": "2022-06-07T17:03:42.519Z",
      "auid": 4294967295,
      "pod": {
        "namespace": "argocd",
        "name": "argocd-repo-server-7db4cc4b45-cpvlt",
        "container": {
          "id": "cri-o://1c361244fcb1d89c02ef297e69a13bd80fd4d575ae965a92979deec74
0711e17",
          "name": "argocd-repo-server",
          "image": {
            "id": "quay.io/argoproj/argocd@sha256:85d55980e70f8f7073e4ce529a7bbcf6
d55e51f8a7fc4b45d698f0a7ffef0fea",
            "name": "quay.io/argoproj/argocd:v2.3.4"
          },
          "start_time": "2022-05-31T16:57:53Z",
          "pid": 319
        }
      },
      "docker": "1c361244fcb1d89c02ef297e69a13bd",
      "parent_exec_id": "MTAuMC4xMC4yMTg6MzA4OTk3NTAyODQyMTEzOjExMjQ3",
      "refcnt": 1
    }
  },
  "node_name": "10.0.10.218",
  "time": "2022-06-07T17:03:42.519Z"
}
```

The event stream as JSON output is verbose and hard to understand, but it is information dense. You have several ways of ingesting this JSON data and deriving analytical information from it. The obvious one is to use the Tetragon CLI tool. Isovalent, the company behind Cilium and Tetragon, also offers a full-featured commercial product that can analyze and visualize this data, to make it more actionable and easier to assimilate.

Installing the Tetragon CLI

The Tetragon CLI is useful to filter events by pod, host, namespace, or process. The CLI can be downloaded from the GitHub releases page. Simply download the tool based on your operating system and CPU architecture, and untar it to a standard location such as /usr/local/bin, or add the path to the binary to your PATH variable for your shell. Alternatively, if you have go installed on your workstation where you want to run the CLI, you can download and install it with the commands in Listing 8-5.

Listing 8-5   Installing the Tetragon CLI

```
GOOS=$(go env GOOS)
GOARCH=$(go env GOARCH)
curl -L --remote-name-all https://github.com/cilium/tetragon/releases/download/
   tetragon-cli/tetragon-${GOOS}-${GOARCH}.tar.gz{,.sha256sum}
sha256sum --check tetragon-${GOOS}-${GOARCH}.tar.gz.sha256sum
sudo tar -C /usr/local/bin -xzvf tetragon-${GOOS}-${GOARCH}.tar.gz
rm tetragon-${GOOS}-${GOARCH}.tar.gz{,.sha256sum}
```

With the Tetragon CLI installed, the events from the log files can be pretty printed simply by sending the JSON output to the CLI command tetragon observe, as shown here:

```
kubectl logs -n kube-system ds/tetragon -c export-stdout -f | tetragon observe
```

TracingPolicies for FileAccess and Network Observability

TracingPolicies are custom resources that make it easy to set up real-time filters for kernel events. A TracingPolicy can not only match and filter system calls for observability, it can also trigger an action on these matches. Tetragon offers a few examples that showcase this capability, to inspire your own TracingPolicies.

Apply the example tracing policies for file access and network observability, as shown here:

```
kubectl apply -f https://raw.githubusercontent.com/cilium/tetragon/v0.8.0//crds/
   examples/sys_write_follow_fd_prefix.yaml
kubectl apply -f https://raw.githubusercontent.com/cilium/tetragon/v0.8.0/crds/
   examples/tcp-connect.yaml
```

With these additional TracingPolicies enabled, Tetragon starts tracing file access and network activity, as demonstrated in Listing 8-6.

Listing 8-6 An Example Showing the Tetragon CLI Displaying Events Such as File Access and Network Calls

```
$ kubectl logs -n kube-system ds/tetragon -c export-stdout -f | tetragon observe

...[output truncated]
🏃 process default/xwing /bin/bash
📖 open    default/xwing /bin/bash /etc/passwd
📕 close   default/xwing /bin/bash
📖 open    default/xwing /bin/bash /etc/terminfo/x/xterm
📕 close   default/xwing /bin/bash
🏃 process default/xwing /bin/cat /etc/passwd
📖 open    default/xwing /bin/cat /etc/passwd
📕 close   default/xwing /bin/cat
💥 exit    default/xwing /bin/cat /etc/passwd 0
🏃 process default/xwing /usr/bin/curl -Lv https://cloud.oracle.com
📖 open    default/xwing /usr/bin/curl /etc/ssl/openssl.cnf
📕 close   default/xwing /usr/bin/curl
📖 open    default/xwing /usr/bin/curl /etc/hosts
📕 close   default/xwing /usr/bin/curl
📖 open    default/xwing /usr/bin/curl /etc/resolv.conf
📕 close   default/xwing /usr/bin/curl
📡 connect default/xwing /usr/bin/curl tcp 10.244.1.152:65175 -> 23.212.250.69:443
📖 open    default/xwing /usr/bin/curl /etc/ssl/certs/ca-certificates.crt
📕 close   default/xwing /usr/bin/curl
📤 sendmsg default/xwing /usr/bin/curl tcp 10.244.1.152:65175 -> 23.212.250.69:443
   bytes 517
📤 sendmsg default/xwing /usr/bin/curl tcp 10.244.1.152:65175 -> 23.212.250.69:443
   bytes 126
📤 sendmsg default/xwing /usr/bin/curl tcp 10.244.1.152:65175 -> 23.212.250.69:443
   bytes 109
📤 sendmsg default/xwing /usr/bin/curl tcp 10.244.1.152:65175 -> 23.212.250.69:443
   bytes 31
✂ close    default/xwing /usr/bin/curl tcp 10.244.1.152:65175 -> 23.212.250.69:443
📤 exit    default/xwing /usr/bin/curl -Lv https://cloud.oracle.com 0
📤 exit    default/xwing /bin/bash  0
...[output truncated]
```

These events are monitored directly from within the kernel, so very little can be obfuscated or masked by a malicious actor.

The primary downside to this approach is that actions you can take (such as killing a process that reads a file) are reactionary: You know about the event as it is happening, not beforehand. Still, it is extremely powerful to be able to have a low-overhead solution for filtering and matching events at the kernel level and being able to create policies that can help you observe and act on them.

Summary

This chapter covered several services and choices that enable you to observe both your infrastructure and your applications in OCI. OCI services always emit metrics and logs that can be captured and analyzed. The services that enable this functionality can also do it for your applications. OCI Monitoring can capture, store, and search through the metric data that OCI services and your applications generate. Monitoring is also integrated with alarms that can trigger other systems by creating notifications. OCI Logging can capture, index, and search through logs generated by OCI services and your application. This can help you understand patterns in application use and behavior. OCI Logging also includes audit logging and support for custom logging for your applications. Apart from these services, the OCI Logging Analytics service has features that can ingest metrics and logs from a multitude of services and provide deep insights into your applications and infrastructure, with minimal configuration. You can also bring in your own tools and processes to monitor your OCI resources and assets. For most cloud native applications running on Kubernetes, the Prometheus and Grafana stack is a popular choice for gathering and visualizing metrics. This chapter included an overview of setting up this popular set of tools on OKE, including how to set up OCI plug-ins for Grafana. eBPF is an emerging technology that is often used for observability, and this chapter also covered its installation and use on OCI with the popular open-source project Tetragon.

References

1   Supported monitoring services: https://docs.oracle.com/en-us/iaas/Content/Monitoring/Concepts/monitoringoverview.htm#SupportedServices

2   SDK example for posting metric data for your application to OCI Monitoring: https://github.com/oracle/oci-java-sdk/blob/master/bmc-examples/src/main/java/MonitoringMetricPostExample.java

3   CloudEvents: https://cloudevents.io/

4   OCI Logs data source for Grafana: https://grafana.com/grafana/plugins/oci-logs-datasource/

5   OCI Metrics data source for Grafana: https://grafana.com/grafana/plugins/oci-metrics-datasource/

9

DevOps and Deployment Automation

Automation is a key element of building and managing cloud native applications at scale. Cloud platforms and cloud native architecture patterns have more loosely coupled moving parts than a traditional monolithic application deployed on persistent legacy hardware platforms. Although cloud native architecture provides unprecedented development velocity, resilience, and cost optimization, it also introduces additional operational overhead. Automation is an essential component to overcome this overhead and realize the benefits of a cloud native approach to application development.

Automation systems are not a new concept; many have existed since long before cloud native development was a mainstream idea. Several of these platforms have introduced support for working with cloud platforms and environments such as Kubernetes clusters. The advent of cloud native development has also given rise to a new breed of tools and approaches for continuous integration/continuous deployment (CI/CD) systems that embrace DevOps culture. One example is building infrastructure as code, a type of automation that enables you to use code to express the flows that build, test, deploy, and manage your applications as well as infrastructure. Managing these automation flows as definitions that describe the automation flow in an easy-to-read format is one way to introduce DevOps practices to CI/CD systems. These codified automation flows can be source controlled, making them easy to replicate and to use for tracing changes and making the automation platform itself more resilient to failures. A traditional system might rely on an always active pool of agents that are kept around indefinitely to perform the various tasks of a CI/CD system, such as to compile applications, run tests, and orchestrate deployment jobs. In a traditional environment, this is acceptable because operations teams are working with preprovisioned capacity that is specifically allocated for the CI/CD system. In a cloud-based environment, however, this leads to a massive waste of resources because these resources could have been requested just-in-time, allowing the system to optimize on cost while also being able to scale well beyond the preprovisioned capacity by which a traditional CI/CD system is limited.

Several of the tools that embrace a DevOps approach are themselves cloud native. Some are cloud-based services, such as GitHub actions; others are self-hosted platforms that support cloud native deployment models, such as ArgoCD and Jenkins. Jenkins, one of the most popular CI/CD platforms, has evolved from its on-premises origins to a modern cloud-aware platform. This also puts Jenkins in a unique position to handle non-cloud native pipelines and targets (such as building, testing, and deploying a monolithic application to an on-premises server) just as well as it can handle cloud native pipelines and targets (such as building and pushing container images and deploying microservices to a Kubernetes cluster). Because Jenkins is based on a plug-in model, it can be extended, and new functionality can be added quite easily. A thriving plug-in ecosystem is one of the main advantages of using Jenkins. OCI has plug-ins that help integrate Jenkins with the OCI platform as well. Tools such as ArgoCD and Flux take an opinionated approach to continuous deployment, called GitOps.

This chapter explores different automation platforms and methods, such as Jenkins, GitOps, ArgoCD, GitHub Actions, and OCI's native DevOps service, and how they work with OCI.

OCI DevOps Service

The OCI DevOps service is a fully managed CI/CD service that helps developers get started quickly and reap the benefits of a DevOps-oriented software development culture using OCI. The service includes everything required for building and delivering software, including managed Git repositories, build pipelines, repositories for build artifacts and Docker images, and sophisticated deployment management tools. As with most other OCI services, the DevOps service provides an open platform. The DevOps service can integrate with a variety of external tools to enable developers to choose the specific features of the service that give them the most benefit, instead of asking them to use the entire platform. For instance, a developer might have an existing Git repository and build tools within the enterprise for compliance reasons, but might use the DevOps service deployment tooling for its capability to integrate with private OKE clusters. This section introduces the DevOps service and examines some of the most common integrations and workflows when building cloud native applications.

The OCI DevOps service relies on several concepts that should be familiar to most developers. Nevertheless, it pays to introduce these concepts and how they relate to each other. This way, you can start to see the service as a set of capabilities to choose from and integrate with your favorite tools and open-source solutions.

The fundamental grouping construct in DevOps is that of a *project*. A project provides a common space for grouping DevOps capabilities that work in concert to build and deliver a related set of applications. The project can group DevOps resources such as code repositories, build pipelines, artifacts, triggers, deployment pipelines, and environments that are related to a set of applications that are managed together, typically by the same team. Figure 9-1 illustrates the components and overall workflow in the DevOps service:

1. Code is committed into a *code repository*. The code repository could be mirrored from an external repository using a DevOps connection.
2. Committing code can *trigger* a *build pipeline*.

3. A *build pipeline* executes a *build specification*.

4. Execution of the build pipeline typically creates *artifacts*.

5. A build can trigger a *deployment pipeline*.

6. The *deployment pipeline* delivers artifacts to a target *environment*.

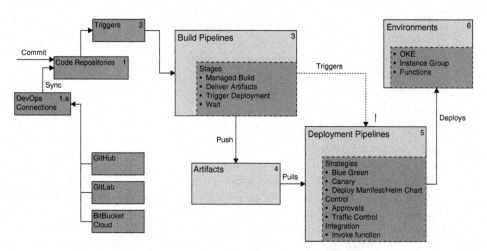

Figure 9-1 DevOps Service Components and Workflow

Code Repositories

Code repositories are Git repositories that are hosted and managed by the DevOps service. You can access these repositories using SSH or HTTPS; the access is controlled through OCI Identity and Access Management (IAM). The SSH mode of access uses an SSH key pair that is configured as OCI API keys. Although you can use the same key pair for multiple uses (say, for the CLI as well as Git access), using separate key pairs for groups of resources is typically a good way to isolate and even remove access to specific sets of resources, and it limits the reach of any one key pair.

When using SSH, the username you specify is in the format
`[federation_provider/]user_name@tenancy_name`

The HTTPS mode of access uses Auth Tokens, which are also managed through OCI IAM. When using HTTPS, the username you specify is in the format
`tenancy_name/[federation_provider/]user_name`

In either case, the federation_provider is optional and used only when using federated identities.

External Connections and Mirroring Repositories

In many scenarios, especially when transitioning from an existing source control provider to OCI DevOps, you might want to use the existing repo as the primary repository. In these cases, you can choose to *mirror*, or periodically sync, the commits from the existing repository to the DevOps platform so that you can set up and validate any automation processes without impacting developers' workflows until you are ready to make a switch.

Mirroring works with both GitLab and GitHub using personal access tokens (PATs). These tokens are generated on the respective platforms and should have the capability to read the repositories; they are stored as secrets in an OCI vault. An *external connection* is a DevOps resource that can connect and access external services such as GitHub or GitLab on behalf of the user.

External connections can be used for build source integration when a build pipeline can use the external repository directly. External connections can be used by repository mirroring as well, which updates your code repository in OCI with commits from an external repository. Repository mirroring uses the external connection resource to query and access external repositories using the personal access token associated with that external connection. The steps to set up mirroring are as follows:

1. Create an access token in GitHub/GitLab.
2. Add it as a secret to an OCI vault.
3. Create an external connection.
4. Create a dynamic group for external connections.
5. Create a policy to grant it read permissions on vault secrets.
6. Choose the external connection for mirroring a repository. The console lists the external repositories available.
7. Choose the repository to mirror, and set the interval for the sync operation.

Triggers

As the name suggests, *triggers* in the DevOps service are a way to start build pipelines in response to an event in the source management system, such as pushing new commits to a branch. The most common use for a trigger is to start a build when a new commit is pushed to the repository or when a Pull Request is merged. The type of events that can be used in a trigger depends on the type of the repository. GitHub and GitLab repositories have collaboration flows that use Pull Requests (also known as Merge Requests in GitLab). When using these repositories, triggers can be based on events related to Pull Requests, such as when a Pull Request is opened, updated, merged, or reopened.

Note

Deployment triggers are stages in the build pipelines and are similar in naming to triggers within a DevOps project. However, these are stages that the build service supports to trigger external workflows.

Build Pipelines

Build pipelines are one of the most central constructs in the DevOps service. At a high level, build pipelines provide a fully managed continuous integration environment within OCI that consists of an orchestration model and a managed environment for building application code into artifacts. Build pipelines also integrate with artifact repositories and deployment tooling.

The build pipeline uses a set of *stages* to describe the build process and to allow the developer to control its flow. A typical build pipeline executes multiple stages, such as running a build tool (which performs the actual build), storing the artifacts (such as application bundles or container images) into an artifact repository, and triggering other processes. Stages in a DevOps pipeline are predefined and represent the various actions, such as compiling source code, running vulnerability checks, and delivering artifacts that form the overall build process. Stages can be executed in sequence or in parallel. For instance, if a single source repository contains the source code for multiple microservices, you can make the build process more efficient by building the microservices in parallel. In such cases, the DevOps pipeline can perform complex orchestrations, such as performing multiple builds in parallel, storing the individual artifacts, and handling multiple deployments.

Build pipelines provide the following stages:

1. Managed Build
2. Deliver Artifacts
3. Trigger Deployment
4. Wait

Of these, the *Managed Build* stage is the heart of the build pipeline. This stage provides a managed build environment, an ephemeral compute instance for running builds—a build runner. The build process for running a build is described as code that uses a build specification that you commit to your source repository. The Managed Build stage is simply pointed to the repository and told where to expect the build specification; the service does the rest. The build specification describes the build environment and the build process in a sequence of steps that is executed by the build runner.

The other stages provide supporting control flow, such as delivering the artifacts generated by the Managed Build stage to appropriate repositories. If the managed build generates a container image, the *Deliver Artifacts* stage can move that image in to OCIR; similarly, if the managed build produces a language-dependent artifact, such as a `.jar` file or similar generic artifact, it can deliver those to the Artifact Registry.

The *Trigger Deployment* stage can trigger a deployment pipeline, typically after a managed build has run and the artifacts it created have been delivered to a repository.

The *Wait* stage pauses the pipeline for a specific duration. This is useful when interacting with external systems that might take a few moments to process an action. For instance, an artifact repository might want to run a vulnerability scan on every new artifact before allowing users to pull that artifact from the repository.

Understanding the `build_spec` Structure

The build specification describes how a build runner should run a build. It is a YAML document that describes how the build runner should be configured and what steps should be run by the build, in what order. The default name for the build specification is either `build_spec.yaml` or `build_spec.yml`, and the managed build looks for it in the root of the source repository. If the file is located in a nonstandard location, the Managed

Build stage configuration can specify a relative path to it. When a Managed Build stage is executed, the service performs the following sequence of actions:

1. Provisions a build runner. An ephemeral instance is provisioned to perform the build.
2. Sets up the build environment. The build runners are configured with tools and runtimes, such as the JDK or Android runtimes, source control utilities, CLIs, and tools such as gradle, Docker, and the OCI CLI.
3. Downloads the source code onto the build runner.
4. Locates, parses, and validates the `build_spec.yaml` file.
5. Executes the build_spec configuration, including handling the environment setup, downloading input artifacts, performing the build steps, and saving the output artifacts.

If multiple artifacts must be built from the same source repository, one strategy to consider is to use multiple build spec files that can be run in parallel stages within the build pipeline. Parallel managed build steps are run on separate build runners. This typically speeds up the overall build process for when multiple artifacts need to be built. The builds can be executed in isolation, without depending on artifacts from each other. Listing 9-1 shows a sample `build_spec.yaml` file.

Listing 9-1   Sample `build_spec.yaml` File

```
# Metadata section

version: 0.1
component: build
timeoutInSeconds: 6000
runAs: root
shell: bash

# Environment section

env:

  # these are local variables to the build config
  variables:
    key: "value"

  # the value of a vaultVariable is the secret-id (in OCI ID format) stored in the
  OCI Vault service
  # you can then access the value of that secret in your build_spec.yaml commands
  vaultVariables:

  # exportedVariables are made available to use as parameters in successor Build
  Pipeline stages
  # For this Build to run, the Build Pipeline needs to have a BUILDRUN_HASH
  parameter set
  exportedVariables:
```

```
      - BUILDRUN_HASH
steps:
  - type: Command
    name: "Export variables"
    timeoutInSeconds: 40
    command: |
      export BUILDRUN_HASH=`echo ${OCI_BUILD_RUN_ID} | rev | cut -c 1-7`
      echo "BUILDRUN_HASH: " $BUILDRUN_HASH
      uname -a
      docker --version
    onFailure:
      - type: Command
        timeoutInSeconds: 40
        command: |
          echo "Handling Failure"
          echo "Failure successfully handled"
        timeoutInSeconds: 400
        runAs: root

  - type: Command
    timeoutInSeconds: 1200
    name: "Build container image"
    command: |
      cd ${OCI_PRIMARY_SOURCE_DIR}
      docker build -t demo-hugo-site:${BUILDRUN_HASH} -f Dockerfile .
    onFailure:
      - type: Command
        command: |
          echo "Handling Failure"
          echo "Failure successfully handled"
        timeoutInSeconds: 60
        runAs: root

outputArtifacts:
  - name: output01
    type: DOCKER_IMAGE
    location: <region>.ocir.io/<tenancy_namespace>/demo-site:${BUILDRUN_HASH}
```

The example shows that the build spec is divided into multiple sections. The first section shows metadata about the build spec itself. The version indicates the version of the build spec used; at the time of writing, the only supported value is 0.1. The component indicates the kind of spec file this is; for build spec files, the only applicable value is build, as shown. The default shell used for running builds on a build runner is bash, and this can be overridden to use sh with the shell attribute. Build runners do not support sudo; for scenarios that need superuser privileges, the runAs attribute can be set to root to execute either the whole build or an individual step as the root user. The timeoutInSeconds sets the timeout for steps at the build scope. If the timeout is not specified, the implicit default is 8 hours, which is also the maximum value allowed for timeouts.

The env sections hold environment variables that can be used during the build. env can have three types of variables, named variables, vaultVariables, and exportedVariables. variables are key-value pairs that are declared and whose values can be updated by any build step. vaultVariables are OCI vault secrets that can be used during the build process. The typical purpose for these is to reference a password or an auth token used to log into a private OCIR registry so that images that are built by a build pipeline can be uploaded to the registry. In the build spec, the value of this variable is an OCID that represents the vault secret. When the build runner executes the build, it fetches the actual secret and provides it to all the build steps that reference this variable. This avoids having to create build_spec.yaml files that embed secrets. exportedVariables are a list of variables that are declared and whose value can be set in any stage of the build. A value set for the variable is available in all subsequent steps of the build spec. In the example, BUILDRUN_HASH is an exported variable whose value is set in the first step. It is then used in the subsequent step to tag the container image that was built.

The steps section of the build spec specifies the commands that are to be sequentially executed for running the build. The command can be a multiline command or a single-line command, and each command can be accompanied by a timeout value that overrides the timeout for this step from the one set at the build spec scope. The name is a descriptive field that can be used to trace the progress of the build or to troubleshoot the build using logs. Every step can also have an optional onFailure attribute that is also of type Command, which runs the specified command to perform cleanup or otherwise gracefully exit the build step in the event of a failure. The runAs and timeoutInSeconds values can be overridden at each step from the build scoped values set in the metadata section.

The outputArtifacts identifies the artifacts produced by the build. Artifacts can be of either BINARY or DOCKER_IMAGE type. For a BINARY artifact, the location points to where the artifact can be found. If the artifact cannot be found in the specified location, the build fails. If the artifact is of type DOCKER_IMAGE, the image needs to have been either built or pulled by one of the build steps, or the build fails. The location attribute for an artifact of type DOCKER_IMAGE is the image name and tag.

Artifacts

Artifacts in DevOps are resources that identify entities that can be deployed. Artifacts are typically created by a build pipeline as its output. However, they can also exist independently and be created or managed outside a build pipeline because the build and deploy aspects of the DevOps service can be used independently. This is usually the case for artifacts that are created by external build tools, which can be represented in the deployment service using the artifact resource. Likewise, the artifacts that are produced by the build pipelines can be represented by the artifact resource, and their deployment can be handled using external tools.

Artifacts can be of various types, including a container image in OCIR, a generic artifact such as a .jar file that is stored in the Artifact Registry, Kubernetes deployment manifests, or Helm charts. For most cloud native applications, developers will be building their applications as container images and deploying to platforms such as OKE using a Kubernetes manifest or a Helm chart.

To use the OCIR container image repository with a build pipeline, the user first creates an *artifact* that represents this image repository. This creates the artifact resource that the DevOps build pipeline can use to interact with the container image repository to push the image that the build generates. The build service includes a stage called *Deliver Artifacts* that can be used after the Managed Build stage to deliver the artifacts created from a managed build to an artifact repository. The Deliver Artifacts stage maps the outputArtifacts identified in the build spec with artifact resources in the DevOps service. This mapping ensures that the artifacts created in the build are propagated and delivered to the appropriate artifact stores.

Figure 9-2 shows a build pipeline with a Managed Build stage that uses a build spec from a source repository. The Managed Build stage uses the build spec to execute the various steps in the build and produces artifacts such as a container image. The outputArtifacts section of the build spec identifies the artifacts that are created by the build. The subsequent Deliver Artifacts stage associates the artifacts identified in the outputArtifacts section of the build to a DevOps artifact resource. The stage then delivers the artifact (such as the container image) to the artifact store (such as OCI Container Image Registry).

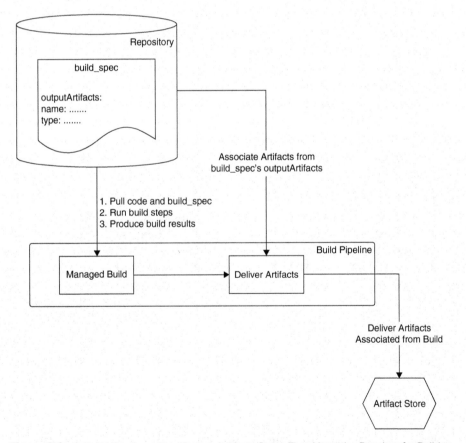

Figure 9-2   A Build Pipeline with a Deliver Artifacts Stage That Maps the Results of a Build to Artifact Resources and Delivers the Artifacts to the Artifact Store

Artifact references are most used by deployment pipelines to represent and identify the workload that is to be deployed to a target platform. Helm charts and Kubernetes manifests are typical examples of artifacts that are not generated by a build process; instead, they are stored either as an inline artifact (Kubernetes manifest) or in OCIR (Helm chart). These artifacts are referenced by deployment pipelines during deployment.

Environments

Environments are resources in DevOps that represent the target platforms or execution environments for deploying your artifacts. They identify a target platform, such as an OKE cluster, and the environment reference is used to interact with these target platforms when deploying artifacts to them. The DevOps service supports multiple OCI services, such as OKE, Compute Instance Groups, and OCI Functions, to be represented as environment resources. The kind of artifact is related to the kind of environment in which artifacts have a natural deployment target type. For instance, a Kubernetes manifest or a Helm chart is always deployed to a Kubernetes cluster, whereas an instance group deployment configuration is targeted at a compute instance group.

The environment reference is most used from the deployment pipeline, as a way to identify an execution environment for a deployment. The target environment can be in any region that the tenancy is subscribed to. This enables the DevOps service to roll out changes to global/multiregion applications with ease and precision.

Deployment Pipelines

A deployment pipeline is the feature that provides the continuous deployment capability in the DevOps service. Deployment pipelines can be used to construct deployment workflows that push artifacts onto environments. Like the build pipelines, deployment pipelines consist of stages that can be run serially or in parallel. A deployment pipeline's stages can be categorized as stages that perform workflow control, perform integrations, or do deployments to target environments. Each group offers various strategies that can be used to form a complete workflow. For instance, control stages provide control flow in the deployment process, such as when getting approvals for deployments or performing traffic shift between environments. Deployment pipelines natively support advanced deployment strategies such as blue-green deployments or canary deployments out of the box. This native support for these deployment models makes it easy to implement them in application deployment workflows using deployment pipelines. The build pipeline and deployment pipeline can be used independently or with each other. They are loosely coupled, to allow developers to use their proffered tools for each job. For instance, an enterprise might mandate that its builds be done on existing on-premises environments and tooling. A build pipeline also offers integration between build and deployment pipelines, allowing variable export and triggering deployments on successful builds.

In a cloud native environment, the most common deployment environment is an OKE cluster. For a better security posture, OKE clusters are usually configured with private API endpoints that are accessible only from within the tenancy or from an on-premises network that is peered with the VCN. This limited visibility for the Kubernetes API endpoints can add configuration steps to the deployment tool that needs to access these APIs. Deployment pipelines can also easily deploy to private OKE clusters. To set up deployments to private OKE clusters, at the time of creating the OKE environment, select the VCN and the subnet where the Kubernetes API endpoint has been created (see Figure 9-3). Access can further be controlled using the security lists or NSGs on the subnet.

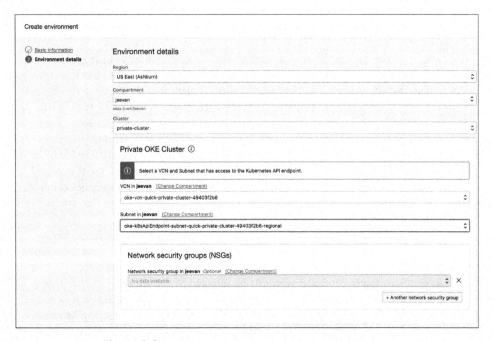

Figure 9-3 Setting Up Deployments to Private OKE Clusters

Understanding Deployment Strategies

Consider an application that is deployed to OKE. The deployment process applies the application definition, which could be a set of Kubernetes manifests, to the OKE cluster. In this process, the build system is not involved, and it is assumed that the container images that are required for the application are already built and available at the repository URL that is referenced in the manifest files. These images could have been built by the DevOps build pipeline, or they could have been built by other tools, perhaps on an on-premises build system. How the application was built and packaged does not matter to the deployment tooling because the deployable artifacts here are either a set of Kubernetes manifests or a Helm chart. These deployable artifacts can reference the container images needed to run the application.

The deployment offers three kinds of deployment strategies for OKE-based environments:

- In-place deployments
- Blue/green deployments
- Canary deployments

In-place deployments are the most basic: This type of deployment simply amounts to redeploying an application over the existing one. In-place deployments are optimal, in terms of resource usage, but they also afford lesser control over the rollout (and potential rollback) of the changes because the newly deployed changes are made available to all users at the same time.

A *blue-green deployment model* maintains two identical environments. One is considered the blue (live traffic) environment, and the other is the green (no live traffic) environment. New versions are deployed to the green environment, and regression tests and sanity checks are performed. When everything looks good, the traffic is switched from the blue environment to the green environment; the green environment is then considered to be the new blue environment. Although this strategy requires more resources (a second environment), it affords much better control over the transition. If the sanity checks fail, the traffic switch does not have to happen. If an issue is detected, even after the traffic has switched, a rollback process is simple and just switches the traffic back to the old environment. This strategy is more suited to applications that are highly sensitive to disruptions.

Finally, *canary deployments* offer a strategy to gradually move traffic from one version to another. When deployed to OKE environments, the canary and blue-green strategies use namespaces within the same cluster. They also rely on an ingress resource, for which a NGINX ingress controller needs to be installed in the cluster. In OKE-based environments, the primary difference in the way these two strategies operate is how the traffic is shifted from the old deployment to the new deployment. In the blue-green strategy, the traffic is switched from one environment to another, based on validation and approval, and all the traffic is switched. This means that users experience either the old application or the new one.

The canary strategy, by contrast, temporarily shifts a specific percentage of traffic from the production version to the new version until approval to deploy to production is received. Once the approval to deploy to production is received, the production deployment is replaced and all traffic then is restored to the production deployment. While the canary version is deployed and waiting to be approved for production deployment, users can experience both versions of the application.

Setting Up a Canary Deployment

Performing a canary deployment to an OKE cluster is one of the most common tasks for developers to carry out when working with deployment pipelines. To get started, first deploy the NGINX ingress controller on to the OKE cluster using the Kubernetes manifests that the project publishes:

```
kubectl apply -f https://raw.githubusercontent.com/kubernetes/ingress-nginx/
  controller-v1.2.0/deploy/static/provider/cloud/deploy.yaml
```

Note

The installation instructions for the latest version can be found at https://kubernetes.github.io/ingress-nginx.

This creates the `ingress-nginx` namespace and installs the NGINX ingress controller. The ingress controller uses a LoadBalancer to expose the ingress resources externally. Its IP address can be retrieved from the service object in the `ingress-nginx` namespace using the following command:

```
kubectl get svc/ingress-nginx-controller -n ingress-nginx
```

Next, create an artifact. The artifact in Listing 9-2 deploys an Apache Tomcat container with six replicas. This Kubernetes deployment can be exposed to other resources using a ClusterIP service. Finally, an ingress resource exposes the service externally under the path `/tomcat` using the NGINX ingress controller. This can be created as an inline artifact.

Listing 9-2 An Example Apache Tomcat Deployment

```
apiVersion: apps/v1
kind: Deployment
metadata:
  name: tomcat
  labels:
    app: tomcat
spec:
  replicas: 6
  selector:
    matchLabels:
      app: tomcat
  template:
    metadata:
      labels:
        app: tomcat
    spec:
      containers:
        - name: tomcat
          image: tomcat:9
```

```
        ports:
          - containerPort: 8080
---
apiVersion: v1
kind: Service
metadata:
  name: tomcat-service
  labels:
    app: tomcat
spec:
  ports:
  - port: 80
    name: http
    targetPort: 8080
  selector:
    app: tomcat
  type: ClusterIP
---
apiVersion: networking.k8s.io/v1
kind: Ingress
metadata:
  name: ingress-tomcat
spec:
  rules:
  -   http:
        paths:
        - path: /tomcat
          pathType: Prefix
          backend:
            service:
              name: tomcat-service
              port:
                number: 80
  ingressClassName: nginx
```

Next, add a deployment pipeline and add a canary deployment stage to the pipeline. The canary deployment stage prompts for the environment reference, the artifact reference, and the canary namespace, as shown in Figure 9-4.

Optionally, you can validate the deployment using a function that can run tests against the new version and return a `true` or `false` response to the deployment pipeline. You can also see the traffic limits for the canary. This is the percentage of traffic the canary deployment will receive; it can range from 1% to 25% of the traffic. You can also set the number of approvals required to perform the production deployment. When the required approvals have been received, the deployment is made to the production namespace of your choice in the cluster. A basic canary deployment with all its steps looks like Figure 9-5.

Figure 9-4   Adding a Canary Deployment Stage to the Pipeline

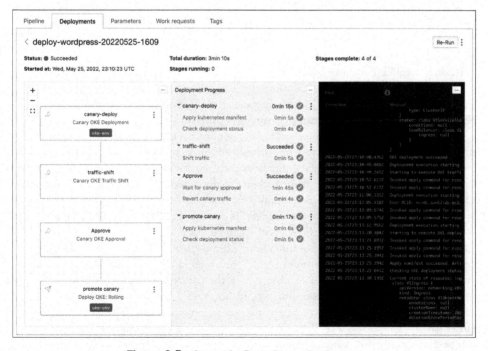

Figure 9-5   Steps of a Basic Canary Deployment

When the deployment pipeline runs, it deploys the artifact (the manifest) to the canary namespace. It then performs the traffic shift step, which annotates the NGINX ingress with canary annotations that direct a percentage of traffic to the canary deployment. The ingress resource for the canary deployment would be annotated as shown in the following example. These annotations cause the ingress controller to ensure that only the predefined percentage of traffic is sent to the canary deployment:

```
nginx.ingress.kubernetes.io/canary: true
nginx.ingress.kubernetes.io/canary-by-header: redirect-to-canary
nginx.ingress.kubernetes.io/canary-weight: 25
```

The deployment process blocks and waits on the approval stage. When the approval has been received, the deployment pipeline resumes by reverting the traffic shift and promoting the canary deployment to production. The blue-green strategy also works in a similar fashion: The artifacts described in the previous listings can be used to replace the canary build stage with a blue-green deployment that deploys the new version of the application to a separate namespace in Kubernetes and switches traffic after an optional verification step.

Elastically Scaling Jenkins on Kubernetes

Jenkins[1] is probably the most well-known CI/CD server today. The long history of Jenkins as an active open-source project has led it to continuously evolve and integrate new technologies such as Kubernetes. Jenkins uses a plug-in model for extensions, and its plug-in ecosystem boasts a vibrant community that is continuously adding and extending capabilities. Some Jenkins plug-ins, such as BlueOcean, offer an opinionated CI/CD workflow with a simplified user interface; others, such as the Kubernetes plug-in, fundamentally change how Jenkins operates. Jenkins itself can be deployed on to a Kubernetes cluster, for better management and elasticity.

At a high level, Jenkins operates on the concept of having a controller and having multiple agents. This is similar to Kubernetes itself, in some respects. The controller in Jenkins manages the various agents, monitors them, and schedules jobs on the agents under its management. The agents in Jenkins are the worker nodes that perform jobs. Continuous delivery in Jenkins is typically done using Jenkins pipelines. The pipeline is the definition of the steps that are needed for code in a code repository to be built into software packages and for those packages to be delivered to your end users. Jenkins uses a text file named `Jenkinsfile` to express these steps and is typically source controlled alongside the application source. When a build job is started, the steps in the `Jenkinsfile` are executed on an agent to which the controller assigns the job.

In traditional on-premises environments, Jenkins uses a system in which a set of controllers is configured with a predefined set of Jenkins agents. The agents are either bare metal machines or VMs that are preconfigured for certain use. They can be preconfigured in a homogeneous way, in which an enterprise has a baseline configuration for all build jobs; they also can have specific configurations or software packages, such as compilers or other build tools, preinstalled on them. These static installations usually do not get a lot of utilization because an agent that has been configured for a specific project with specialized tooling will not typically be used 24×7 unless it is a very high velocity project. Keeping track of the configuration on the agents can also be cumbersome over time.

Jenkins does not require agents to be static. An agent can be a bare metal machine, a virtual machine, or a container. This can be a machine on-premises, or it can be in the cloud. The only real requirement for an agent is that it must be any type of compute that can run Java. This is because the component that runs on the agent and communicates with the controller requires Java. Applying the cloud native best practices and principles to the Jenkins model and leveraging the plug-in model in Jenkins, the Kubernetes plug-in allows Jenkins to operate using Kubernetes primitives.

Note

Oracle has made an OCI plug-in available that can provision OCI compute instances of any shape and dynamically connect them as agents to a Jenkins controller.

Setting Up Jenkins on OKE

Setting up a scalable Jenkins environment on OKE is as easy as installing the Jenkins Helm chart. The command in Listing 9-3 adds the Jenkins Helm chart repository and installs Jenkins in a namespace called jenkins; then it overrides the serviceType and servicePort to use a load balancer listening on the default HTTP port. Running the commands displays further commands to be run that show the default generated password for the default user admin, how to identify the load balancer IP address, and how to access the Jenkins login page.

Listing 9-3 Adding the Jenkins Helm Repo and Configuring the Namespace serviceType and servicePort

```
helm repo add jenkins https://charts.jenkins.io
helm repo update
helm install jenkins jenkins/jenkins -n jenkins --create-namespace \
--set controller.serviceType=LoadBalancer \
--set controller.servicePort=80
```

Note

This installation is a good starting point for exploring how to run Jenkins on OKE. The Jenkins Helm chart gives the developer a lot of control. Developers should refer to the official documentation to implement security and configuration practices that are suited for production use.

The Helm chart installs the Kubernetes plug-in and configures it for using the same Kubernetes cluster where you are installing Jenkins. The Kubernetes plug-in enables a Jenkins server to create agents that are pods. As pods, these "agents" are created when they are needed and discarded when the job is completed. The Kubernetes plug-in has a configuration that points it to a target Kubernetes cluster where new pods will be created to serve as Jenkins agents. Each project defines the agent configuration as a pod template in the Jenkinsfile that is associated with that project. When the Jenkins pipeline executes, a new pod is created in the Kubernetes cluster using the configuration in the Jenkinsfile. This configuration can include the specialized tools required for each project. For instance, one project could be using Java 11 and another could be using Java 15, and you no longer must have agents that are preconfigured with these tool chains always on standby. Instead, the agent configuration is expressed as a pod that can be based on container images that have the required tooling. Listing 9-4 shows an example of this configuration in a Jenkinsfile.

Listing 9-4   Example Pod Template in a Jenkinsfile

```
podTemplate(yaml: '''
    apiVersion: v1
    kind: Pod
    spec:
      containers:
      - name: gradle
        image: gradle:7-jdk11
        command:
        - sleep
        args:
        - 99d
''') {
    node(POD_LABEL) {
        stage('Clone repo') {
            git 'https://github.com/oracle-quickstart/oci-cloudnative.git'
            container('gradle') {
                stage('Clean'){
                    sh 'cd src/orders &&  gradle clean '
                }
                stage('Build app') {
                    sh 'cd src/orders &&  gradle  compileJava '
                }
                stage('Run Tests') {
                    sh 'cd src/orders &&  gradle  test '
                }
                stage('package app') {
                    sh 'cd src/orders &&  gradle bootJar'
                }
```

```
            }
        }
    }
}
```

> **Note**
>
> The build stages are split into separate steps, to demonstrate nested stages. In most builds, this can be a single nested step.

The `podTemplate` defines a pod for running as an agent. The example in Listing 9-4 shows a single container that uses the `gradle:7-jdk11` image. The pod definition can have multiple containers as well. The Kubernetes plug-in always has one container named `jnlp` in the pod; that container runs the Jenkins JNLP agent service that connects to the Jenkins controller and registers the pod as an agent. The first stage clones the Git repo for the application source code. The `container('gradle')` construct selects the container named `gradle` from the `podTemplate` to run its nested stages. The next few stages run inside the `gradle` container; they run the build and unit tests before packaging the application as a JAR file. Figure 9-6 shows the pipeline execution in Jenkins.

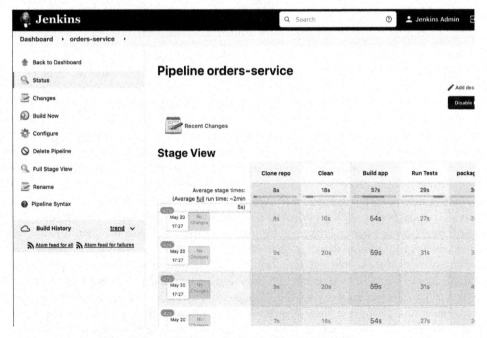

Figure 9-6 Example Jenkins Pipeline Execution

This means that each project can define its build environment and use tools and configurations that are unique to it without having to maintain a large fleet of agents. Because these dependencies are also described as code in the `Jenkinsfile` that is source controlled, developers can easily implement changes to the build environment and tools with the complete traceability that the source control system provides. As the job is queued in Jenkins, perhaps because of a new commit in the source control, the Kubernetes plug-in spawns a pod as an agent and executes the pipeline on that pod. When the job is complete, the pod or that agent is terminated. In this way, Jenkins can truly become elastic, running on a smaller fleet with better utilization rates and using the underlying capabilities of Kubernetes. It also opens the doors to using Kubernetes-based scaling (such as cluster autoscaling) to grow and shrink the Jenkins fleet when required.

GitOps with ArgoCD

Developer workflows are centered on source control systems (usually Git) for application code and infrastructure expressed as code. GitOps is a set of practices that expand on developers' Git-based workflows to provide automated workflows for applications as well as infrastructure. This enables every change in the system, application, or infrastructure to be traced back to a Git commit. Developers can keep track of changes and known good configurations while simplifying and standardizing the workflows for both infrastructure and application changes. Ops and support teams get better visibility into changes and can quickly re-create configurations to help troubleshoot issues. This makes deployments and rollbacks clear and predictable.

With GitOps, a desired configuration is described as code in the Git repository. This could be an application expressed as a Kubernetes manifest or infrastructure expressed as Terraform code. Changes to this configuration are detected by a tool such as ArgoCD[2] or Flux,[3] which can trigger a synchronization or reconciliation of the target environment to the new definition. This enables you to build a completely Git-based workflow using existing practices that developers are accustomed to. For instance, opening a pull request can be detected, and the result could be deployed to a test environment to have automated tests run on it, to ensure that the merge of the pull request will not cause regressions. A merge of that pull request then could deploy the now-tested code to the production environment.

Kubernetes can express applications and infrastructure through Kubernetes manifest files. This makes it an ideal candidate to be operated using the principles of GitOps. Kubernetes is not a hard requirement for implementing a GitOps model, but it makes for a natural fit. Other tools can implement GitOps as well. For instance, automation frameworks such as Ansible and Terraform can also be used to achieve GitOps principles. Regardless of the tools used or the platforms targeted by the deployment process, the essential concept in GitOps is that the Git repository acts as the single source of truth for configurations. Changes to these configurations are propagated to target environments by tools that interface with the Git repository and leverage Git-based workflows.

We chose to show how to deploy ArgoCD onto an OKE cluster and create a GitOps pipeline to describe how you can achieve GitOps practices in OCI. The choice to use

ArgoCD was arbitrary, and other tools (such as FluxCD) are equally applicable. Tools such as ArgoCD have one fundamental difference in how they operate, when compared to other tools in the space, such as Jenkins or GitLab: ArgoCD is Kubernetes focused, has Kubernetes-specific workflows, and understands Kubernetes objects natively. Tools such as ArgoCD are typically deployed on the Kubernetes cluster and work on the principle of pulling changes into a cluster. This is contrary to general-purpose tools such as Jenkins or GitLab that can exist outside the cluster as an independent system and push changes onto one or more target clusters when changes are detected in the Git repository.

ArgoCD itself runs on the Kubernetes cluster. The application controller in ArgoCD continuously monitors running applications and compares the live application state against the desired application state that is defined in the Git repository. This is what lets ArgoCD act when the configuration on the cluster diverges from what is in the Git repository. If a new configuration change has been pushed to the Git repository, ArgoCD detects that there is a difference between the desired state in Git and the current state in the cluster and then acts. It works in the reverse direction as well. Because the configuration contained in the Git repository is the source of truth, any changes on the cluster that Argo CD detects are a deviation from the desired configuration in the Git repository and cause ArgoCD to act as well. Running within the cluster also lets ArgoCD visualize the various Kubernetes objects that make up entire application deployments and their relationships.

Note

Although it is not mandated by GitOps principles, a best practice when using GitOps is to separate the code repositories from the configuration repositories. This allows the typical application workflow to be undisturbed, and perhaps even use existing tooling to build the code, test it, and archive the artifacts. However, once this has been done, a separate workflow can be kicked off to update the configuration that is updating the Kubernetes manifests or the Helm charts to reference the newly built images or configuration values. This allows the CI and CD portions of the workflow to operate completely independently from each other. Developers thus have more freedom when it comes to modifying the tools or workflows, without having to worry about cascading changes to other workflows. This separation of the application configuration from the application code also lets multiple teams collaborate effectively without stepping on each other's toes.

Setting Up Argo CD on OKE

Setting up Argo CD on OKE is as simple as deploying the ArgoCD manifests. The official documentation for deploying ArgoCD covers the steps in detail and also provides additional and optional tools for managing your deployment flow. To get started, create a namespace for ArgoCD and deploy the stable manifests from the ArgoCD GitHub project:

```
kubectl create namespace argocd
kubectl apply -n argocd -f https://raw.githubusercontent.com/argoproj/argo-cd/
  stable/manifests/install.yaml
```

This sets up ArgoCD on the cluster. By default, the ArgoCD server is exposed as a service of type `ClusterIP`. To access the server, developers can either create a port-forward for temporary access or change the service to use a `LoadBalancer` or ingress to expose the server more permanently.

The following command sets up a port-forward that listens on port 8080 on `localhost` and forwards to port 443 on the service:

```
kubectl port-forward service/argocd-server 8080:443 -n argocd
```

While the port-forward is running, developers can access `locahost:8080` to access ArgoCD. Using a port-forward can potentially result in a warning from the browser about the service using a self-signed certificate. The port-forward is temporary and is available only on the environment where `kubectl` is running. This can be useful for testing but not suitable for long-term or multiuser access.

To use a public LoadBalancer resource for the service, and to expose it externally and more permanently, the service object can be patched as follows:

```
kubectl patch svc argocd-server -n argocd -p '{"spec": {"type":
  "LoadBalancer"}}'
```

Alternatively, if the developer is using a private load balancer (in a private subnet) to limit exposure of services, as is popular in many enterprise environments, the annotations for a private load balancer can be added to the patch command as well. The additional annotation that follows creates an internal or private Load Balancer:

```
kubectl patch svc argocd-server -n argocd -p '{
   "metadata":{
      "annotations":{
         "service.beta.kubernetes.io/oci-load-balancerinternal":"true"
      }
   },
   "spec":{
      "type":"LoadBalancer"
   }
}'
```

When the ArgoCD service is exposed, developers can log into the ArgoCD UI. Visit `https://localhost:8080` if you are using port-forwarding, or use the IP address of the ArgoCD server if you are using a LoadBalancer. To log into the UI, you can retrieve the password for the default user. During installation, this password was generated by ArgoCD and stored as a Kubernetes secret. To retrieve the value, use the following code snippet:

```
kubectl -n argocd get secret argocd-initial-admin-secret -o jsonpath="{.data.
  password}" | base64 -d; echo
```

ArgoCD extends Kubernetes with custom resources such as *Application*. After logging into the ArgoCD UI, developers can create an Application in ArgoCD. These custom resources follow the GitOps model and define an application and its expected configuration using the deployable resource definitions stored in a Git repository. The *Application* resource in ArgoCD identifies the Git repository URL, the branch in the git repository to track changes from, and the path to the resource definition files, among other metadata. These resource definitions can be plain manifest files, Helm charts, or kustomize[4] overlays. Figure 9-7 shows an application that is managed by ArgoCD.

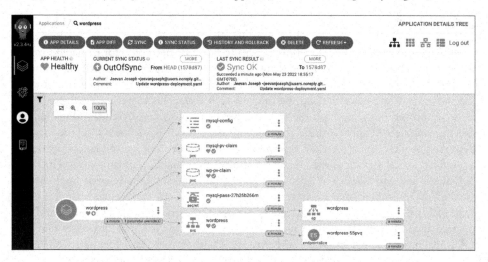

Figure 9-7   Managing an Application Using ArgoCD

ArgoCD runs a controller, named the Application Controller, in the OKE cluster and constantly monitors for changes between the live state and the target state. The live state is the state of the application deployed on the cluster. It can include the number of replicas or whether a service is of type `LoadBalancer` or `ClusterIP`. The target state is the desired state of the application, and it is defined by the resource definitions and values that are stored in the Git repository in the branch that the ArgoCD *Application* resource is tracking. The live and target state can diverge if someone pushes a new commit to the branch that the *Application* is tracking or if someone updates the live state using `kubectl` commands such as `patch`, `scale`, `create`, `delete`, or `apply`. If the live state and target state have diverged, regardless of where the change originated, ArgoCD considers this Application `OutOfSync`. Applications that are `OutOfSync` can be `Synced`, which essentially applies the definitions and values in the Git repository to converge the live state to the target state. This is because, when using GitOps practices, the Git repository is considered the source of truth.

Because ArgoCD constantly compares the live state with the desired state, it can also visualize the live state with several views. This can be a useful tool for visualizing applications and their topology. ArgoCD tracks the desired state in Git, so it can also create *diffs* between the live state and the desired state. This can help developers and ops teams trace application changes, troubleshoot issues, or roll back deployments.

Apart from the CD tooling, the Argo project offers tools such as Argo Rollouts and Argo Workflows. Argo Rollouts support multiple deployment strategies, such as canary deployments and blue-green deployments for Kubernetes. Argo Workflow provides a workflow engine that can be used to manage and scale data processing or similar workflows.

Summary

This chapter looked at a set of automation platforms and approaches for managing cloud native applications at scale. As cloud native applications get more distributed and loosely coupled, these options make it easy to build a loosely coupled fleet of applications that can move at various velocities and use the best-of-breed technologies for what they need to do. However, this also makes the task of building, deploying, patching, and upgrading this growing fleet of applications a challenge in itself. Automation tools and processes described in this chapter focus on this problem; they range from native platforms that are offered by OCI (such as the DevOps platform) to open-source platforms (such as Jenkins) and systems such as ArgoCD that embrace newer methodologies (such as GitOps). With its built-in feature set that supports OCI native services and integration with external tools and systems, the OCI DevOps platform offers a way to build and manage applications within OCI. This helps you consolidate tools and processes onto OCI, making management simple and effective. On the other hand, for users who already have a well-established process of managing cloud native applications, cloud native platforms in OCI (such as OKE) can seamlessly integrate with open-source tools such as Jenkins or ArgoCD so that you can bring your tools of choice and operate without altering your workflows.

References

1 Jenkins: https://www.jenkins.io/
2 Argo: https://argoproj.github.io/
3 Flux: https://fluxcd.io/
4 https://kustomize.io

10

Bringing It Together: MuShop

Throughout this book, we've examined many cloud native development principles, techniques, and technologies. In this chapter, we describe a sample application, MuShop (pronounced Mew-Shop), that puts several of these notions and services in OCI into practice. The goal of this application is to provide a working example that implements the cloud native application design principles and technologies and showcases the operational model for such an application. It can act as a reference point for implementation concepts ranging from application development patterns to infrastructure and deployment automation, or it can act as inspiration for your own microservices. The complete source code for the example application is available on GitHub.[1]

It can be daunting at first for enterprise application developers to shift perspective to cloud native processes and practices, and it is common to view them with a healthy dose of skepticism. Yet cloud native applications are evolving and growing in scale all around us every day. As enterprises increasingly move to cloud providers for infrastructure, applications teams often face the tough choice of whether to refactor an enterprise application to a cloud native model or to simply "lift and shift" to cloud infrastructure. Many application teams choose to "lift and shift" because it offers the path of least resistance, short-term cost savings, and lower risk. The long-term costs, however, typically uncover the design shortcomings of the original application, which was never designed to be computationally elastic or to minimize operational cost. This is natural because these applications were designed for a CapEx[2] world, with an upfront infrastructure cost. The possibility of further cost optimization on the cloud invariably forces development teams to look for an operationally efficient model and to refactor the applications to achieve that elasticity. This path of lift-and-shift followed by planned optimization has proven to be a successful playbook for many organizations.

MuShop fits that traditional notion of a data-driven, transactional application, but reinvented as a set of distributed microservices and operated using cloud native principles and technologies. The reason to choose a transactional application for this example and not something more esoteric is to keep it within the realm of these everyday enterprise applications.

The motivation to build this application as a reference sample and demonstrate the various concepts and services covered in this book is twofold:

- To demonstrate the concepts to users who are new to cloud native development and to provide a deployable reference point that acts as a sandbox and a learning tool. Deploying code to a sandbox and examining how each component works is one of the best learning tools for developers.
- For experienced cloud native developers who are new to OCI, it provides a familiar application construct while introducing them to platforms and services within OCI.

MuShop showcases concepts, practices, and OCI services that are commonly used for cloud native development. In some respects, it has been overengineered, to prove a point or demonstrate features. For instance, most microservices in MuShop use a different programming language, framework, or technology stack. This is simply to demonstrate the polyglot possibilities with microservice architecture and the freedom it affords developers to choose the right tools for the job. This is not intended to suggest that all cloud native applications should consist of polyglot services. This chapter calls out these design choices and discusses them in detail. The name MuShop is a tongue-in-cheek reference to using micro (μ, mu) services to implement an e-commerce site that sells products for cats (mew!).

Architecture

Microservices architecture breaks down complex software systems into smaller, independent application processes. These smaller applications focus on some specific functionality that they can provide as a service, exposed through a well-defined interface. These applications are independently deployed and operated, but they communicate with each other over the interfaces they expose. The originally complex system now consists of much smaller entities that focus on very specific areas and functionality, so it becomes easier to isolate bottlenecks, scale the system, rearchitect just parts of it (maintaining the interface contracts), and more. This is not just an architectural approach to building modern applications that are scalable, portable, and resilient; it is also a software development methodology, in that it enables independent teams to build, test, and release software in relative isolation. This approach also allows teams to implement functionality, using any tools or technology stacks of their choice, as long as the interface contracts and API protocols are honored. Many of these applications also leverage the twelve-factor application methodology,[3] which is a set of popular guiding principles to implement software that is to be delivered as a service. Because most microservices are implementations in which some functionality is delivered as a service, the twelve-factor methodology is great at providing implementation guidance.

MuShop implements an e-commerce use case—a website that delivers a shopping experience for products, carts, order management, and more. MuShop consists of several microservices written in various languages, using frameworks and libraries that are popular in their respective communities. Each service exposes or provides a REST API that makes up the features of the service. The choice to use REST as the API protocol in these services (instead of other choices, such as gRPC) is a conscious one; although gRPC offers several advantages over REST in terms of efficiencies and performance, REST is more familiar to the wider audience and makes the examples more relatable for users. Figure 10-1 shows the high-level architecture of MuShop.

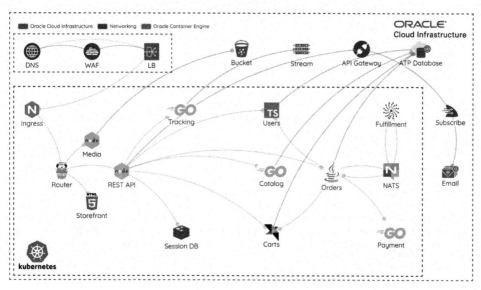

Figure 10-1   High-Level Architecture of the MuShop Example Application—Each Microservice Uses Its Own Stack to Demonstrate the Polyglot Nature of This Application

It might not look like a typical *n*-tier architecture of a traditional data-driven application; instead, it could look like a web of dependencies. The tiered model still exists within these applications; however, it has been up-leveled to show the individual services and the interactions between them. A quick glance can show you the critical services that many other services depend on and illustrate what each service interacts with. The diagram also separates the applications and services that are deployed to a Kubernetes cluster from platforms and services outside the cluster. All the components that are deployed to the cluster are component services and supporting services of MuShop, and these services depend on external services that are outside the cluster. Examples of these external dependencies include an autonomous Oracle database and object storage buckets.

Most architectures have external dependencies that are managed cloud services, legacy systems, or self-managed systems that are run outside the cluster itself. Although this is natural and common, care should be taken to decouple them from the applications using configuration. Strong dependence on these external services can introduce vendor lock-in and make the application less portable. Therefore, it is key to design applications so that these dependencies can be managed as externalized configuration or using standard interfaces and APIs. These could be a standard object storage API or an Object Relational Mapping (ORM) framework, such as JPA in Java-based applications, to abstract your applications from hard dependencies on the underlying database.

MuShop manages these external dependencies through configuration that can be provided to the individual containers. This configuration can be in the form of environment variables or configuration files that are provided to the containers at runtime (such as a config map in Kubernetes). This allows the same containers to be run with different configuration options, such as for development environments and production environments.

An architectural goal of adopting a cloud native development model is to improve system resilience. One way to do that is to eliminate single points of failure in the system. A single service that is used by several other services has the potential to become a bottleneck. Microservice architectures make it easy to identify these services and plan accordingly. External dependencies pose a similar challenge, as with dependence on a single database. Microservice architectures often recommend a database-per-service model, with each service using its own database on a dedicated infrastructure. MuShop, however, opts for a slightly modified take on this pattern by using separate database schemas on a shared database infrastructure in its default configuration. This is done to demonstrate application-level isolation while keeping the infrastructure needs of a sample application to a minimum. From a service perspective, and for implementation purposes, this is close to the database-per-service pattern. A mere configuration change to how the application connects to databases can switch from multiple schemas to completely separate databases. Because configuration is external to the application containers for the services, switching between a shared database infrastructure and dedicated databases for each service can be achieved without requiring code changes or rebuilding the container images. When appropriate, this pattern can also be used to share database resources in dev/test environments; then a switch can be made to use dedicated databases for more critical environments, simply using external configuration.

Source Code Structure

The source code for MuShop is managed in a single repository, to make it easier to work with and understand the entire system in the same context. This style of using a single source code repository to store multiple projects is sometimes called a monorepo. The typical manner of source-controlling an individual project in its own repository is called a multirepo in this context.

Multirepos are familiar to most developers and are the norm. The choice to use a monorepo or multirepo for your microservices applications depends on a set of factors that should be carefully considered. By their nature, microservices have a smaller codebase, fewer developers, and fewer dependencies than the system as a whole. A multirepo typically gives these teams more autonomy, and these projects can move independently. The commit histories for each project look clean, with commits related to just that project or service. Additionally, code reviews are streamlined and focused, and CI/CD configurations are simple because they focus on building just a single service or application. In sensitive environments, multirepos can meet compliance and security needs around who has access to sensitive code. On the other hand, multirepos can silo developers, and when a single small team works on several services, multirepos have to work across repositories, which can be counterproductive as the number of repositories increases. The drawbacks are easily understood with an example. Consider a team that uses a multirepo to implement a new feature. If a feature is to be implemented across three separate services, then, by extension, it is spread across three separate repositories. This can make it difficult to see the whole feature in its entirety because its code is spread across the repositories. This approach might also be overkill when the same team members are forced to switch among the three repositories to make quick changes that are then tracked as three separate code commits. Multirepos can also act as an organization barrier, siloing developers into their own corners and features.

A monorepo, on the other hand, can encourage consistency of coding standards and styles when using the same programming language and comparable tech stacks. Additionally, you get a complete view of the larger system as a whole. The dependencies of the whole system can be analyzed at once, and useful reports can be generated easily in a monorepo. Above all, a monorepo breaks down organizational walls between developers and promotes collaboration. On the flip side, with large teams and complex systems comprised of numerous microservices, a monorepo can be quite chaotic, with the commit history muddled by commits, merges, and conflict resolutions across teams. Care also needs to be taken to craft your CI/CD pipelines so that the changes to the repository trigger the appropriate build and deployment workflows.

Beyond these pros and cons, organizational and compliance requirements might dictate the choice of source code structuring. MuShop uses a monorepo primarily because of its role as an example application. As such, we wanted to make it easier for users to get started with MuShop; not having to clone multiple repositories was a choice we made to support that.

Within MuShop, the source code is primarily organized into two groups:

- Code that automates the deployment, including infrastructure automation. This can be found under the directory `deploy`.
- The source code for each of the microservices. This can be found under `src`. MuShop uses a variety of programming languages and frameworks for its services. Each service under the `src` acts as an independent project, with its own dependency management, build tools, tests, and packaging. The common aspect is that all the services are packaged as container images and follow the general principles of the twelve-factor application methodology.

Figure 10-2 shows the high-level view.

📁	.github/workflows	ignore stack versions	last year
📁	ci	merge-ci-and-ignores	3 years ago
📁	deploy	complete stack version bump	5 months ago
📁	images	dark mode mushop logo	last year
📁	src	Merge pull request #350 from oracle-quickstart/dependabot/npm_a...	2 weeks ago
📄	.dockerignore	dockerignore update	2 years ago
📄	.gitignore	gitignore update	5 months ago
📄	CONTRIBUTING.md	Added a CONTRIBUTING.md	3 years ago
📄	LICENSE	Initial spin off of MuShop demo	3 years ago
📄	README.md	dark mode notation for logo on readmes	last year
📄	THIRDPARTY.md	version licence updates	2 years ago
📄	wercker.yml	merge-ci-and-ignores	3 years ago

Figure 10-2   The Layout of the MuShop Code Repository

To familiarize yourself with MuShop, clone it to your workstation. You need to have Git[4] installed. If you are new to using Git, a client such as the GitHub desktop (https://desktop.github.com)[5] is highly recommended.

To clone the repo, run the following command:

```
git clone https://github.com/oracle-quickstart/oci-cloudnative.git
```

This clones the repository to your workstation, and you should be able to browse the source code.

Services

The source code for every service that makes up MuShop can be found in the `src` folder. MuShop takes a polyglot approach to microservices, with each service choosing a different programming language and framework and having its own stack. Some of these services are built for both the x86 (`amd64`) and ARM (`arm64`) platforms, which enables more portability for workloads as ARM-based compute platforms are becoming more mainstream with cloud providers. This offers an example of how to implement a development workflow to target multiple architectures for your workloads and effectively package them as containers that support these multiple architectures. Each service is responsible for a single function; their nuances are described in the sections that follow.

Storefront

Technology stack: JavaScript
   Target architecture: amd64/arm64

Description: The Storefront is a responsive single-page web application that implements the MuShop storefront. This is the web page that users visit to shop at MuShop. As the user browses the store, adds items to the cart, and creates orders on the browser, this web application makes calls to the other services that expose these respective services. Instead of having the storefront depend on and know about every back-end API and how to access it, these APIs are aggregated by the API service, which becomes the single entry point for the storefront to access all services. The API service acts as a facade for the APIs provided by the various microservices.

The application uses UIKit (https://getuikit.com) for the UI components. It also uses axios (https://axios-http.com) as its HTTP client to make API calls to the API service.

API

Technology stack: nodeJS

   Target architecture: amd64/arm64

   Description: This service acts as a storefront back end. It is written in Node.js and orchestrates services for consumption by the Storefront web application. The storefront UI makes its API calls to the API service, which then passes these along to the respective implementations. The API service acts as a facade for the APIs provided by the various microservices, such as the Catalog service for browsing the store, Carts service for adding items and keeping track of them across sessions, and Orders Service to create and manage orders. Its role is similar to that of a reverse proxy, or a very lightweight API gateway. The design choice of not using a managed full-featured API gateway service such as the OCI API Gateway was made simply because it does not require most of the features offered by such platforms. Implementing a service discovery mechanism and using that directly from the client (storefront) is another way to get a similar effect without the added facade, and this could be more efficient in some circumstances. However, this shifts the API orchestration overhead to the client and removes the capability to have centralized management for API endpoints.

The API service also supports a "mock mode," which completely mocks the services underneath. This is generally useful for the development and testing of the API consumers (such as the storefront web application) without having real implementations for the actual microservices. Most API gateways can also provide similar functionality, to enable these use cases of parallel development.

Catalog

Technology stack: Go

   Target architecture: amd64/arm64

   Description: The Catalog service provides an API for querying the catalog/product information. The product data is stored on Oracle Autonomous Database. The service uses the GOdror (Go Driver for Oracle DB) with GoKit to interact with the Oracle DB from Go. The API exposed by the service is read only, and the sample application uses an SQL script that is run at application deployment time to seed the catalog data into the database.

Carts

Technology stack: Java, using the Helidon framework
    Target architecture: amd64/arm64
    Description: This service provides a cart that users can use while shopping. The cart is tied to the user profile and is persisted in an Oracle database. The Carts service uses the Autonomous Database's JSON features to store cart data as JSON documents instead of relational tables. This service provides an example for building a Java-based microservice using the Helidon framework (https://helidon.io/), as well as demonstrating the features of the Oracle database for JSON document storage, queries, and joins across document and relational data models.
    It is built using the maven build tool.

User

Technology stack: TypeScript, NextJS, and TypeORM
    Target architecture: amd64/arm64
    Description: The User service manages customer accounts, customer profile data, and authentication. The User service provides the capability to create new user accounts and update their profile information. It also handles authentication in MuShop because introducing an identity-management solution would have been overkill for a sample application. Identity information maintained by other services (such as the order created by a user) can reference user identifiers (such as a user ID) provided by the User service. It is important to note that MuShop uses a slightly modified version of the database-per-service pattern, which is essentially that every microservice has its own database. As an example application, to keep resource usage minimal while promoting the architectural patterns that promote data isolation and better resiliency than, say, using multiple databases, MuShop uses multiple schemas. This means that services that use user information, such as the orders service, maintain its data in a separate schema or database from the user service. Validation of identifiers is done across services, not by a traditional foreign key relationship that is common in monolithic applications.
    The users service is built in TypeScript using the NestJS (https://nextjs.org/) framework, which uses progressive JavaScript to build efficient Node.js server applications. It also uses TypeORM, which is an Object Relational Mapper for TypeScript and JavaScript. Oracle DB connectivity is enabled by the official node-oracledb package from Oracle, for Node.js.

Orders

Technology stack: Java, using the SpringBoot framework

Target architecture: amd64/arm64

Description: The orders microservice is a lightweight application built using SpringBoot (https://spring.io/projects/springboot) that leverages Spring JPA for database connectivity. It exposes a REST API for order management operations. The application is typical of a spring JPA application and exposes CRUD operations on orders. It interacts with the user service over the REST API to track and validate users for whom the orders are created.

It also interacts with the Fulfillment service over an asynchronous message bus (NATS. io). As orders are created, it sends messages to the fulfillment service to fulfill them. This interaction is meant to showcase a messaging-driven pattern, which is common in microservices and many modern reactive architectures. Messaging systems promote elasticity, scaling, and loose coupling for services that operate at different velocities in a cloud native environment. If the order volume spikes, the service can scale up, but a related service can be cushioned from these spikes using the message bus, which buffers the increased order flow to a rate that the fulfillment service is capable of. More importantly, messaging systems can set failure boundaries. If the fulfillment system goes down, that failure should not cascade onto other services, such as orders. The messaging service that sits between microservices and the asynchronous communication model prevents these cascading failures.

It uses gradle (https://gradle.org/) as its build tool.

Fulfillment

Technology stack: Java, using the Micronaut framework

Target architecture: amd64/arm64

Description: Fulfillment application models an asynchronous service that models a fulfillment workflow based on incoming messages that represent orders that have been placed. The messaging platform used is nats.io, and the fulfillment application listens for messages appearing on a topic. The application reads these messages and sends reply messages to indicate the processing of orders on a separate topic that the orders application listens to. The orders application updates the status of an order based on the messages it receives from the fulfillment service. This message-driven flow between the orders and fulfillment applications showcases the asynchronous patterns that can be used in cloud native applications.

The Fulfillment application is written in Java and uses the Micronaut (https:// micronaut.io/) framework. It is built using the gradle build tool. This application is built as a native binary using the GraalVM (https://www.graalvm.org/) native image compiler. The GraalVM native image compiler can create platform-specific native binaries for several languages, including Java. The native image is machine code, and no traditional Java Virtual Machine (JVM) is required to run it. This improves the performance of the application, in most cases. The gradle build included can be configured to switch between creating a standard Java bytecode and using the native image. For the Fulfillment application, there is an order of magnitude difference in the performanc due to its use of the GraalVM Native Image compiler.

Payment

Technology stack: Go

  Target architecture: amd64/arm64

  Description: This is a bare-bones service written in Go that performs a simple validation out of the box and can be expanded to cover new use cases and integrations. Because MuShop was built to showcase microservices architectures and was often used in hands-on workshops and meetups, the payment service scaffold primarily acted as the bare-bones service to expand on and make code changes to these settings.

Assets

Technology stack: Node.js

  Target architecture: amd64/arm64

  Description: This is a container used during deployment of the application that pushes the image assets used by the application to OCI object storage. It contains a Node.js OCI client and the images used in the application. These images are uploaded to the object storage bucket that is provided as a parameter. It runs only during deployment and exists after the images are uploaded to the object storage. The object storage bucket to use for the images is typically created by infrastructure automation such as Terraform, and the URLs are provided to the Helm chart. Users can optionally override this as well.

DBTools

Technology stack: None. This is a collection of utilities.

  Target architecture: amd64/arm64

  Description: This container packages common runtime tools for database interactions that are used across services to interact with the database. For instance, MuShop services that interact with the database might need to set up or update the database schema when a new version is deployed or seed data into the database when first run. This container packages the tools used to execute database scripts so that they can be run as Kubernetes jobs when required.

Edge Router

Technology stack: None

  Target architecture: amd64/arm64

  Description: This is an optional container running the Traefik proxy, for use in development environments.

Events

Technology stack: Go

 Target architecture: amd64/arm64

 Description: The Events service is an optional service that captures events from the storefront and sends them to an event stream. Stream-processing applications can listen on this stream and react to it. This service is intended to showcase integration with the OCI streaming service.

Newsletter Subscription

Technology stack: Node.js

 Target architecture: amd64/arm64

 Description: The newsletter subscription is a serverless function that is hosted on the OCI Functions platform. When users sign up for the MuShop newsletter, the storefront captures the email address and invokes the function through the OCI API gateway. The function sends an email to the recipient, informing them that they are subscribed to a newsletter. Note that the subscription is not tracked or stored anywhere; the sample application simply showcases how to invoke a function through an API gateway and how to send emails using the Oracle Email Delivery service.

Load

Technology stack: Python

 Target architecture: amd64/arm64

 Description: The load directory contains a set of test scripts that use the locust.io stress-testing tool. The tool lets developers define user behavior using Python scripts. The scripts themselves send HTTP requests and receive responses much like the Storefront. Locust.io lets developers define user flows by creating conditional logic based on the responses received and creating more requests based on values from previous requests. Flows can be randomized as well. When the flow is defined, the locust.io tool can spawn multiple instances that simulate users and hit the services concurrently. MuShop uses these load scripts to test the functionality, as well as simulate users for creating realistic load conditions to test scaling operations and the resiliency of the microservices.

Building the Services

The source code for every service that makes up MuShop can be found in the src folder. Microservices consist of multiple smaller applications that are each built independently. Compared to a traditional monolithic application, building microservices can often be complex, with each application having subtle nuances in its build processes. On top of this, for a polyglot application such as MuShop, in which each service is built using separate tool chains, maintaining these build tool chains can become overwhelming. Imagine maintaining a local build environment with the compilers and tools to build Go applications, Java applications (some using maven, others using gradle), TypeScript applications, and more. Now consider every team member who needs to build these applications maintaining a similar setup on their workstations and the whole team being in lock-step with upgrades to all versions of compilers and tools. Even though these microservices vary widely in the build tools they use, they all share a common packaging format of a container image. Ultimately, the end result of each of these build processes is a container image.

To address the complexity of the build tooling and standardize it for teams, it is a common and preferred practice for containerized application development to also containerize the build tools and processes. Instead of requiring developers to maintain these tool chains, the build tools and processes are contained within a container, the application code to be built is mounted onto a container, and the build and packaging are executed within the container. This makes the build process smooth and extremely portable because the build tools and build environment no longer need to be maintained locally. Because the containers that provide the build environment are built from Dockerfiles, it helps to codify the build environment and the tools it is expected to have and to maintain a history of how the build environment changes over time. Docker also provides support for multistage builds that help with adding software and build tools for build stages, but basing the final output image on a slimmer base image that includes only the runtime dependencies. For instance, the final image for an application need not include a package manager or build tools when the build stages use containers that have these components. Avoiding image bloat by retaining only runtime dependencies for the applications optimizes the image for its size and minimizes its attack surface.

MuShop takes this approach, and each microservice describes how it is built by providing a Dockerfile. These Dockerfiles also take advantage of Docker's multistage builds to optimize the final images. Listing 10-1 shows an abbreviated version of the Dockerfile for the Orders service.

Listing 10-1   An Example Showing the Multistage Builds Using Docker

```
# Stage 1 : Setup the build environment

FROM gradle:6.5 as buildenv
RUN mkdir -p /usr/src/app
WORKDIR /usr/src/app
COPY settings.gradle /usr/src/app
COPY build.gradle /usr/src/app


# Stage 2 : Build the application

FROM buildenv as appbuild
COPY src /usr/src/app/src
RUN gradle clean test bootJar

# Stage 3 : Application container
```

```
FROM openjdk:13-slim
COPY --from=appbuild /usr/src/app/build/libs/orders-1.0.0.jar /app/orders-
  1.0.0.jar
EXPOSE 80
ENTRYPOINT java $JAVA_OPTS -jar /app/orders-1.0.0.jar --port=80
```

The build process is divided into three stages. The first stage sets up the build environment. It starts off by choosing the gradle container image as the base image because the application uses gradle as its build tool. It then adds the gradle settings file and build file for the application. This is set up as a single stage, to take advantage of how Docker runs multistage builds. When this build is run by Docker, it creates an intermediate container for this stage, and this can be cached. If there are no changes to the files in this container—that is, the gradle settings and the build file (which includes library dependencies)—then this container does not have to be re-created in subsequent builds, making those subsequent builds faster.

The second stage adds the application source code and runs the actual gradle build. This works because this stage is based on the intermediate container created in the first stage, which includes the gradle build tools and settings required for this build. This container gets updated every time the source code changes, which is expected because you need to rebuild the application when you make changes to the code.

The last stage builds the final application container. Notice that it starts with a new base image. It does not carry on from the build environment you set up and used in the first two stages because when you run the application, you do not need the build tools (such as gradle). You can keep the image small and lightweight by including only the runtime components you need. Because Orders is a Java application, you need a Java runtime, and this is why here you base the final application container on the openjdk:13-slim base image. It provides the basic Java runtime needed for this Java application. This stage simply copies the executable JAR file you built during the previous stage and then sets up the container to run the application.

Once again, the multistage build optimizes the build process here. If changes are made to the command-line flags or other parameters that are passed to the application, then a change to the final stage of the build without any source code changes will be very fast. This is because the first two stages are unaffected and the previously cached intermediate containers are still up to date; the build can then skip to the third stage directly without actually rebuilding the application.

The build flow for each application might be different and is based on the build process for the respective programming language and packaging models for the frameworks used. Because the builds are run in containers as well, automation systems can easily build these images and integrate with image repositories or sophisticated deployment models. MuShop is published on GitHub, so it uses GitHub workflows to automate the application and image build processes. MuShop also uses GitHub workflow features to support multiple CPU architectures for images so that these can be even more portable. The complete GitHub workflow for the applications can be seen by examining the .github/workflows directory. Here the containers.yaml workflow lays out the automated process that builds and pushes container images when their source code is updated. The `docs.yaml` file lays out the process for publishing docs to the GitHub site. There is a workflow to manage stale open issues on GitHub as well.

Infrastructure Automation

Infrastructure automation is a key operational characteristic in cloud native application architectures, and MuShop demonstrates these concepts using the OCI Terraform provider. The infrastructure management code is in the `deploy/complete/terraform` directory. The infrastructure automation flow covers the creation and management of resources such as the virtual network, the OKE cluster, and the worker node pool. The code is split into multiple files that work with specific resource areas, for better readability and maintainability. Module usage was consciously avoided for this Terraform configuration, for a few reasons. First, this approach would provide a more complete example of how these resources are used. Second, modules would have introduced external dependencies that are more difficult to control.

As with IAM policies, some OCI resources are always created in the home region for a tenancy. For this reason, you will notice that the Terraform configuration uses multiple `provider` definitions, one for the home regions and the other for the region where resources are deployed. Listing 10-2 demonstrates multiple providers to interact with multiple regions at the same time.

Listing 10-2   An Example Showing Multiple Terraform Provider Definitions to Work with Multiple Regions Simultaneously

```
provider "oci" {
alias = "home_region"
tenancy_ocid = var.tenancy_ocid
region = lookup(data.oci_identity_regions.home_region.regions[0], "name")
user_ocid = var.user_ocid
fingerprint = var.fingerprint
private_key_path = var.private_key_path
}

provider "oci" {
alias = "current_region"
tenancy_ocid = var.tenancy_ocid
region = var.region
user_ocid = var.user_ocid
fingerprint = var.fingerprint
private_key_path = var.private_key_path
}
```

The Terraform configuration also uses the `kubernetes` and `helm` providers to deploy the application after the infrastructure resources are built. The default configuration values and parameters are provided in the included `terraform.tfvars.example` file. This file should be renamed to `terraform.tfvars` before use. The Terraform configuration can be customized by changing the values in this file. Listing 10-3 shows the boilerplate code that contains placeholders that should be replaced with actual values.

Listing 10-3   An Example `terraform.tfvars` File with Placeholder Values—the Content of This File Determines How Terraform Authenticates with OCI

```
# OCI authentication
tenancy_ocid = "ocid1.tenancy....."
fingerprint = "" # e.g.: "5f:53:..." or leave blank if using CloudShell
user_ocid = "" # e.g.: "ocid1.user..." or leave blank if using CloudShell
private_key_path = "" # e.g.: "/users/user/.oci/oci_api_key.pem"

# Deployment compartment
compartment_ocid = "ocid1.compartment...."

# region
region = "us-ashburn-1"
```

The Terraform configuration can also be directly imported into the OCI Resource Manager service. The resource manager can load the Terraform configuration from a remote URL and generate a user interface for users to provide custom values for the `terraform.tfvars` configuration file. This provides a one-click experience for managing the infrastructure deployment and the application deployment. The direct link to import a stack into resource manager can be used for any Resource Manager Stack and can be used as an example to provide templated environments for team-based development. For instance, if the platform engineering team wants to standardize infrastructure topologies, it can provide a standardized stack that application teams can use that is guaranteed to have the topology and configuration that the platform team approved.

Helm Charts

As with most microservice applications on Kubernetes, MuShop consists of multiple pods, replica sets, services, config maps, and other Kubernetes resources. Each service in MuShop offers multiple configuration options that determine the behavior of the system. This configuration can be maintained in the Kubernetes manifests, but doing so for applications that have numerous moving parts and configuration options can be a challenge. Apart from becoming verbose and growing in complexity over time, this approach comingles the configuration data with the Kubernetes resource definitions.

In a typical development workflow, as you release new versions of your software, you want to build your containers once but then configure these containers and your Kubernetes deployments differently in your test and production environments. For instance, with MuShop, several of the services use databases; which database to connect to is a configuration option for these services. In a development environment, the service might use a shared database, whereas in production it might get a dedicated database. As developers, we want to make sure that the code that we build and test is exactly the code that we run in production. By decoupling the configuration from the code, we can ensure that the same application and the same container can be configured to run in various environments. However, maintaining a set of Kubernetes manifests for each deployment environment becomes hard to scale and keep track of.

A Helm chart provides a templating mechanism for Kubernetes manifests so that you do not have to maintain separate manifests for various configurations. Helm charts separate the Kubernetes resource definitions from the configuration values. The resource definitions are maintained in a template form with placeholders that can be replaced for actual values. The configuration values are separated from resource definitions, and this configuration is maintained in a human-readable YAML document, commonly referred to as a `values` file. Having configuration values consolidated like this makes it easy to understand the configuration values and maintain them over time. Because the configuration values are separate, it is also easy to keep track of changes by simply storing the configuration in a source control system. When a Helm chart is installed to a cluster, Helm replaces the placeholder values in the manifest templates using the configuration values from the `values` file provided to it. This effectively creates a complete manifest using these values. This generated manifest is applied to the Kubernetes cluster. Listing 10-4 shows a deployment manifest template (truncated, for brevity), and Listing 10-5 shows a `values.yaml` file helm parameter. Listing 10-6 shows the full manifest file.

Listing 10-4   An Example of a Deployment Manifest Template

```
apiVersion: apps/v1
kind: Deployment
metadata:
  name: api-server
spec:
  replicas: {{ .Values.replicaCount }}
  template:
    spec:
      containers:
        - name: api-server
          image: "{{ .Values.image.repository }}:{{ .Values.image.tag }}"
          imagePullPolicy: {{ .Values.image.pullPolicy }}
```

Listing 10-5   `values.yaml` File

```
replicaCount: 1
image:
  repository: iad.ocir.io/oracle/ateam/mushop-api
  tag: 2.3.2
   imagePullPolicy: IfNotPresent
```

Listing 10-6   Resulting Deployment Manifest

```
apiVersion: apps/v1
kind: Deployment
metadata:
  name: api-server
spec:
  replicas: 1
  template:
    spec:
      containers:
        - name: api-server
          image: iad.ocir.io/oracle/ateam/mushop-api:2.3.2
          imagePullPolicy: IfNotPresent
```

As shown in Listing 10-4, the manifest template has several placeholder values. The YAML-based `values.yaml` file shown in Listing 10-5 defines these values in a way that is easy to navigate, read, and understand. The YAML format also makes this a well-organized format. At runtime, the placeholders in the template are replaced by the values from the `values.yaml` file, to generate a full manifest as shown in Listing 10-6.

The Helm charts for MuShop are responsible for deploying and configuring each of the services in the system. Helm charts can reference other Helm charts from within it. This makes it easy to compose an application out of independent Helm charts. Every microservice in MuShop provides its own Helm chart, which exposes its configuration parameters in a well-defined form. This Helm chart for an individual service can be used to configure and manage that service alone. Several of these Helm charts can be pulled together to create a higher-level Helm chart that configures and manages multiple services. MuShop is organized in this manner, and the MuShop Helm charts are found under the path `<repository_location>/deploy/complete/Helm-chart/mushop/`. Here you will find the top-level chart, which is made up of multiple subcharts, one for each service. The subcharts can be found under the `charts` directory, as Figure 10-3 illustrates.

charts	helm updated deprecated notation	10 months ago
templates	cluster certificate issuer selfsigned option	last year
.helmignore	Introducing complete deployment mode	3 years ago
Chart.yaml	storefront chart version bumps	last year
requirements.yaml	storefront chart updates for ODA	last year
values-dev.yaml	values-dev comment update	last year
values-mock.yaml	Fixed review comments	2 years ago
values-prod-reference.yaml	storefront new values for oda	last year
values-prod.yaml	catalogue vs catalog (service catalog)	last year
values-test.yaml	values-test.yaml clusterissuer fix	last year
values.yaml	chart updates to include events	3 years ago

Figure 10-3   The MuShop Helm Chart Consists of Multiple Subcharts—the Application Can Be Configured Differently for Various Environments by Using Customized `values.yaml` Files

Each application or microservice has its own configuration and resources that are modeled by a Helm chart that can provision and manage that application. Each of these subcharts contains a `values.yaml` file that provides sensible and secure defaults for the application. The top-level MuShop Helm chart is composed of the subcharts for each of the microservices, along with some global resources and templates. Even though each microservice (subchart) provides its own values, the top-level chart can override values that are set by them. This enables developers to manage the configuration centrally. Finally, the user can provide a fully customized YAML file that fully expresses the configuration and overrides any of the configurations that have been set underneath. Figure 10-3 shows several of these values-files for various environments such as `values-dev.yaml`, `values-test.yaml`, and `values-prod.yaml`. When changing values for a subchart, only the elements that need to be changed are specified in the top-level values-file; the values not specified are not overridden, and the defaults from the chart's values-file are still applied.

If you are new to using Helm charts with subcharts, this might seem confusing at first. Consider this example. The Orders Service has its default values defined within the orders subchart by the developers of the Orders Service, who have provided some sensible defaults. In this example, the application expects environment variables to be set for the container. Listing 10-7 shows the default `values.yaml` that the orders subchart provides, with its defaults. Note the `newOrdersSubject: mushop-orders`, which determines the name of the subject onto which messages are posted when new orders are created. The developers of the orders service have set the default to be `mushop-orders`, which is a reasonable default.

Listing 10-7   The Values File in Each Subchart Sets the Defaults for All Configuration Parameters—This Example Shows a Snippet from the `values.yaml` for the Orders Chart

```
env:
  zipkin: zipkin.jaeger.svc.cluster.local
  javaOpts: -Xms32m -Xmx150m -XX:MaxRAM=150m -Djava.security.egd=file:/dev/urandom
  -Doracle.jdbc.fanEnabled=false -XX:+UnlockExperimentalVMOptions -XX:+UseZGC
  -Dlogging.level.mushop.orders=INFO -Dspring.zipkin.enabled=false
  natsHost: "nats"
  natsPort: 4222
  newOrdersSubject: mushop-orders
  shippedOrdersSubject: mushop-shipments
```

However, when deploying MuShop to a development environment, you might need to override this. At the time of performing a Helm install, the user can provide a customized `values.yaml` file, such as `values-dev.yaml`. This file would contain only the configuration parameters that need to be overridden, nothing else. Listing 10-8 shows such a value file in which the `newOrdersSubject` is overridden to have a value of `test-env-orders`. The other values in the orders Helm chart are still in effect, but the value for the `newOrderSubject` has been overridden.

Listing 10-8   An Example Showing Selective Values from the Underlying Chart Being Overridden

```
... (truncated for brevity)
# The environment specific override.

orders:
  env:
    newOrdersSubject: test-env-orders


...
```

Utilities and Supporting Components

As with most applications, MuShop also uses third-party open-source software, where required. Within the application, MuShop uses the NATS messaging system to asynchronously connect microservices and set failure boundaries. MuShop also uses software that is outside the core application, to support its functionality. The monitoring stack is a good example. Observability is essential to smoothly running a microservices-based application because of the sheer number of moving parts in the system. MuShop uses the Grafana and Prometheus stack for monitoring and installs these to the Kubernetes cluster as well. To keep the code well organized, the core application Helm chart is separate from the supporting software. This helps to easily keep track of application changes, separate from changes to the supporting software. MuShop maintains these in a separate chart called MuShop Utilities. The MuShop Utilities chart includes the following components:

- **Prometheus:** Monitoring system and time series database for monitoring events from the workloads running in the cluster.
- **Grafana:** Utility for querying, visualizing, and alerting based on metrics data. It integrates with Prometheus as the data source.
- **metrics-server:** Metrics Server, which collects resource metrics from kubelets and exposes them.
- **ingress-nginx:** Kubernetes ingress controller implementation, which uses Nginx as its reverse proxy and load balancer.
- **cert manager:** A certificate controller that obtains certificates from issuers and periodically renews them. MuShop uses it to issue and manage SSL certificates when you configure your own domain name with MuShop.
- **Jenkins:** A popular CI/CD tool. It is not installed by default, but it can be enabled. If it is installed, it will be preconfigured to run builds by spinning up a pod to run the build and tearing it down after the build is complete.

Deploying MuShop

MuShop is designed to showcase multiple deployment options for your cloud native applications in OCI. The process is fully automated and covers both infrastructure and application deployments because the sample is designed to be deployed with no prior knowledge about tools and services in OCI. When building your own applications, you should consider whether this is the right approach for you. Most enterprise organizations tend to separate infrastructure management and application development. In these cases, infrastructure teams might use automation tools such as Terraform or the OCI Resource Manager service, and application teams might be using continuous delivery tools such as Jenkins or the OCI DevOps service.

The default MuShop deployment itself is a simple but highly coordinated affair, and it is worthwhile to dive into the details of how the process works. As described in earlier sections, the infrastructure is managed by a Terraform configuration packaged as an OCI Resource Manager stack. The application is packaged as a Helm chart that can be deployed to a Kubernetes cluster using Helm. The process can be kicked off simply by using the Deploy button on the GitHub page. Figure 10-4 shows the Deploy button on the GitHub page.

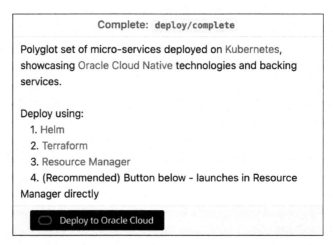

Figure 10-4   Deploy Buttons Can Be Embedded Anywhere and Can Launch the OCI Resource Manager to Deploy Infrastructure and Applications

Clicking the button takes you to the OCI Resource Manager service where the stack will be imported. The button is simply an HTML link to the Resource Manager service, with a query parameter that points at the stack that needs to be deployed. In the case of MuShop, new versions are released as stacks (zipped Terraform configuration with a `schema.yaml`) through GitHub releases. You can create links or buttons like these that point to your stacks as well.

Some application configuration is exposed to the user, and these cases are captured by Terraform. Terraform passes these to the Helm chart using the `values.yaml` file used for the Helm chart. Figure 10-5 and Listing 10-9 showcase how some of these Helm chart values are set from Terraform based on user input in the OCI Resource Manager service.

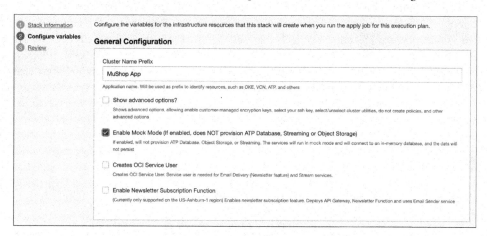

Figure 10-5 The OCI Resource Manager Can Provide an Intuitive User Interface for the Terraform Code

Listing 10-9 The OCI Resource Manager Supplies the User-Provided Values to the Terraform Code

```
# Create namespace mushop for the mushop microservices
resource "kubernetes_namespace" "mushop_namespace" {
  metadata {
    name = "mushop"
  }
  depends_on = [oci_containerengine_node_pool.oke_node_pool]
}

# Deploy mushop chart
resource "helm_release" "mushop" {
  name      = "mushop"
  chart     = "../helm-chart/mushop"
  namespace = kubernetes_namespace.mushop_namespace.id
  wait      = false

  set {
    name  = "global.mock.service"
    value = var.mushop_mock_mode_all ? "all" : "none"
  }
  # ...[truncated for brevity]
}
```

When the Terraform configuration is applied, it uses the OCI provider for Terraform to create the basic infrastructure components, such as networks, databases, and the Kubernetes cluster itself. After the infrastructure components are created, the Terraform configuration uses the Kubernetes and Helm providers for Terraform to interact with the cluster that was created and installs the Helm chart to the cluster to complete the deployment.

You can access additional instructions regarding the deployment options and variations of MuShop on the documentation website.[6] This includes deploying with Istio[7] Service Mesh and integrating with OCI Logging and Analytics. Additionally, there is a variation of MuShop[8] where all services use Micronaut.[9]

Summary

This chapter took a deep dive into MuShop, a reference application that applies the concepts described throughout this book. From structuring source code for your microservices to exploring the various build practices and deployment models that improve development velocity, the example application (and its more than a dozen services, all built using a variety of technologies) showcases how you can effectively compose a complex application from a set of microservices and manage it effectively. This chapter also provided a walk-through of the deployment automation using Terraform and Helm charts, which can hopefully inspire your own Helm charts for your applications.

References

1 MuShop Source Code on GitHub: https://github.com/oracle-quickstart/oci-cloudnative

2 CapEx, which stands for capital expenditures, pertains to the financial resources a company puts into physical assets like properties, equipment, or infrastructure. These assets are anticipated to bring advantages to the company over a few years and are not regarded as expenses in the current period.

3 The Twelve-Factor Methodology: https://12factor.net/

4 Git: https://git-scm.com

5 GitHub Desktop: https://desktop.github.com

6 MuShop Documentation: https://oracle-quickstart.github.io/oci-cloudnative/

7 Istio: https://istio.io/

8 MuShop Variation using Micronaut: https://github.com/oracle-quickstart/oci-micronaut

9 Micronaut: https://micronaut.io/

Index

ORACLE

Get answers to your technical questions

—

Find getting started guides, documentation, tutorials, architectures, and more at Oracle Help Center – Oracle's #1 hub for technical documentation.

ORACLE

Get architectural guidance from Oracle experts

Design, develop, and implement your cloud and on-premises workloads with guidance from Oracle architects, developers, and other experts versed in Oracle technologies and solutions.

ORACLE
CLOUD
Infrastructure

Learn.
Build.
Launch.

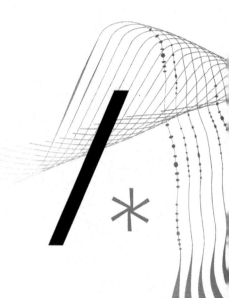

(And don't forget to BYOOST*)

Consider this an open invite to join developers like you to pick up new skills—and pick your favorite language—to build whatever you want on OCI.

Check us out and meet new friends at developer.oracle.com.

*Bring your own open source tools. We'll bring the fun-sized ideas.